Women's Studies Quarterly

An Educational Project of the Feminist Press at the City University of New York in Cooperation with Rochester Institute of Technology

Guest Editor for Current Issue
Wendy Kolmar, Drew University

Editor
Diane Hope, Rochester Institute of Technology

Editors Emerita
Nancy Porter, Portland State University
Janet Zandy, Rochester Institute of Technology

Publisher
Jean Casella, the Feminist Press and the Graduate School and University Center, CUNY

Editorial Board
Lynne Derbyshire, University of Rhode Island
Jean Douthwright, Rochester Institute of Technology
Lisa Freeman, Kansas State University
Edvige Giunta, New Jersey City University
Dorothy O. Helly, emerita, Hunter College and the Graduate School, CUNY
Barbara Horn, Nassau Community College, SUNY
Alice Kessler-Harris, Columbia University
Wendy Kolmar, Drew University
Linda Layne, Rensselaer Polytechnic Institute
Tobe Levin, University of Maryland, European Division, and J.W. Goethe University, Frankfurt am Main, Germany
Kit Mayberry, Rochester Institute of Technology
Carol J. Pierman, University of Alabama
Lee Quinby, Hobart and William Smith Colleges
Carol Richardson, Rochester Institute of Technology
Deborah S. Rosenfelt, University of Maryland, College Park
Sue V. Rosser, Georgia Institute of Technology
Carole Anne Taylor, Bates College
Mari Boor Tonn, University of Maryland
Bonnie Zimmerman, San Diego State University

Managing Editors
Livia Tenzer and Molly Vaux

Copy Editor
Romaine Perin

Editorial Assistants
Bridget Cross, Deveryle James, Kristin Leong

Administrative Assistant to the Editor
Cassandra Shellman

Contents

6 Editorial
Wendy Kolmar

FILM AND FEMINIST THEORY: WIDENING THE LENS

15 On the Existence of Women: A Brief History of the Relations Between Women's Studies and Film Studies
Tania Modleski

25 The Gaze As Theoretical Touchstone: The Intersection of Film Studies, Feminist Theory, and Postcolonial Theory
Corinn Columpar

45 Viewing in the Dark: Toward a Black Feminist Approach to Film
Janell Hobson

GENDER AND FEMINISM ON THE SCREEN: APPROACHES TO INDIVIDUAL FILMS

60 The Cyborg Mystique: *The Stepford Wives* and Second Wave Feminism
Anna Krugovoy Silver

77 *Girls Town*'s Challenge to "Do It Yourself" Feminism
Angela E. Hubler

88 Creating the Lesbian Mammy: *Boys on the Side* and the Politics of AIDS
Katie Hogan

103 Re-scripting History and Fairy Tales in Brigitte Roüan's *Outremer*
Dominique Licops

120 Views from "The Other Side": Theorizing Age and Difference in Yvonne Rainer's *Privilege*
Gwen Raaberg

131   "I'm a Wheelchair Girl Now": Abjection, Intersectionality, and Subjectivity in Atom Egoyan's *The Sweet Hereafter*
Vivian M. May and Beth A. Ferri

WOMEN FILMMAKERS AND THEIR FILMS

151   Films by Tracey Moffatt: Reclaiming First Australians' Rights, Celebrating Women's Rites
Cynthia Baron

178   Political Filmmaking: Talking with Renee Tajima-Peña
Interview by M. Rosalind Sagara

189   Remembering *Barbie Nation:* An Interview with Susan Stern
Susan Stern with Wendy Kolmar

196   María Novaro on the Making of *Lola* and *Danzón*
Interview by Isabel Arredondo

213   Documenting Race and Gender: Kym Ragusa Discusses *Passing* and *Fuori/Outside*
Interview by Livia Tenzer

TEACHING FILM AND FILMS FOR TEACHING: REFLECTIONS AND RESOURCES

221   Women Make Movies Responds to Hate
Xochitl Dorsey

227   Uncovering the Harem in the Classroom: Tania Kamal-Eldin's *Covered: The Hejab in Cairo, Egypt* and *Hollywood Harems* Within the Context of a Course on Arab Women Writers
Diya Abdo

239   Motherhood, Desire, and Intimacy: Teaching Mexican Women's Film (with syllabus)
Isabel Arredondo

255   Whose Naming Whom: Using Independent Video to Teach about the Politics of Representation
Megan Boler and Katherine R. Allen

271   Women's Stories, Women's Films: Integrating Women's Studies and Film Production (with syllabus)
Anne Orwin

285 Teaching What We're Not: Using Videos to Diversify the
Women's Studies Curriculum
Ann Schonberger, Nancy Lewis, Mazie Hough, and Leslie King

296 The Films We Teach: Using *Rosie the Riveter, Global
Assemblyline, Dreamworlds II,* and *Fast Food Women* in the
Women's Studies Classroom
*Wendy Kolmar, with teaching guides by Caitlin Killian,
Debra Liebowitz, Lynne Derbyshire, and Carol J. Pierman*

312 Women, Film, and Feminism: A Course Syllabus
Walter Metz

319 Feminisms on Film (with syllabus)
Carol J. Pierman

BOOK REVIEWS

324 Diana Robin and Ira Jaffee's *Redirecting the Gaze:
Gender, Theory and Cinema in the Third World*
Rama Lohani Chase

328 E. Ann Kaplan's *Feminism and Film* and Sue Thornam's
Feminist Film Theory: A Reader
Anahid Kassabian

Editorial

Wendy Kolmar

When I first proposed that *Women's Studies Quarterly* do an issue on film and women's studies, the "and" in the title and the relationship it suggests seemed quite unproblematic to me. Film and women's studies were connected in my mind in myriad ways. Women's studies courses make extensive use of documentary and feature films as class material. Courses linking gender/feminism and film are common in women's studies curricula. Film series are a staple of campus programming by feminist student groups and women's studies programs alike. For me and for my students, ready references to images from popular Hollywood film—from Disney's *Little Mermaid* to *Thelma and Louise* to *Basic Instinct*—make convenient illustrations of dominant ideologies of gender. Film, particularly documentary film, has been a medium for exploring women's lives, presenting historical and sociological research, raising consciousness, and doing political organizing. Film, and increasingly other new media, are also a medium for women's creative expression and exploration of the world. Feminist perspectives have become part of the conversation in film theory and criticism. Questions and concepts from feminist film theory, "the gaze" in particular, have gained currency in the discourse of women's studies outside the pages of film journals and have provided crucial tools for thinking about gender and power in discussions of visual culture—advertising, rock video, visual art, and mass media.

The essays, reviews, syllabi, and teaching materials we've included in this issue, as well as the substantial amount of material we were unable to include, bear out in many ways my initial thoughts about these myriad connections. Taken together, the contents of the issue lay out multiple, layered connections between film, its makers, viewers, and teachers, and feminism, feminist theory, women, gender, and women's studies. The essays collected here raise a variety of questions and suggest multiple engagements between the terms on either side of the "and." How have the fields talked to each other? How has the development of a women's movement and feminist thought influenced popular film? Influenced independent and documentary film? How has film served as a medium through which to explore questions of gender raised by women's movement activists and by feminist scholarship? Does film represent an intentional response to cultural change or a sort of cultural sponge that soaks up and purveys gender ideology within the mix of understandings about culture, society, power, and politics? What my work on the issue has also revealed for me are the disconnects and discontinuities between and among the terms I list above. We use film a lot in women's studies, but we often treat it as a transparent window into other women's lives—in other words, without much awareness of it as film. At the same time, as Tania Modleski's essay suggests, film studies has raised questions about film that come out of the insights and discussions within feminist theory but has perhaps lost in the process the sense that "real women" exist as viewers, students, and filmmakers, let alone as people whose lives film may in some way represent.

Certainly the issue and its contents suggest that—whatever the uneasinesses in these multiple engagements—the conversations generated have been and continue to be well worth having.

Film and Feminist Theory: Widening the Lens

The essays in this section engage in a collective rethinking of Laura Mulvey's groundbreaking essay "Visual Pleasure and Narrative Cinema." First published in the British film journal *Screen* in 1975, it has been at the center of discussion about gender and film spectatorship since its appearance. The essays in this section attest to its continued power to provoke discussion. Based in the concepts of Lacanian psychoanalysis, Mulvey's essay argues that popular cinema is formed around a set of "looking relations" which are also power relations in which the always male gaze dominates, controls, and contains the "to-be-looked-at" female. The exercise of subjectivity as women is impossible within this system, Mulvey argues. A woman takes pleasure either in her own fetishized passivity or in gazing through a male eye at her own victimization. Mulvey's work provided feminist scholars with a strong explanatory paradigm for thinking about gender and power in many areas of visual culture, but at the same time posed troubling challenges for those who had imagined that film might also be a tool for women's visibility, organizing, consciousness raising, and creative expression.

Tania Modleski's lead essay traces the history of the relations between and among feminist theory, women's studies, and film studies and suggests that that history has been, at least in part, a long series of engagements with Mulvey's compelling and troubling arguments.

Modleski's essay makes visible the ways in which Mulvey's argument sidelines many of the functions of film that feminists and women's studies students and teachers have found and find most important (a point which is reinforced by their substantial representation among the contributions to this issue): to represent the lives of women as a means of communication, education, political organizing, and consciousness raising, and to explore the work of women filmmakers. Modleski's history shows us the ways in which evolving theory within feminism and film studies that increasingly problematized gender and the category "woman" helped to reinforce the marginalization of these ideas as simplistic or passé. Her critique of the gaze and her argument that "real women" do exist, watch movies with pleasure, make movies, and appear on screens, not only as fetishes but as women, set the stage for the two other pieces in this section and, in one way or another, for every essay in the issue.

Janell Hobson's and Corrinn Columpar's essays both engage Mulvey's paradigm and challenge it, looking at the structures and people that are made invisible by it. These essays take up the challenge that Jane Gaines poses in "White Privilege and Looking Relations" to "rethink film theory along more materialist lines" and argue that the gaze, as Mulvey defines it, hides the complex relations of race, class, nation/colonialism, and sexuality that structure both visual pleasure and who is to be looked at in popular film.

Columpar contests Mulvey's work on two grounds: first, in terms of questioning Mulvey's tools of analysis—the limitations of psychoanalysis and anthropology as grounding theories and methods for film theory and the problem of the visual as its central metaphor for knowledge and power; and second, the ways in which Mulvey's analysis of the gendered gaze obscures other systems of domination, race, and colonialism in particular, that must also be understood as structuring relations of power and the visual. Columpar's essay argues for "theoretical frameworks pragmatic enough to respond to a variety of visual texts and flexible enough to accommodate the complexities of multiple identities" (20).

Janell Hobson's essay "Viewing in the Dark" shares many of Columpar's concerns. Hobson argues that the gaze is of limited usefulness because the female bodies it identifies as "to be looked at" are never black female bodies; in fact, she argues, black female bodies on the screen are most often coded as "to be looked away from." Hobson also counters the centrality of the visual in film analysis, noting that it is often as voices and not as bodies that black women enter mainstream cinema; we hear rather than see them. Hobson, drawing on the films of African American filmmaker Julie Dash, contests the notion that female presence and subjectivity are impossible in the process of filmmaking and film viewing. She highlights both Dash's critique, in her short film *Illusions,* of Hollywood's use of black women and their voices to sing for white women and Dash's defiance, in her feature film *Daughters of the Dust,* of the structure of pleasure Mulvey theorizes. Black female bodies are at the center of Dash's film. In that film, Hobson argues, "the black female spectator repositions herself as viewer and critic by centering black female subjectivity in the arena of visual pleasure," and the black female filmmaker "gains authority" to "reshape the gaze" and "redefine such pleasure for her audience."

Taken together, the three essays in this section indicate the continuing power of Mulvey's analysis of patriarchal looking relations. The simultaneous processes of thinking through and contesting her paradigm have clearly helped to expand the theoretical and methodological approaches feminist film critics and viewers bring to thinking about film.

Gender and Feminism on the Screen: Approaches to Individual Films

The essys in the second section represent the breadth of feminist approaches to film and the multiple ways in which gender enters interpretive activities. One might say that this section answers the call of the first essays for a complex and diverse set of reading practices among feminist film critics. The essays in this section demonstrate that variety along a number of overlapping and intersecting trajectories in terms of both what they examine and the tools with which they work. Considered here are films by both male and female directors, both Hollywood and independent films, and films made inside and outside the United States.

The translation of feminist thinking onto the screen in popular film is explored in the essays by Anna Krugovy Silver on *The Stepford Wives* and Angela Hubler on *Girls Town.* Silver's essay argues that Bryan Forbes's 1975 film is a "feminist allegory" threading together, through its parody of middle-class suburban life, second wave feminism's critiques of housework, the nuclear family, and beauty culture. In the Stepford wives, Silver suggests, we see the literalization, and simultaneously the effective popularization, of the ideas of such second wave thinkers as Betty Freidan, Pat Mainardi, and the Redstockings. Two decades later, Jim Mckay's 1996 film, as Hubler reads it, makes an argument for the necessity of feminist collective action in a film about four adolescent girls who, in taking action against the man who raped their friend, develop and share a common understanding of the oppression in their own lives.

The tools of feminist film analysis have perhaps most often been turned to scrutinizing Hollywood film. Beginning with Marjorie Rosen's *Popcorn Venus* and Molly Haskell's *From Reverence to Rape*, feminist scholars have examined popular film's construction and dissemination of ideologies of gender through its perpetuation of cultural stereotypes of women as desirable object, victim, or whore. Katie Hogan's "Creating the Lesbian Mammy: *Boys on the Side* and the Politics of AIDS" examines this film's deployment of hegemonic ideologies of gender, race, and sexuality. Hogan defines what she calls the "the lesbian mammy" figure as the key to the race and gender politics of Herbert Ross's 1995 film. Ostensibly a film about AIDS and female bonding, *Boys,* Hogan argues, uses the desexualized black lesbian (played by Whoopi Goldberg) to contain the threat to white heterosexual viewers of "black female sexuality, lesbian sexuality, and AIDS" and at the same time to make invisible the impact of AIDS in the lives of African American women.

The final three essays in this section have in common an interest in film as a site of feminist theorizing, particularly theorizing that thinks at the intersections of gender and other markers of difference. These three essays are also particularly attentive to film form and the use of repetition, fragmentation, and disruption to realize narratives. The essays by Dominique Licops and Gwen Raaberg examine the work of two independent women filmmakers, Brigitte Roüan and Yvonne Rainer, as examples of consciously feminist filmmaking. Both essays are interested in the ways that the two filmmakers destabilize dominant meaning systems in their films: Roüan in her film *Outremer,* set in Algeria during the years of its struggle for independence from France, makes visible the ways in which "colonialist and patriarchal scripts function together to reproduce the social order"; Ranier in her avant garde film *Privilege* "counters the cultural invisibility of women," particularly older women and women of color, and "challenges viewers to rethink their relation to power."

Both Raaberg's essay and the final essay in this section, Vivian May and Beth Ferri's examination of Atom Egoyan's 1995 film *The Sweet Hereafter,* see film as a site for acts of feminist theorizing in which the viewer and the filmmaker share. Like the two preceding essays, May and Ferri's essay deploys an intersections analysis to show us how the film deconstructs dominant structures of meaning, specifically the ableist stare and the patriarchal gaze, in Egoyan's film. They argue that Egoyan's fragmented narrative about a teenage girl—an incest survivor disabled by a bus acccident—shows us "disability and gender as interdependent sites of both agency and marginality." Finally, their essay argues explicitly what several others in the section imply: that film is a site for testing out theoretical tools and methodological practices. As a group, the essays in this section propose a broad range of fruitful questions and methods for feminist approaches to film. How does popular film reflect and help to perpetuate dominant ideologies and stereotypes of gender? How does popular film absorb and deploy the insights and objectives of feminist movement? In what ways does the work of feminist filmmakers, both in form and substance, work to destabilize dominant cultural meaning systems? Does film offer a particularly fruitful site for feminist theorizing both by filmmakers and film spectators?

Women Filmmakers and Their Films

The five pieces in this section indicate continued interest in women filmmakers and their work despite the increasing complexity of our understandings of gender and of the relationship between artistic production and gendered experience. Through their films, women directors of both documentary and fiction films have engaged in the political and intellectual work of twentieth-century feminism and other movements for social change. The four interviews and one essay in this section make this plain while focusing our attention on the work of five quite different women filmmakers. Cynthia Baron's essay looks at the work of Australian Aboriginal photographer, video artist, and filmmaker Tracey Moffat, particularly at three films, *Nice Coloured Girls, Bedevil,* and *Night Cries.* Moffat, Baron argues, creates extraordinarily complex, rich, and beautiful films that challenge their audiences' conventional viewing habits and offer them "an Aboriginal view of Australia's internecine history and fraught national identity." Asian American independent filmmaker Renee Tajima-Peña, interviewed here by M. Rosalind Sagara, surveys her own career and reflects on the relative centrality of race and gender politics in her films in light of her work on her most recent film, *Labor Women,* a film commissioned by Asian Women United. Susan Stern, in my interview with her, relates the story of the making of her first film *Barbie Nation* from its conceptualization in response to her daughter's "Jealous Barbie" game to the politics surrounding its completion and attempted marketing to cable stations. Filmmaker Kym Ragusa, interviewed here by Livia Tenzer, explores the relationship between "personal memory and 'official history'" in two films about her two grandmothers: *Passing,* about an incident in the life of her African American grandmother, and *Fuori/Outside,* about her Italian American grandmother. Finally, in her interview with Mexican filmmaker María Novaro, Isabel Arredondo invites her to talk particularly about the themes, structure, and production of two of her feature films, *Lola* and *Danzon*.

The pieces in this section not only turn our attention to the work of the five filmmakers represented here, but they also give us glimpses, through the careers of these five women, into the professional politics of filmmaking and film production and the challenges women filmmakers still face in the development and dissemination of their creative work.

Teaching Film and Films for Teaching: Reflections and Resources

The essay that opens this section, "Women Make Movies Responds to Hate," describes the initiative that Women Make Movies (WMM), the New York City–based distributor of women's films, took after September 11 to make films related to the Arab and Muslim community available free of charge. WMM staff member Xochitl Dorsey speaks compellingly for the power of film as an organizing and educational tool, a power that many of us tap every day in a variety of ways in our classroom and campus uses of films and videos.

The balance of the section offers teaching resources in two general areas: one group of essays and syllabi describes courses focused particularly on feminist approaches to film and film theory, while the other group of materials examines the use in women's studies and discipline-based courses of specific films to teach about women, gender, and intersecting differences. Many of the uses of film described here re-assert the importance of Modleski's point about real women; film remains a powerful way to make women's lived experience present to our students, even as we try also to make them critical viewers of film visual culture, aware that film is always re-presenting and re-framing that experience.

Four of the contributions included here describe feminist film courses. Isabel Arredondo's essay presents her course Motherhood, Desire, and Intimacy, in which she explores those three concepts through comparison of recent films by Mexican women directors and the classic Hollywood films of the 1930s and 1940s. Anne Orwin's essay describes her course Women's Stories, Women's Films, in which she uses films by women directors and film theory to explore the question "Are there uniquely women's stories?" Walter Metz's course Women, Film, and Feminism, laid out in the detailed syllabus included here, looks at the work of women directors in a variety of periods and locations, among them avant garde, early, and recent U.S. cinema, and

European art cinema. The course approaches the films through a range of feminist and film theories and asks students to use those theories in applied exercises. Carol Pierman's course Film and Feminism attempts to teach women's studies graduate teaching assistants to approach film as film, rather than just use film as an information source. Pierman's syllabus introduces graduate students to film theory and a variety of documentaries and feature films directed by women and then asks the students to develop a teaching exercise which uses these newly learned approaches.

The remaining essays in this section, taken together, seem to me to provide an excellent teaching resource for anyone working in women's studies. As a group they detail classroom uses of fourteen different, currently available, documentary films. Diya Abdo's essay "Uncovering the Harem in the Classroom" discusses her showing of Tania Kamal-Eldin's films *Hollywood Harems* and *Covered: The Hejab in Cairo, Egypt* in the context of a course on Arab women writers. The films complement the texts in Abdo's course by making visually present for students both Orientalist images of Arab women in Western popular culture, as *Hollywood Harems* does, and Arab women's experience of the hejab, or veil, as *Covered* does. (*Covered* was available through the Women Make Movies initiative.) Megan Boler's and Katherine Allen's essay "Whose Naming Whom: Using Independent Video to Teach About the Politics of Representation" sets out their use of the documentaries *Girls Like Us, Tongues Untied, The Color of Fear,* and *It's Elementary: Teaching About Gay Issues in Schools*. Through these films, they introduce an intersections analysis of race, class, gender, and sexuality and help students examine the ways in which "individuals and communities are named by the dominant culture and resist those namings" in a range of courses they have taught in education, human development, and women's studies. Ann Schonberger and her colleagues provide in their collection of short essay examples of films they use to introduce issues of diversity into core women's studies courses at the University of Maine, a campus with an overwhelmingly white student and faculty population. Finally, four additional short essays on four films used frequently in women's studies classrooms suggest contexts for teaching these films and rethinking the material they offer. Caitlin Killian essay discusses her use of *Rosie the Riveter* in sociology courses to examine a range of issues including women's employment patterns, racial differences in hiring and employment conditions, gender socialization, and backlash. Debra Liebowitz's essay revisits *Global Assemblyline* in light of a series of questions she poses about the changing situations of workers in the developing world. She argues that the film can still be used effectively to challenge our students' "assumed hierarchies of gender, race, and nation." Lynne Derbyshire's essay sees Sut Jhally's *Dreamworlds II* as providing "a welcome route to examining media representations of women and their sexuality," but, Derbyshire cautions, for the film to be effective it is essential to find ways to break through students' resistance to Jhally's analysis and promote critical viewing among students saturated by their culture with the images that the film examines. Carol Pierman's short essay describes her use in women's studies courses of *Fast Food Women,* Anne Lewis Johnson's film about Appalachian women working in fast food restaurants. For Pierman, the film is a way to make vivid for her students the exploitation of women in low-wage service jobs as it lets a group of women from Whitesburg, Kentucky, most of them laid-off coal miners' wives, relate their experiences of working in fast food franchises.

Taken together, the work of the contributors to this issue bears out, I believe, my initial thought: that the connections between women's studies and film are myriad. While the richness and complexity of the theoretical and pedagogical questions raised in the engagements between women's studies and film are evident in the pieces here, some of the gaps and silences that Tania Modleski's lead essay identifies may also be present. I hope the issue provokes for other readers, as it has for me, a range of questions about both film and women's studies and the ways in which we move theoretical approaches, epistemologies, and pedagogical strategies between them to enrich our thinking on both sides of that "and."

REFERENCES
Gaines, Jane. "White Privilege and Looking Relations: Race and Gender in Feminist Film Theory." *Screen* 29: 4 (1988): 12–17.
Haskell, Molly. *From Reverence to Rape: The Treatment of Women in the Movies.* New York: Holt, Rinehart and Winston, 1973.
Mulvey, Laura. "Visual Pleasure and Narrative Cinema." *Screen.* 16: 3 (1975): 6–18.
Rosen, Marjorie. *Popcorn Venus.* New York: Avon Books, 1973.

Wendy Kolmar is professor of English and director of women's studies at Drew University. Her most recent book is Feminist Theory: A Reader *(1999), coedited with Fran Bartkowski.*

Copyright © 2002 by Wendy Kolmar

On the Existence of Women

A Brief History of the Relations Between Women's Studies and Film Studies

Tania Modleski

I'm honored to have been asked to write a brief history of the dialogue between women's studies and film studies to help introduce this issue of *Women's Studies Quarterly*. That the history of the relations among film, women's studies, and feminist theory (note I've added a third term) hasn't always been polite enough to be characterized as a "dialogue" (not to mention the fact that a lot of the time we got so mad or so full of ourselves we weren't even on speaking terms) makes the task all that much more compelling. I hope the reader will indulge me in a little personal reminiscence, since I was present when women's studies was just beginning to get institutionalized, when film studies programs were proliferating, and when continental film theory first came to the United States.

In 1973 I was teaching, with a master's degree in English, as a lecturer at Old Dominion University in Norfolk, Virginia. The young lecturers, who were all hired on three-year terminal contracts, began introducing women's studies– and cultural studies–type courses into the curriculum. What had happened was that the university, which had previously required students to take twelve units of composition and literature, reduced the number of required credits to three units of composition, or, in other words, one English course. Jobs were on the line, and the majority of regular faculty bowed with ill grace to new courses that would up the English department's enrollments, thus preserving their now underenrolled courses—which they saw as maintaining the highest standards of Western civilization.

For our part we were delighted to play the role of barbarians at the gates. We giddily proposed courses called Women in Literature, Black Literature, Madness in Literature, the City in Literature, and a host of others. In my courses on women in literature, I taught novels, supplemented with films, explicitly as consciousness-raising devices, and indeed, saw no difference at that time between teaching and consciousness-raising. At times I would go into the community and take films with titles like *Growing Up Female* to various women's groups so we could compare our lives with those depicted on the screen, and so I could (woman of the world as I was at twenty-three) educate them about their status as an oppressed group. I wrote little short pieces for local publications on stereotypes (or "images") of women in literature and film. Molly Haskell's book *From Reverence to Rape,* published in 1974, provided me with material to use in these discussions and in my mini-manifestos.

In those heady days, women were organizing unofficially in universities all around the country, and soon women's studies was beginning to become institutionalized. Many of these programs tended to be sociological in nature, but those of us in literary or film studies generally felt comfortable in them, because we ourselves were oriented towards sociological approaches to the study of literature and film.

When my three-year stint at Old Dominion was over, I returned to graduate school, entering the Modern Thought and Literature program at Stanford, where I was in for a shock. Students had taken over the program and were introducing Marxism, feminism, poststructuralism, and deconstruction into the graduate curriculum by way of what were called "ad hoc seminars." Those of us still stuck in certain older ways of understanding film and literature were summarily dismissed for not understanding the complex workings of language and representation and for our naive belief that literature and film did or could (insofar as it presented positive role models for women) reflect reality. I recall the moment when I felt the full force of the powerful sea change.

I had had, and was thrilled to have had, my first film paper published by *Jump Cut,* a publication that emphasized Marxist and feminist approaches to film and that tended to focus on the reactionary ideology in Hollywood films and held up as exemplary foreign art films, particularly those produced in countries with Marxist and socialist regimes. The title of my article was "Swept Away by the Usual Destiny," and the paper excoriated Lina Wertmuller for perpetuating negative images of women in her films.

My friend Dana Polan, who was on the editorial board of *Jump Cut,* suggested I accompany him to a board meeting. In the middle of the meeting a group of young women on the board lambasted editor John Hess for running a cartoon in the recent issue of *Jump Cut* in which a picture of a tin can on a small plate was captioned "La can est sur la saussure." In their view, the new psychoanalytic and structuralist/poststructuralist methodologies were having a difficult time getting a toehold in the academy, and it was irresponsible of *Jump Cut* to mock approaches that could add so much to our understanding of the workings of language and ideology. Shortly after this meeting the women broke from *Jump Cut* and founded their own high-theory feminist film journal, *Camera Obscura.*

As for me, I had no idea what was going on. But I got the message that my recent publication, for which I was still hugging myself with pride (and for which I was expecting great adulation from the *Jump Cut* group) was obsolete even as it hit the stands.

I got my first tenure-track job teaching film and literature at the University of Wisconsin–Milwaukee. I was still struggling with the newer theories, and here I was at the place that had put continental theory on the map. Michel Benamou had headed the Center for Twentieth-Century Studies and introduced many French theorists to this country by putting on prestigious conferences there. A couple of these highly visible conferences were devoted to film theory and had galvanized the world of film studies. Teresa de Lauretis, a professor at Milwaukee, and Jaqueline Rose took on their conferees, making important interventions in film theory by showing how much the use of Lacanian theory by film theorists like Christian Metz and others involved concepts (like fetishism) central to the position of women in the male unconscious. Yet these theorists never discussed the position of women in film.

That such interventions were being made very early in the evolution of the latest film theories made feminism a more integral part of the field than was typically the case with more established fields and disciplines.

But feminist film theory's road was by no means smooth. In many universities around the country, a kind of split occurred between sociologists, who still seemed dominant in women's studies programs (although I have no figures on this), and at least some of the humanities scholars working with the newer French theories. The perception was that women's studies programs and courses, some of which were highly resistant to theory, were devoted to the study of "real women," while literary and film theorists as well as some philosophers were concerned with the *representation* of women. And representation was, believe me, no simple matter. The reflection theory of representation—the notion that art reflected reality—which had been so useful to feminism in its consciousness-raising phase was discredited: Jacques Lacan showed us that language prevented us from having access to the real; no one had mastery over language. Instead, language mastered us. For these and other reasons, the author as origin and producer of language was declared dead. It followed, of course, that the question of the author's gender was moot. This point was driven home to me when a high-powered feminist who was my unofficial mentor explained to me what kind of work she did on texts—and what she most certainly did not do, she said, her voice dripping with disdain, was analyze texts *by* women as if they had some sort of privileged relation to women's experience. Knees knocking, I emphatically agreed, "Of *course* not" (although in fact discovering, reading, and writing about women writers and women filmmakers had been my delight up until then).

Some years of pretty bad teaching on my part ensued, as I struggled to explain that we were not masters of language, cinematic or otherwise. Sadly enough, I was a case in point back then: I might not be able to explain this doctrine to my satisfaction, but I certainly exemplified it.

In those days, I would start all my film courses in women's studies with Laura Mulvey's essay "Visual Pleasure and Narrative Cinema" and then proceed to slog through theories even *more* difficult as the course went on. Mulvey's essay further "disappeared" women by suggesting not only that the female, like the male, author was dead but (1) that woman as spectator was an impossibility in a cinema so oriented toward male fantasy and (2) that woman (as woman) was in an important sense absent from the screen as well, appearances to the contrary notwithstanding. Mulvey drew heavily on Lacanian psychoanalysis to argue that woman represents a threat to men: she signifies castration, and thus is the bearer not the maker of meaning. Images of women on screen are coded not as female but as not-male. Films work to contain the threat women pose, according to Mulvey, by investigating and punishing them or turning them into fetishes.

I always dreaded fetish day in the courses I taught. That's when I had to tell the males (or I should say the male) in the Feminism and Film class that he had been traumatized by the sight of his mother's genitals, which, since he understood the penis to be standard equipment for the whole human race, he perceived as missing, and so he leaped to the conclusion that his dad had lopped hers off and could do the same to him at any time. Thus the sight of the mother's lack was so terrifying he had to repress it. The fetish—a shoe perhaps or a piece of underwear he had seen just before he encountered the sight of the lack—enabled him unconsciously to disavow what he had just (not) seen.

No, I would say to the male in the class, *of course* you don't remember looking up at your mother's naked body—that's the point. The sight was so frightening you had to repress it. All right, yes, it is theoretically possible, so let's *say* you really, really never saw your mom naked—you saw some female naked at some point, right? No, of course you wouldn't have suspected your dad of cutting off the penis of a little girl you're pretty sure he'd never seen. But I don't think I like your *hostile tone;* so let's move on. Okay, then. We've established that because the sight of women's genitals is so traumatic to men, women in cinema are fetishized—glamorized and made into two-dimensional icons, cut up into body parts (legs, breasts, etc.), or their entire bodies made to resemble the phallus through use of costume, furs, etc. Woman as woman—as three-dimensional, whole human being—does not exist within filmic representation. Arethereanyquestions? okaythenseeyounexttime.

By this point feminist film, literary, and cultural studies were moving into a phase in which women were thought not to exist even *off-screen.* Thus the late '80s and early to mid '90s marked the period of the great essentialism debates. Attacks on the category of women were marshaled by historians like Denise Riley, philosophers like Judith Butler, and many others. Any claims made on behalf of women were greeted with suspicion by theorists who saw "gender" as a "regulatory fiction" that often policed the boundaries between men and women, gays and straights, and even women and women. Needless to say, such a critique threatened to render the *women* in *women's studies* an outmoded, not to say a reactionary, concept.

While Butler and others were questioning the category of woman from their positions as philosophers, some lesbians, women of color, and working-class women were also concerned to "trouble" notions of gender by insisting on the differences between themselves and middle-class white women, rather than focusing on the commonalities among women, as feminists had previously tended to do. This trend was occurring in women's studies at large, and feminist film theory was no exception

Lesbian feminist Sue-Ellen Case wrote an article on the butch/femme aesthetic in which she argued that key concepts of heterosexual white female film theorists—in particular Mary Ann Doane's concept of female film spectatorship as masquerade—had been ripped off from lesbian practices. An article by Jane Gaines took white female film theorists to task for remaining blind to questions of race. In the course of the article Gaines makes important points about the very different status of looking in and at films when the subjects and objects of the gaze are Black. Others took up the question of race to note that (as I myself put it) if women as women don't exist in mainstream cinema this absence is far more literally the case with women of color than with white women.

Part of Gaines's agenda was evidently to discredit white feminist uses of psychoanalysis in cinema studies. (To my mind, Gaines was correct in claiming that psychoanalysis hasn't sufficiently accounted for race and the history of racism in American films, but she has not proved it *cannot* do so.) At the end of the essay Gaines specifically pits psychoanalysis against "historical materialism," thereby joining in the growing chorus of scholars in both literary and film studies decrying psychoanalysis as ahistorical. At least one high theorist—Ben Brewster, an editor at *Screen*, the British film journal that had imported French theory into Anglo film criticism and had first published Laura Mulvey's essay—repudiated theory altogether and virtually disappeared into the archive.[1] A dogged insistence that nothing mattered beyond the empirical history that could be extracted from the archive began to hold sway in some quarters of film studies.

Additionally, some major film scholars like David Bordwell and Noel Carroll who apparently felt left in the dust by psychoanalytic critics, particularly feminist ones, began insisting on the appropriateness of a different methodology to the study of film, cognitive philosophy. That cognitivism, with its emphasis on awareness, reasoning, and judgment, was meant not to supplement psychoanalytic theory, with its emphasis on the psyche and the unconscious, but to replace it is announced by the title of a book that the two men edited, *Post-Theory*.

Bordwell himself had long been denouncing the very enterprise of interpretation, frequently singling out examples from feminist work to ridicule. Indeed, some might be tempted to say that his and his cohorts' concern with hard, solid, empirical data and with the workings of reasoning and judgment are very male defenses against the messiness brought to the critical task by women who have focused on the often unsavory contents of the psyche and the unconscious. But to make such a claim would brand me as old-fashioned and essentialist, so I won't go there. Suffice it to say that I myself detect behind one of Bordwell's favorite injunctions—to treat "film as film"—an attitude of "woman as woman" be damned.

To return to the debates that took place *within* feminist film studies, they increasingly, as I have discussed, centered on the question of the existence of women on screen and off. A sizable number of feminist critics (many of them initially coming out of the British cultural studies tradition, like cultural critic Angela McRobbie and film and television critic Charlotte Brunsdon) reacted against the idea that woman was nothing but a signifier *in* films and nothing but a male in drag *at* films—in short that she was nothing at all in and of herself. Critics started to insist on the necessity of studying not only the female spectator as she is constructed by the text but also the female social subject, and they began examining the reactions of real female spectators, seeking out historical evidence of women's responses to particular films (see Stacey) and conducting ethnographies of women viewers—one of the most notable of these studies in this country is Jacquelyn Bobo's analysis of Black women's reactions to *The Color Purple*, among other literary and film texts. Unfortunately, some ethnographies were explicitly pitted against psychoanalysis. But, I think, nothing in principle stands in the way of joining these two modes of inquiry—other than a misguided fear on the ethnographer's part of appearing elitist by going beyond the subject's own self-understanding.

All these debates within feminist film studies have, I think, made us strong.

White middle-class feminist critics are much more aware of the blind spots of theory, particularly those with respect to race, class and sexuality. At the same time, many ideas that once appeared esoteric and difficult to assimilate have filtered into mainstream film and feminist studies. Students no longer seem so baffled by arguments of the constructionists, or by certain psychoanalytic concepts (some students actually become such avid fetish finders that they must be restrained). On the contrary, film studies has conferred on women studies' professors the tools with which to demonstrate how women *are* constructed by various techniques in film and television—those media that most powerfully shape our perceptions of ourselves and others.

To use an example from my own experience: teaching *Top Gun* to a class of freshmen as part of their general education requirement, I realized I was taking on a film that has been a favorite of young people for an astonishing number of years now. When I finished showing clips of the various encounters between the Tom Cruise character, a pilot, and the Kelly McGillis character, an instructor at the flight training school called Top Gun, one of my women students playfully bemoaned the fact that she could no longer see the movie as a great love story between equals. By excerpting the clips the way I had, I had shown the movie to be less about love and more about the man's need to gain power over the woman and to undermine her authority. The student now saw that the threat posed by the woman in the film had to be neutralized in order for her to be reconstructed as subordinate love object. Later in the class, with still a few minutes left to go, the student, again playfully, pleaded with me to play the volleyball scene "one more time"; the other female students enthusiastically seconded the idea. I was happy to oblige, happy to see real women become desiring subjects fully appreciating the half-nude, gleaming male bodies coded for erotic pleasure.

In such ways, students can be made to realize that, especially with respect to Hollywood film, we are involved in contradiction—even when we recognize it as retrograde, film moves us; it works on us; it manipulates us, and we need to recognize how this happens. It is hard for us to disconnect ourselves from the apparatus once we are caught up in it, hard to refuse utterly the pleasures of the text, but analysis makes total innocence and dupery impossible. Furthermore, as real women we bring our own desires to a film and these desires affect the way we see it: interpretation, even for untutored filmgoers, is almost always more than interpellation.

Recognizing real spectators requires us, I think, to recognize real women directors. We won't (I hope) make the mistake of seeing the female author as master over language and art, and we won't assume that because she's a woman she will necessarily create certain kinds of films with specific sensibilities that differentiate her from male authors. But we surely can at times factor her into our analyses. Nancy Miller's idea of feminist analysis of women's work as a collaboration between critic (or viewer) and author gets the formula, I think, exactly right (although the unconscious comes into play in ways that render interpretation unstable).

Finally, there are times when we are even obliged not to let our guards down completely, but to see certain films as reflecting lives of those whom we wish to know better. Take, for example, the documentary film *Behind the Veil*, which shows us a glimpse of the horrors suffered by Afghani women and girls. It would be fatuous to condemn such a film on the grounds that it naively purports to "reflect" the lives of girls and women, that it is not properly self-reflexive, that it doesn't call into question its own truth claims, that the lives it seeks to depict are constructions. So again, I'm not saying that we should abandon our skepticism about claims to truth, objectivity, and the like, only that we should be open enough to see that film can perform all kinds of functions, including didactic and informational ones. To refuse to acknowledge as much would be to consign all women to the *burqa*— to the position of enigma, the space of unknowability she has occupied in much male cinema—for all time.

So, yes, I remain convinced that women exist. I have doubt about some other categories. Feminist theorists and film theorists have gradually turned my thinking around 180 degrees. Judith Butler's demonstration that heterosexuality is derivative of homosexuality; Richard Dyer's work (among that of others) showing how whiteness is constructed against blackness; the studies of feminists maintaining that men define their identities against women (they are everything woman is not)—all have persuaded me that despite men's perception of woman as lack, as not-male, it's white heterosexual men who don't exist. But let's not pop open the champagne too soon. Despite the fact that these chimerical beings are defined by their negativity as not-gay, not-woman, not-Black (except insofar as the traits of these groups are expropriated, in which case we can still say straight white man *as* straight white man doesn't exist), they have a lot of power. This power must continually be contested. So even if you don't agree with me about the existence of women, why don't we adopt a strategic essentialism, pretend we exist, and keep fighting the good fight.

NOTES

1. For a scathing criticism of Brewster's retreat from theory and his conversion into a "pure historian," see Zizek 13.

REFERENCES

Bobo, Jacquelyn. *Black Women as Cultural Readers.* New York: Columbia UP, 1995.

Bordwell, David, and Noel Carroll, eds. *Post-Theory: Reconstructing Film Studies.* Madison: U of Wisconsin P, 1996.

Brunsdon, Charlotte. "Crossroads: Notes on 'Soap Opera'." *Screen* 22.4 (1981): 32–37.

Butler, Judith. *Bodies That Matter.* New York: Routledge, 1993.

———. *Gender Trouble: Feminism and the Subversion of Identity.* New York: Routledge, 1989.

Case, Sue-Ellen. "Towards a Butch-Femme Aesthetic." *Discourse: Journal for Theoretical Studies in Media and Culture* 11.1 (1988–89): 55–73.

de Lauretis, Teresa. "Through the Looking-Glass." *The Cinematic Apparatus.* New York: St. Martin's Press, 1980. 187–202.

Doane, Mary Ann. "Film and Masquerade: Theorising the Female Spectator." *Screen* 23.3–4 (1982): 74–88.

Dyer, Richard. *White.* New York: Routledge, 1997.

Gaines, Jane. "White Privilege and Looking Relations: Race and Gender in Feminist Film Theory." *Screen* 29.4 (1988): 12–17.

Haskell, Molly. *From Reverence to Rape: The Treatment of Women in the Movies.* 2nd ed. Chicago: U of Chicago P, 1987.

Inside Afghanistan: Behind the Veil. Prod. Cassian Harrison. Channel Four (UK), 2001.

McRobbie, Angela. *In the Culture Society: Art, Fashion, and Popular Music.* London: Routledge, 1999.

Miller, Nancy K. "Emphasis Added: Plots and Plausibilities in Women's Fiction." *PMLA* 96.1 (1981): 36–48.

Mulvey, Laura. "Visual Pleasure and Narrative Cinema." *Screen* 16.3 (1975): 6–18.

Rose, Jacqueline. "The Cinematic Apparatus: Problems in Current Theory." *The Cinematic Apparatus.* Ed. Teresa de Lauretis and Stephen Heath. New York: Saint Martin's Press, 1980. 172–86.

Stacey, Jackie. "Feminine Fascinations: Forms of Identification in Star-Audience Relations." *Stardom: Industry of Desire.* Ed. Christine Gledhill. London: Routledge, 1991. 141–63.

Top Gun. Dir. Tony Scott. Paramount, 1986

Zizek, Slavoj. *The Fright of Real Tears: Krzysztof Kieslowski Between Theory and Post-Theory.* London: BFI, 2001.

Tania Modleski *is the Florence R. Scott Professor of English at the University of Southern California. Her publications include* Feminism Without Women: Culture and Criticism in a "Postfeminist" Age, The Women Who Knew Too Much: Hitchcock and Feminist Theory, *and* Loving with a Vengeance: Mass-Produced Fantasies for Women.

Copyright © 2002 by Tania Modleski

The Gaze As Theoretical Touchstone
The Intersection of Film Studies, Feminist Theory, and Postcolonial Theory

Corinn Columpar

A theory is exactly like a box of tools. It has nothing to do with the signifier. It must be useful. It must function. And not for itself. If no one uses it, beginning with the theoretician himself (who then ceases to be a theoretician), then the theory is worthless or the moment is inappropriate. We don't revise a theory, but construct new ones; we have no choice but to make others. It is strange that it was Proust, an author thought to be a pure intellectual, who said it so clearly: treat my book as a pair of glasses directed to the outside; if they don't suit you find another pair; I leave it to you to find your own instrument, which is necessarily an instrument for combat.

—Gilles Deleuze[1]

Visuality: A Site/Sight for Converging Histories

As a scholar working both within and between the fields of film studies, women's studies, and postcolonial studies—three "disciplines" that are all rigorously interdisciplinary in their concerns and methodologies—I am no stranger to the theoretical toolbox. With its emphasis on the local over the universal and the pragmatic over the programmatic, Deleuze's description of that box resonates with the experience of producing criticism at sites where multiple bodies of knowledge intersect and new methodological approaches are needed, for such experiences demand that the critic be, above all else, resourceful. Yet transgressing disciplinary boundaries begs the question of whether theory can travel. In other words, one of the greatest challenges posed by interdisciplinary work is that of translation. Which theoretical frameworks, explanatory concepts, and research practices are applicable and, moreover, useful in contexts other than those out of which they developed? What ideological assumptions inform a given theoretical practice and thus determine its political effects and analytical efficacy? How do various intradisciplinary and interdisciplinary discourses complement, supplement, revise and challenge one another? In short, what tools does the box contain and how do they work independently and in conjunction with one another? Feminist film theory has, for the most part, taken shape around the notion of the male gaze, and while early formulations of this concept facilitated a sustained engagement with questions regarding the impact of gender on one's relationship to the act of looking, they often failed to account for other key determinants of social power and position. The influence of postcolonial studies on film theory, however, has allowed for the creation of a series of theoretical concepts that foreground issues of racial and national difference and acknowledge the role that race and ethnicity play in looking relations. More specifically, postcolonial critics have posited the existence of an ethnographic gaze and a colonial gaze—both of which have complicated the male gaze as monolith and allowed for the emergence of a more nuanced feminist practice within film studies. Critics who have simultaneously explored the sexual and racial politics of representation within a variety of national cinemas include Ella Shohat, Jane Gaines, Christine Holmlund, E. Ann Kaplan, Lola Young, Gina Marchetti, and Fatimah Tobing Rony. With their pioneering work these scholars have created a space for analyses of visual culture that are both feminist and postcolonial in nature and have restored to critical visibility women of color, who are routinely left out of discussions governed by the assumption that, to paraphrase the title of a popular anthology of womanist writings, all the women are white and all the blacks are men (Hull, Smith, and Scott). Rather than review or comment upon this body of work, however, I want to engage in a (meta-)analysis of how these gazes—which are some of the most important tools in the contemporary feminist film critic's box—have been theorized.

At the same time, however, that the male, ethnographic, and colonial gazes demand consideration as related analytical concepts, they also do so as historical phenomena that are similar (all three consolidate a relationship between power and visuality), yet distinct (each has its own ideological and institutional origins). In surveying American and European film history, it becomes quite clear that film is not a window onto the world, nor has its use historically been ideologically neutral; rather it is a signifying system with its own representational legacies, established tropes, industrial constraints, and political baggage. In particular, as that which has, more often than not, consolidated, initiated, or perpetuated various stereotypes as well as a visual economy that privileges a white, male perspective, dominant Western cinema is profoundly implicated in both sexist and racist practice. Consequently, in the words of E. Ann Kaplan, "looking relations are never innocent" (6). While reference to a Western artistic tradition in part explains its aesthetic and ideological development, cinema's birth at the end of the nineteenth century additionally bound its history up with that of other fields of knowledge (for example, anthropology and psychoanalysis), political institutions (for example, colonialism), and social discourses (for example, biological racism and the cult of domesticity)—all of which were, even before the invention of moving pictures, dependent to some extent on the visibility of difference and the overidentification of certain groups of people with their bodies. As the technology that ushered in what Rey Chow calls a "modernity . . . specifically grounded in visuality" (5), cinema further entrenched that dependency by institutionalizing existing looking relations and conventionalizing certain objects of sight. By exploring various writings within film theory that have brought the converging histories cited above to bear upon discussions of cinema, I foreground questions of power, visuality, and corporeality in order to understand the gaze as a theoretical touchstone, a critical tool continually under negotiation.

The Male Gaze: A Return to Theoretical Origins

With the publication of her groundbreaking essay "Visual Pleasure and Narrative Cinema" in 1975, Laura Mulvey set the agenda for the burgeoning field of feminist film criticism and set the stage for a wide array of subsequent musings on the mechanics of the gaze within cinema. Drawing selectively on an Althusserian concern with ideology; Jacques Lacan's rereading of Freud through the lens of structural linguistics; and the emerging body of film theory grounded in psychoanalysis being produced in the early 1970s by scholars such as Jean-Louis Baudry, Christian Metz, Pam Cook, and Claire Johnston, "Visual Pleasure and Narrative Cinema" politicizes the gaze by defining the act of looking as an exercise of power. In particular, Mulvey traces cinema's complicity with patriarchy, positing it as catering to specifically male (unconscious) pleasures and as structured by a sexual division of labor in which men are invested with the power to look while women function primarily as image or object of sight. Elaborating on John Berger's incisive formulation "men act and women appear" (Berger 47), she writes, "In a world ordered by sexual imbalance, pleasure in looking has been split between active/male and passive/female. The determining male gaze projects its fantasy onto the female figure, which is styled accordingly" (Mulvey 33). Yet at the same time that the spectacle of femininity incites pleasure in the male spectator, it is also a potential source of male anxiety given the fact that, within psychoanalytic discourse, woman signifies lack and thus evokes the horrific threat of castration. In order to suppress any anxiety and allay any threat that the male spectator may feel at the unconscious level when contemplating the female body, film, according to Mulvey, employs two principle strategies: fetishistic scopophilia, whereby the specularized woman is made reassuring through her hyperglamorization, and sadistic voyeurism, which entails the investigation of a female character by a male representative of the Law.

Even though almost twenty-five years have passed since the publication of "Visual Pleasure and Narrative Cinema," most of us feminist film critics still feel the need to preface our own remarks by reproducing well-rehearsed synopses of Mulvey's argument such as the one above. While this near compulsive return to a hypothetical theoretical origin certainly attests to the fact that Mulvey's discussion of the male gaze laid the foundation for an entire field of critical inquiry (if not by inspiring disciples, then by providing a paradigm against which to write), it also constitutes an ongoing attempt to come to terms with the legacy engendered by a seemingly provisional, yet ultimately enduring alliance of feminist and psychoanalytic methods. Appropriating psychoanalysis as, in her words, a "political weapon" and approaching issues of representation by way of Freud and Lacan's designation of woman as lack, Mulvey centers psychoanalytic discourse in a way that forces a consideration of whether the analytical ends justify the methodological means. Furthermore, the article begs the question of how invested Mulvey is in Lacan's theoretical model. That is, does she make reference to psychoanalysis because she believes it to be the purveyor of some transhistorical truth (be that truth one of essences or social convention) or because she regards it as an historically specific discourse uniquely qualified to analyze film form given the degree to which it has consciously or unconsciously influenced filmmaking practice and twentieth-century culture at large? In other words, does Mulvey impose a psychoanalytic spin on questions of film form, or does she expose psychoanalysis to be a structuring discourse of cinema?

These same queries emerge when one takes into consideration Mulvey's "Afterthoughts on 'Visual Pleasure and Narrative Cinema' Inspired by *Duel in the Sun*," for in this follow-up to her landmark essay it is once again difficult to ascertain the extent to which the author maintains a critical distance from psychoanalytic theory. In "Afterthoughts" Mulvey attempts to redress certain lacunae in her earlier work by foregrounding the issue of female spectatorship and drawing on examples from the female-centered genre of melodrama. Invoking Freud's characterization of women's lives as an ongoing oscillation between an active, phallic masculinity and a passive, conditioned femininity, Mulvey examines the ease with which the female spectator engages in transvestism in order to participate in the pleasures offered by dominant cinema. As a means of exploring both the rewards and difficulties of such strategic "masculinization," she uses as a point of comparison the characters of Pearl from *Duel in the Sun* and Stella from *Stella Dallas*, both of whom must choose between two men and, by extension, the poles of male and female identification that they represent. In the process of her analysis Mulvey enacts a close reading of Freud's article titled "Femininity" that culminates in her identification of a certain slippage with regard to how Freud conceives of the relationship between masculinity and activity on the one hand, and femininity and passivity on the other. What Freud initially labels as associations of "convention" are eventually essentialized as he invokes "biology" and "nature" when discussing libidinous drives and male aggression. While Mulvey's concern with this slippage is born of a desire to theorize female agency as something other than a regressive masculinity, her subsequent reliance upon Freud's ideas for their power to explain the female spectatorial experience makes her a participant in his psychoanalytic paradigm. That is, even though she peppers her writing with quotation marks, throwing into question the terms *femininity, masculinity, active,* and *passive* as well as the notion of a "correct" femininity, Mulvey still structures her argument around these terms, thus reifying more than problematizing them.

Of course, this concern with the spirit in which an author appropriates a certain discourse for the purposes of analysis is one raised not only by Mulvey's work or, for that matter, even all work grounded in psychoanalysis; yet I would argue that part of the reason that Mulvey's institutional model of the cinema has been hashed and rehashed so many times is that it constitutes a theoretical primal scene involving strange bedfellows. That is, for many feminist scholars, Mulvey's coupling of political concerns and psychoanalytic methods is an uneasy one that has, nonetheless, set a particular precedent. For others, that coupling is a logical response to the historically coincident emergence of both cinema and psychoanalysis at the end of the nineteenth century and to the number of resultant congruencies between the way women are positioned within film on the one hand, and within Freudian and post-Freudian discourse on the other. One author who quite persuasively attends to the subject of these congruencies in a number of her projects and, at the same time, remains self-reflexive in her methodological choices is Mary Ann Doane. Defining her relationship to psychoanalysis as ambivalent, Doane openly advocates a degree of disobedience to the texts of Freud and Lacan while simultaneously acknowledging the crucial importance of psychoanalysis insofar as it "enhances the legibility of the ideological effects of Western culture's construction of femininity" and, furthermore, seems a "perfect fit" with film studies given its unique capacity to explain spectatorial experience and representational conventions (Doane, "Introduction" 7–8).

In her most canonized article, "Film and the Masquerade: Theorizing the Female Spectator," Doane draws upon psychoanalytic accounts of female specificity as a lack of distance from one's body and, thus, one's self (produced not only by Lacan, but also by certain key figures in the theoretical corpus known as "French feminism," such as Michele Montreley, Sarah Kofman, and Luce Irigaray) in order to theorize female spectatorship in terms of a certain proximity that inspires a narcissistic response to the image. Although she is careful to qualify her argument as an engagement with discursive constructions of femininity rather than a treatise on female essence, she must nonetheless clarify her project for the sake of her critics in a later work thus:

> My point in the essay was not that this [designation of femininity as closeness] is an adequate definition of femininity but that it is a persistent one both in various theories of discourse informed by psychoanalysis and in cinema itself (particularly in its alignment of the female spectator with genres such as the "weepie" or tearjerker). These discourses assign to the woman a *position,* a *place* within patriarchal culture. Certainly the position is unreal—in the sense that it does not specify all behaviors or particular differences of individual women. But an admission of its unreality does not constitute a denial of its forcefulness, its effectivity. (Doane, "Masquerade Reconsidered" 35)

Foregrounding her interest in the material effects of discursive constructs, Doane states in no uncertain terms the fact that cinema and psychoanalysis are concurrent examples of the same Western episteme. Yet even a cursory review of film history and criticism reveals a more complex relationship between the two—that is, that psychoanalysis is also implicated in and constitutive of cinema in highly significant ways. One need look no further than the appropriation of Freudian symbolism in surrealist cinema of the 1920s, on the one hand, or the incorporation of the talking cure as therapeutic process into Hollywood melodramas of the 1940s, on the other, in order to surmise that psychoanalysis has had a significant impact on the explicit content of film.

Additionally, the precision with which Mulvey's model describes the work of Alfred Hitchcock, for example, does indeed suggest a less overt and therefore more insidious influence whereby the form of certain films has, perhaps unwittingly, been informed by psychoanalysis and is consequently structured by the threat of castration, the association of woman with lack, and the visibility of sexual difference. Finally, even if one refuses to concede that Mulvey's adoption of psychoanalytic methods was, at least in the case of some films, textually warranted, the institutionalization of film studies as an academic discipline, which has allowed for a systematic dissemination of film theory, guarantees some degree of exchange between psychoanalysis and contemporary film production as (future) filmmakers are exposed to film criticism infused with a psychoanalytic orientation.

Thus it is possible to locate at the site of cinematic textual production the influence of psychoanalysis, be it conscious or unconscious, systematic or idiosyncratic. However, the extent of that influence and, by extension, the limits of psychoanalytic theory as method of analysis are made glaringly clear by Doane in "Dark Continents: Epistemologies of Racial and Sexual Difference in Psychoanalysis and Cinema." In this article, which approaches the intersection of race and gender on screen through Freud's use of the trope of the "dark continent," she writes, "Psychoanalysis can . . . be seen as a quite elaborate form of ethnography—as a writing of the ethnicity of the white Western psyche" (211) With this statement Doane defines psychoanalysis to be a racially specific discourse that draws on blackness as metaphor (in other words, female sexuality as the "dark continent") while normalizing whiteness and the European/American nuclear family as setting for Oedipality. For some scholars such as Jane Gaines, this assessment is grounds for an argument about the utter inadequacy of psychoanalytic methods; for others, most notably Franz Fanon and Homi Bhabha, it demonstrates issues of racial difference not to be outside the scope of psychoanalysis, but rather to be the site of a self-defining repression, a type of structuring absence at the very center of psychoanalytic discourse. For all these critics it attests to the need for a historicization of psychoanalysis in conjunction with a consideration of historical factors in the production and consolidation of racial identities. As explored in the following section, such historicizing impulses have taken shape in film studies around two distinct, yet related, areas of inquiry: imperialism and anthropology or, more specifically, the colonial gaze and the ethnographic gaze generated, respectively, by each. But before going any further, it is necessary to return to Mulvey yet again.

Blind Spots and the Race to Learn to See

Attacked by its detractors as deterministic at best and prescriptive at worst, "Visual Pleasure and Narrative Cinema" has provoked countless challenges and revisions. While the majority of critiques have taken as their starting point the article's failure to account for the experiences of actual filmgoing women and its inability to conceive of a female act of spectatorship, I want to bracket those concerns for the moment in order to approach them in a more roundabout manner—that is, through a focus on the ways that critics have problematized Mulvey's conceptualization of the gaze itself. As I stated above, the gaze that Mulvey theorizes is one that controls; to be precise, it is one that not only objectifies women, but also aligns itself with the power to act, to move the narrative forward, and to exact punishment for transgressions against phallic Law. As the lynchpin of her theory of the cinema as apparatus, it emerges in "Visual Pleasure and Narrative Cinema" as one that programmatically privileges all men and institutionalizes a monolithic male perspective. Under challenge in certain subsequent writings, however, is this assumed identity between the look, mastery, and masculinity. For instance, critiques from within a psychoanalytic framework have questioned Mulvey's characterization of the gaze as necessarily controlling and supportive of sadism. In this vein, D. N. Rodowick argues that the political and polemical nature of her argument leads Mulvey to ignore the masochistic components of the gaze, while Gaylyn Studlar seizes upon this "blind spot" in order to construct a theoretical model featuring a "masochistic aesthetic," a focus on pre-Oedipality and the oral mother, and a submissive gaze that counters Mulvey's gaze point for point.

Yet it is those critiques that highlight the limitations of psychoanalysis as methodological tool by demanding a consideration of how factors other than gender determine one's access to the gaze that have paved the way for a whole new avenue of inquiry within film theory. In "White Privilege and Looking Relations: Race and Gender in Feminist Film Theory," Jane Gaines foregrounds the historical prohibition of the black gaze and stresses the need to "rethink film theory along more materialist lines, considering for instance, how some groups have historically had the license to 'look' openly while other groups have 'looked' illicitly" (208). Contending that psychoanalysis is ill-equipped to deal with issues such as race and class because of its universalizing  premises and disregard for actual historical experience, Gaines argues that a feminist film theory grounded in psychoanalysis operates ideologically insofar as it perpetuates a white feminist perspective and agenda by failing to address structures of oppression other than patriarchy. Furthermore, she cites the ahistorical nature of not only Mulvey's work, but also that of a number of contemporary feminist theorists, as responsible for creating a model of patriarchy that is unable to accommodate either female agency in the face of oppression or differences over time and across space in the way that patriarchy functions. As such, she advocates the adoption of a historical materialist perspective (derivative of Marxism) that is concerned more with social reality and ideological ruptures than with theoretical abstractions and the ideological rigidity attributed to certain signifying practices. With such a methodological shift Gaines throws a wrench into the workings of what Constance Penley calls "the bachelor machine" (the cinema as patriarchal apparatus), and issues a call for film criticism that takes as its starting point the plurality of historical experience and the recognition of multiple axes of oppression.

Since 1986, when Gaines's article first appeared in an issue of *Cultural Critique,* many film scholars have responded to her call by exploring the role of race in cinema both historically and textually. That the issue of class has received far less attention, at least in the context of film criticism and production in the United States, is no doubt largely attributable to the fact that the entrenched myth that every American is middle class has bred a silence around the topic that few have felt compelled to break. Yet at the same time, with regard to questions of visual representation, race has a salience that class lacks given the extent to which it is dependent upon a scopic regime of difference. In *American Anatomies: Theorizing Race and Gender,* Robyn Wiegman discusses the process by which race has come to be "constituted as a visual phenomenon, with all the political and ideological force that the seemingly naturalness of the body as the locus of difference can claim" (22). Building upon Michel Foucault's *The Order of Things,* which takes as its subject the various ways that knowledge has been organized in the West since the Renaissance, Wiegman examines how the rise of the discipline of natural history in the seventeenth century served to align vision with scientific authority and set the stage for the emergence of a racial taxonomy based on corporeality. While initially constructed to be nonhierarchical and divested of any assumptions regarding people's innate worth, this taxonomy was eventually co-opted by certain researchers in the name of race science and transformed definitively into a racial hierarchy constructed out of the assumption of white supremacy. With this transformation, interest in the superficial effects of the body gave way to a concern with the essential self expressed by such effects such that the visible body gained the status of a text to be read only by scientists who, armed with various mechanical apparatuses, were practiced in the search for some invisible interiority. What these professionals found in the course of their search, however, speaks volumes about their own subjectivity and very little about their subjects/objects of scrutiny, for, in the words of Jacqueline Urla and Jennifer Terry, bodies became "surfaces onto which physicians, scientists, and lay people [could] inscribe and project powerful cultural meanings and moral prohibitions" (6). Given the need to justify European imperialist expansion and the systematic enslavement of certain populations, what was inscribed and projected onto nonwhite bodies with regularity were assumptions about their inherent inferiority and "primitive" nature.

Thus, while the naturalists relied upon the objective eye for its ability to discern difference between entities and to envision taxonomic schemas, the ascendancy of race sciences established a tautology of authority in which to see was to know and to know was to have institutional control of the gaze. This scopic regime fed both colonialist politics and anthropological practice in the nineteenth century insofar as it served to maintain the distance upon which colonialism's claim to political authority and anthropology's claim to discursive authority rested. In short, it posited an insurmountable difference between white people and the nonwhite people under their rule, tutelage, or scrutiny, and thus provided the necessary justification for a whole range of politically and personally invasive acts. Not surprisingly, given the extent to which biological racism, anthropology, and colonialism were grounded in a visual economy, cinema was complicit in these regimes from the moment of its birth. By institutionalizing looking relations forged in other contexts (namely, the colonies, laboratories, museums, world fairs, and the anthropological "field"), it has perpetuated the hegemony of certain racial constructs and consolidated what Sander Gilman describes as an ideologically charged iconography in which the representation of individuals "implies the creation of some greater class or classes to which the individual is seen to belong" (223). Contemporary film scholars have traced the historical collusion between visuality, anthropology, and colonialism by discussing, alternately, the ethnographic gaze and the colonial gaze as the mechanisms by which the nonwhite subject has been and continues to be fixed in his/her otherness. In other words, like Mulvey's male gaze, which "projects its fantasy onto the female figure," the ethnographic and colonial gazes project their own fantasies, the most salient of which revolves around the notion of authenticity.

The Racialized Gaze: A Return to Evolutionary Origins

Assuming psychoanalysis to be, as Doane suggests, an ethnographic writing of the white subject, anthropology emerges as its counterpart within Western thought to the extent that "[its] historical unity lies in its subject matter: dark-skinned people known as 'savages' or 'primitives.'"[2] Much of contemporary anthropological work has responded to poststructuralist critique with a self-reflexive interrogation of its methods, scientific status, assumptions regarding cultural translation, and constructions of local place/global space (see, for example, Clifford and Marcus; Gupta and Ferguson; Lavie and Swedenburg; Clifford) At its outset, however, anthropology was propelled by the positivist impulse that Foucault and, in turn, Wiegman associate with the emergence of biology in the nineteenth century and, thus, conceived of itself as a science of racial difference, an objective evaluation and classification of cultures other to that of the white Westerner. For this reason Trinh T. Minh-ha defines it as a brand of gossip engaged in by white men. She writes,

> A conversation of "us" with "us" about "them" is a conversation in which "them" is silenced. "Them" always stands on the other side of the hill, naked and speechless, barely present in its absence. Subject of discussion, "them" is only admitted among "us," the discussing subjects, when accompanied or introduced by an "us," member, hence the dependency of "them" and its need to acquire good manners for the membership standing. The privilege to sit at table with "us," however, proves both uplifting and demeaning. It impels "them" to partake in the reduction of itself and the appropriation of its otherness by a detached "us" discourse. (Trinh 67)

While this passage is part of a wholesale condemnation of anthropology that is problematic in its failure to account for the type of autocritical work invoked above, it foregrounds the alienating, compromising, and polarizing effects of a classical anthropology both informed by and productive of assumptions about the absolute difference between self and other.

The consolidation of this difference into a visual shorthand or racial iconography was greatly facilitated by photography and eventually film, both of which were held in high regard by the scientific community because of their assumed transparency, objectivity, and ability to save for posterity visual documentation of races considered to be always, already vanishing. In fact, the history of early cinema is in many ways a history of scientific method, for it was in order to document and study human and animal locomotion that Étienne-Jules Marey and Eadweard Muybridge experimented with series photography in the 1890s, and thereby paved the way for both motion picture technology and the realist aesthetic best exemplified by the Lumiere Brothers' actualités and travelogues. Ethnographic (pre-)cinema got its start as early as 1895 when a student of Marey's named Félix-Louis Regnault turned his teacher's chronophotographic gun on "the other" for the first time, thus making the analysis of images of movement and, in time, moving images central to anthropological method. Regnault produced a variety of chronophotographic studies of West African performers at the Paris Ethnographic Exposition of 1895 with the conviction that "by filming the movements—walking, running, jumping, climbing—of West Africans, and comparing them with films of the movements of Europeans, one could establish an evolutionary typology of the races. Human history could be read in locomotion" (Rony 14).

In her book *The Third Eye: Race, Cinema, and Ethnographic Spectacle*, Fatimah Tobing Rony examines this early work by Regnault, as well as his subsequent use of motion picture technology, in order to trace the birth of the scientific research film and demonstrate the extent to which cinema was, from its inception, a persuasive means of visualizing and inscribing race. Expanding her definition of ethnographic cinema to accommodate not only scientific and educational films, but also fictional narrative films, Rony explores certain formal and thematic continuities between Regnault's corpus and later films such as *Nanook of the North* and *King Kong* in order to posit first the process of racialization and second an implicit narrativization of evolution as the defining elements of ethnographic cinema. That is, as ethnographic cinema denies the anthropological subject historical agency, individual voice, and psychological complexity, it reduces him/her to a racial "type" and constructs him/her as "ethnographiable," as one existing outside of or, more accurately, prior to history. As such, the mise-en-scène of ethnographic cinema is what Anne McClintock calls anachronistic space. Defined as "a permanently anterior time within the geographic space of the modern empire" (McClintock 30), anachronistic space is created by mapping difference onto a diachronic axis whose teleology posits the white male as the crowning achievement of historical progress and the racialized native as the embodiment of his evolutionary past.

Because of its need to primitivize native cultures and locate them in a space of difference, classical anthropology has been reluctant to acknowledge change within those cultures, be the cause of that change some force from within the community or the disruptive presence of the anthropologist him/herself. As a result, ethnographic cinema constructs an ahistorical image of the native around which a discourse of primitive purity is generated and through which the actual effects as well as the imperialist underpinnings of the anthropological process are effaced. Contrary to its self-image as a science practiced by disinterested experts, anthropology benefited the white community out of which it developed. Ethnographic cinema, like museums and world fairs, allowed for the consumption of cultural difference, even by those living nowhere near the borderlands of the colonies, and thereby facilitated the formation of what Deborah Root dubs a white "cannibal culture" (*Cannibal Culture*). Ella Shohat touches upon one of the visual pleasures enjoyed by the presumably white, Western consumer of ethnographic cinema when she contends that "the mimetic capabilities of the cinema satisfied the three-dimensional need for gazing at the 'other,' bridging, as it were, the spatial gap between the Western spectators and the objects of their gaze" ("Imaging" 68). Yet at the same time that cinematic documentation in the name of science closed a geographical gap, it manufactured the theoretical gap upon which the power of the gaze rests and by which people from other cultures were rendered reassuringly distant, yet utterly knowable. Furthermore, in watching these ethnographic films, the viewer was taught how to "read bodies" and, in the process, was reassured of his/her superiority: while the established iconography of race fixed nonwhite bodies as an immediately recognizable sign of the primitive and as "the essential index of authenticity" (Rony 195), whiteness came to be synonymous with modernity, historical progress, and a civilizing influence. In defining the other, white culture defined itself such that the native functioned not only to provide a glimpse into a remote prehistory of humanity, but also to embody difference from a white norm that was constructed retroactively as "historifiable."

Given the above account of looking relations at work in ethnographic cinema and scientific discourse, it should be readily apparent that anthropology and colonialism are thoroughly implicated in each other.[3] While anthropology provided the rationale for the "white man's burden," colonialism was its modus operandi; as a result, it was the construction of racial difference forged within anthropological discourse that fortified colonialist ideology and informed colonialist practice during the heights of imperialism. The specularization of racialized bodies positioned white Western viewers not only as ersatz scientists and subjects reassured of their race-less-ness, but also as, in the words of Robert Stam and Louise Spence, "armchair conquistadors" (4). In terms of its mechanics, the look associated with colonialism by various film theorists such as Kaplan (the "imperial gaze"), Reina Lewis (the "orientalist gaze"), and Shohat (the "disciplinary gaze of empire") is one that is functionally synonymous with Rony's ethnographic gaze, in that it systematically empowers white culture and reduces indigenous bodies to static icons of difference. Yet by foregrounding the context of imperialist politics, the "colonial gaze" mandates a consideration of film's role in the creation of not only the fiction of race, but also that of nation.

The majority of scholars interested in the relationship between colonialism and the cinema have focused their attention primarily on fictional narrative films, since their status as "entertainment" (as opposed to "science") usually guarantees that they are more widely distributed, enthusiastically received, and frequently viewed than ethnographic cinema. Furthermore, because they deliver an ideological message that, while less overt, is often all the more insidious than that of films made in the name of anthropological inquiry, narrative films are the venue where myths around the issue of national identity are not only most widely disseminated, but also most persuasively presented. Because those European powers with the most expansive colonial empires—namely, Britain, France, and Germany—were also home to some of the most prolific and commercially successful film industries of the silent period, they ensured that when their white audiences could not come to the European cinema, the European cinema would come to them. In this way, they were able to create a sense of national community and racial solidarity within a scattered populace. As Shohat and Stam write, "Given the geographically discontinuous nature of empire, cinema helped cement both a national and an imperial sense of belonging among disparate people. For the urban elite of the colonized lands, the pleasures of cinema-going became associated with the sense of a community on the margins of its particular European empire (especially since the first movie theaters in these countries were associated with Europeans and Europeanized local bourgeoisie)"(102).

The success of such constructions of nation can be measured most readily by the extent to which they consolidate a sense of national identity not only among the colonizing population, but also among the colonized. In *Black Skin, White Masks* Franz Fanon employs psychoanalysis in the theorization of the self-alienated colonial subject in Africa who either must identify across racial boundaries and with the nation of his/her oppressors or submit to a socially induced self-loathing. Explaining the impact of imperialism on the psychological as well as the political life of the colonized, Fanon writes of the "black schoolboy in the Antilles, who in his lessons is forever talking about 'our ancestors, the Gauls'" (147) and who, upon attending a Tarzan film with his friends, readily identifies with the only character whom both colonial society at large and that film in particular empower: the white hero. As suggested by Fanon's comments and as made explicit by Shohat's choice of nomenclature when describing imperial looking relations, the colonial gaze contains a disciplinary component that the ethnographic gaze lacks because of anthropology's investment in maintaining (what is believed to be) an authentically primitive object of study. This is not to say that ethnographic cinema does not construct (as opposed to reflect) bodies in its imaging of cultural purity and regressive savagery, but rather that that construction depends upon the dissuasion of change and a minimization of Western influence. In the majority of fictional narrative films produced during the heights of imperialism, however, nonwhite characters function as mere foils for a white protagonist in that they are either vilified, reduced to self-effacing sidekicks, or relegated to the background as "local color." Making indigenous people's access to subjectivity contingent on a self-regulation of their otherness, these films rendered native bodies docile by issuing a mandate for imitation of the dominant culture.

Although it is misleading to speak of a colonial cinema per se given the shifts in global power that have ushered us into a "postcolonial" present, the ethnographic gaze and colonial gaze still structure most mainstream films in the anglophone world (if not the world over) and, thus, define a colonialist aesthetic. Furthermore, in spite of shifts in actual ethnographic practice and academic anthropology, the ethnographic impulse discussed by Rony primarily in relation to films made before 1940 continues to hold sway over the Western imagination, since "the episteme of the Ethnographic is still alive and well, especially in popular media" (Rony 197). While a change in the political climate, borne of the various decolonization struggles and civil rights movements since the 1950s, has resulted in a positioning of the native as an object of romanticization and yearning more than derision and aggression, the tendency to relegate indigenous cultures to a temporal space outside history and to a textual space outside narrative persists nonetheless. A particularly salient case in point is the epic of colonial nostalgia, which has proved remarkably compelling to Western audiences in recent years, as evidenced by the overwhelming success, critical, popular, or both, of films such as *Out of Africa* (Sydney Pollack, 1985); *The Piano* (Jane Campion, 1993); and *The English Patient* (Anthony Minghella, 1996). While all these movies are marked by the historical moment of their production and, thus, characterized to varying degrees by a critical stance toward the institution of colonialism, they also bear traces of a colonial legacy insofar as they capitulate to certain colonialist tropes and racialized fantasies.

Multiple Identities, Multiple Gazes

As demonstrated by the preceding discussion of race and visuality, the colonial and ethnographic gazes are like the male gaze insofar as they accord their bearers a position of mastery and designate their objects as the site/sight of difference. Moreover, when considered in conjunction with one another, the three gazes can be seen as colluding in a single ideological project: the interpellation of the film spectator into a hegemonic viewing position in which the Western, white, male identity is normative.[4] Despite the convergences of the three discussed gazes, however, it is necessary to resist the temptation to conflate them or reduce them to an identical logic given their distinct histories, legacies, and mechanics; to fail to do so can severely limit one's critical approach. Take, for example, Homi Bhabha's argument for a reading of the stereotype in terms of a fetishism wherein that which is simultaneously acknowledged and disavowed is racial rather than sexual difference (see "The Other Question"). In suggesting that the racialized gaze (in other words, the ethnographic and colonial gazes) and the male gaze are comparable insofar as they are both structured by a perceived lack—of the penis on the one hand and the dominant skin/race/culture on the other—Bhabha creates a provocative theoretical model that addresses the normalization of whiteness and the persistence of racial stereotyping. Yet he does so at the expense of women, since his model is unable to take gender into consideration or even to recognize the unique predicament of the colonized woman. As Christine Anne Holmlund points out, "Even when read as metaphors for psychic interactions, the decision to posit racial/ethnic difference as *analogous* to sexual difference invariably makes it hard for Bhabha to think the two categories together and against each other, with the result that, once again, the voices of women as colonizers and colonized are distorted or silenced" (7). In other words, the problems arising from Bhabha's analysis-by-analogy are the same problems posed by feminist theories that discuss the "colonization" of women or patriarchy as a form of "slavery," and thereby reduce to metaphor the experiences of women who have been victims of racist institutions and, consequently, produce an analysis of gender relations that applies only to white women. That is, in forging a comparison between multiple axes of oppression, Bhabha is unable to account for the intersection of those axes.

This oversight, however, does not mean that Bhabha's comments are not useful, for they most certainly are; rather, it suggests the need for theoretical frameworks that are pragmatic enough to respond to a variety of visual texts and flexible enough to accommodate the complexities of multiple identities. Only after acknowledging the respective histories (both theoretical and practical) of the male, ethnographic, and colonial gazes as well as the ways in which the institutions out of which those gazes developed (patriarchy, colonialism, anthropology, psychoanalysis) diverge as well as converge historically and substantively, can one explore the various ways in which they intersect. For example, they may collude in the reproduction of an order that is imperialist, racist, and patriarchal, as demonstrated by a number of westerns, such as the archetypical *The Searchers* (John Ford, 1956), which envision American identity in terms of a manifest destiny that depends upon xenophobia with respect to native people and the mastery of space that masculine privilege affords; or it may be the case that the subversion of one depends upon or is tempered by the realization of another, as in the case of *The Piano*, where a stereotypically primitive native culture contributes to the sexual "liberation" of a white woman, or *Dances with Wolves* (Kevin Costner, 1990), which delivers a critique of imperialism yet relies upon the trope of the noble savage in order to do so; or, finally, the potential for radical critique may be opened up by a simultaneous challenge to all three, as in Tracey Moffatt's experimental short *Nice Coloured Girls* (1987), which employs a variety of anti-illusionistic representational techniques to deconstruct accounts of female Aboriginal identity produced by colonizers of the past and to examine female Aboriginal subjectivity in the present. The tip of the iceberg, the preceding examples can only hint at the myriad ways that the discourses of sexual, racial, and national difference intersect in film. Only with our continual exploration and interrogation of these intersections will our understanding of the male gaze, that cornerstone of feminist film theory that is continually being perpetuated and subverted, negotiated, and challenged, remain vital.

NOTES

1. "Intellectuals and Power: A Conversation Between Michel Foucault and Gilles Deleuze" in Michel Foucault, *Language, Counter-memory, Practice* (Ithaca: Cornell UP, 1977), 208.
2. In making this assertion, Rony draws upon the work of the anthropological historian George W. Stocking, Jr. See *The Third Eye*, 7.
3. In the introduction to his anthology *Colonial Situations: Essays on the*

Contextualization of Ethnographic Knowledge (Madison: U of Wisconsin P, 1991), George W. Stocking, Jr., presents a very cursory, yet informative, overview of the disciplinary crisis sparked in the late 1960s when scholars began to force the anthropological community to acknowledge the extent to which ethnography and colonialism were/are historically related to and dependent upon one another.

4. Laying bare the national, racial, and gender components of this viewing position in a most striking way is the trailer for Nicholas Roeg's *Walkabout* (1971), an Australian film about an urbanite teenaged girl and her little brother who, while stranded in the outback, meet up with an Aboriginal boy in the midst of a walkabout. Declaring via voice-over "The Aborigine and the girl—30,000 years apart—together. *Walkabout*. Just about the most different film you'll ever see," the trailer displaces onto the film itself ("the most different film") the radical otherness of its two protagonists vis-à-vis the white, Western, male norm. While the difference of the black Aboriginal male is romanticized throughout the film, it is nonetheless produced by a racist model of evolutionary progress that relegates him to the anachronistic space discussed by McClintock. In contrast, the white girl's difference is sexual in nature and consequently sexualized throughout the film so as to incite desire on the part of both her traveling companion and the film viewer.

REFERENCES

Berger, John. *Ways of Seeing*. London: British Broadcasting Corporation and Penguin Books, 1972.

Bhabha, Homi. "The Other Question: The Stereotype and Colonial Discourse." *The Location of Culture*. New York: Routledge, 1994. 66–84.

Chow, Rey. *Primitive Passions: Visuality, Sexuality, Ethnography, and Contemporary Chinese Cinema*. New York: Columbia UP, 1995.

Clifford, James. *The Predicament of Culture: Twentieth-Century Ethnography, Literature, and Art*. Cambridge: Harvard UP, 1988.

Clifford, James, and George Marcus. *Writing Culture: The Poetics and Politics of Ethnography*. Berkeley and Los Angeles: U of California P, 1986.

Doane, Mary Ann. "Dark Continents: Epistemologies of Racial and Sexual Difference in Psychoanalysis and Cinema." *Femmes Fatales: Feminism, Film Theory, Psychoanalysis*. New York: Routledge, 1991. 209–48.

———. "Introduction: Deadly Women, Epistemology, and Film Theory." *Femmes Fatales: Feminism, Film Theory, Psychoanalysis*. New York: Routledge, 1991. 1–14.

———. "Masquerade Reconsidered: Further Thoughts on the Female Spectator." *Femmes Fatales: Feminism, Film Theory, Psychoanalysis*. New York: Routledge, 1991. 33–43.

Fanon, Franz. *Black Skin, White Masks*. New York: Grove Press, 1967.

Gaines, Jane. "White Privilege and Looking Relations: Race and Gender in Feminist Film Theory." *Issues in Feminist Film Criticism*. Ed. Patricia Erens. Bloomington: Indiana UP, 1990. 197–214.

Gilman, Sander. "Black Bodies, White Bodies: Toward an Iconography of Female Sexuality in Late Nineteenth-Century Art, Medicine, and Literature." *Race, Writing, and Difference*. Ed. Henry Louis Gates, Jr. Chicago: U of Chicago P, 1986. 223–61.

Gupta, Akhil, and James Ferguson. *Culture, Power, Place: Explorations in Critical Anthropology*. Durham: Duke UP, 1997.

Holmlund, Christine Anne. "Displacing Limits of Difference: Gender, Race, and Colonialism in Edward Said and Homi Bhabha's Theoretical Models and Marguerite Duras's Experimental Films" *Quarterly Review of Film and Video* 13.1–3 (1991): 1–22.

Hull, Gloria, Barbara Smith, and Patricia Bell Scott. *All the Women Are White, All the Blacks Are Men, but Some of Us Are Brave*. New York: The Feminist Press, 1981.

Kaplan, E. Ann. *Looking for the Other: Feminism, Film, and the Imperial Gaze*. New York: Routledge, 1997.

Lavie, Smadar, and Ted Swedenburg. *Displacement, Diaspora, and Geographies of Identity*. Durham: Duke UP, 1996.

Marchetti, Gina. *Romance and the Yellow Peril*. Berkeley and Los Angeles: U of California P, 1993.

McClintock, Anne. *Imperial Leather: Race, Gender, and Sexuality in the Colonial Context* New York: Routledge, 1995.

Mulvey, Laura. "Visual Pleasure and Narrative Cinema." *Issues in Feminist Film Criticism*. Ed. Patricia Erens. Bloomington: Indiana UP, 1990. 28–40.

Rony, Fatimah Tobing. *The Third Eye: Race, Cinema, and Ethnographic Spectacle*. Durham: Duke UP, 1996.

Root, Deborah. *Cannibal Culture: Art, Appropriation and the Commodification of Difference*. Boulder, CO: Westview Press, 1996.

Shohat, Ella. "Gender and Culture of Empire: Toward a Feminist Ethnography of the Cinema." *Quarterly Review of Film and Video* 13.1–3 (1991): 45–84.

———. "Imaging Terra Incognita: The Disciplinary Gaze of the Empire." *Public Culture* 3.2 (1991): 41–70.

Shohat, Ella, and Robert Stam. *Unthinking Eurocentricism: Multiculturalism and the Media*. New York: Routledge, 1994.

Stam, Robert, and Louise Spence. "Colonialism, Racism, and Representation." *Screen* 24.2 (1983): 2–20.

Terry, Jennifer, and Jacqueline Urla. "Introduction: Mapping Embodied Deviance." *Deviant Bodies*. Ed. Jennifer Terry and Jacqueline Urla. Indianapolis: Indiana UP, 1995. 1–18.

Trinh, T. Minh-ha. *Woman, Native, Other*. Indianapolis: Indiana UP, 1989.

Wiegman, Robyn. *American Anatomies: Theorizing Race and Gender*. Durham: Duke UP, 1995.

Young, Lola. *Fear of the Dark: 'Race', Gender, and Sexuality in the Cinema*. New York: Routledge, 1995.

Corinn Columpar *is currently assistant professor in film studies and women's studies at Keene State College in Keene, New Hampshire, and is in the final stages of earning her doctorate in women's studies from Emory University. Her dissertation, titled "Hybridity as Spectacle: The Inscription of Difference in Contemporary Cinema," explores the impact of gender and race on the cinematic representation of cultural hybridity in contemporary films from the United States and New Zealand.*

Copyright © 2002 by Corinn Columpar

Viewing in the Dark
Toward a Black Feminist Approach to Film

Janell Hobson

In the spring semester of 2000, when I taught my first Introduction to Women's Studies course, I introduced Laura Mulvey's "Visual Pleasure and Narrative Cinema" during a unit on images of women in popular culture. To illustrate Mulvey's analysis of the *scopophilic* instinct, in which she defines "looking . . . [as] a source of pleasure," I showed my class a clip from Alfred Hitchcock's *Rear Window*, since she had examined in her essay how the male voyeuristic gaze was used in this film.[1] In a "point of view" shot, the camera's gaze frames a close-up of Grace Kelley as she bends down to kiss James Stewart, the character we assume to hold the point of view. My students at least understood how the "look"—as it entailed the power dynamic of "woman as image, man as bearer of the look"—was constructed in cinema once we established this gender paradigm.

However, when I assigned Julie Dash's groundbreaking black feminist film *Daughters of the Dust* for a screening, my students were unable to comprehend how Dash altered not only the essential gender paradigm but also the racial paradigms of looking relations.[2] Somehow, they could not interpret Dash's techniques of African aesthetics: her use of visuals and sounds, her focus on images of black people—especially close-ups of African American women—and her revolutionary form of narrative and cinematography that displaced the white male gaze as "bearer of the look." It was not just that Dash removed this privileged gaze from her frame of reference; she also challenged the "visual pleasure" we expect to gain from watching a film. In short, my students, who were primarily white, middle class, and female (give or take three male students) were "visually" challenged by the shift from Hollywood filmmaking models. The three African American female students in this class were an exception; while "confused" by the narrative, they were nonetheless appreciative of the "beautiful" appearances of the black women in this film.

Although I realize that a viewing of *Daughters of the Dust* would have been difficult for any student unused to such projects as Dash's in restructuring the racial and gender hegemonic practices of filmmaking,

I did not prepare them well for Dash's radical departure, even with a feminist film critique such as Mulvey's. While Mulvey's essay provides a convincing feminist analysis of film that moves away from a simple examination of visual images of women and focuses instead on the male-identified gaze of the camera, it falls short of any analysis of racial factors and how they might shape the "looking relations" in cinema. However, therein lies the problem—in "looking." Whereas the construction of the white female body in film can be viewed, studied, and deconstructed, often in Hollywood cinema there *is* no black female body that we can analyze.[3] Or so we think.

In her essay Mulvey describes the sexual imbalance that structures the cinematic frame and, hence, the world as we know it. She suggests:

> [Pleasure] in looking has been split between active/male and passive/female. The determining male gaze projects its fantasy onto the female figure, which is styled accordingly. In their traditional exhibitionist role women are simultaneously looked at and displayed, with their appearance coded for strong visual and erotic impact so that they can be said to connote *to-be-looked-at-ness*. Women displayed as sexual object is the leit-motif of erotic spectacle: from pin-ups to strip-tease, from Ziegfield to Busby Berkeley, she holds the look, plays to and signifies male desire. (750)

While we may argue that, when black women *are* included in film, they certainly inhabit this function in the same way as their white female counterparts, the "to-be-looked-at-ness" embodied in erotic pleasure functions differently with regard to the racial dynamics of the gaze. For the black female body may incorporate the "erotic pleasure" of the white/nonwhite male gaze through the image of a "Jezebel" or "tragic mulatto," but there is also "displeasure" in such cases as grotesque "mammies" and "Sapphires," who functioned in early Hollywood films—and to some extent, in contemporary cinema—as the antierotic and the antithesis to the white female body and, hence, as the signifier for a blackness that shapes a more palatable representation of whiteness.[4]

Nonetheless, what are we to make of their absence, or should I say their "disembodied" presence, since there is still a dearth of images of black women in cinema? For even as Mulvey effectively analyzes how Grace Kelly is framed for the camera's voyeurism in her role as Lisa in *Rear Window*—in which her "exhibitionism . . . establishe[s] . . . her obsessive interest in dress and style, in being a passive image of visual perfection"—she makes no reference to the one instance of the black (female) presence in this film (755).

To be sure, the presence is so fleeting that one would have to be obsessively searching for it, as I began doing while viewing films and detecting the ways in which black bodies surface. Given the brevity of this presence, I cannot criticize Mulvey too severely for failing to comment on it. Perhaps there really isn't anything to say, but having realized that filmmakers—especially one as compulsive and fastidious in his constructions of mise-en-scène and narratives as Hitchcock—do not include diegetic and nondiegetic items in their films accidentally, I feel I must provide commentary. I am referring to a pivotal scene in *Rear Window* when Jeffries (played by James Stewart) makes an urgent phone call to his detective friend Sergeant Boyle. Much to his dismay, Boyle is not available for his call, as is made known to him by Boyle's "babysitter," who answers Jeffries in a voice that is noticeably female, black, and Southern in dialect.

We may well ask why Hitchcock chose to insert this small presence of the black female when he rarely includes black bodies in his films, perhaps with the exception of background servants who function as components of the luxurious surroundings of his middle- and upper-class white protagonists. Moreover, the sound of the babysitter precipitates much of the climactic action that later unfolds in the narrative. It is as if, just as the white characters are jolted into uncertainty and danger, they must be reassured of their racial, class, and gender status through the voice of the black female, comfortably placed (even though we never see her) in a role of servitude. A voice that reminds the characters, as well as the audience, of the dominance and normalcy of whiteness—even when that representation of normalcy takes on voyeurism, burglary, and murder.

Toni Morrison offers a critique of the absence-presence of blackness, which she calls the "Africanist presence," in American culture and literature, in her work *Playing in the Dark:*

> There seems to be a more or less tacit agreement among . . . scholars that . . . [white male] views, genius, and power are without relationship to and removed from the overwhelming presence of black people in the United States . . . These speculations have led me to wonder whether the major and championed characteristics of our national literature . . . are not in fact responses to a dark, abiding, signing Africanist presence . . . Through significant and underscored *omissions,* [italics added] startling contradictions, heavily nuanced conflicts, through the way writers peopled their work with the signs and bodies of this presence—one can see that a real and fabricated Africanist presence was crucial to their sense of Americanness. And it shows. (5–6)

Through this Africanist presence, the norm of white maleness is buttressed, as the constructions of race and gender difference reinforce the meanings of whiteness and masculinity. Such a reading then indicates that although visual theory relies on our ability to interpret and deconstruct the visual stimuli created in images and through the gaze, it must also incorporate an analysis of the *in*visible, or the *dark* presence, as Morrison suggests in her critique of literature. Consequently, I advocate a feminist film theory inclusive of race, class, and gender analyses that integrate an examination of "looking relations" with a search for the invisible but *felt* presence that frames the visual and cultural scene.

Although Mulvey's treatment of gender is significant in our feminist analyses of film, I argue that we need to turn our attention not just to "image" and "gaze," but also to sound. In a media-saturated, visually oriented society, we must learn both how to become visually literate and how to move beyond the visual. This literacy calls for our understanding of visual "absence" and auditory "presence," or the "disembodied presence." As such, in our critiques of film, our attention needs to be placed not just on the visual, but also on the unseen and the heard, the Africanist presence that is made known through sound.

For the remainder of this essay, I will consider how the black female body—as represented through her disembodied voice—is used in mainstream cinema by way of supporting and defining the normalized white (male) body. I will further determine how this off-screen blackness shapes and characterizes the dominance and normalcy—even the morality—of whiteness in cinema. I will then conclude by examining the ways in which black women fit into and displace these paradigms in films and, hence, by calling for a black feminist approach that continuously probes these issues of race, gender, and class.

Offscreen Blackness

Although the black female body in American popular cinema is often rendered "invisible," its presence is often detected in subtle ways, through a process perhaps functioning in the realm of the subconscious. When they do appear in film, even in many guises, black women can often fit into two main types: the asexual and nurturing mammy or the tragic mulatto/Jezebel, the sexualized black woman "out of control of her emotions, split in two by her loyalties and her own vulnerabilities" (Bogle 33). The former represents strength and devotion in ways that pose no sexual or emotional threat to the white world, while the latter represents a wildness that signifies the nonwhite, often read in contrast to the "white," who is orderly, controlled, neat, virtuous, and pure (which of course a "mulatto" is not; and she is "tragic" because she cannot attain such purity).

Certainly, black women's roles have become more complex since early Hollywood cinema with the advent of more black female actors and producers, filmmakers, and writers functioning behind the cameras. However, the industry still continues to be predominately male, white, and upper class, a fact which has limited the growth and depth of such roles in film and, more important, the existence of such roles.

Yet even when she is not in a film, the meanings ascribed to the black woman's body are so inherent in supporting notions of whiteness and masculinity that her presence can be clearly invoked. One example that comes to mind is Terry Gilliam's 1991 *The Fisher King*. An eccentric comedy starring Jeff Bridges and Robin Williams, the film tells the story of a successful New York City radio DJ named Jack (played by Bridges), who makes his living insulting people on his radio show. Inevitably, he loses his soul, so to speak, and Perry (played by Williams), a college professor who is now homeless as a direct result of a tragedy spawned by Jack's callous remarks to an emotionally unbalanced caller, will help him recover it.

Even this morality tale of class oppression and urban isolation functions through the Africanist presence of the dark, dirtied, chaotic world of "blackened" homeless white males, first signified by the early appearance of a homeless black man rapping earnestly on the window of Jack's limousine to panhandle. In this simplistic shot, when Jack does not open his window, we are to understand that he is a cold, unfeeling man of wealth. It is only when he is toppled "from the top" and wallows "at the bottom" that he begins his journey of recovery.

Because in Hollywood movies black male bodies are relegated to minor roles—either homeless men or, in *The Fisher King*, the super of a decrepit building where Perry dwells—they alone function as the Africanist presence, often rendering the black female invisible, since the quota of racial inclusiveness is already filled through the black male. In the case of *The Fisher King*, it was only when I asked myself, "Where are the black women?" that I found them. They were *off*screen. With the exception, in one shot, of an extra whose role was that of a nurse/*mammy* wheeling a disabled elderly white woman on a city sidewalk (interestingly, both bodies are usually invisible in film and relegated to the background, though here they significantly enhance the plot of the "wounded" king motif in the movie title), black women are the "voice" of this film.

The voice is captured in the refrain of the song "I Got the Power," as the black female vocalist in the rap group Snap belts out this phrase in the movie soundtrack during significant scenes in which Jack has "power" that he is using either destructively or ineffectively. An example of his destructive use of power comes when Jack's angry, insulting radio "voice" instigates a violent confrontation in a trendy restaurant—during which Perry loses his wife and ultimately his mind. His ineffective use of power is illustrated in a scene where Jack has the opportunity to intercede on behalf of a transvestite "queen" (played by Michael Jeters) who is facing arrest.

What is clear from Jack's actions—or his lack of action—is that Jack has the power and the "voice of authority" to influence events. What is also clear is that Jack's voice of authority is supported by and contrasted to the "disembodied" voice of the black female, the "voice of soul" in the "I Got the Power" refrain. In both instances of this refrain, Jack fails to listen to the voice that says, "I got the power," and so the film renders this voice as ironic. Interestingly, we may assume that this voice is Jack's inner voice or subconscious, while we—the viewers—realize it is the nondiegetic voice of the soundtrack, coming from a black female body. Another refrain on the soundtrack is the chorus, sung by black female backup singers, of Ray Charles's "Hit the Road, Jack," which again highlights the black female voice as the singers provide the emotional and "soulful" track of the narrative of the white male protagonist in search of his soul.

The use of the black female voice as a literal and figurative "sounding board" for the white male protagonist who struggles toward emotional and morally grounded decisions further implies how the black woman's presence ensures the identity of white masculinity. Her invisible blackness signifies in polarity with his visible whiteness, as Morrison suggests, "the projection of the not-me" (38). As his racial and sexual "Other," she symbolizes what is most foreign to him—both in embodiment and in behavior. Such contrast further reflects his internal struggles and the contradictions of his hegemonic status.

Another illustration of the disembodied black female voice, though quite brief, comes in the pivotal scene in Stephen Spielburg's 1993 *Schindler's List*. The turning point for Oscar Schindler, who makes the life-changing decision to use his money to save as many Jews as possible from the death camps of World War II, is dramatized in a scene of contemplation. After lovemaking, we are led to assume, as his blonde white female partner lies asleep in bed, partially nude and serving as a "sex object" for the camera, Schindler gazes out the window while listening to the diegetic sound on the radio of Billie Holliday's sad, meditative "God Bless the Child." Holliday's voice in this scene serves two purposes: to sexualize the white woman in Schindler's bed with sultry vocals and to raise the conscience of Schindler himself, as Holliday sings a song of salvation and self-reliance.

In such ways, the voice of black women can serve as a sort of Greek chorus, the background array of characters in ancient Greek theater representing the everyday people who narrated or "translated" for the audience the actions of the main characters. Ironically, this is not far from Disney's interpretation of the Greek chorus as the "Gospel Chorus" of black women seen in Disney's 1997 animated film *Hercules*. In animation, or caricature, the women's corporeality is still displaced from the screen, and they exist primarily as cartoon voice-overs.

Even when black women do appear on screen as a Greek chorus-turned-hip-hop group in Warren Beatty's 1998 *Bulworth*, they function as satirical caricatures, the ghettoized hip-hop backup singers to Bulworth's outrageous "rap" at a political fundraiser. Their bodies literally disrupt the organized conservative affair, as much as does the profanity and slang in Bulworth's lyrics. They also rejuvenate the title character, another white male (played by Beatty) who has lost his political "soul" but found it again with a little soul singing and rapping from the young, the black, the female, the poor, and the marginal. In short, he has an opportunity, as a black homeless man (played by Amiri Baraka) admonishes him, "to be a spirit, not a ghost." Or, to be more corporeal and less "white"—to be a "soul."

This enigmatic phrase highlights another aspect of white masculinity, which functions as ghostlike or as "death," in contrast to a black femininity that represents flesh and life. As film theorist Richard Dyer explains:

> Death may in some traditions be a vivid experience, but within much of the white tradition it is a blank that may be immateriality (pure spirit) or else nothing at all. This is within the logics of whiteness even if it is not at the forefront of white identity. White people have a colour, but it is a colour that also signifies absence of colour, itself a characteristic of life and presence. . . . If it is spirit not body that makes a person white, then where does this leave the white body, which is the vehicle for the reproduction of whiteness, of white power and possession, here on earth? (207)

To answer Dyer's question, this leaves the white constructed body very dependent on an Africanist presence that has meaning through its very corporeality. The black body as fleshy, sexualized, earthy, and—if feminine—the epitome of womblike "life" polarizes the white body as spiritlike and deathlike: rigid and divorced from "soul." Hence, Bulworth's process of "descent" and rebirth in South Central L.A. occurs first in an African American church, where he begins to confront political "truths"; he is further rejuvenated by his infatuation with the black female protagonist, Nina (played by Halle Berry).

Ultimately, Bulworth's public display of his affection for Nina toward the end of the film culminates in his assassination. This "kiss of betrayal" (that is, the betrayal of the white race)—no longer "hidden" and contained in the tradition of white supremacist discourse on "miscegenation" but open and witnessed by the flashing bulbs of the media's cameras—indicates Bulworth's symbolic destruction of his status as a "white man." He no longer rigidly upholds the white capitalist patriarchal system, as he embraces the working-class black female body which threatens the very system and his own identity.

The Politics of Visibility

Because the black female body poses such a threat to the white patriarchal system, it has been rendered invisible, for fear that the visibility of a sexually desirable woman would disrupt the accepted constructions of whites as beautiful, as the norm. Ironically, this invisibility began in Western culture with the *hyper*visibility of the black female body: in particular, in the display of the black woman as slave on the American auction block and as Venus figure in European sideshow exhibitions.

Whereas her status as slave relegated her visibility to the "safe" confines of servitude and chattel, her status as "freak"—as embodied in the figure of South African Saartjie Baartman, the "Hottentot Venus," who was exhibited in London and Paris from 1810 to 1815—allowed Europeans to publicly mock and ridicule her body, in the case of Baartman, because of her well-endowed derriere. Furthermore, they reduced Baartman's body to fragments, objectifying her buttocks as grotesque in cartoons and dissecting her genitalia as essentially "different," for scientific preservation and public spectacle.[5] This refusal or inability to "see" the black female body in its entirety culminates in white discomfort and "displeasure" at viewing her body as holistic or desirable.

Another body publicly displayed and therefore publicly "disruptive" to the white viewing audience was that of Elizabeth Taylor Greenfield, a famous black singer of the antebellum period, who was revered by audiences for her "purity" and beauty of *voice* but was repulsed for the blackness of her body.[6] As such, she was called such admiring names as "Black Swan," even as the appellation *black* marked her racial difference, but was also called an "African cow" and a "biped hippopotamus." Carla L. Peterson further notes:

> [Greenfield's audience's] solution to this perceived incongruity of body and voice was to *deemphasize* the body. Indeed . . . Greenfield sought to make her body "quiet" . . . For its part, her audience sought to *obliterate* the body altogether: "Upon the suggestion of another, we listened to her without looking toward her during the entire performance . . . and were at once and satisfactorily convinced that her voice is capable of producing sounds right sweet." (124) [Italics added]

What distinguishes Greenfield from Baartman—who, although considered a "freak" because of her "protruding buttocks," never provoked any of her audience members to "look away" or obliterate her body—is the "voice." Baartman also sang and performed with musical instruments during her exhibition, but her audience accepted her performance as an ethnological construction of her racial, sexual, and cultural "difference."

Greenfield, by contrast, sang classical music from the Western tradition and had a voice that was classically trained. As such, her voice *transcended* her status as a black female, and it is this transcendence that her audience found threatening. Hence, to contain her within a white patriarchal hegemony, her voice had to be disembodied from her blackness—thus inviting the audience to accept the voice but to render the body invisible.

Cinematic "Pleasure" and the Black Feminist Gaze

In examining this history of visualizing and erasing black female bodies within the politics of "visual pleasure," we may come to understand how cinema adapted similar attitudes into their own practices. Subsequently, those of us who study film and wish to incorporate black feminist analyses still confront the cinematic construction of black female bodies as stereotyped, marginalized, or invisible. It is because of these challenges that I find it imperative to analyze beyond the visual and consider all the elements within the cinematic frame—especially when the voice of the black female, disembodied as it may be, can be found outside the visible while maintaining significance to the film narrative. Nonetheless, as we begin to explore these issues in black feminist film criticism, we are still faced with the dilemma of redefining cinematic pleasure and restructuring the cinematic gaze—both of which have been shaped by white male hegemony. Because of this hegemony, black feminist film theory and practice must function in opposition, or as bell hooks has suggested, through an "oppositional gaze," which she declares has the ability to convey "Not only will I stare. I want my look to change reality" (116). Hooks further asserts:

> It was the oppositional black gaze that responded to [white supremacist] looking relations by developing independent black cinema. . . . Black looks, as they were constituted in the context of social movements for racial uplift, were interrogating gazes. We laughed at television shows like *Our Gang* and *Amos 'n' Andy*, at these white representations of blackness, but we also looked at them critically. Before racial integration, black viewers of movies and television experienced visual pleasure in a context where looking was also about contestation and confrontation. (117)

Here hooks suggests that black (and) feminist viewing combines visual pleasure with confrontation and interrogation. Such viewing practices resist the construction of what Mulvey describes as the scopophilic act of the audience, in which the viewers are relegated to the role of voyeur, looking at the screen with pleasure but rarely with any criticism. This look merely serves to objectify, whereas the "oppositional gaze" that hooks advocates confronts for subjectivity.

Hence, the visual pleasure of the "oppositional gaze" does more than replicate voyeurism; it probes, revises, and inspires to see differently. It hints at the possibilities of interpreting the world, and in this context, the world of cinema—as white identified and male oriented as it often is—through an empowered sense of pleasure and looking. Here the black female spectator repositions herself as a viewer and critic by centering black female subjectivity in the arena of visual pleasure. However, the black female filmmaker can advance this position even further once she gains authority behind the camera to reshape the gaze and redefine such pleasure for her audience.

Giving Body to the Voice

One of Julie Dash's earlier films, her 1983 short *Illusions*, reflects the black feminist goal of repositioning for black female subjectivity. Dash not only achieves this objective through her short, but also manages to restore the visibility of the black female body to its vocal presence, thus uniting corporeality and voice while rejecting the mainstream cinematic practice of obliterating the body as it maintains the diegetic or nondiegetic black female voice.

In the narrative, Dash goes behind the Hollywood scene of the 1940s and inserts two black female protagonists in her fictional revision of the classic Hollywood era. One character, Ester Jeeter, represents the traditional displacement of the black female body in the industry, as she is hired as a singer to overdub a musical voice-over in place of a white woman. Through her juxtaposition of Ester, emerging from the dark in the backdrop as she prepares to provide sound to the image, with the white female body on screen, Dash refocuses the black female body, in particular through her camera close-up on Ester. She also confronts what Gwendolyn Audrey Foster calls the "common practice" in the '30s and '40s of synchronizing the black female voice with the white female body in cinema, thus relegating women as "substitutable fragmented constructions" (45). In this practice, the sensuality of the black female voice is appropriated, as Foster notes, "to construct the female sexuality of the white singer," not unlike the ways in which this voice is often used to construct the moral conscience and emotional feelings of the white male protagonist in contemporary cinema.

The other significant black female character in this short is Mignon Dupree, an executive assistant at the film studio who is light enough to "pass" for white. Her motives for passing, however, differ significantly from those of other black female characters in Hollywood "passing drama" films, such as *Imitation of Life* and *Pinky*. Whereas the passing-for-white heroines in these dramas transgress the color line for love and acceptance in the white social world, Mignon seeks to pass in order to participate in the power structure of the Hollywood film industry. Hers is not the goal of submerging her identity in the limited role of passive white female. Rather, she passes to transcend both her race and her gender as she works side by side with Hollywood's "bigwigs," even rebuffing the sexual advances of white men. In these ways, Mignon represents the filmmaker Dash herself, as Mignon accuses the Hollywood film industry at the end of the film by commenting, "Your scissors and your paste methods have eliminated my history, my participation in this country," and as she resolves to correct and revise this erasure.

In her first feature-length film, *Daughters of the Dust* (1991), Dash's efforts to reclaim black women's history and black female bodies are signified in every scene through the theme of loss and recovery. The opening sequences not only reclaim earth-mother archetypes through images of black female hands holding the earth or the matriarch of the Peazant family, Nana, washing fully clothed in a stream, but the ancient text of *Thunder: The Perfect Mind*—a Gnostic gospel recovered in the twentieth century—is invoked in a female voice-over. The text itself invokes the feminized Savior, speaking with ambiguity in such phrases as "I am the First and the Last... I am the honored one and the scorned one." That the speaker of this text is usually recognized as female further supports Dash's attempts at refocusing the cinematic text on black femininity, especially as she glamorizes the image and the sensuality of the black female body, young and old, impoverished and bourgeois, pregnant and childless.

Toward the end of the film, as the main character, Eula, pulls the women in the family together and urges them to confront their judgments of the "ruint" woman in the family, named Yellow Mary, she argues, "If you love yourself, love Yellow Mary 'cause we're *all* good [women]." Such a statement radically defies not only the tradition of rendering the black female invisible in film but also the judgments often made of black women in public, which tend to devalue our bodies and our character. Ten years later, Dash's first feature film still stands unrivaled in American cinema for its complex and profound depictions of sensual and diverse black female bodies.

Conclusion

While *Daughters of the Dust* continues to be a groundbreaking black feminist film, Dash certainly operates within a tradition of black female filmmakers, and some have gone on to success, such as Kasi Lemmons with her 1997 film, *Eve's Bayou*.[7] Yet even these small successes are not enough to cause a shift in mainstream cinema. As America's film industry continues to measure the "success" of a film by the size of the audiences it attracts rather than by its artistic achievement, marginal filmmakers who choose to film marginal stories and images face a long struggle in earning support for their craft, as this particular art requires an immense amount of money just to sustain itself. This reality must also be analyzed in our assessment of films, as the number of filmmakers who are women, people of color, and representatives of other marginal groups is limited by the difficulty of raising funds to film a project. As much as Dash received success with her first feature film, it took her more than ten years to make *Daughters,* and even then, she was told by those who control film finances that "there was no market for the film" (Dash 16).

As Audre Lorde asserts, even choices of art are based on economics: she recognizes that such an art form as poetry proves the "most economical" craft, thus accounting for the numerous women, people from the working class, and people of color who have access to writing this genre (116). Lorde's point about choice suggests that those of us in film studies and women's studies must constantly confront economics and issues of class in our film criticism as much as we analyze artistic constructions of race, gender, and sexuality. Consequently, I envision a black feminist approach to film that raises issues not only of the use of visual pleasure and invisibility in cinema, but also of the politics and economics behind the filmmaking process, in terms of whose films get made and how such films are received.

I imagine that the next time I teach *Daughters of the Dust*, I will continue to illustrate Mulvey's points in clips from *Rear Window*, but I will also have to include the scene featuring the diegetic sound of the black female voice. Juxtaposing the visible white female body with the invisible black female body may enable students to appreciate the efforts Dash makes in her films. They may also appreciate the struggles that she faced in making a film over the space of ten years—and for less than one million dollars—that resists mainstream cinematic models, compared with the efforts of her white male counterparts, who can gain access to millions and produce films with less artistic vision, in just one year.[8]

Perhaps it is the "market" that governs the Hollywood filmmaking hegemony, but as feminist scholars and instructors, especially those of us venturing to find a larger audience beyond the classroom through film festivals and the like, are able to influence that market, we may encourage radical ways in which spectators can look at a film. Not just for "visual pleasure" but also for interrogation.

JULIE DASH FILMOGRAPHY

The Rosa Parks Story. Original movie for network television. CBS. 2002
Love Song. Original movie for cable. MTV. 2000.
Incognito. Original movie for cable. Imani Pictures. 1999.
Funny Valentines. Original movie for cable. Showtime. 1998.
Subway Stories. Original movie for cable. HBO. 1996.
Breaths. Written and performed by Sweet Honey in the Rock; made for television. 1994.
Daughters Of The Dust. Feature film. American Playhouse/Kino International Theatrical Release. 1991.
Praise House. Written and performed by Urban Bush Women; made for television. 1991.
Relatives. Written and performed by Ishmael Huston Jones, made for television. 1990.

Preventing Cancer. Morehouse School of Medicine. 1989.
Breaking the Silence. National Black Women's Health Project. 1988.
Illusions. Short. 1983.
Diary of an African Nun. Short. 1977.
Four Women. Short. 1975.
Working Models of Success. Documentary. 1973.

Projects in Development

The Colored Conjurers. Feature film.
Digital Diva. Feature film and interactive CD-ROM.
Enemy of the Sun. Feature film.
The Reader. Feature film.

NOTES

1. I would like to thank Robin Blaetz for modeling similar teaching strategies with these texts while I served as her teaching assistant in an Introduction to Film class at Emory University in the spring semester of 1999.
2. In preparation for the screening of *Daughters of the Dust,* I tried to give my students some perspectives in feminist film criticism, thus beginning with the canonical essay by Laura Mulvey. I used various film clips to illustrate the male gaze and female image, from classic Hollywood films to recent mainstream films. What I had hoped my students would notice is the normative construction of white bodies in film, and, in comparison, recognize what Dash was doing differently with her own film.
3. This is not to suggest that racial analysis cannot be employed in the absence of nonwhites in cinema. On the contrary, some film theorists, such as Richard Dyer have contributed significant analyses of the hegemonic construction of whiteness in film.
4. Such figures as "mammies" and "Sapphires" did provide pleasure but in the context of ridicule and mockery or comfort. Even as there was supposed to be no "erotic pleasure" in looking at these figures, as they were traditionally defined as "asexual," the emphasis on their sexual parts, such as enormous breasts and buttocks, basically rendered such display of exaggerated female sexuality as nonthreatening because of their racial difference and, hence, because such bodies need not be taken seriously.
5. Saartjie Baartman was a Khoisan woman (called Hottentot by her European contemporaries) who was brought to London in 1810 at age twenty to be exhibited because of her "protruding buttocks," a condition considered pathological by the Europeans and referred to as steatopygia. Baartman was displayed in sideshows in both England and France, and when she died in Paris in 1815 at age twenty-five, a natural scientist, George Cuvier, took a plaster cast of her body and dissected her sex organs, which became the subject of a thesis that he wrote and that formed the basis for much of race science. Her genitalia were placed in

a bell jar and remained on public display at the Musée de L'homme in Paris until the 1970s.

6. I am grateful to Kimberly Wallace-Sanders at Emory University, who, in her spring 1998 graduate seminar The Black Female Body in American Culture, first introduced this historical figure to me and made this analysis of the dichotomy between Greenfield's body and voice.

7. This tradition can be traced back to 1922 when Tressie Souders became the first African American filmmaker with her silent film *A Woman's Error*. The work of black women filmmakers is documented by Yvonne Welbon in her forthcoming film *Sisters in Cinema*. See Welbon's Web site www.sistersincinema.com for additional information.

8. This struggle continues as Dash's attempts to follow up on the success of *Daughters* have resulted primarily in the relegation of her subsequent film projects to cable television.

REFERENCES

Bogle, Donald. *Toms, Coons, Mulattoes, Mammies, and Bucks: An Interpretive History of Blacks in American Films*. 2nd ed. New York: Continuum, 1990.

Dash, Julie. *Daughters of the Dust: The Making of an African American Woman's Film*. New York: New Press, 1992.

Dyer, Richard. *White*. New York: Routledge, 1997.

Foster, Gwendolyn Audrey. *Women Filmmakers of the African and Asian Diaspora: Decolonizing the Gaze, Locating Subjectivity*. Carbondale: Southern Illinois UP, 1997.

hooks, bell. *Black Looks: Race and Representation*. Boston: South End P, 1992.

Lorde, Audre. *Sister/Outsider*. Freedom, CA: Crossing P, 1984.

Morrison, Toni. *Playing in the Dark: Whiteness and the Literary Imagination*. Cambridge: Harvard UP, 1992.

Mulvey, Laura. "Visual Pleasure and Narrative Cinema." *Film Theory and Criticism: Introductory Readings*. Ed. Gerald Mast, Marshall Cohen, and Leo Braudy. 4th ed. New York: Oxford UP, 1992. 746–57.

Peterson, Carla L. *"Doers of the Word": African-American Women Speakers and Writers in the North (1830–1880)*. New York: Oxford UP Press, 1995.

Janell Hobson received her Ph.D. in women's studies from Emory University and is a visiting assistant professor of women's studies at the State University of New York, Albany. She has coordinated film festivals and series on black and third world women filmmakers.

Copyright © 2002 by Janell Hobson

The Cyborg Mystique
The Stepford Wives and Second Wave Feminism

Anna Krugovoy Silver

Bryan Forbes's 1975 suburban gothic film *The Stepford Wives* has been almost uniformly neglected in film criticism in the past two decades.[1] Recent genre studies of horror and science fiction ignore the film, as have collections of feminist film criticism. Although *The Stepford Wives* is in part a science fiction rewrite of Betty Friedan's pioneering 1963 liberal feminist polemic *The Feminine Mystique*, Friedan lambasted it as "a rip-off of the women's movement," a surprising indictment considering the film's obvious debt to her work (Klemesrud 28). The themes of *The Stepford Wives* dovetail so closely with those of second wave feminism that the film can be viewed as a popularization of some of the most persistent concerns of the women's liberation movement of the 1960s and early 1970s.[2] The film's examination of the plight of the dissatisfied middle-class housewife, its parody of the fetishization of housework, its explicit critique of the nuclear family, and its relentless focus on the constructedness and artificiality of female beauty are key issues to which second wave feminists—particularly radical feminists—drew public attention. *The Stepford Wives*, I argue, is a feminist allegory that stems from the ideological and political concerns of feminists as diverse as Friedan, Pat Mainardi, the Redstockings, and The Feminists. The film's popularity thus attests to the diffusion of feminist theory from smaller, loosely connected consciousness-raising and activist groups to mainstream American culture as a whole. By translating essential ideas found in such radical feminist documents as the "Florida Paper" into film, *The Stepford Wives* indicates that by 1975, these ideas had, through widespread media coverage, become common currency; the film thus suggests not the failure and perversion of feminist rhetoric, as Friedan implies, but its success and popular appeal.[3] In this essay I will briefly examine the film's reception, and then read it as an important cultural document of second wave feminism that addresses three main issues drawn from the women's movement: a woman's domestic labor, a woman's role in the nuclear family, and a woman's control over her body.

First, since the film was unavailable for rental for many years, let me provide a brief plot summary. *The Stepford Wives* takes place in the mythical middle-class suburb of Stepford, where Walter, Joanna, and their two children have recently moved from New York City. Joanna and her new friend Bobbie, also a young wife, quickly notice how strange their neighbors are: the women are all "superhousewives," who cook, clean, and are devoted to their husbands, but also seem oddly placid, passive, and unwilling to express opinions. Their husbands, by contrast, spend a great deal of time with the mysterious Stepford Men's Association. Eventually, Joanna and Bobbie discover that women, shortly after arriving in Stepford, change from being energetic and independent to being zombies with no clear personalities of their own; Bobbie suggests that Stepford water may be poisoning them. After the "change" occurs in Bobbie, Joanna becomes suspicious, confronts her friend, and discovers that Bobbie has been replaced by a robot. Although she now tries to escape Stepford, Joanna is tricked into entering the mansion that houses the Stepford Men's Association, where the head of the association, Dis, explains that the men of Stepford have found the technological means to create perfect wives. Joanna then meets her own uncanny double, who murders her by strangling her with a pair of pantyhose. As the film ends, the viewer realizes that Joanna, like the other women of Stepford, has been killed with the full knowledge and complicity of her husband.

Critics of *The Stepford Wives* either derided it, on the one hand, as anti-male or, on the other hand, as a misrepresentation of feminist goals and cultural critiques. Richard Schickel, of *Time* magazine, chastises the film because it "never shows a single man whose feminine ideal exceeds gatefold dimensions. That too is a form of dehumanization" (4); while P. Zinnerman's *Newsweek* review calls *The Stepford Wives* "a shallowly satiric suburban joke that says some ugly and unsupported things about what kind of women men really want" (70). Such critiques are almost identical to the critiques of 1970s feminist-consciousness novels and are thus unsurprising.[4] Others found the film's feminist message muddled, simplistic, or downright offensive. Pauline Kael in her *New Yorker* essay concludes that the film's aggressively pro-woman stance places too much blame on men and not enough on women. "If women turn into replicas of the women in commercials, they do it to themselves," she claims. "Even if the whole pop culture weighs on them—pushing them in that direction—if they go that way, they're the ones letting it happen" (112). Although she clearly simplifies the power of cultural gender norms, ignoring the ways that women internalize gender expectations, Kael does not reject the notion of a feminist film outright; however, in the tradition of liberal feminism, she believes that *The Stepford Wives* is too critical of men and presents "educated American women" only as victims, rather than as actors (113). Herbert Gans, writing in *Social Policy*, sets forth a similar liberal feminist critique: "The film sees the movement as setting women against men, thus ignoring the many feminists who have argued that women's liberation cannot be achieved without larger social change that also liberates men" (59–60). Gans, who conflates men's and women's needs for liberation, also criticizes the representation of men in the film as "hicks" who are "so weak that they must murder their wives and live with robots to achieve their wants" (60).

Perhaps the most outspoken critic of *The Stepford Wives*, however, was Friedan herself, who walked out of an "awareness session" that followed a special screening of the film, announcing that "I think we should all leave here. I don't think we should help publicize this movie. It's a rip-off of the women's movement" (Klemesrud 28). Is Friedan correct, however, that the film is a "rip-off"? Other women at the screening disagreed. Writer Gael Greene, for instance, "loved it—those men were like a lot of men I've known in my life. . . . They really do want wives who are robots"; while Eleanor Perry had expected "Betty Friedan [to] stand up and say, 'Yes, this is just the way that men treat women'" (Klemesrud 28). Friedan's dismissal of the film suggests her discomfort with some of the same characteristics that Kael and Gans disliked, particularly the way that the film implicates *all* men in the destruction of women's lives: not one man in Stepford moves away from the town or attempts to save his wife. The political context in which Friedan was operating may have influenced her response to *The Stepford Wives*. By the mid 1970s, the liberal feminist movement, as institutionalized in the National Organization for Women (NOW) and *Ms.* magazine, was concerned with consolidating power as the best way to continue the dissemination of its goals into legislation and the culture at large. NOW's membership, for instance, had grown from 3,000 in 1970 to more than 50,000 in 1974 (Hogeland 20). Analyzing the reviews of feminist-consciousness novels published in *Ms.*, Lisa Marie Hogeland argues that the reviews assume that "[n]ot only . . . are (all) men not that bad, but no men are really all that bad: all men can and must be saved for feminism. Any overstepping of the bounds of feminist realism—any negative or shallow portrayals of men characters— threatened the claims to centrality of *Ms.*'s cultural feminism" (90).[5] Although Friedan did not specify exactly what she hated about the film, she may well have objected to the representation of such weak, selfish, and evil men. *The Stepford Wives* does not offer a vision of men and women working together for the betterment of both women's and men's lives; rather, it envisions men who are willing to kill in order to preserve their male prerogative. Friedan may also have interpreted the film as parodying, or co-opting, important tenets of feminism. The fact that the film is science fiction, in particular, enables the resistant viewer to conclude that the oppression of women within the home is simply a fantasy. One could argue, therefore, that Forbes uses feminist critique simply to create a sensationalistic Hollywood film. However, the themes that Forbes's film articulates are so closely related to Friedan's own work that *The Feminine Mystique* is central to an understanding of *The Stepford Wives* as sociocultural document. Forbes's dystopic vision of suburban America ultimately owes too much to feminist theories to be merely a parody of those theories.

The Stepford Wives and "The Problem That Has No Name"

The Feminist Mystique explores the phenomenon that Friedan famously labels "the problem that has no name": the widespread dissatisfaction, anxiety, and low self-esteem that Friedan observed among American housewives of the 1950s and 1960s. Friedan chronicled the unhappiness of the middle-class suburban housewife for whom marriage, maternity, and domesticity failed to provide a compelling purpose in life, arguing that prosperity and economic security were not bringing these women the happiness that a career or extrafamilial activities might. On the one hand, stifling conceptions of femininity conceptualized women as frivolous and passive, while on the other hand, a woman's role as nurturer and moral center of the family left her nothing for herself. Friedan writes:

> If a woman had a problem in the 1950's and 1960's, she knew that something must be wrong with her marriage, or with herself. Other women were satisfied with their lives, she thought. What kind of woman was she if she did not feel this mysterious fulfillment waxing the kitchen floor? She was so ashamed to admit her dissatisfaction that she never knew how many other women shared it. If she tried to tell her husband, he didn't understand what she was talking about. She did not really understand it herself. . . . "There's nothing wrong really," they kept telling themselves. "There isn't any problem." (19)

Forbes replicates Friedan's concern with housewives' depression and nervous breakdowns in *The Stepford Wives* as Joanna and Bobbie constantly question their dislike of Stepford and, ultimately, their sanity. "It's perfect!" Joanna exclaims to Bobbie at Dis's pool party. "I just don't like it."[6] Later, Bobbie wonders aloud, "Maybe we're the crazy ones." And finally, after Bobbie has been replaced by a robotic double, a desperate Joanna tells her psychiatrist, "If I'm wrong, I'm insane, and if I'm right, it's worse than if I'm wrong." The implication, in the film, is that Stepford's "feminine mystique" erodes a woman's mental health even before she is physically destroyed. The woman, like Bobbie or Joanna, who does not find pleasure and satisfaction in endlessly baking and cleaning the floor is a deficient woman within the value structure of suburban Stepford and, by analogy, in 1970s America. When Bobbie exclaims, "I'm not gonna end up like one of those pan scrubbers!" she encapsulates the fears of Friedan's educated, intelligent, bored housewife.

Friedan and other second wave feminists focused much of their theoretical energies on analyzing the role of housework in women's lives. Friedan, for instance, contends that regardless of how much time busy housewives spend shopping, cooking, and cleaning, their work is never done. She famously concludes, therefore, that because housewives have nothing to do but housework, they must find more and more to do in order to give their lives structure and meaning. "The more a woman is deprived of function in society at the level of her own ability," Friedan writes, "the more her housework, mother-work, wife-work, will expand—and the more she will resist finishing her housework or mother-work, and being without any function at all. (Evidently human nature also abhors a vacuum, even in women.)" (239). In addition, housework is invested—by a woman, her family, and the culture at large—with tremendous importance, so that women keep their energies focused on the home rather than looking for a more personally and intellectually fulfilling career. As Friedan claims, "Housework, washing dishes, diaper-changing had to be dressed up by the new mystique to become equal to splitting atoms, penetrating outer space, creating art that illuminates human destiny, pioneering on the frontiers of society" (239).

Of course, Friedan was only one of many second wave feminists who examined the gender politics of housework, particularly who in the home does what, and what those divisions suggest about the power dynamics of the family. Pat Mainardi's 1970 essay "The Politics of Housework," perhaps the best-known examination of the subject, brilliantly details her own struggles to divide the housework with her husband, and his various efforts to avoid domestic drudgery. Mainardi analyzes each of his excuses. "'I don't mind sharing the work, but you'll have to show me how to do it'" translates, for Mainardi, to "I ask a lot of questions and you'll have to show me everything everytime I do it because I don't remember so good" (449). The bottom line, for Mainardi, is that something as "trivial" as housework is intensely political, because it reinforces the private sphere as woman's particular area of expertise, keeping the public sphere secure for men. When women do housework, it both enables men to do other, more "important" things, and at the same time prevents women, who are busy scrubbing the toilet, from doing those same things. Mainardi articulates a key second wave feminist thesis by concluding that women thus constitute an oppressed servant class. Her essay was enormously influential at its publication, mining women's previously unexplored resentment and rage. Novelist and Redstocking Alix Kates Shulman remembers that through reading "The Politics of Housework," she "had become sensitized to the issue of traditional divisions of labor" (284); feminist activist Barbara Winslow "applauded" the broadside in her consciousness-raising group, though she "continued to do all the housework" (240).

Bryan Forbes places housework at the very center of conflict in *The Stepford Wives*. The film nicely parodies Friedan's feminine mystique during the ill-fated Stepford Wives meeting, a consciousness-raising session at which the robots enter into an animated conversation about the pleasures of Easy On Spray Starch, recalling Friedan's statement that "the really important role that women serve as housewives is *to buy more things for the house*" (206). Moreover, even robot housewives never get the chance to relax: they are forever cleaning, polishing, and baking, and they derive almost beatific pleasure from it. Stepford defines the "bad" wife as the one who keeps a sloppy house. Bobbie, for example, jokes about the smears of peanut butter on her cabinets, and comments, when she first enters Joanna's home: "A messy kitchen! How beautiful!" After she has been murdered, robot Bobbie, by contrast, declares, "I just want to look like a woman and keep a clean house." Bobbie's newfound enjoyment of domesticity precipitates Joanna's decision to consult a psychiatrist and to attempt to flee Stepford.

Robot Bobbie is clearly an exaggerated version of the suburban housewife who has been brainwashed into thinking that cleaning house is the epitome of a woman's existence. The men of the film, of course, are not bothered with any domestic work, and Dis even admits that he enjoys watching a woman do her "chores." Cleaning the house is thus framed by Dis, as well as by other characters in the film, as service to the husband and family that epitomizes wifely submission by enabling men to pursue their work and leisure. Walter, for instance, chastises Joanna for the time that she spends on her photography, asking her, "When are things going to start sparkling around here?" Robotic Joanna will no longer ask Robert to watch the children while she develops her photographs or travels to galleries in New York; rather, she will subsume her own interests entirely to Walter's, and her care of the house will confer prestige upon him. Forbes's (and Levin's) metaphor of the housewife as robot, moreover, is not anomalous; many second wave feminists emphasize the monotonous, robotic nature of housework. Merely as an example, Beverly Jones writes, "One of the definitions of automation is a human being acting mechanically in a monotonous routine. Now, as always, the most automated *appliance* in a household is the mother" (56). *The Stepford Wives* literalizes what second wave feminists—including Friedan—had argued for more than a decade, namely, that fetishizing housework turns women from individuals with goals and ambitions into cleaning appliances: robots.

Forbes's parody of the cult of cleanliness, in which women are literally transformed into what Florynce Kennedy calls "dirt searchers" (442), is part of the film's overall criticism of the nuclear family, which is represented as not only oppressive, but actually murderous. Again, Forbes merely literalizes what radical second wave feminists were articulating in their essays, manifestos, speeches, and demonstrations. That the patriarchal family was the linchpin of institutional and social patriarchy had become axiomatic in feminist theory by the film's release in 1975. Even the mainstream, liberal NOW includes, in its "Statement of Purpose," the assertion that "the laws and mores governing marriage. . . [discriminate] against both men and women, and [are] the cause of much unnecessary hostility between the sexes" (101). More radical feminists, of course, were vocally and vociferally anti-marriage. Ti-Grace Atkinson's group The Feminists, which demonstrated at a marriage license bureau because "We can't destroy the inequities between men and women until we destroy marriage" (The Feminists 537), was perhaps the most critical of sex and marriage of the radical feminist groups. More dramatically, a WITCH coven invaded a bridal show in Madison Square Garden, released white mice to symbolize the brides, and performed an "unwedding ceremony" in which they pledged to "smash the alienated family unit" (Baxandall 215). Personal narratives and memoirs reveal that the decision about whether or not to marry, and how to constitute marriage, were pressing and painful issues for feminists in the 1960s and 1970s, as consciousness-raising groups politicized the personal and asked women to examine the ways that their own marriages functioned as microcosms of larger social inequalities. *The Stepford Wives* arose out of these feminist critiques of marriage, but rather than simply exploiting the feminist critique, as Friedan implies, the message of Forbes's suburban gothic is consistent with that of many second wave feminists. His conclusions about the family are indebted to, and consequently reinforced, the popularization of feminist rhetoric and theory.

The sinister Stepford Men's Association is housed in a Victorian mansion that was once falling apart but is now being restored. The mansion clearly symbolizes the Victorian home, with its separate-spheres ideology, in which men work in the public sector while women remain at home, creating a safe domestic haven for their families. The home, however, is not a safe place for women in Stepford. Throughout the film, Forbes uses cage and prison images to make the suburban home *unheimlich* and foreboding. Joanna is often framed by walls and doors that seem to constrict her. When she walks into Bobbie's kitchen, about to discover her best friend's transformation, Forbes shoots her as walled in from both sides. Later, returning to Bobbie's house on the night when she herself will be murdered, Joanna is framed by Bobbie's window as though she were in a prison cell. Perhaps most dramatically, Joanna's physical struggle with Walter is shot through the staircase bars. Later, when she sneaks from her room, the bars fill up the entire horizontal and vertical frame, so that Joanna appears completely hemmed in, again imprisoned. Forbes therefore likens her escape from the house to a prison escape and Walter to her jailer.

Finally, of course, Joanna is killed in the old Victorian mansion after being lured into the building by the taped voices of her children, which recalls the metaphorical imprisonment in her home that Forbes has suggested throughout the film. When Joanna first walks into the house, the audience views her from above, in a position that emphasizes the viewer's panoptic vision of Joanna as hunted prey. Again, the dominant piece of scenery in the mise-en-scène is the staircase, with its heavy wooden bars. The camera then pans around in a circle to show that Joanna is not only surveyed but completely surrounded. Walking up the stairs, she is constricted by the staircase on one side and the wall (with the shadows of bars playing against it) on the other. As Joanna steps into Dis's office, Forbes frames her in the doorway, revealing that she is completely ensnared. As she desperately runs through the house, realizing that she is to be killed, the walls form a maze around her, with the doors and narrow hallways leading only to more rooms, but never to exits. At one point, Joanna opens a cabinet to reveal a porcelain doll, a shot that cleverly symbolizes the Men's Association's conceptualization of woman as beautiful and passive object. In a device recalling cyber-Bobbie's inability to define the word *archaic*, the doll is, of course, an antique, a Victorian relic.

Forbes also explicitly links the Victorian and modern homes through the eerie reconstruction of Joanna's bedroom in the old mansion. By rebuilding the contemporary suburban bedroom in a Victorian house, the Men's Association indicates its adherence to nineteenth-century ideals of marriage, neatly and effectively symbolized by the bedroom in which Walter and the new Joanna's marriage will be consummated. Moreover, Joanna, through her death and replacement with a robot, will be "reborn" as a more perfect woman, no longer the biological offspring of a mother and father, but the product of a group of men. During the climactic scene in which Joanna confronts her double, she represents all those women who are trapped by a feminine mystique that (in this case, literally) kills women.

By introducing the viewer not only to Walter but also to the other men in the Stepford Men's Association, Forbes blames not simply the *institution* of marriage for the Stepford women's oppression, but, specifically, the men of Stepford, who work actively and plan carefully the murder of their wives and the mothers of their children. The viewer witnesses, for instance, Ike sketching Joanna during the meeting at her home, and sees the men of the Association inspecting Joanna's and Walter's bedroom in cool preparation for her violent death. Thus, Forbes does not merely posit an abstract, institutional, or economic force behind the women's deaths, but individual, flesh-and-blood men. Moreover, Forbes implicates *all* the men of Stepford, not only ringleaders such as Dis. Forbes's vision of a universal male subjugation of women shares with radical feminism the concept that the patriarchy begins in the home, and that it is perpetuated, to differing degrees, by all men, even "good" husbands, and even those who themselves suffer discrimination. As the "Redstockings Manifesto" reads: "*All men* receive economic, sexual, and psychological benefits from male supremacy. *All men* have oppressed women" (Redstockings 534). Before women can achieve true equality, Forbes indicates, the whole family structure, from which men benefit, must be changed.

Of course, *The Stepford Wives* is primarily concerned with the experiences of the middle-class, educated woman, a focus shared by *The Feminine Mystique*. Criticizing Friedan for her lack of attention to working-class and black women, bell hooks has argued, "The racism and classism of white women's liberationists was almost most apparent whenever they discussed work as the liberating force for women. In such discussions it was always the middle-class 'housewife' who was depicted as the victim of sexist oppression and not the poor black and non-black women who are most exploited by American economics" (146). The presence of a young black couple in the grocery store at the end of the film implies that black women, too, are subject to the normalizing pressures that white women face. Although the film thus erases the important differences between black and white women's racialized experiences, suggesting a cross-racial "sisterhood," it does include black women in its vision of oppression. The black woman is wearing a bandana, just as Joanna was at the opening of the film. By linking Joanna and the other woman, the bandana thus reminds the audience of how much Joanna has changed, and foreshadows the newcomer's fate. In addition, because black women—most notoriously Mammy in *Gone With the Wind* and Aunt Jemima—have traditionally been represented as wearing bandanas, the bandana indicates that the young woman will be forced to take on a retrograde role as housekeeper and as the nurturer of others, to the exclusion of her own needs. The film suggests, albeit in passing, that all women, regardless of their racial and socioeconomic background, are oppressed by men, and that all men, regardless of their racial and socioeconomic background, oppress them.

The Female Body and Feminine Beauty

Second wave feminists articulated a woman's ability to control her own body as a fundamental right, a right most often rhetorically invoked in efforts to decriminalize abortion. Alice Echols argues that "abortion loomed so large in the early radical feminist agenda [because] without it there could be no such thing as sexual freedom or self-determination for women" (175); Cindy Cisler, a member of New York Radical Women who also helped found New Yorkers for Abortion Law Repeal, states that "abortion is a woman's right . . . no one can veto her decision and *compel* her to bear children against her will" (Echols 141). Reproductive freedom—most specifically the decision whether or not to have children and the ability to terminate an unwanted pregnancy—were thus linked by second wave feminists to larger issues of sexual choice and pleasure and to a woman's ability to shape her own life. *The Stepford Wives,* which was released two years after the *Roe v. Wade* decision, indirectly alludes to the struggle for women's autonomy over the decision of when, or whether, to give birth, although the film does so indirectly and in a way that allies itself more with cultural feminism than with radical feminism. In *The Stepford Wives,* men control not only their wives' behavior (by murdering and replacing them), but also their ability to reproduce. By killing their wives, the Stepford men break the biological link between women and childbirth, wresting reproduction from women's control, even as they make child care one of women's main duties. Robots, separated from all human physiological processes, do not menstruate and cannot have children. When Joanna confronts Bobbie after her children have disappeared, she finally, in frustration, takes a kitchen knife and plunges it into Bobbie's belly. The symbolism here is overt: Joanna proves Bobbie's nonhumanness and nonfemaleness by striking her in the part of the body in which Bobbie would carry a child. Earlier in the film, Bobbie drew attention to her reproductive capability by commenting that she always carries tampax. Now, her inability to bleed (surely an allusion to menstruation), as well as her uterine wound, speak to her separation from "nature." Though she looks like the perfect woman, cleans and has sex like the perfect woman, Bobbie is in fact a sterile, unnatural nonwoman.[7] In this instance, then, Forbes seems to ally himself less with social constructionist radical feminists than with those cultural feminists who accept and celebrate women's association with her reproductive capability. *The Stepford Wives* associates human women in part with their reproductive systems and views masculine control over reproduction as a particularly aberrant aspect of Stepford: men, in effect, become "fathers" to their own wives, who are no longer able to reproduce. The film's emphasis, then, is not on women's choosing *not* to have children, but rather on women's losing the choice to *have* children; nevertheless, the focus on women's control over their bodies is maintained.

The men of Stepford, however, find the robots more beautiful than they do their human wives. Unlike women, robots do not age, wrinkle, or gain weight. Many feminist theorists have recently analyzed the ways that the body, which requires constant discipline and control to maintain, is unceasingly scrutinized and judged, always at risk of being found lacking. In *Unbearable Weight: Feminism, Western Culture, and the Body*, Susan Bordo writes, "The construction [of the female body] . . . is always homogenizing and normalizing, erasing racial, class, and other differences and insisting that all women aspire to a coercive, standardized ideal" (169). Normalizing processes, of course, guarantee most individual women's failure to achieve body expectations; nevertheless, this constant threat of failure keeps most women, at differing levels of consciousness and activity, on the treadmill of physical discipline.

Before Foucault and others, however, second wave feminists were already enormously concerned with the disciplining processes that women undergo in order to be considered beautiful and feminine, processes that range from dieting, exercise, and cosmetics, to adopting particular ways of walking and taking up space that are considered womanly or ladylike. Robin Morgan's bestselling anthology *Sisterhood is Powerful* includes several essays on the tyranny of beauty, as well as the famous "No More Miss America!" manifesto of 1968. The Miss America protest, at which demonstrators crowned a sheep Miss America and unfurled a banner that read "Women's Liberation," drew a great deal of media coverage and brought the women's liberation movement into the forefront of public attention. Arguments presented in the manifesto and at the protest, most basically that women are "enslaved by ludicrous 'beauty' standards" ("No More Miss America!" 522) had, by 1975, become current enough to make their way into *The Stepford Wives*.

Explaining the rationale behind the robots to Joanna, Dis suggests that she "think of it the other way around. Wouldn't you like some perfect stud waiting on you around the house, praising you, servicing you, whispering how your sagging flesh was beautiful, no matter how you looked?" In addition to the submissiveness at the heart of the robot's attractiveness to the Stepford men, the robots enact, in grotesque exaggeration, the cultural desire to keep the body in perfect discipline. Machines, after all, are much more easily shaped and maintained than human bodies: why use a treadmill or a stair master when your body *is* a treadmill or a stair master? Joanna's robot double has much larger breasts than Joanna does, and they stand straight up as if surgically altered—the robot will, apparently, never grow old, never suffer from "sagging flesh."

Moreover, in addition to being judged by its shape and size, the female body is what Sandra Bartky has called "an ornamented surface": a woman's hair, makeup, and clothing are as important to her overall feminine appearance as her exercise regimen (31). The robots in *The Stepford Wives* conform to cultural norms of feminine appearance not merely through their slim bodies (because, after all, human Bobbie and Joanna are slim themselves) but in their overall appearance. After their "transformations," Bobbie's overalls and Joanna's pants disappear, replaced by ruffled aprons and dresses. Bobbie begins to wear makeup, curl her hair, and wear a "padded uplift bra." Forbes emphasizes the artificiality of the robots' appearance by bathing their faces in light and filming them in soft focus. The soft focus is particularly significant in three key scenes: first, when Carol welcomes Walter with a casserole at the beginning of the film; second, when Bobbie and Joanna discover that Charmaine has "changed"; and third, when Joanna encounters her own double. In each instance, the robots are filmed in soft focus and the humans in sharp focus. Recalling Bobbie's flippant comment about "those good old days when *Playboy* used the airbrush," Forbes has metaphorically "airbrushed" the robots to emphasize their status as literalization of male fantasies. Joanna's double then kills her, appropriately, by strangling her with a pair of pantyhose, which clearly symbolizes the constricting norms of female beauty that Joanna tried to reject. Joanna's murder—which is not included in Ira Levin's novel—suggests the popularization of feminist claims that pantyhose are "barbarous rituals" that, along with girdles and stiletto heels, should be thrown in a "freedom trashcan" and burned ("No More Miss America!" 521).

Sexually, also, the robots are designed only to cater to their husbands' sexual desires and to have no desires of their own: they are sexual objects rather than sexual subjects. The human Joanna, Bobbie, and Charmaine all criticize their husbands sexually. Bobbie jokes that her husband Dave is "best in bed when the market's up." Charmaine confesses that Ed married her for her beauty, and contemptuously refers to the rubber suit that he had made for her (foreshadowing, of course, her replacement by a "rubber" woman). Joanna several times alludes to her premarital sexual life: for example, when Walter asks her if she's ever "made it in front of a log fire," she caustically replies, "Not with you." Female sexuality in the film is aggressive and disruptive. The robots, however, murmur sexual platitudes to their husbands, as Joanna and Bobbie discover when they boldly enter a house to hear a woman moaning, "You're the king, Frank. You're the master." Earlier, Joanna had seen Ted walk up to his wife in the yard and peer beneath her blouse; in response, Carol simply walks towards the house, her face expressionless except for a bland smile. Although the female robots claim to have good sex lives, the film makes it clear that their sexuality is thoroughly circumscribed by their programmed desire to serve their husbands. Female desire has been washed out of them. As Charmaine says, while her beloved tennis court is ripped up to make way for a heated swimming pool, "I want to please him now. . . . All I ever thought about before was just me."

The film's last scene, in which the Stepford Wives stroll through the supermarket to the familiar sounds of piped music, is perhaps its most haunting. The camera follows Charmaine, then Carol; then it meets Bobbie and, finally, Joanna. The women are almost identically dressed in huge hats and long dresses, and they speak in soft, well-modulated voices, repeating pleasantries to one another. The wives are essentially interchangeable, each of them conforming to exaggerated images of feminine beauty and behavior. Bobbie, with her bouncy, assertive walk and loud voice, has been replaced by a gliding figure in a low-cut dress, speaking softly: she now takes up only as much space as a woman should. Joanna has lost any distinguishing characteristics that might separate her from Carol or Marie. The final nightmare of *The Stepford Wives* is a vision of women who all have exactly the same vocabulary, the same interests, even the same clothing. Within the supermarket, Forbes underscores the women's status as their husbands' commodities: they are beautiful objects bought with the deaths of the human wives, with no subjectivities of their own.[8]

The New York Radical Feminists' 1969 manifesto claims that a

> [m]an establishes his "manhood" in direct proportion to his ability to have his ego override woman's, and derives his strength and self-esteem through this process. This male need, though destructive, is in that sense impersonal. It is not out of a desire to hurt the woman that man dominates and destroys her; it is out of a need for a sense of power that he necessarily must destroy her ego and make it subservient to his. (New York Radical Feminists 380)

The similarity between the final message of *The Stepford Wives* and the arguments set forth in the manifesto reinforces the debt owed by the film (and, for that matter, Levin's novel) to the ideologies and theories of the second wave feminist movement. The women of Stepford are represented as an oppressed class of people who are ultimately destroyed by their husbands' need to "dominate" and "destroy" them in maintenance of their own egos. The robots, unlike liberated women, do not argue for their own sexual pleasure, do not attempt to pursue their own careers, do not ask their husbands to share the housework, and, finally, remain beautiful even as their husbands age. The failed consciousness-raising session that Joanna and Bobbie organize suggests that a woman's consciousness of her own subservience within the home and within society is so threatening to men that the latter will fight back with murderous hostility. When Betty Friedan walked out of the discussion about *The Stepford Wives,* she publicly rejected the very notion that the film draws from the feminist rhetoric that she herself inspired. Nevertheless, *The Stepford Wives* is an important document of second wave feminism, and it deserves reexamination by feminist cultural and film critics and a place in the women's studies classroom.

NOTES

This article was originally published in *Arizona Quarterly* 58.1 (Spring 2002).
1. The movie's invisibility in critical discussion may stem in large part from its lack of availability as a videocassette; now, however, it has been released in a new letterbox DVD format, which should ensure its return as an iconic film of the 1970s.

2. I will be referring in this essay to events and dialogue from the film *The Stepford Wives*, rather than from Ira Levin's novel. The screenplay, written by William Goldman, differs in several important respects from the novel. Goldman's most startling and effective departure from Levin's novel is his decision to have Joanna's robot double kill her. In the novel, Joanna is presumably killed by Bobbie, though this is not stated explicitly in the text.
3. The "Florida Paper" is the term popularly given to Beverly Jones and Judith Brown's "Toward a Feminist Liberation Movement," published in June 1968. For a full discussion of the article, see Echols 62–65. Parts of the article have been reprinted in Robin Morgan's *Sisterhood Is Powerful: An Anthology of Writings from the Women's Liberation Movement* (1970) and in Miriam Schneier's *Feminism in Our Time: The Essential Writings, World War II to the Present* (1994). I have relied on the two most important second wave anthologies for my primary documents: *Sisterhood Is Powerful*, and Anne Koedt, Ellen Levine, and Anita Rapone's *Radical Feminism* (1973). Some of these documents, and others not included in the two anthologies, have been reprinted in *Feminism in Our Time*. Rachel Blau DuPlessis and Ann Snitow's recent anthology *The Feminist Memoir Project: Voices From Women's Liberation* (1998) is an invaluable source for oral histories of the movement, and Echols is an essential historical analysis of radical feminism.
4. Christopher Lehmann-Haupt wrote, of *The Women's Room*, "Men can't be that bad.... There must be room for accommodation between the sexes that you've somehow overlooked" (qtd. Hogeland 84). Hogeland notes, "What is particularly striking in these reviews is that none of the reviewers attempted to argue that some men were oppressive (or dull) and that most men or men in general were not. Instead, any negative or shallow depiction of any male character was made to stand in for all men. Even the most minor of such depictions, in other words, signaled to reviewers the eruption of 'ideology' into 'objective' or 'fair' realist fiction" (85). Reviewers of *The Stepford Wives* ignore the fact that it is not a realistic film, but is clearly a feminist, science-fiction allegory set within contemporary suburbia. Writers who critique the wholly negative representations of men in the film often ignore its genre, which focuses less on well-rounded, subtle character construction than on its an overt social, political, and moral message.
5. *The Stepford Wives* is quite similar to the consciousness-raising, or CR, novel: like the CR novel, *The Stepford Wives* includes a consciousness-raising scene, and, more important, is structured around the awakening of the protagonist's consciousness and her realization of her own personal and political oppression.
6. All film quotes are from *The Stepford Wives*.
7. My use of the word *sterile* does not signify my acceptance of the term; this is, however, the implication of the film.

8. The supermarket finale also reveals that female friendship has been destroyed in Stepford. Alliances between women (such as that envisioned by Joanna, Bobbie and Charmaine) might conceivably have interfered with the Men's Association's monolithic control over Stepford, but now that the ties of understanding and sympathy have been destroyed between the women, no threat exists to the men's hegemony.

REFERENCES

Bartky, Sandra Lee. "Foucault, Femininity, and the Modernization of Patriarchal Power." *The Politics of Women's Bodies.* Ed. Rose Weitz. Oxford: Oxford UP, 1998. 25–47.

Baxandall, Rosalyn. "Catching the Fire." *The Feminist Memoir Project: Voices from Women's Liberation.* Ed. Rachel Blau DuPlessis and Ann Snitow. New York: Three Rivers P, 1998. 208–24.

Bordo, Susan. *Unbearable Weight: Feminism, Western Culture, and the Body.* Berkeley and Los Angeles: U of California P, 1993.

Echols, Alice. *Daring to be bad: Radical Feminism in America, 1967–1975.* Minneapolis: U of Minnesota P, 1989.

The Feminists. "Women: Do You Know the Facts about Marriage?" *Sisterhood Is Powerful: An Anthology of Writings from the Women's Liberation Movement.* Ed. Robin Morgan. New York: Random House, 1970. 536–37.

Friedan, Betty. *The Feminine Mystique.* New York: Dell, 1984.

Gans, Herbert. "Gans on Film: 'The Stepford Wives'—Killing Off Women's Lib," *Social Policy* 6 (1975): 59–60.

Hogeland, Lisa Maria. *Feminisms and Its Fictions.* Philadelphia: U of Pennsylvania P, 1998.

hooks, bell. *Ain't I a Woman?* Boston: South End P, 1981.

Jones, Beverly. "The Dynamics of Marriage and Motherhood." *Sisterhood Is Powerful: An Anthology of Writings from the Women's Liberation Movement.* Ed. Robin Morgan. New York: Random House, 1970. 46–61.

Kael, Pauline. "The Current Cinema." *The New Yorker* 24 Feb. 1975: 110+

Kennedy, Florynce. "Institutionalized Oppression vs. The Female." *Sisterhood Is Powerful: An Anthology of Writings from the Women's Liberation Movement.* Ed. Robin Morgan. New York: Random House, 1970. 438–46.

Klemesrud, J. "Feminists Recoil at Film Designed to Relate to Them." *New York Times* 26 Feb. 1975: 28.

Mainardi, Pat. "The Politics of Housework." *Sisterhood Is Powerful: An Anthology of Writings from the Women's Liberation Movement.* Ed. Robin Morgan. New York: Random House, 1970. 447–54.

New York Radical Feminists. "Politics of the Ego: A Manifesto for New York Radical Feminists." *Radical Feminism.* Ed. Anne Koedt, Ellen Levine, and Anita Rapone. New York: Quadrangle Books, 1973. 380.

The National Organization for Women. "Statement of Purpose." *Feminism in Our Time: The Essential Writings, World War II to the Present.* Ed. Miriam Schneir. New York: Vintage Books, 1994. 95–102.

"No More Miss America!" *Sisterhood Is Powerful: An Anthology of Writings from the*

Women's Liberation Movement. Ed. Robin Morgan. New York: Random House, 1970. 521–23.

Redstockings. "Redstockings Manifesto." *Sisterhood Is Powerful: An Anthology of Writings from the Women's Liberation Movement.* Ed. Robin Morgan. New York: Random House, 1970. 533–35.

Schickel, Richard. "Women's Glib." *Time* 3 Mar. 1975: 4.

Shulman, Alexis Kates. "A Marriage Disagreement, or Marriage by Other Means." *The Feminist Memoir Project: Voices from Women's Liberation.* Ed. Rachel Blau DuPlessis and Ann Snitow. New York: Three Rivers P, 1998. 284–303.

The Stepford Wives. Screenplay by William Goldman. Dir. Bryan Forbes. Perf. Katharine Ross, Paula Prentiss, Peter Masterson, Nanette Newman, Tina Louise, Carol Rossen, and Patrick O'Neal. Anchor Bay, 1975.

Barbara Winslow, "Primary and Secondary Contradictions in Seattle: 1967–1969." *The Feminist Memoir Project: Voices from Women's Liberation.* Ed. Rachel Blau DuPlessis and Ann Snitow. New York: Three Rivers P, 1998. 225–48.

Zinnerman, P. "Suburban Gothic," *Newsweek* 3 Mar 1975: 70.

Anna Krugovoy Silver *is assistant professor of English and interdisciplinary studies and director of the Women's and Gender Sudies Program at Mercer University. Her book,* Victorian Literature and the Anorexic Body, *is forthcoming from Cambridge University Press.*

Copyright © 2002 by the Arizona Board of Regents

Girls Town's Challenge to "Do It Yourself" Feminism

Angela E. Hubler

The recognition that "the personal is political" was central to the second wave of the women's movement. Women were radicalized by the notion that what they had understood as their private experience was, in fact, "characterized by power and fraught with political meaning" (Mandle 2). Founders of consciousness-raising groups believed that once women realized that their problems "had political, social origins, they would move on to consider what kind of collective, political action to take" (Davis 89). Now, in the first years of the twenty-first century, while this slogan retains much of the rhetorical power with which it resonated in the late 1960s, it can also echo some of the most antifeminist, reactionary tendencies within American culture, in particular, the ideology of individualism. In contrast to feminism, which entails at least a partial critique of social hierarchy, this ideology asserts that society, as it currently exists, (almost invariably) offers personal and economic success to the talented, hardworking individual. Because this ideology ascribes failure to strictly personal shortcomings, it is extremely conservative on an explanatory level. It is conservative and apolitical in a more proactive sense as well, as it focuses on the isolated individual, rather than on the group; it is this latter focus that is necessary for any sort of political transformation.

Sociologist Ruth Sidel found that the ambivalence that vitiates the potential radicalism of the notion "the personal is political" also characterized the consciousness of the adolescent girls she interviewed in writing *On Her Own: Growing Up in the Shadow of the American Dream*. On the one hand, Sidel found that the girls' aspirations for the future had been profoundly shaped by feminism. Most influential was what she calls "career feminism," which seeks "equality in the workforce," and which led many girls to seek careers in law, journalism, and business and, significantly, to "focus on material success" (17–25). Thus, the new feminist message melded with the much older "pull yourself up by your own bootstraps" vision that characterizes the American dream. This ideology, or unified set of beliefs about American society, results

Patti (Lili Taylor) and Emma (Anna Grace) confront Richard Helms (Tom Gilroy) in a scene from *Girls Town*, directed by Jim McKay.

Copyright © 1996 by October Films/USA Films

in the girls' notion that "they can and must make their own way in life, can and must provide for themselves materially, can and must take control of their own lives" (Sidel 9).

Sidel's description of the young women she interviewed would serve just as well for many of the young women who take women's studies and English courses with me. While they have internalized many of the demands of feminism, they are confident that they will be rewarded for individual fortitude and effort, rather than penalized for being female. They assure me that things have changed, so that further social and political transformation is not needed. To a great extent, their confidence is a result of the accomplishments of second wave feminists, who did, to a significant degree, achieve abstract equality for women by altering both legal and informal barriers to greater participation in economic, political, and educational institutions and by gaining access to abortion. However, such students fail to realize that in addition to the more obvious obstacles posed by sexist employers, co-workers, teachers, and partners, a variety of durable structures and institutional obstacles, such as the differential responsibility for child rearing and housework, confront them. Thus, it is clear that one of the fundamental challenges for the women's movement—and the women's studies classroom—remains critical: to enable women and girls to see that only by collectively resisting oppression can they be liberated. *Girls Town*, the 1996 film directed by Jim McKay, powerfully depicts this process.[1]

Girls Town confronts, both narratively and technically, the ideology of individualism that infects so many young women today. Narratively, the film focuses on the aftermath of a rape. Shortly before her high school graduation, after which she was to attend Princeton, Nikki (played by Aunjanue Ellis) commits suicide, after being raped. While shocking, the suicide is plausible. According to Lori Heise, rape victims are nine times more likely than nonvictims to attempt suicide.[2] The film focuses on the consequences of the rape not for Nikki, but for her friends, Angela, Emma, and Patti (played by Bruklin Harris, Anna Grace, and Lili Taylor). Nikki's friends arrive at an understanding of their shared experience of male violence and come to identify with Nikki and with one another. Consequently, they begin to resist that violence.

Not only does the narrative stress the girls' recognition of the inadequacy of individual responses to male violence and spotlight the development of a collective response to this violence; in addition, the making of the film itself was a collective process. McKay, the director, and Denise Casano, the co-writer, drafted an outline that was developed into a script in workshops with the actors (Wilson). In this way, as in others, McKay's film resembles those of British director Mike Leigh. Neither filmmaker glamorizes his characters, but instead realistically depicts a gritty world populated by ordinary people. Both, too, make films that engage political issues without presenting any easy answers.

Girls Town begins with a close-up, slow-motion shot of striding feet. As the camera moves up, we see that the feet belong to a teenage girl, whom we later learn to be Nikki. The soundtrack, which initially consists of instrumental music into which street noise intrudes, shifts from exterior to interior, so that film viewers hear what Nikki does as she relives being raped. While viewers hear Nikki's desperation, fear, and anguish, the filmmaker resists the direct depiction of her rape. In doing so, he avoids the danger of paradoxically positioning the film viewer as a voyeur in a scene of violence against women.

This strategy is almost certainly in response to a landmark essay by film theorist Laura Mulvey, who argues that realist film techniques reproduce gendered hierarchies of power. These techniques emerge from a social world in which men are active and women passive, men look and women are looked at. She asserts that film spectators, who take the point of view of the camera, are invariably positioned as active and male, regardless of their biological sex, thereby making a passive object of the female film "icon" (436). While Mulvey's arguments are grounded in the controversial complexities of psychoanalysis, her conclusion is compelling: the formal aspects of film tend, despite the narrative content, to reinforce the subjection of women. Linda Lopez McAlister, for example, notes reports that at showings of *The Accused* (Jonathan Kaplan, 1988), which sympathetically depicts the struggles of the survivor of a gang rape to achieve legal justice, "groups of young males . . . cheered the rapists on during the rape scene" (343).

Despite her agreement with Mulvey's thesis, McAlister notes the difficulties it presents for the feminist filmmaker. Whereas Mulvey calls for the abandonment of the codes of cinematic realism and an alternative cinematic practice, McAlister rejects this, pointing out that such films "strike the uninitiated as strange, boring and unpleasant to watch" (342). McAlister offers several examples of films about violence against women that are "accessible" but that do not permit "audience identification with the abuser and his violence" (343, 344). Although the films are realist, the filmmakers use "techniques that minimize, stylize, or dramatize the violence rather than depicting it in a naturalistic fashion" (346–47). McKay's filmic technique does just this: by choosing not to depict the rape visually, he conveys the trauma of the rape in such a way that the viewer must take the point of view of the victim rather than of the perpetrator. The kind of identification that is encouraged in the film, however, is not typical. The initial scene's focus on Nikki encourages the viewer's assumption that she will be the main character, with whom viewers typically identify. Early in the film, however, this identification is frustrated by Nikki's suicide. To put the matter starkly, by removing the rape victim from the screen, the film avoids the pitfalls of an audience identification that becomes itself a species of individualism. Rather than encouraging passive identification with a single, larger-than-life character, the film focuses on an ensemble of characters.

After learning of Nikki's suicide, the three friends read her diary, which Emma has stolen from Nikki's house during a sympathy visit to her mother, and discover that Nikki has been raped. The friends are appalled by what they learn and incredulous that she had not told them. Patti exclaims, "She fuckin' didn't say nothin'. We could'a helped her. Man, she should have said something. . . . That makes me wonder, you know. I thought I knew Nikki. And I don't know Nikki." Emma replies, "It makes sense to me. Well, you know how she was like always totally in control of everything. Like Miss Perfect. She thought she would handle it for herself. And she couldn't. . . . People don't talk about that shit." Emma, who volunteers at a women's shelter, acknowledges the inadequacy of individual responses to male violence, and introduces a major theme in the film, the powerful change that would result if, in the words of poet Muriel Rukeyser, "one woman told the truth about her life" (Rukeyser 103). In fact, the film goes on to quote Audre Lorde's insistence that "it is not difference which immobilizes us, but our silence."[3]

Rukeyser claims that if we break that silence "the world would split open" (103). As the conversation among the three friends proceeds, however, it becomes apparent why Nikki, like 42 percent of rape victims in one survey, told no one about her rape (Warshaw 50). For when Emma, in response to Patti's demand that Patti be told about the "more major events" in her friends' lives, tells her friends that she had been raped on a date the previous year, Patti first minimizes the situation and then holds Emma, as an individual, responsible: "What do you expect. . . . If you call that rape, I've been raped by just about every guy I've gone out with. . . . Look. You just don't get in that situation in the first place. If I don't want to have sex with somebody, I don't get in a car with my tits hanging out." A heated argument among the three ensues in which Patti is forced to confront that she, as were Emma and Nikki, is in a situation in which she has "no control": her relationship with an abusive ex-boyfriend, with whom she has a child. Angela has the final words in the scene: "Talking about it is cool, don't get me wrong. But what . . . is it doing—to do something, to fight back. You know what I'm saying, saying I'm not going to take this . . . anymore."

In the scenes that follow, however, the three do fight back, earning the title's (loose) allusion to *Boys Town* (Norman Taurog, 1938), the Spencer Tracy film about juvenile delinquents and other troubled boys. First, when Patti, Emma, and Angela walk by the car in which Emma was raped, Patti keys it and punctures a tire. While Emma and Angela first watch in shock, they soon join Patti, breaking off the sideview mirror, breaking the window, and spray-painting *Rapist* on the hood. This is significant because in taking these actions, the girls not only wreak vengeance on Josh, the rapist, but also publicly censure male violence and warn others that though their violence may take place in private, it may not remain hidden. As the girls damage the car, they curse Josh, expressing their outrage at his violence. Their emotions change from rage to victory, however, as they take a picture of their handiwork. Later, they rob the apartment of Eddie, Patti's ex-boyfriend, and pawn what they steal in order to buy food and clothes for his child. In another scene—inspired by an actual incident at Brown University—the girls begin a list of rapists on the wall of the girls' bathroom in their high school to encourage others to break the silences that divide them, and they write next to the list, "Subvert the patriarchy!"

The movie climaxes when the girls confront Nikki's rapist, an employee at the magazine where she was an intern. When he challenges their assertions that he raped Nikki, Emma pushes him down and kicks him. Here, unlike the restrained depiction of Nikki's rape, the camera does not hesitate to graphically depict this scene of female violence, anger, punishment, and retribution. Like other less personal female violence played out earlier in the film (against property, for example), this violence is shocking, partly because, unlike other, similar female revenge films such as *Set It Off* (F. Gary Gray, 1996) and *Thelma and Louise* (Ridley Scott, 1991), it is realistic rather than hyperbolic. As Patti remarks, "If this was a movie, we would'a shot fifty people by now." Of course, it is a movie, but one with a realist, documentary aesthetic rather than a Hollywood one.[4] Thus, viewers respond to the girls' behavior not in relation to screen fantasies of female violence—Thelma and Louise blowing up the semi of a sexist, obnoxious trucker, for example—but in relation to the fact that men are overwhelmingly those responsible for violence. Sociologist Michael Kimmel notes, "Men constitute 99 percent of all persons arrested for rape; 88 percent of those arrested for murder; 92 percent of those arrested for robbery; 87 percent for aggravated assault; 85 percent of other assaults; 83 percent of all family violence; 82 of disorderly conduct" (243). In terms of our knowledge about women's typical behavior, then, to see these actors behave as they do on screen is extraordinary. Even the film characters must reassure themselves that they haven't gone too far as they leave the rapist lying in the street and walk away: Angela repeats, "It's all right."

At the same time that the violence in this scene is disturbing, it is also emotionally gratifying. The purpose of this film, however, is not to encourage women (or girls) to become violent. Rather, in depicting the way that the recognition of a shared experience of male violence can catalyze female solidarity, the film is part of a tradition in feminist film and literature that includes Dutch director Marlene Gorris's *A Question of Silence* (1983), Susan Glaspell's one-act play *Trifles*, and poet Gwendolyn Brooks's "A Bronzeville Mother Loiters in Mississippi. Meanwhile, A Mississippi Mother Burns Bacon." In such works, the emphasis falls upon the shared experience and emotional reactions of the female characters, a commonality that points implicitly to a structural, transindividual cause.

Furthermore, although the film certainly validates the girls' righteous anger, it is clear that their actions are insufficient to overcome the problems that confront them. Their response to the violence and oppression that they experience has gone beyond silent, passive endurance (or even acceptance), but their politics, in order to be truly effective, require further development. In evaluating their behavior, however, it is important to understand the context for the actions they take. Had they chosen to pursue justice with the police and in the courts, for example, the chances of succeeding would have been very slim. The conviction rate for rape in the United States in 1994, to take one year, was only 20 percent (U.S. Department of Justice 3). Even this abysmally low rate is called "inflated" by the U.S. Department of Justice because it is based "on the number of convictions divided *not* by the total number of rapes but by just the number recorded by police" (3).

The end of the movie reflects the fact that a fully worked-out solution to male violence has not been delivered to viewers. The anticlimactic final scene takes place on the day of the senior prom, on top of the high school baseball dugout. The girls joke about the upcoming prom, which they won't be attending; the impending last week of school; and their plans for the future. As a train whistle blows in the distance, the camera slowly moves away from the girls and toward the train tracks. Emma says, "I wanna get on it!" Patti replies, "Damn, that train's running through my head"; and Emma exclaims, "Let's get on it, you guys!" The film concludes with a shot of the train as the soundtrack breaks into Queen Latifah's "U.N.I.T.Y." The final shot of the train suggests movement, but the destination remains undefined, as the solutions to the problems represented in the film have no simple answers that a film can neatly deliver to its audience. The train, a powerful and complex symbol in American culture, suggests more than a simple desire for escape. The train has symbolized a desire for freedom and movement since before the Civil War. In music, for example, from African American spirituals to country to rock and roll, singers have expressed the longing to leave limitation and sorrow behind and move forward into some better place. The music of social change and protest has also utilized this symbol in songs such as "Get on Board, Little Children," a spiritual that refers directly to the Underground Railroad and that was sung by Civil Rights workers. Thus, the girls' longing to get on the train is, in fact, a poignant expression of their still unrealized yearnings for liberation. "Let's get on it, you guys," invites viewers on board to join the collective movement for social justice in transforming society.

Despite, and in a certain way because of, its irresolution, then, the conclusion of *Girls Town* is far more politically hopeful and suggestive than the joint suicide that ends *Thelma and Louise*. In this latter film, the final image of a car flying through the air, seconds from crashing to earth and killing the two women in it, powerfully protests male domination of, and violence against, women. As in Kate Chopin's *The Awakening*, however, female self-assertion is ironically depicted as self-destructive. This deeply romantic and individualistic conclusion (despite Thelma and Louise's clasped hands) is a refusal to return to a social world seen as irredeemably hostile. As Thelma explains to Louise, "I feel like something crossed over in me and I can't go back." Such a refusal results from an inability to imagine any kind of social future superior to the one that now exists.

We must attribute this failure of the imagination not to the characters in the film but to the writer, Callie Khouri. Khouri's ability to imagine a different ending to this film was almost certainly stunted by her hostility to the social movement working to eradicate male violence, feminism. Khouri has rejected descriptions of the film as feminist, because, she says in a particularly insightful comment, "the word has a negative stigma attached to it" (Murphy H8). Thus, while she protests male violence, her protest, like the car soaring through the air in the final scene of *Thelma and Louise*, isn't really going anywhere. In this regard, one must grudgingly respect the artistic integrity of

Khouri and director Ridley Scott, as the nihilism of the conclusion manifests the vacuity at the very heart of the film.

This comparison is instructive, for it clarifies the tone of *Girls Town*'s unusually unresolved conclusion. Reviewers have commented on this, typically seeing it as pessimistic. Michael Tanner, for example, notes: "No matter how successful they are with their junior vigilante campaign, the girls end up where they started: stuck in a town they're tired of, with one dead friend and no clear vision of what their future holds. Their realization—that revenge served at any temperature is a dish that doesn't fill you up for long—separates *Girls Town* from the conventional feel-good closure endemic to most films of its ilk"(3–4). While Tanner rightly points out that the conclusion frustrates the desire for a happy ending, he doesn't reflect on the motivation behind this technique.

The film's lack of closure is not merely a negative reaction to typical Hollywood movies, an attempt to indicate the way that "real life" does not have neatly tied loose ends and satisfying conclusions; rather, it is designed to stimulate and engage the political sensibilities of the viewer. In fact, the epilogue to *The Good Woman of Setzuan*, a play by German Marxist Bertold Brecht, would serve *Girls Town* equally well (with the substitution of the words "movie" for "play" and "people" for "men"):

> You're thinking, aren't you, that this is no right
> Conclusion. . . .
> We feel deflated too. We too are nettled
> To see the curtain go down and nothing settled.
> How can a better ending be arranged?
> Can one change people? Can the world be changed?
> It is for you to find a way, my friends,
> To help good men arrive at happy ends.
> *You* write the happy ending to our play!
> There must, there must, there's got to be, a way! (Brecht 96)

Thus, the lack of closure in a work such as *The Good Woman of Setzuan* or *Girls Town* is, in fact, the hopeful indication that human society can and will take up the challenges posed by the film. *Girls Town*'s refusal to satisfy viewers with an artistic performance, the openness of the conclusion, reminds us of the openness of the social. The satisfaction denied by the conclusion can only be achieved by the collective transformation of society.

JIM MCKAY FILMOGRAPHY

Our Song. 2001. IFC Films.
Girls Town. 1996. USA Films.
No Alternative. 1993. Movies Unlimited, Polygram Music Video.

NOTES

Thanks to Tim Dayton, Jill Deans, and Melissa Divine for reading and commenting on an earlier draft of this essay, and to Summer Lewis for secretarial help. Special thanks to the Department of English at the University of Portland for inviting me to deliver this essay as a public lecture.
1. The film won two awards at the 1996 Sundance Film Festival: the Filmmakers Trophy and Special Jury Prize.
2. Statistic cited in *WAC Stats* 50.
3. Several lines from Lorde are shown written in a notebook belonging to one of the girls (Lorde 44).
4. McKay discusses his filmmaking style in an interesting interview with Mia Mask, commenting on the influence of documentary filmmaker Frederick Wiseman (Mask).

REFERENCES

Brecht, Bertold. *Parables for the Theatre.* New York: Grove P, 1961. 96.
Davis, Flora. *Moving the Mountain: The Women's Movement in America since 1960.* New York: Simon and Schuster, 1991. 89.
Kimmel, Michael. *The Gendered Society.* New York: Oxford UP, 2000. 243.
Lorde, Audre. "The Transformation of Silence into Language and Action." *Sister Outsider.* Trumansburg, N.Y.: Crossing P, 1984. 44.
McAlister, Linda Lopez. "Feminist Cinematic Depictions of Violence Against Women: An Analysis of Three Representational Strategies." *Krieg/War: Eine Philosophische Auseinandersetzung aus Feministischer Sicht.* Ed. Charlotte Annerl and Sophia Gabriel Panteliadou. Munich: Wilhelm Fink Verlag, 1997. 341–47.
Mandle, Joan. "How Political Is the Personal? Identity Politics, Feminism, and Social Change." 12 July 2000. Online. Available: <http://research.umbc.edu/~korenman/wmst/identity_pol.html. 2. 2 Feb. 2002.
Mask, Maria. "ND/NF Interview: Girls 'Hood; Realist Jim McKay Returns with 'Our Song.'" Online. Available: <http://www.indiewire.com/film/festivals/fes_00NDNF_000405 _McKayint.html. 5 Feb. 2002.
Murphy, Ryan. "Writer Hits a Nerve with Revenge Movie." *Kansas City Star* 30 June 1991: H8.
Rukeyser, Muriel. "Kathe Kollwitz." *The Speed of Darkness.* New York: Random House, 1960. 103.
Sidel, Ruth. *On Her Own: Growing Up in the Shadow of the American Dream.* New York: Penguin, 1990. 17–25.
Tanner, Michael. "Joan of Arc Rule." 17 September 1998. Online. Available:

<http//www.hotwired.lycos.com/movies/96/35/index3a.html. 3–4. 5 Feb. 2002.
U.S. Department of Justice, Bureau of Justice Statistics. "Crime and Justice in the United States and England and Wales, 1981–96: Convictions per 1,000 offenders." Online. Available: <http:www.usdoj.gov/05publications/05_3_c.html. 3. 5 Feb. 2002.
Warshaw, Robin. *I Never Called It Rape.* New York: Harper and Row, 1988. 50.
Wilson, Brandon. "Lili Taylor Captures Talk of the Town at This Year's Sundance Film Festival." 25 Aug. 1995. *Daily Bruinonline.* Online. Available: <http://www.dailybruin.ucla.edu /db/issues/96/8.26/ae.taylor.html. 24 Sept. 1997.
Women's Action Coalition, ed. *WAC Stats: The Facts about Women.* New York: New P, 1993. 50.

Angela E. Hubler *is an assistant professor of women's studies at Kansas State University. Her recent essay publications focus on the culture of female adolescence and can be found in* Delinquents and Debutantes: Twentieth-Century American Girls' Cultures, Children's Literature Association Quarterly *25.2,* NWSA Journal *12.1, and the forthcoming* Growing Up Postmodern.

Copyright © 2002 by Angela E. Hubler

Creating the Lesbian Mammy
Boys on the Side and the Politics of AIDS

Katie Hogan

Postmodern film theorists often dismiss film criticism that focuses on stereotypes and images of socially marginalized groups as naive and outdated. Ellis Hanson's *Outtakes: Essays on Queer Theory and Film* characterizes such a focus as oversimplified and theoretically and aesthetically "impoverished" (5). But the virtue of using the images/stereotypes method is in its rendering of historical and political context—a particularly useful tool in studying films about AIDS. In addition, as Suzanna Walters points out, a blind spot of postmodern "signification theorists" is that they downplay, and sometimes even ignore, how social and political contexts are intertwined with the construction of film narratives (26).

In analyzing one of Hollywood's first responses to the topic of women and AIDS, Herbert Ross's 1995 film, *Boys on the Side,* I neither dismiss this commercial film as trivial or lacking in artistic skill nor denigrate the importance of the emotional outlet and visual pleasure the film provides the spectator. *Boys* is clearly a potential source of catharsis for an audience/spectator, and few people with personal experience of AIDS would easily reject discourses that allow people with the disease and those who love them some narrative release and identification.[1] However, as with most cultural and artistic works, this one possesses multiple strands and meanings. One meaning notable in *Boys* comes from the way AIDS and the cultural idea of the black woman as "mammy" dramatically collide in the film in the figure of a newly created role—the "lesbian mammy." This figure emerges in a film about AIDS in order to do what the mammy figure has always done: reassure white spectators that black women's sexuality is under wraps and that the racial boundaries between "white" and "black" are firmly intact. The lesbian mammy figure also manages the boundaries between heterosexuality and homosexuality at the same time that it offers a message of tolerance and acceptance of AIDS and gay people.

This white heterosexual fantasy expresses the dominant culture's fear of black female sexuality, lesbian sexuality, AIDS, and any demonized sexualities and cultural behaviors that are seemingly linked with the epidemic. The multiple anxieties associated with the epidemic are eased through a nonthreatening, desexualized, maternal, African American lesbian character. In order to address the existence of AIDS in American women's lives, its potent web of stigma must be tempered and made palpable. The result is a plot in which a black lesbian cares for a white, heterosexual, middle-class, HIV-positive woman while putting on hold her own desires and ambitions.

One crucial effect of such a framework is that the impact of AIDS on the material lives of African American women of all sexual identities is strategically erased and displaced onto white heterosexual women. Although "[t]hree-fourths of women with AIDS are women of color," the one (and, to my knowledge, only) commercial film on women and the epidemic organizes the story around the classic figure of the suffering white woman (Denison 4). This interpretation of the film is not meant as moral chastisement of white women or popular feminism; rather it illustrates how the white female heterosexual body is also symbolically used in mainstream film to mediate a threatening social stigma. Such a practice transforms HIV-positive white heterosexual women's experiences and lives into a useful iconography that erases not only the realities and contradictions of HIV-positive white women's lives, but the very fact of HIV and AIDS in African American women.

Black Woman as Mammy

The first identification of black woman as mammy is often pinpointed to the publication of Harriet Beecher Stowe's *Uncle Tom's Cabin,* in which, as Patricia Turner explains, "Stowe's physical description of Aunt Chole, the faithful wife to Uncle Tom and loyal servant to the Shelby family, set the standard for future fictional representations of mammy figures" (46). Stowe's novel influenced how black women would be imagined in dominant fiction and visual representations throughout the nineteenth century and provided a legacy that continues to this day. For this reason, Turner argues, *Uncle Tom's Cabin* "is virtually impossible to ignore in a study of race and American popular culture" (67).[2]

The mammy/auntie figure of Stowe's famous novel reappeared in nineteenth-century theatrical adaptations of *Uncle Tom's Cabin,* and in the twentieth century in films and material culture—salt and pepper shakers; cookie jars, napkin holders, and almost any object associated with the kitchen. Turner has found that

> [m]ammy/auntie figures constitute the most frequently depicted character.... Draped in calico from head to toe, Aunt Jemima and her cronies pose no sexual threat to their white mistresses. They want to nourish rather than seduce white men. The artifacts they grace belong almost exclusively to the kitchen.... The mammy figures convey the notion that genuine fulfillment for black women comes not from raising their own children or feeding their own man (black [heterosexual] families are rarely featured) but from serving in a white family's kitchen. (25)

This all-too-familiar cultural fantasy of the black woman as "the mighty nurturer" continues to permeate American culture, particularly in the kinds of roles black female actors play in American films (Bogle 298). The only black female actors to win Academy Awards to date are Hattie McDaniel and Whoopi Goldberg, both of whom won in the best supporting actress category for "mammy" roles.

Aside from appearing in the controversial film *The Color Purple*, Whoopi Goldberg has been repeatedly cast in films in which she is the sole black character surrounded by an all-white cast. In addition, Goldberg is often presented in an updated version of the mammy/servant role. In *Ghost*, her Oscar-winning role, she plays a wacky medium who is compelled to reunite a grief-stricken white woman with her dead, yuppie husband (Bogle 329). In *The Long Walk Home*, she plays a domestic servant who "humanizes" her white southern employer, and in *Clara's Heart* she assumes the role of a beautifully dressed, wise, live-in Jamaican maid who nurtures a neglected, rich, white boy. In the 1996 film *Bogus*, Goldberg once again portrays a single woman who, after the sudden death of her best friend, becomes guardian of her late friend's child. As in *Clara's Heart*, the little boy is white and emotionally distraught.

Although Goldberg's characters are portrayed as the moral center in these films, and, as in *Clara's Heart*, the character's own personal struggles are slightly developed, her characters are consistently without a separate romantic/personal/communal life of their own. In almost all her movies, Goldberg is consistently denied an on-screen romance. As Donald Bogle notes, "The very idea of Whoopi Goldberg as a romantic film personality was unacceptable to certain audiences. Filmmakers seemed to view her as an asexual creature from another universe" (298). Goldberg's role as a black lesbian character, Jane DeLuca, in *Boys on the Side* follows this dominant pattern of the desexualized, updated mammy.[3]

The American film industry's transformation of black women's bodies into icons of benevolence and self-sacrifice serves as the "solution" to the threat of black women's sexuality and, in the case of *Boys*, black lesbian sexuality. The same "mammy" strategy that was employed in the presentation of Hattie McDaniel's character, Mammy, in *Gone With the Wind* is similarly evoked for a black lesbian character in *Boys on the Side*. This pattern suggests an inextricable link between racial ideas and ideas about human sexuality. As Kobena Mercer and Isaac Julien argue, "The prevailing Western concept of sexuality . . . *already contains racism*" (qtd. in Somerville 5). Likewise, Siobhan B. Somerville explores the idea of racial and sexual difference as interrelated: "It was not merely a historical coincidence that the classification of bodies as either 'homosexual' or 'heterosexual' emerged at the same time that the United States was aggressively constructing and policing the boundary between 'black' and 'white' bodies" (3). *Boys* also presents a linked racial and sexual hierarchy, one expressed in terms of women and AIDS and a nostalgic universal feminist solidarity.

From Angry Black Woman to Feminist Sister: The Transformation of Jane

Hailed by *New York Times* film critic Janet Maslin as "one of the strongest Hollywood movies to deal with AIDS thus far," *Boys on the Side* is the first commercial film with well-known actors—Whoopi Goldberg, Mary-Louise Parker, and Drew Barrymore—to address the neglected issue of women and AIDS and to present an out, black lesbian character (Maslin C3). *Boys* attracted a mixed audience, but it was primarily marketed as a women's/gay film. Lesbians and bisexual women were anxious to see a major star play "gay," while heterosexual women of varied racial and cultural identifications were drawn to the topic of AIDS and to the women's bonding theme made popular by the film *Thelma and Louise* (1991).

The story begins with Goldberg's character, Jane DeLuca, as an angry, isolated, unsuccessful lead singer for an otherwise all-white, all-male rock band. In the opening scene, Jane is singing a rendition of Janis Joplin's "Piece of My Heart" before an indifferent audience in a seedy New York nightclub. One of the club's intoxicated patrons, a young white woman, is laughing and flirting with her male date and disturbing Jane's concentration. Insulted by this woman's rude behavior, Jane boldly approaches her after the set. The woman immediately assumes that Jane is a waitress who has come to clear away the bottles and glasses. Jane explains that she is the singer in the band and humorously confronts the woman's annoying behavior.

Throughout the first forty minutes of the film, Jane is smart, confrontational, and sarcastic. She swears unflinchingly at a New York City cab driver; wears a black leather jacket, a symbol of "toughness"; and is forceful and opinionated. When Jane's co-worker informs her that the band has lost its gig at the club, this seventeen-year veteran of the music club scene swiftly decides to quit the band and move to Los Angeles in search of new work and a new life. She answers an ad for a ride share placed in the newspaper by Robin, played by Mary-Louise Parker, and Jane and Robin meet for lunch.

Robin and Jane are the archetypal odd couple. Whereas Jane is abrasive, tough, and "butch," Robin, a successful real estate agent, is controlled, ultrafeminine—she's often dressed in soft cashmere and angora—and fastidious. With great reluctance (and with no real options) Jane agrees to the ride share with Robin, whom she calls "the whitest woman on the face of the earth."

The movie charts the growth and transformation in Jane's and Robin's unlikely friendship as they travel across the country accompanied by Jane's cute, but goofy, friend, Holly, played by Drew Barrymore. Together the three women bond as they confront Holly's experiences with domestic violence, Robin's struggle as a woman with AIDS, and Jane's encounters with racism and homophobia. The film ends with Robin's death from AIDS, the birth of Holly's biracial baby, and Jane being devoted to the memory of Robin.

One interpretation of the film is that it presents a poignant tale of women's solidarity and power. Indeed, the film is a statement about women bonding, forged in a popular feminist style. Some clear markers of this are the title, which evokes the idea of women's friendship as central, whereas women's interest in men is "on the side" or ancillary; the all-women's soundtrack featuring the work of Melissa Etheridge, the Indigo Girls, Annie Lennox, and Bonnie Raitt; Robin's reference to Anne Sexton's "In Celebration of My Uterus"; and occasional nods to *Thelma and Louise.* Yet the notion of women's cross-racial and cross-cultural bonding that accompanies these signposts minimizes many experiences and identities while magnifying others. Human difference, conflict, and contradiction are constructed as divisive and "unsisterly."

From Maslin's perspective, however, *Boys on the Side* is a successful film: it is "sharp" and funny" and "creates an unexpected groundswell of real emotion" (C3). Comparing it with *Thelma and Louise* and *Terms of Endearment,* Maslin celebrates *Boys on the Side* for its ability to "blur [. . .] lines of race and gender with surprising ease" (C3)[4]

But does the film blur the lines of race and gender, or does it deny race in favor of white heterosexual gender? It is important to point out that blurring lines of race and gender is not the same as acknowledging human difference, and this is a distinction that both Maslin and the movie miss. For "blurring" race and gender often fails to decenter whiteness and heterosexuality—Goldberg's character, despite the "blurring," is still marginalized.

Maslin does note, however, that Jane is "the quintessential outsider as the film begins" and that Goldberg herself is "Hollywood's most uncategorizable star" (C3). Yet this inexplicable outsider status seems irrelevant to Maslin, who declares that *Boys on the Side* has finally provided Goldberg with "a role that suits her talents" (C3).[5]

In a sort of quick afterthought, Maslin does comment on the "small irony" that *Boys on the Side* "depicts [AIDS] in terms of a straight white woman," and on the unfortunate decision to present Jane's sexuality "in terms of metaphor and wisecracking rather than actual physicality" (C3). But for viewers with even the slightest awareness of the politics of AIDS in America, this choice will not be surprising: a white, heterosexual, middle-class woman, even one who contracts HIV as Robin does through a one-night stand with a bartender, is more likely, given racial, class, and sexual politics, to garner visibility than a black or working-class woman who contracts HIV in exactly the same way.

Robin's inevitable death from AIDS takes on broad, heroic meanings; she becomes a symbol of lost youth, unrealized young motherhood, and the impossibility of heterosexual love and marriage. In one scene, Robin can't get HBO in her motel room, so she asks Jane if she can watch *The Way We Were* on the television in hers. Jane joins her in a tearful viewing, during which Robin confesses that she's not "very liberated . . . . I want a husband with a decent job. I want two kids, a boy and a girl, in that order. And a salt-box Colonial with three bedrooms, a sun porch, a stairway with a white banister, and a convertible den." Through her association with Jane, Robin gradually develops a feminist consciousness, but it is one that aggressively includes traditional (white) motherhood, heterosexual marriage, and monogamy above all else. Robin symbolizes "valuable" heterosexual womanhood and the American Dream in a way that outsider Jane cannot.

Running parallel to the film's vision of women and AIDS are facts such as that black women constitute 57 percent of the cases of all U.S. women with AIDS, and that in 1993 a study conducted in San Francisco indicated that "HIV seroprevalence was more than three times higher among lesbian and bisexual women than for all women" (Groeger 4–5). Had Maslin been aware of such facts, perhaps her discussion of the "small irony" of Robin and the elision of Jane's "actual physicality" would have been more complex.

To Elizabeth Pincus, *Boys on the Side* may be "brash" and "ballsy," with Whoopi Goldberg "bursting onto the screen as a full-blown, not-shyof-the-'L'-word lesbo," but the film's desexualization of Jane concerns Pincus (26). Goldberg's Jane "is granted a platonic crush on the movie's tragic heterosexual, turning a heretofore bawdy romp into a picture that's maudlin and sterile" (26). Sharing Pincus's frustration were several lesbian viewers who voiced their discontent on an America Online message board: "The lesbian was cynically rendered unlucky-in-love as to make her more palpable for a general audience. Wouldn't the movie have done just as well if Whoopi Goldberg's love life was healthy?"; "In film, lesbians are usually a sexual void"; "My friend said she was sick of seeing Hollywood portray lesbians as 'women who always fall in love with straight women;' " "I am also tired of unrequited lesbian love stories."

These viewers' frustrations with the film's (and society's) inability to allow Jane a love life echo Donald Bogle's observations about the persistent construction of Whoopi Goldberg's characters as "asexual creature[s] from another universe" (298). Again, the desexualization of Jane occurs in terms of both racial and sexual politics: the fact that Jane is a black woman surrounded, for the most part, by white people is just as significant as the fact that Jane is a lesbian surrounded, for the most part, by heterosexuals. Pincus, unlike Maslin and the viewers quoted above, questions the film's overly idealized multiracial, intergenerational sisterly solidarity, which she dismisses as "hokey" and "def[ying] belief " (Pincus 26). But Pincus's discussion of lesbian representation overlooks the historical process of what Wahneema Lubiano refers to as racialized gender. In *Boys,* Jane is stripped of a romantic life not only because of her lesbian identity, but also because she is black. Jane is certainly neither celibate by choice nor romantically shut down, as her wistful, sexual-emotional longing for the heterosexual Robin and Holly makes evident. But the fact that she's a black woman *and* a lesbian explains her nonexistent love life.

Jane's lack of "actual physicality" exists within the larger historical framework of the black woman as innately immoral or as the sign and practice of hypersexuality. And as a black lesbian, Jane experiences her sexuality, to borrow from Evelynn Hammonds's theories on black lesbian sexuality, as a "deviant sexuality [that] exists within an already pre-existing deviant sexuality" (137). Jane is unconsciously associated with historical narratives of black women's sexuality as excessive, illicit, and taboo coupled with the unspeakableness of homosexuality.[6] Homophobia clearly contributes to the desexed, nurturing features of Jane, but homophobia and racism are inseparable in her characterization, as theoretical work on black women's sexuality makes clear. In fact, *Boys* articulates the need for further development of the study of the interrelationship between race, racial discourses, and discourses on homosexuality and heterosexuality (Somerville 1–14).

Unlike the role of the traditional mammy, Goldberg's mammy role in *Boys on the Side* incorporates her lesbian identity, and her white family consists of two single women under thirty, one of whom has AIDS. Nevertheless, Goldberg's lesbian persona possesses the subordinating traits of the traditional black mammy. Jane nourishes and comforts Robin and Holly through each individual life crisis. She is the rock, the all-giving mother who never asks for nourishment, so devoted is she to these two characters' needs. Jane is stripped of emotional needs in addition to sensuality and desire, for she is an emblem of selfless, sentimental nurturance. The film's refusal to give Jane an interior life of her own, one composed of desires, rage, dreams, memories, pleasure, and fears, and her lack of a visible community, make this clear. Devoted, celibate, lesbian friend/mammy and second-class citizen is the only possible role available. Jane is repeatedly depicted as comforting and emotionally attentive to her adopted white family, yet she is rarely the recipient of their tenderness and care. And while it is true that Goldberg plays Jane as an opinionated, forceful woman, Jane's forcefulness is often in response to these two women and their predicaments. On the whole, Jane's own needs are pushed aside and never articulated.

With each scene, Jane's initial preoccupation with finding work in Los Angeles as a musician and with healing her own broken heart evaporates as she is pulled into the dilemmas of Robin's and Jane's circumstances. Shortly after their dramatic narrow escape from Holly's brutish, violent boyfriend, Holly begins to have second thoughts about leaving him and considers returning to this drug-addicted, physically abusive man. Even though Jane is appalled by Holly's decision to return to Nick, she stays by her side and watches Holly cry. Frustrated, Jane walks into the bathroom to enlist Robin's help, only to find Robin collapsing onto the cold floor. Jane's attention shifts from Holly to Robin, who is immediately rushed to the hospital in an ambulance. The next scene depicts the worried, exhausted Jane sitting in a hospital waiting room, the sweet little Holly sleeping in her lap, as the doctor informs Jane that Robin has AIDS. In the following scene, Jane is shown comforting Robin as Robin cries and pulls at the tubes in her nose and arms.

Jane's friendship with these women would not be so stereotypical if the screenplay provided her with other friends and a chosen community; instead Jane has been plunged into the drama of these women's lives unwittingly. But it is what she does with this situation that is disturbing: she inexplicably abandons her former plan to start over in L.A. in order to help Robin and Holly. Three months later, the women are living together in a beautiful house in Tucson, Arizona, and Jane has hooked into a lesbian bar community, but she is still focused on Robin's needs, in terms of both romance and health. In addition to experiencing constant stress and anxiety, associated with Robin's AIDS diagnosis, Robin and Jane's idealized friendship deteriorates as a result of misunderstandings about Jane's "crush" on the heterosexual Robin. Meanwhile, the pregnant Holly becomes involved with an idealistic, naive, conservative cop named Abe Lincoln, who turns Holly over to the authorities once he learns that she may have been involved in the murder of her battering boyfriend. Janet Maslin refers to this part of the plot and the courtroom sequence that follows as clumsy and "contrived." But the courtroom drama allows Jane to come out as "gay," in response to an arrogant, feminist-bashing, homophobic prosecutor, and it provides Robin with the opportunity to present her ideas on feminism as sisterly solidarity before she dies.

Significantly, when Robin shows up to testify on Holly's behalf, Robin says to her now estranged friend, Jane, "You are my family and I love you." Jane responds by bending over and picking up Robin's luggage.[7]

In *Boys on the Side*, it is a black, unattractively dressed, desexualized lesbian who, in taking care of a slender, white, middle-class woman with AIDS, serves as a nonthreatening moral compass and role model to an AIDS-phobic audience and society. Similar to Harriet Beecher Stowe's Topsy, Jane is a mischievous entertainer, who, through her contact with the more delicate and dying Robin, transforms into a lesbian mammy/caretaker.

Black Women, AIDS, and Silence

Through the fake visibility of the sentimentalized lesbian mammy, *Boys* addresses the still unspeakable topic of AIDS, and in so doing obscures its problematic assumptions of sexuality, race, and gender behind the cloak of breaking silence.[8] As Evelynn Hammonds argues, "Visibility in and of itself does not erase a history of silence nor does it challenge the structure of power and domination, symbolic and material, that determines what can and cannot be seen" (141).[9] A black lesbian character is the ostensible protagonist in *Boys on the Side*, but in terms of a subtle, contemporary reworking of the good mammy figure who is isolated from communities of color and denied a sexual/romantic relationship. Although Jane is more likely to be HIV-positive than Robin is, the complex experiences of black women in the epidemic are silenced by the spectacle of a supposedly neutral and "natural" feminist emotionality, complete with an updated beloved black servant figure and a feisty, dying, white heroine.[10] As bell hooks points out, "The racial politics of Hollywood are such that there can be no serious representations of death and dying when the characters are African Americans. Sorrowful black death is not a hot ticket" (35).

Another telling contradiction arises when Robin's demise from AIDS is juxtaposed with the antics of Holly, a sexually active childlike woman who seems to have never heard of safer sex or contraceptives—she's eight weeks pregnant when the film opens and won't consider abortion because "it's murder." Maslin describes Holly as possessing the luscious flirtiness of a 1940s pinup girl, but Holly's position in this film is a bit more complex. The film ends with Holly married to the conservative white cop, who, miraculously, accepts her biracial baby. The plight of Robin suggests that yes, even white, heterosexual, educated, "valuable" women contract HIV and develop AIDS; but this same message is then repeatedly undermined by the experiences of Holly, who has more unsafe sex than any other character in the entire film and never once considers HIV a threat—even though her symptomatic housemate contracted HIV through a one-night stand.

On one level, Holly can be read as comic relief from the "heavy" issues so that the movie itself can have a sexy and fun side. But the underlying effect is to reinforce the idea that even though HIV leads to the death of one of the film's main characters, the epidemic is not really of concern to heterosexuals. It's another instance in which the boundaries between heterosexuality and homosexuality are reinforced. The decision to break silence on women and AIDS is so fraught with anxiety about sexual and racial categories that the narrative makes up for its own bravery by mitigating its message of risk.

Breaking silence and creating visibility are not enough to challenge underlying cultural assumptions. On the whole, Whoopi Goldberg's Jane loses her critical ability to resist the dominating effects of white heterosexual power. Jane initially feels put off by Robin's white-bread physical appearance, her adoration of Carole King and the Carpenters, and her penchant for women's heterosexual romantic "weepies," such as *The Way We Were* and *An Officer and a Gentleman*—examples of white, straight romantic culture that Robin cherishes and that Jane finds incomprehensible and offensive. But before too long, Jane is humming, and even singing and playing, Carpenters songs. Viewers are asked to celebrate Jane and Robin's reconciliation, which symbolizes that these two otherwise incompatible women/cultures have forged a bond despite insurmountable odds. However, the burden of change and compromise fall on Jane. Since Jane barely has a world of her own, the more she becomes immersed in the world of Robin, the less she seems like the independent, East Village musician we meet when the movie opens.

Following in the mammy tradition, Jane does emerge as an influence on the white heroine, when Robin admits in front of an entire courtroom that she's not gay but "at times I understand the inclination." In another instance, Jane's "influence" is more problematic. In one of the film's many intertextual references, Jane directly evokes *Gone with the Wind*'s Mammy and Scarlett, although with a twist.[11] Here, the film breaks from its own pattern and "humorously" constructs Jane as the hypersexual black woman while comically parodying the figure of the sentimentalized mammy. She persuades the prudish, uptight Robin to utter the word *cunt*, liberating Robin from her nice, sexually repressed, white girl training—"You free, Miz' Scarlett, you free!" Yet it's impossible not to read this scene as that of the black woman as stand-in for the "good" white woman's repressed sexuality.

Overall, *Boys* does succeed in breaking the resounding silence on women and AIDS in mainstream film, and it eschews the marginal positioning of women in the epidemic by giving the central role to a woman character who falls outside the ideological "risk group" fabrication. But it also operates with both candor and conformity, resulting in competing political and aesthetic elements; it both resists *and* conforms to traditional racial, sexual, and gender roles for women.

For example, the film uses the classic Hollywood education plot. By the movie's end, Jane changes from a wisecracking skeptic to a caretaking desexualized "sister." The inciting incident that leads Jane down a different path and alters her life forever occurs when she quits the band and agrees to drive across the country with Robin and Holly. Jane, the protagonist of this education plot, learns how to be less gruff and more tender, and that racism and homophobia are her problem; if only Jane weren't so angry and sarcastic, the film suggests, then she would be a happier woman. The initial racial-sexual-cultural tension with which the film opens and the continual focus on the "working out" of that tension through rigid racial and sexual roles is the film's underlying project.

NOTES

Parts of this essay originally appeared in a slightly different form in Katie Hogan, *Women Take Care: Gender, Race, and the Culture of AIDS*. Ithaca: Cornell UP, 2001.

1. For further elaboration of this idea, see Hogan 95–99.
2. See also Manring 149–83.
3. Goldberg has also played a space age mammy on television, on *Star Trek: The Next Generation*. "The character of Guinan, who seems to have existed for centuries and in several dimensions, is the ship's bartender. And, while she does not have the official rank of ship's 'counselor' (another female, a white, bosomy member of an 'empathic' species, is ship therapist and basically points out the obvious), Guinan does provide insight all the time in the manner of a guru; she never has romantic or sexual liaisons; and is the Captain's special friend, giving him sage advice, protecting him, looking out for him. Also, Guinan's race has enslavement in its past" (Ian).
4. *Thelma and Louise* is a far more complex film in its treatment of popular feminism than either *Boys on the Side* or *Terms of Endearment*. *Terms of Endearment*, similar to many film and fictional treatments of AIDS, uses the occasion of a white dying mother as a springboard for antifeminist backlash and mandatory gendered caretaking. *Thelma and Louise*, by contrast, shocked cultural commentators, resulting in widespread condemnation and debate about the film. For a good summary of the debate surrounding *Thelma and Louise*, see Suzanna Danuta Walters's introduction, "On Outlaw Women and Single Mothers," in her book, *Material Girls: Making Sense of Feminist Cultural Theory* (Berkeley and Los Angeles: U of California P, 1995) 1–28.
5. Contrast Maslin's discussion of Goldberg's portrayal of Jane as an "outsider" with Patricia Hill Collins's views on African American women as strangers in their own land: "The status of African-American women as outsiders or strangers becomes the point from which other groups define normality. . . . As the 'Other' of society who can never really belong, strangers threaten the moral and social order. But they are simultaneously essential for its survival because those individuals who stand at the margins of society clarify its boundaries. African-American women, by not belonging, emphasize the significance of belonging" (68). Collins goes on to explain that African American women's "outsider" status often provides them with a powerful, critical point of view that allows them to dismantle conventional and dominant ways of thinking. Yet for Maslin, the meaning of Goldberg's—and Jane's—outsiderness is both mundane and mysterious.
6. As Hammonds argues, from "the production of the image of a pathologized black female 'other' in the eighteenth century" to the myth of the "loose," hypersexual black female that was produced during and after slavery and Reconstruction, representations of black women's sexualities have been fraught with silence, unease, and racist mythologies (Hammonds 132–33).

One strategy developed by late nineteenth-century and early twentieth-century black women social reformers in response to racist representations of black women's sexuality was to counter the myth of the black woman as the "embodiment of sex" with the image of black women as the embodiment supermorality—an image that still has a far-reaching impact on contemporary representations of black women, as Donald Bogle's history of black actors in film suggests (Hammonds 133).

7. While white female caretaking is often presented in AIDS discourse as involving HIV-negative and -positive women whose love and tenderness rescue the stigmatized gay male from the realm of total abjection, no one performs this function for HIV-infected poor women or women of color on a representational level. The white middle-class female character may even possess a nonconventional trait, as in the case of the imaginative, eccentric, drug-addicted Harper Pitt of Tony Kushner's *Angels in America,* or of the funky lesbian helpmates in Paul Monette's novel *Halfway Home* and Nisa Donnelly's *The Love Songs of Phoenix Bay;* but these female characters are nevertheless constructed in terms of the traditional idea of the good woman as the woman who cares. They act as "white" mammies, but because of their class and race privileges they are more often constructed as slim, ethereal "ministering angels" rather than as the sentimentalized figure of the hefty, black mammy. However, women of all races, classes, ages, and religions grapple with the construction of "bad" women or "good" women in AIDS discourse. Good women function as didactic role models to a heartless AIDS-phobic society; bad women shore up the division between those who deserve sympathy and services and those who do not. Rarely are complex women located in diverse communities where they struggle with homophobia, racism, and sexism as well as with HIV. Even when a woman herself is HIV positive, women's actual experiences in the epidemic are often treated as peripheral and incidental.

8. For a discussion of fake visibility, see Schulman; in particular, "Conclusion: The Creation of a Fake Public Homosexuality."

9. Evelynn Hammonds observes that, in terms of representation in the AIDS epidemic, "black women are victims that are once again the 'other' of the 'other,' the deviants of the deviants, regardless of their sexual identities and practices" (141).

10. Emotional white femininity incased in sentimental novels is addressed in Danica. Danica offers an example of how white sentimental glorification masks class politics and childhood sexual abuse: "I push myself to read harder books. Nothing gives me a hint of a life like mine. Nothing is even close. There are saints, there are Alcott's *Little Women* and there are holy martyrs. There is nothing else. I am wrong" (19–20). Similarly, Dorothy Allison's *Bastard Out of Carolina,* described by one reviewer as "one of those unusual books that show childhood abuse without sentimentality or simplicity," similarly reveals class politics embedded in sentimental narrative.

11. Helen Taylor points out that some white feminists have consistently celebrated the novel and film in terms of Scarlett O'Hara's determination and leadership, while black feminists "are left to point to the political problems" (114). Taylor explains that such celebrations would require "both turning a blind eye to [the novel's and film's] white supremacist

southern propaganda, and entering into an unholy alliance with the crudest southern chauvinism and the activities of the Ku Klux Klan" (115). Simply put, what some feminist critics and readers interpret as women's resistance to domination, other feminist critics and readers interpret as reactionary racial stereotypes and class ideology. This tension within a white, middle-class feminist sensibility that challenges patriarchal dominance yet capitulates to reductive constructions of racial, economic, and sexual inequalities and identities has been vigorously exposed by numerous critics, including bell hooks, Audre Lorde, Hazel Carby, Patricia Hill Collins, and Barbara Smith, to name just a few. Barbara McCaskill and Layli Phillips assert, "We're downright weary of our typecast roles as the laughable Topsies of women's lib or the Beulahs who breast-feed the feminist imagination" (117).

REFERENCES

Bogle, Donald. *Toms, Coons, Mulattoes, Mammies, and Bucks: An Interpretive History of Blacks in American Films.* New York: Viking, 1994.

Boys on the Side. Dir. Herbert Ross. Perf. Whoopi Goldberg, Mary-Louise Parker, Drew Barrymore, Matthew McConaughey, Anita Gillette, James Remar, Amy Aquino, Dennis Boutsikaris, and Estelle Parsons. Warner Brothers, 1995.

Collins, Patricia Hill. "Mammies, Matriarchs, and Other Controlling Images." *Black Feminist Thought: Knowledge, Consciousness, and the Politics of Empowerment.* New York: Routledge, 1991. 67–90.

Denison, Rebecca. "Understanding HIV and AIDS: The Basics." *World* 110 (June 2000): 4.

Danica, Elly. *Don't—a Woman's Word: A Personal Chronicle of Childhood Incest and Adult Recovery.* Pittsburgh: Cleis, 1998.

Groeger, Anne. "Women and AIDS: Get the Facts!" *World* 56 (Dec. 1995): 4–5.

Hammonds, Evelynn. "Black (W)holes and the Geometry of Black Female Sexuality." *differences* 6.2–3 (1994): 126–45.

Hanson, Ellis. Introduction. *Outtakes: Essays on Queer Theory and Film.* Durham: Duke UP, 1999. 1–19

Hogan, Katie. *Women Take Care: Gender, Race, and the Culture of AIDS.* Ithaca: Cornell UP, 2001. 95–99.

hooks, bell. *Reel to Real: Race, Sex, and Class at the Movies.* New York: Routledge, 1996.

Ian, Marcia. Personal communication to author. August 1993–August 1997.

Manring, M. M. *Slave in a Box: The Strange Career of Aunt Jemima.* Charlottesville: UP of Virginia, 1998.

Maslin, Janet. "Another Buddy Story, with a Twist or Two." Rev. of *Boys on the Side,* dir. Herbert Ross. *New York Times* 3 Feb. 1995: C3.

McCaskill, Barbara, and Layli Phillips. "We Are All 'Good Woman!': A Womanist Critique of the Current Feminist Conflict." *Bad Girls/Good Girls: Women, Sex, and Power in the Nineties.* Ed. Nan Bauer Maglin and Donna Perry. New Brunswick: Rutgers UP, 1996. 106–22.

Pincus, Elizabeth. "Side Dish." Rev. of *Boys on the Side,* dir. Herbert Ross. *Gay Community News* Winter 1995: 25–26.

Schulman, Sarah. *Stagestruck: Theater, AIDS, and the Marketing of Gay America.* Durham: Duke UP, 1998.

Somerville, Siobhan. *Queering the Color Line: Race and the Invention of Homosexuality in American Culture.* Durham: Duke UP, 2000. 1–14.

Stowe, Harriet Beecher. *Uncle Tom's Cabin or, Life among the Lowly.* 1852. New York: Penguin, 1981.

Taylor, Helen. "*Gone with the Wind:* The Mammy of Them All." *The Progress of Romance: The Politics of Popular Fiction.* Ed. Jean Radford. London: Routledge and Kegan, 1986. 113–36.

Turner, Patricia A. *Ceramic Uncles and Celluloid Mammies: Black Images and Their Influence on Culture.* New York: Anchor, 1994.

Walters, Suzanna Danuta. *Material Girls: Making Sense of Feminist Cultural Theory.* Berkeley and Los Angeles: U of California P, 1995. 1–28.

Katie Hogan *is associate professor of English and director of the Student Center for Women at Fiorello H. LaGuardia Community College of the City University of New York. She is co-editor of* Gendered Epidemic: Representations of Women in the Age of AIDS *(Routledge) and author of* Women Take Care: Gender, Race, and the Culture of AIDS *(Cornell).*

Copyright © 2002 by Katie Hogan

Re-scripting History and Fairy Tales in Brigitte Roüan's *Outremer*

Dominique Licops

In *Outremer* (1992), French actress, film director, and script writer Brigitte Roüan offers a feminist, postcolonial revision of the history of "French Algeria" in the years between 1946 and 1964.[1] Instead of focusing on the political events, the Algerian anticolonial struggle that led to independence in 1962 and France's violent repression of this struggle, Roüan draws on family memories to portray the lives of three *pieds-noirs* sisters, Zon (Nicole Garcia), Malène (Roüan) and Gritte (Marianne Basler).[2] The screening of what Catherine Portuges has called the *colonial féminin* allows Roüan to reveal how colonial women contributed to the sociopolitical landscape of Algeria and how this in turn shaped their destinies (82). It is significant that each sister's suitor holds a stereotypical colonialist role: thus, Zon, the eldest, is married to a navy officer; Malène marries a farmer who exploits both the land and the native population; and Gritte, the youngest, is engaged to a diplomat. However, as we shall see, they do not remain the passive adjuncts of their husbands; rather they actively contribute to either maintaining or undermining the existing colonial and gendered order.

The film is composed of three sections, each covering the same period of time (1946–64) but each focusing on a different sister. This structure of illusive repetition provides a multifaceted critique of how the politics of gender and colonialism intersect in shaping a society and its history.[3] Each section of the film reveals the way in which each sister's consciousness is shaped by certain cultural "scripts" that allots her a place in the society according to gender, race, and class.[4] Roüan encodes these scripts in a subtle visual and narrative "grammar" that combines Catholic iconography, fairy tale elements, history, and romance. These scripts not only prescribe social roles; they also shape memory and history. Thus, each section reprises key events of the family history, such as Gritte's engagement party, a family gathering at Malène's farm, and Zon's death, and yet the chronology remains uncertain, because each sister remembers these events differently. The film exposes the illusion of chronology by showing how each sister inscribes the events within the logic of her own story instead of remembering a story with its own inherent chronology. In this essay, I analyze the way in which the combination of the repetitive structure with a syncretic visual and narrative grammar both highlights the fact that history is structured by memory and reveals that memory and consciousness are themselves conditioned by cultural scripts that encode the society's sociopolitical order.

Gender Scripts: Heroic Men and Romantic Women

In *Outremer,* Roüan uses various cultural scripts, such as Catholicism, fairy tales, romance, and history, in order to comment on the gendering and racializing of the colonial society she depicts, what Gayatri Spivak describes as "a worlding of a world," that is, the textual organization of the practical world (Spivak and Grosz 1). Roüan herself comments on this "worlding" when she explains how education and social expectations affected the people who are the inspiration for the film:

> I wanted to show people hemmed in by inherited property and preconceived notions, occupying prearranged positions, . . . the men of that time were not allowed to cry, they were placed on pedestals, forced to be virile and magnificent statues. . . . The women were addicted to one man. Such an education creates neurotic women, of which I am one. I was brought up to be married, so of course I never married.[5]

The gendering of the society is made very clear: men are meant to be heroes, whereas women are meant to marry them. This gendering is reflected in the film's intertwinement of two discourses, history and romance, that are complimentary in configuring gender roles. Since Roüan focuses on the *colonial féminin,* history—a male discourse written by men and about men and a discourse that prescribes male roles (the heroes of colonial history are the officer, the settler, the diplomat)—is only referred to in voice-off. For instance, we hear about historical events on the radio, and we hear de Gaulle's famous speech of 4 June 1958, but we do not see him.[6]

The romance, on the contrary, is a central structuring device that Roüan highlights by interspersing elements from the fairy tale of Sleeping Beauty and Prince Charming. She in turns associates these elements with Catholic images and discourse, in order to suggest how religion contributes to the imposition of gender roles. For instance, when her daughter cannot remember her catechism, Zon pricks her with a needle, an allusion to Sleeping Beauty. This suggests that

Catholicism puts the young girl to sleep, in other words, teaches her to forget her own self in order to conform to the role of wife.

Roüan further inscribes the fairy tale and Catholic subtexts into the film's structure by having the first two sections begin with a shot of the prospective husband crowned by a halo of light. Thus Paul and Gildas appear as the sanctified Prince Charming for Zon and Malène, respectively. Roüan thereby suggests that, if the adult life of Sleeping Beauty starts with the prince's kiss, the lives of women were considered significant only when they met their future husband.

However, at the beginning of the third section, Maxime, Gritte's suitor, first appears half-naked on the stairs in a more diffuse spotlight. This undignified apparition indicates the debunking of the romantic script and its demotion into comedy. As each section of the film depicts the development of the respective couples' romance, the complementarity of history and romance is highlighted.

By endorsing their husband's colonialist roles, Zon and Malène contribute to maintaining both the gendered and the colonial order of their society. The two sisters' complicity is enhanced when they have to compensate for their husbands' inability to fulfill their role as either splendid officer or hardworking farmer. Thus, when Paul laments that he has "des nerfs de femme" [women's nerves][7] and wants to resign from the navy, Zon convinces him not to by telling him: "Je suis fière de votre promotion . . . je vous aime, vous n'avez pas le droit de me décevoir, j'ai besoin de vous admirer" [I am proud of your promotion . . . I love you, you cannot disappoint me, I need to admire you]. As for Gildas, he just sits and reads, while Malène does all the farmwork, as well as taking care of the children.

The two sisters' active contribution to maintaining this social script has tragic consequences. Shortly after Paul returns to sea, he is reported missing in action. Zon is therefore partly responsible for his death. Her inability to understand herself other than as Paul's lover leads to her own death, which, she thinks, will reunite her with her husband. The romantic script is thus morbid, since the woman's need for her husband completely eclipses other dimensions of life, such as that of being a mother. Moreover, Zon's belief in paradise as a place where she will join her husband underlines the collusion between the romantic script and the discourse of Catholicism.

Zon's own comments about her imminent death offer further insight into the consequences of gender scripts on women's sense of self:

> Contrairement aux apparences, je ne suis pas enceinte. J'ai un crabe dans le ventre c'est un cancer. Ils croient tous que je ne le sais pas. Ils disent que c'est le trac du combattant. Je vais enfin rejoindre mon mari.

[I may look pregnant, but I'm not. I have a crab in my tummy, it's a cancer. They all think that I don't know. They say its fighters' nerves. I will join my husband at last].[8]

The equation between the cancer and the "trac du combatant" comments on her identification with her husband, which is graphically represented in the scene in which she dies while wearing his uniform. This suggests that women were not allowed to have an identity of their own and that their lives only had meaning in relation to their husbands. Zon's death takes this social script to its logical end. Her lack of self-definition makes her death inevitable. Therefore Djebar's neologism "nécrose" [necrosis] seems appropriate to describe Zon's neurosis (Djebar 132). Zon's cancer adequately metaphorizes the internalization of social prescriptions that do not allow women to develop an identity of their own and therefore lead to their metaphorical and literal death.

Malène's response to social prescriptions also has tragic consequences. If, for Zon, it is a matter of making reality correspond with the plot of the fairy tale by forcing her husband to live up to her socially inculcated expectations, for Malène, fairy tale–like romance is an unattainable ideal. In the opening scene of the second section, in a conversation with Zon, Malène expresses her doubts about the possibility of this plot being realized, when she considers the fact that for the rest of her life she will lean on Gildas's shoulder with foreboding rather than joy. The man's fall from his pedestal is graphically represented in a scene in which she tells him how much she longs to look up at him standing rather than down at him sitting.

Malène attempts to save the script by assuming her husband's role. She practically takes her husband's place as head of the farm, even though she tells her sisters that she has to do all this work because her husband is so busy. However, she, to use her own words, is ashamed to be "celle qui porte la culotte" [the one who wears the pants]. Her inability to cope with this situation leads her to set fire to the farm, and when Lakhdar, a young worker who has grown up on the farm, is wrongly accused, she is unable to defend him. When Gildas suggests that they leave Algeria, she refuses in spite of a farmworker's warning that "they" are going to kill her husband.[9] Shortly afterward, she takes Gildas's place in the car and gets shot instead of him. As Malène first figuratively then literally takes Gildas's place, the gender expectations of her society lead her to become thoroughly implicated in the maintenance of the colonial order.

Zon and Malène appear as the latter-day equivalent of those French women whose men conquered Algeria in the 1830s, and whom Algerian novelist Assia Djebar describes as follows:

> Les femmes françaises parcourent la correspondance des vainqueurs, quasiment les mains jointes: et cette dévotion familiale *auréole* le mouvement de séduction censé se dérouler de l'autre côté de la Méditerranée. (70; my emphasis)[10]
> [French women religiously read the conquerers' letters: and this familial devotion *crowns with glory* the movement of seduction that is allegedly taking place on the other side of the Mediterranean.]

Roüan's portrayal, however, goes one step further than Djebar's description, since she shows how women actively partook in the maintenance of the colonial order.

By showing the tragic outcome of historical and romantic gender roles, *Outremer* criticizes these social scripts, which elevate men on pedestals and prescribe that women be dependent on them for their identity. *Outremer* not only debunks two colonialist stereotypes, those of the officer and the settler, but also reveals, through Paul's doubts concerning his abilities to be an officer and Gildas's unwillingness to fulfill his role, that gender roles can be as restrictive for men as they are for women. In fact, Zon and Malène's unhappiness and deaths stem not only from the gap between their expectations and reality, but also from their inability to create new positive roles for themselves and their husbands.

This debunking of romantic and historical scripts is taken one step further in the third section of the film, which focuses on the youngest sister, Gritte. Her relationship with Maxime, Paul's younger brother and a diplomat, is cast from the start at the level of comedy. The comic effect is introduced by the spotlight being directed at Maxime as he rushes down the stairs, half-dressed, to greet Gritte, who is arriving by airplane for their engagement party. This mood is maintained in scenes in which Maxime leaves Gritte in his car after having failed to get her to either marry him or have sex with him, and in a scene in which Gritte spills boiling water on him in order to reject his advances.[11] The interplay between tragedy and comedy further demotes Paul and Gildas's "sanctification," since it suggests that gender expectations are ridiculous.

The fairy tale script undergoes significant transformations in the Gritte section that signal its nuanced demotion into comedy. First, the script becomes more explicit, because Gritte will not submit to it and

Zon and Malène need to convince her to conform to it. This is prefigured at the beginning of the film, when Zon and Malène offer Gritte "une arrivée de princesse" [a princess's arrival] at her engagement party. As Zon explains: "C'est romantique, on voulait faire arriver Gritte du ciel" [It's romantic, we wanted Gritte to arrive from the sky].[12] Unlike her sisters, who accept marriage as the only way of life, Gritte hesitates to marry Maxime. After she postpones her wedding for the second time, the three sisters have a fight as Zon and Malène try to convince Gritte to accept Maxime's proposal.[13] This scene highlights the different status that the fairy tale script has in each protagonist's life. During the argument, Zon and Malène try to force Gritte to conform to the romantic script (marriage), Zon by affirming that it is real: "L'amour seul compte, je suis tombée amoureuse de lui, lui de moi, et on est heureux pour la vie" [Love is the only thing that counts, I fell in love with him and he with me, and we are happy for life]; and Malène by saying that it is an unreal ideal: "Je comprends que tu aies peur, mais ça ne sert à rien d'espérer toute sa vie quelque chose qui n'existe pas" [I understand that you are afraid, but it's no use hoping for something that does not exist]. Gritte replies to both of them that she is fed up with their "histoires de bonheur" [happy stories] and she is not duped by their claims of happiness. This particular version of a feminine mystique—romance encoded as the fairy tale of Prince Charming—is doubly demystified: it is both a lie and a fiction, "des histoires." Gritte goes one step further in exposing the function of the romantic script in restricting women's possibilities, since she does not blame her unhappiness on the lack of a Prince Charming in her life— indeed Maxime would be only too happy to oblige—but on her father's refusal to let her study medicine.

Second, whereas Zon experiences the romantic script as real and Malène sees it as an unattainable ideal, Gritte considers it as a lie/story that she can manipulate. For instance, she uses the rhetoric of the fairy tale to ward off unwelcome suitors such as Antoine Pélissier, a young architect from France, to whom she explains: "J'attend l'homme qui m'enlèvera sur son cheval" [I am waiting for the man who will take me away on his horse]. Gritte's awareness of the social function of the romantic script allows her to resist familial pressures to marry and thus to escape the fate of her sisters, who are, at different levels, trapped within this script.

Significantly, Gritte is the only sister who survives, while her two sisters' entrapment within the patriarchal script leads to their death. In the last scene, which takes place in a church in Paris in 1964 and in which Gritte is on the verge of pronouncing marital vows, the film lapses into the fairy tale genre that typifies patriarchal gender prescriptions: the two dead sisters appear as fairies or angels whispering to Gritte, who is standing at the altar, in a scene that intertwines national iconography (French flag) with the romantic and religious scripts (Catholic wedding ceremony). The apparition of the two dead sisters as fairies or angels literalizes the romantic and religious scripts and underscores what Caroline Rooney has described as "not only the violent realisations of a constructed truth, but the violence of the construction of its realisation" (110). Up to this point, the film seems to suggest that it is a matter of saving either the script or the heroine.[14] Indeed, both Zon and Malène die in the process of realizing the romantic script, whereas Gritte manages to evade it. However, in the final scene, her acquiescence to the script that she has manipulated remains forever suspended, since the film ends before she pronounces the marital vow. This fantastic and ambiguous ending of an altogether realist film seems to bear witness to the lasting, crippling influence of patriarchal education on women.

The third transformation of the fairy tale script takes place in a scene in which Maxime and Gritte are in the lobby of a hotel in Algiers, listening to Charles de Gaulle's famous speech of 4 June 1958: "Je vous ai compris, je sais ce qui s'est passé ici, je vois ce que vous avez voulu faire . . . jamais plus qu'ici je n'ai compris combien c'est beau, combien c'est grand, combien c'est généreux la France" [I have understood you, I know what happened here, I see what you want to accomplish . . . never more than here have I felt the beauty and the generosity of France (subtitles)]. As Gritte gets all excited about de Gaulle's promises, Maxime rebukes her with a comment that conflates the discourse of the fairy tale and that of history, represented by de Gaulle's speech in voice-off: "Tu as trente ans et . . . tu crois encore au prince charmant?!" [You're thirty and . . . you still believe in Prince Charming?!]. If Roüan stages the different attitudes of the sisters toward the Prince Charming subtext in order to criticize the ways in which certain social representations of men as historical agents and women as their adjuncts circumscribe women's and men's lives, the conflation of history with the fairy tale reinforces the notion that history is just one of those social fictions told to legitimize a certain social order. The intersection of history and fairy tale in Maxime's comment suggests that these two discourses are complicit in their definition of gender roles, since the heroes of history function as the Prince Charming of the fairy tale.

The fourth and final transformation of the fairy tale subtext is the discrepancy in Gritte's story between the historical hero (de Gaulle) and the would-be Prince Charming (Maxime), on the one hand, and between the apparent lover (Maxime) and the real one (the *fellagha*, or Algerian rebel), on the other hand. Gritte's belief in this tale on the political level as opposed to her manipulation of it on the domestic level suggests how the patriarchal and colonial scripts intersect. Thus, if Gritte rebels against the patriarchal order, she still hopes for the maintenance of the *pied-noir* community in Algeria, (in the form of a cohabitation symbolized by her love for the fellagha?). Gritte transposes her romantic expectations on both de Gaulle and the fellagha. It is as if she expects de Gaulle's promises to make her relationship with the fellagha possible. Her relative freedom from the romantic script is further qualified by the death of her lover, who gets killed on his way to meet her. As she says, "C'est ma faute" [It's my fault]. Gritte's belief in Prince Charming at the political level and her love for the fellagha indicates the contradictory position of colonial women who believed in the Algerian cause.

Racializing Romance

The discrepancy between the apparent suitor and the real lover in the Gritte section as well as the total absence of Gritte's affair with the fellagha in the first two sections reveal not only that the romantic script is complicit with the historical discourse but also that it is racialized, and therefore doubly implicated in the colonial order. The conflation of history with the fairy tale indicates how colonialist and patriarchal scripts function together to reproduce the social order. Having concentrated on gender roles so far, I will now consider how the gendering of the colonial world depicted in *Outremer* is deeply racialized.

That the romantic script is complicated by racial stereotypes is suggested in the way the sisters' romantic expectations are influenced by racial stereotypes. Zon and Malène's self-perceptions are constructed in relation to certain images of colonized women that are stereotypes of the colonialist imaginary.

In a telling scene, Zon looks at herself in the mirror and holds up the outfit of a belly dancer, thereby disguising herself as the exotic Arab woman, a figure who, Gilles Boëtsch argues, is equated in the Western imaginary with an object of desire and is represented as dancer and temptress (93–93). The film euphemistically implies that this disguise is effective, since the outfit is on the bed after Zon and Paul have just made love.

If Zon defines herself in relation to a stereotype of the Arab woman as imagined by the male colonialist, Malène compares herself to the native servant when she confronts Gildas:

> Je fais tout à la fin . . . je deviens vieille, je suis ridée comme une pomme d'api, j'ai de poil aux pattes, j'ai des cals aux mains. Je ressemble à Zohra, c'est ça que tu veux? Tu crois que j'ai pas honte de porter la culotte?
> [I do everything in the end . . . I am becoming old, I am getting wrinkled, I have hairy legs, callused hands. I look like Zohra, is that what you want? Don't you think I'm ashamed of wearing the pants?]

Malène identifies with Zohra, thereby unwittingly telling the truth of the exploitation of native population. The irony is taken one step further when Gildas says: "On peut plus faire confiance à personne: même Zohra est capable de nous foutre une bombe dans le four" [We can't trust anyone, even Zohra could put a bomb in the oven]. Here is another unwitting truth, since it is the person who compares herself to Zohra, Malène, who starts the fire. The film thereby legitimates the Algerian revolution. Nevertheless, if the film allows us such a subversive reading, we must remember that Zon and Malène themselves do not question the legitimacy of the colonial order. Indeed, their self-definition in terms of colonialist stereotypes in fact supports the colonialist construction of the world. It is the metaphorical and phantasmal encounter, subtly conveyed by the film, which uncannily tells the truth of the situation and critiques it.

The difference between Zon's and Malène's class position in colonial society is evident in the different images they have of the native woman: for Zon she is the exotic dancer, for Malène she is the hardworking servant. It is also conveyed by the spaces the sisters occupy. Zon is seen mainly within the confines of the big house. Malène, for her part, is generally working hard on the farm. Both Zon's house and Malène's farm are part of the Algerian landscape that is occupied by the colonizer. It is only Gritte who wanders in a space coded as that of the colonized: the mud habitation, the local hospital, the local store.

Unlike her two sisters, Gritte has, as a nurse, come face-to-face with the racist violence on which her society is built, and in particular with the reality of French torture. Her rejection of racist stereotypes and colonialist practices is symbolized in a dinner scene in which her father, her two sisters and their husbands, and a couple of friends are commenting on recent events, euphemistically referring to the French policy of torturing Algerian rebels and suggesting that the solution to the war is killing them all off.[15] As the conversation unfolds, Gritte's facial expression changes to one of horror, and she first leaves the table, then comes back and vomits. Her vomiting is symbolic of her rejection of the dominant ideology and becomes particularly significant when contrasted with Zon's cancer, which connotes her internalization of social scripts.

Nevertheless, Gritte cannot articulate this rejection, just as she cannot integrate her affair with the fellagha into the family story. Therefore, her actions and attitudes are constantly misread by her sisters. For instance, when she is crying over the death of her lover, Zon, who brings her a letter from Maxime announcing Maxime's wedding with another, thinks she is crying because of that. Zon can only inscribe her crying within that plot. Similarly, Malène thinks Gritte is crazy to be standing outside behind the sandbags, flashing a light in the middle of the night, and she misunderstands Gritte's reaction at the shots they hear, since she does not know that Gritte was actually signaling to her lover. The events and logic of Gritte's love affair are excluded from Zon's and Malène's stories. Because such an experience is unthinkable for them, they cannot understand the meaning of Gritte's actions and attitudes.[16] Zon's comment on her vomiting—"Mon Dieu, comme on l'a mal élevée" [God, how badly brought up she is]—is an unwitting comment on how colonialist education has failed to make her accept racism.

However, it is disconcerting that within Gritte's own narrative, nearly all the events concerning her relationship with the fellagha (their first encounter, a scene in which he follows her, when they are asleep together, his death) are silent.[17] Rather than suggest, like Naomi Greene, that this is a sign of Roüan's inability to conceive of an interracial relationship (115), I would argue that this silence is a measure of the exclusion of such an experience from the dominant society and the life stories it allows. Thus, should Gritte be able to live such an experience, there are no available narrative forms in which to articulate it. But there are other means of expression, and it is through her body that Gritte expresses her experiences: her kneeling down after the first encounter with the fellagha, her blush when she comes home after their second meeting, her vomiting at the table, her crying after the shots at Malène's house.

Because Gritte chooses to pursue such an experience, her self-definition is doubly untimely, since she both refuses to submit herself to the usual script of marriage and rejects the colonialist beliefs on which the legitimacy of her social circle is founded. Instead, she chooses the most taboo of relationships. With her subtle portrayal of the three sisters' attitudes toward the gender and racial scripts of their society, Roüan stages an evolution of the female colonizer's political awareness. This evolution, like the metaphorical subtext, is an endorsement of the legitimacy of the Algerian revolution, but her portrayal avoids presenting the colonizers as monsters. Her film thus depicts the complexity of the colonial situation, which is too readily dichotomized in historical and official accounts of the war of independence.

Reproducing the Social Order: Children and Social Scripts

Having thus far analyzed how the sisters either support or reject the scripts prescribing gender roles and race relations, I will now discuss the representation of children, which further conveys how this society is gendered and racialized. Roüan critically reflects on the historical reproduction of gendered and racialized identities in French Algeria by portraying children's attitudes toward these various scripts.

Children are portrayed as having internalized sexist attitudes. For instance, the girls tell a little boy to go away because "c'est les filles qui mettent la table d'abord" [it's up to us girls to lay the table]. And a little boy says: "La politique ça vous intéresse pas—vous êtes que des filles" [Politics don't interest you—you are only girls].[18] How does this happen? Several scenes suggest how this gendering is transmitted to children. In the first, Paul is telling his two daughters—both dressed in pink!—the story of Prince Charming. We catch the end of his story: "On l'a appelé charmant, prince charmant. Ils ont eu énormément d'enfants. Très heureux voilà" [He was called Charming, Prince Charming. They had lots of children and were very happy, that's all]. Fairy tales here serve to inculcate gender expectations. The following scene implies that it is the lived experience of a certain order that creates a desire for its imitation. Thus Guénolée, Zon and Paul's eldest daughter, expresses the desire to reproduce her mother's destiny: "Je me marierai avec un officier de marine" [I will marry a naval officer].[19] The interaction between the normative discourse, here exemplified by the fairy tale, and the "real" social order is explained by de Certeau:

> Le discours normatif ne "marche" que si déjà il est devenu un récit, un texte articulé sur du réel et parlant en son nom, c'est-à-dire une loi historiée et historicisée, racontée par des corps. (218)
> [Normative discourse only "works" [literally, "walks"] if it has already become a narrative, a text articulated on reality and talking in its name, that is to say, a historicized law, narrated through bodies.]

Here, the normative discourse is not only told to the children in the form of a fairy tale; it is also narrated to them through their parents' bodies and lives.

However, Guénolée's actions contradict her proffered wish to marry a naval officer: Malène has seen her kiss Lakhdar, a young Algerian who does the gardening.[20] In the gap between Guénolée's wish and her actions, we glimpse the contradictions between a racialized romantic normative discourse and the colonial reality of cohabitation. The racialization of the romantic script is exposed when Malène says that she is sure that Zon will be furious with Guénolée for kissing Lakhdar. Children further provide the candid perspective that exposes the contradictions of racism. For instance, Guénolée suddenly realizes, while reciting her catechism, "Mais alors les Arabes aussi sont nos frères?" [But then, Arabs are also our brothers?]. The ambivalence of Zon's answer, "Non . . . oui, mais seulement en Jésus Christ" [No . . . yes, but only in Jesus Christ], reflects the contradictions of making religion fit into a colonialist ideology.

Childhood and adolescence also function as a shared space between the colonizer and the colonized: *pieds-noirs* and Algerian children are often glimpsed playing together. As they grow up, however, the boundary between colonized and colonizer has to be enforced, for instance, by racializing the romantic script. More tragically, in the scene where Lakhdar is unjustly accused of setting fire to the farm, we witness the moment in which the colonized is constructed as the dangerous other and expulsed from the space of a shared identity. The morning after the fire, the soldiers have come to investigate and, as they stand close to Malène's family in opposition to the workers who are sitting with their arms on their heads, the camera clearly demarcates the two opposing groups.[21] Lakhdar, however, does not sit accused with the other workers: his intermediate position functions as a space of shared identity that lies between the colonizer and the colonized. This makes him conspicuous to the soldier, who asks why he is not sitting with the other workers. Lopez, the foreman, answers that "Lakhdar, c'est comme mon fils, c'est kif-kif" [Lakhdar is a son to me (subtitles)]. The soldier's question suffices to create doubt about Lakhdar's innocence in Lopez's mind. In the following shot, the adolescent is cast as the absolute other, the fellagha. He tries to flee from this dichotomized space, but Lopez catches him and beats him up. Childhood and adolescence are thus not only vehicles through which racist discourse is criticized; the children's precarious position in the adult world also reflects the grown-ups' ambivalence toward racial difference and highlights the mechanism of racial othering. Moreover, the film suggests that racism is something that one is educated into; and the arbitrariness of racial segregation is conveyed in the opening image of the film, a blue sky crisscrossed with barbed wire.[22]

Although children and adolescents have an unwitting yet accurate eye for the ambiguities that undergird the adults' racialization of the world, they are represented as not explicitly questioning the discourse of gender expectations. This might be because gendering is more seamless, because it is "internal" to a group and therefore easier to control, whereas the "racializing" is more of an "external" imposition on a heterogeneous world.

In *Outremer,* Roüan explodes the traditional image of the colonizer by introducing the experience of the *colonial féminin* and of children. She multiplies the gender and racial stereotypes of the colonial situation to suggest how social scripts function to legitimize a dominant order. Roüan not only conveys the variety of the colonizer group in Algeria; she also comments on how it ideologically reproduces itself.[23] Her revision of history through the multiple lens of Catholic iconography, fairy tale, and romance is an effective way of demystifying history and exposing its collusion with a gendered and racialized "worlding of the world." Indeed, history and fairy tale do not stand in opposition. Rather, fairy tales are the basis for a revision of history that itself informs the rewriting of romantic and fairy tale scripts. Thus, the historical collusion between Christianity and colonization is the basis for a very personal and original rewriting of fairy tale figures as Christian icons of saints and angels.[24] This multiscripted re-creation of the interstitial space of the *colonial féminin* allows Roüan to escape "la vision manichéenne du colonialisme . . . [qui] empoisonne souvent la grammaire de la représentation" [the Manichaean vision of colonialism [that] often poisons the grammar of representation] and to offer a humane portrayal of the settlers (Rosello 171).

Outremer exposes the gender, race, and class politics of a specific society to convey how its history is structured by memories that are conditioned by cultural scripts. The manner in which Roüan stages the remembering problematizes the bases of history, namely, objective memory and chronological time. By screening a period of time from three different, feminine (Zon, Malène) and feminist (Gritte), perspectives, Roüan shows that events do not have an inherent meaning or chronology, thus undoing the very notions of perspective and objectivity. She not so much shows that each person remembers *the* story differently, but that each re-members a different story. This point is crucial because not only can the meaning of some events (such as Gritte's crying) be totally misread according to the person who is articulating the story; whole episodes can be occluded. Thus in Zon and Malène's sections, we are given no inkling of Gritte's affair with the fellagha. Furthermore, *Outremer* complicates the notion of history by revealing how remembering itself is based on the social scripts by which a society seeks to reproduce itself and that prescribe that the characters understand their lives according to certain plots, which support their position in the social order.

The precarious nature of any narrative is highlighted in *Outremer*, since the filmic structure leads the viewers to question their expectations about the possibility of writing the story of a family—and by implication of a nation. The landmark events in the family history, such as Gritte's engagement party, the family reunion at Malène's, and Zon's death, figure in each section of the film. Yet these "events" are always different because their meaning changes according to the temporal and emotional logic of each character. Thus, the three sections function much less as a puzzle than as three conflicting narratives that all vie for recognition. The question thus shifts from truth—which is the true or objective story?—to one of power—which is the story that will be remembered and made official? *Outremer* explodes the notions of chronology and objective memory that make traditional history possible. Roüan's reciprocal rewriting of history and the fairy tale accords with the structure of illusive repetition and difference that makes the film so challenging for the viewer, in order to convey the mnemo- and scriptologic nature of history.

NOTES

1. "Algérie Française," as Catherine Portuges explains, was "[a] powerfully charged *mot d'ordre* [that] originated with the European settler community, [and] linguistically suggested an inseparable connection between the territories in question [i.e., France and Algeria]" (99, her emphasis). The year 1946, marking the beginning of the war in Indochina, is a key date in anticolonial struggles. Translations are mine, unless parenthetically indicated as those of the film's subtitles.
2. The Algerian war for independence, at the time euphemistically called "les événements," started in 1954. *Pied-noir* refers to settlers of European descent in Algeria.
3. The film's critique of colonialism is a matter of some controversy. Some critics, such as Catherine Portuges and Naomi Wolf, argue that the film stereotypes the Arab community and obscures the struggle for independence from colonial rule (Portuges 86, 88; Greene, 106), while others, such as Françoise Audé, think that the film presents a "harsh analysis of the patriarchal and colonial system" [l'âpreté de l'analyse du système patriarcal et colonial] (Audé 37). Nevertheless even Portuges agrees that the film "implicat[es the director,] the viewer, and the occupying forces in the violence that remains present but unseen beyond the confines of claustrophobic domestic enclosure" (Portuges 88). For my part, I think it is important to distinguish between the colonialist point of view of the

protagonists (especially Zon and Malène) and the director's point of view, conveyed on the one hand in the evolution in the three sisters' political consciousness and their increasing involvement with Algeria, and on the other, as I argue in this paper, in the imagery of the film and its ironic portrayal of the characters' beliefs.
4. I focus here on gender and race, and indicate in passing her critique of classism.
5. "Press notes, *Overseas:* interviews with Brigitte Roüan (Aries film release)" (New York: Dennis Davidson Assoc., 1991) 3 (qtd. Portuges 85). Roüan suggests that autobiography is a significant source for the film: like Zon's husband, "her father was declared missing . . . when [she] was very young" (ibid). It is therefore not surprising that Zon's youngest child is called Brigitte.
6. For a historical account of this episode, see Stora, *Histoire* 50ff.
7. "J'ai des nerfs de femmes" is translated in the subtitles as "I'm a failure."
8. The first sentence is from the subtitles. The expression *le trac du combattant* has no English equivalent. It designates the fear of soldiers just before they go into battle.
9. This ambivalent portrait of Malène can be seen as an image of the colonial administration in Algeria. This is particularly evident in the scene in which she pays the workers; when they protest at being underpaid, she innocently replies that it is M. Gildas who decides. It is as if, on the one hand, she colludes in exploiting them, and on the other, refuses to take responsibility for doing so.
10. The scene in which Malène and Gritte are standing next to Zon, who is playing the piano, also suggests the political role of French women, since their clothes are the colors of the French flag.
11. The two scenes in which he leaves echo each other, as he grumbles in the car: "Elle me rend fou" [She drives me crazy]; and "La putain de sa mère je l'aurai" [I'll get her yet (subtitles)].
12. There are classist connotations to the notion of princess that become clear when Zon comments about Grace Kelly: "Tu parles d'une princesse. Elle a beau avoir tout l'or du monde c'est jamais qu'une fille de maçon" [Some princess. She may have all the gold in the world, she's only a bricklayer's daughter].
13. Here, archetypal elements from another fairy tale emerge: the fight between sisters, especially of two against one, reminds us of Cinderella and her two ugly sisters.
14. I thank Mireille Rosello for pointing this out to me.
15. Thus the friend says: "Ce ne sont pas des hommes, il suffit de les chatouiller un peu et ils se mettent à table" [They have no guts, tickle them and they squeal (subtitles)], and later suggests the solution of genocide, "la technique du bateau à soupape" [the bottomless boat (subtitles)].
16. Another example is the episode in which Gritte supposedly loses her engagement ring while playing volleyball. We learn in the last section of the film that she in fact lost it much earlier, when she first meets the fellagha.

17. In the second encounter, where Gritte brings the fellagha some medical supplies, he tells her in Arabic: "Finally, I've been waiting for you" (subtitles).
18. It can also be argued, however, that the children don't internalize these codes. They might just adopt them when they are convenient. See Mireille Rosello's discussion of Claire Bretécher's *Les frustrés* in *Infiltrating Culture* (23–52). This scene could be interpreted in this way, since the girls are not actually laying the table, but playing with the reflections that the glasses make on the ceiling: they use the comment about girls laying tables to send the little boy away, because he might interrupt their game.
19. Gender norms are also inculcated through games, as when Zon gives her son a toy boat, telling him it is like his father's.
20. This episode offers an echo to Gritte's affair with the fellagha, especially as Lakhdar, being wrongly accused of setting fire to the farm, is aligned with the rebels.
21. This scene in fact complicates the dichotomization of the colonial space by subdividing these two groups according to gender: the camera alternates between (1) the male colonizer (the soldiers, Gildas, and Lopez); (2) Malène, her sisters, and the children; (3) the workers; and (4) the old Algerian woman.
22. There is another scene in which two boys are playing at war, the *pied-noir* playing the part of the French special forces agent and the Algerian that of the fellagha. The obvious imbalance between the two boys' equipment is a comment on the imbalance of power and resources between France and Algeria. This scene, moreover, is particularly interesting because it is the only one in which an Algerian woman is seen and heard at the same time. During the rest of the film there is always a disjunction: we can either see her or hear her. This dissociation between the soundtrack and the visual track emphasizes the native women's powerlessness that this scene conveys. Indeed, she seems to only have authority over children (whom she is telling to stop playing at war); and Malène undercuts this authority by saying: "Laissez les, ils ne font rien de mal" [Let them play, they are not doing any harm]. The French woman's role in the war is euphemistically conveyed here: she encourages it to go on.
23. Zon is emblematic of the military aristocracy, Malène of the agricultural class; Lopez, of Spanish origin, suggests the various national origins of the settlers. Thus, Roüan goes against "l'image de l'homogénéité des 'pieds-noirs'" [the homogenous image of the *pieds-noirs*], which, Stora argues, constituted itself when they "returned" to France (Stora, *La gangrène* 258).
24. See the earlier discussion of the halos, the catechism scene, and the wedding scene.

REFERENCES

Audé, Françoise. "Domaine Privé." *Positif* 359 (January 1991): 35–37.
Boëtsch, Gilles. "La Mauresque aux seins nus: L'imaginaire érotique colonial dans la carte postale." *Images et colonies*. Paris: Syros, 1993. 93–96.

de Certeau, Michel. *L'invention du quotidien. Tome I. Arts de faire.* Nouvelle édition, établie et présentée par Luce Giard. Paris: Gallimard, 1990.
Djebar, Assia. *L'amour, la fantasia.* 1985. Paris: Albin Michel, 1995.
Greene, Naomi. "Empire as Myth and Memory." *Cinema, Colonialism, Postcolonialism.* Ed. Dina Sherzer. Austin: U of Texas P, 1996. 103–19.
Portuges, Catherine. "*Le Colonial Féminin:* Women Directors Interrogate French Cinema." *Cinema, Colonialism, Postcolonialism.* Ed. Dina Sherzer. Austin: U of Texas P, 1996. 80–102.
Rooney, Caroline. "'Dangerous Knowledge' and the Poetics of Survival: A Reading of *Our Sister Killjoy* and *A Question of Power.*" *Motherlands.* Ed. Susheila Nasta. London: Women's P, 1991. 99–126.
Rosello, Mireille. *Littérature et identité créole aux Antilles.* Paris: Karthala, 1992.
———. *Infiltrating Culture.* Manchester: Manchester UP, 1996.
Roüan, Brigitte, dir. *Outremer.* France. Screenplay (based on a story by Roüan) by Roüan, Philippe Le Guay, Christian Rullier, and Cedric Kahn. Cinematography by Dominique Chapuis. Sound by Dominique Hennequin. Perf. Brigitte Roüan, Nicole Garcia, Marianne Basler, Philippe Galland, Yann Dedet, and Bruno Todeschini. Prod. Daniel Champagnon, with C.N.C. and the Ministère de la Culture et de la Communication. 1990. Aries Film Releasing.
Spivak, Gayatri, and Elizabeth Grosz. "Criticism, Feminism, and the Institution." *The Post-Colonial Critic.* Ed. Sarah Harasym. London: Routledge, 1990. 1–2.
Stora, Benjamin. *La gangrène et l'oubli.* Paris: La Découverte, 1991.
———. *Histoire de la guerre d'Algérie (1954–1962).* Paris: La Découverte, 1993.

Dominique Licops *is a Ph.D. candidate in comparative literary studies and French at Northwestern University. Her dissertation analyzes how Caribbean Francophone and Anglophone writers rework natural images of identification in order to convey nonessentialist forms of identity. She has also published essays on Gisèle Pineau, Maryse Condé, and Assia Djebar.*

Copyright © 2002 by Dominique Licops

Views from "The Other Side"
Theorizing Age and Difference in Yvonne Rainer's *Privilege*

Gwen Raaberg

The films of director-writer Yvonne Rainer, as Teresa de Lauretis points out in her foreword to the published film scripts, are "produced at the intersection of creative and critical practices—the avant-garde and the women's movement, filmmaking and theories of representation and spectatorship, performance art and psychoanalysis, autobiographical writing and the critical study of culture." Indeed, Rainer's films not only arise from the interaction of theory and practice; her experimental practices explore her subjects so intensely and engage the audience so actively that they involve us in the process of analyzing society and constructing theory. Yet because Rainer's work is categorized as avant-garde, "difficult," experimental cinema, it has not received the attention it deserves from feminist scholars and teachers and is seldom viewed in women's studies classrooms. Her filmmaking is complex, but it offers a unique opportunity for viewers to work their way through a feminist analysis of contemporary society to a concrete understanding of theory. In bringing theoretical as well as aesthetic concerns to her exploration of crucial issues and relationships in women's lives, Rainer is able both to actualize theoretical concepts and to enhance the scope and coherence of feminist theory.

Rainer's early career was devoted to performance, and during that time she was a dancer, choreographer, and founder of the pioneering Judson Dance Theater. In 1967 she began experimenting with film and in 1972 began writing and directing full-length films, which have been shown at art theaters and festivals throughout the United States and abroad. Her early works, *Lives of Performers* (1972), *Film about a Woman Who . . .* (1974), and *Kristina Talking Pictures* (1976) are antinarrative films directed to an exploration of the medium and to an analysis of human relationships—physical, psychological, and emotional. Her work becomes increasingly political in *Journey from Berlin* (1980) and increasingly theoretical in *The Man Who Envied Women* (1985). Her most recent films are *Privilege* (1990), which won the Filmmakers'

Trophy at the 1991 Sundance Film Festival, and *murder and murder* (1996), which won the "Teddy" Award at the 1997 Berlin Film Festival. These films, aesthetically experimental, theoretically informed, and significantly concerned with cultural analysis, have established Rainer as a feminist artist at the forefront of independent cinema.

In *Privilege,* Rainer offers a particularly forceful and wide-ranging feminist critique of society. Here she challenges viewers to rethink their own relation to power and privilege and to become actively engaged in the construction of feminist theory. In this film she undertakes an investigation, announced in the opening sequences, of menopause and aging in women. But the topic opens outward to encompass an analysis of power in relation to race, ethnicity, class, and sexual identity, as well as gender and age. Rainer is especially interested in women with a "double difference," such as gender and color, and what Susan Sontag has termed the "double marginality" of gender and age ("Double Standard"). This concern leads her to explore the circumstances in which these women are doubly marginalized and subordinated, and the situations in which young, middle-class, heterosexual, white women may gain privilege by submitting to a patriarchal hierarchy. Since ageism has sometimes persisted even in feminism, Rainer's feminist exploration of aging women is a significant undertaking; and since most work concerning age has focused on mainstream, middle-class, white culture, the filmmaker brings a necessary diversity to the topic. Expanding the purview of feminist critique, Rainer focuses on the interrelation of women of color and aging women, presenting diverse voices and multiple perspectives that provide an incisive analysis of power and privilege from "the other side."

Rainer's focus on power moves the film through an investigation of women's lived experiences to a penetrating analysis of women's unequal and unstable relation to patriarchal power systems. In this critical process, *Privilege* confronts a number of issues, practical and theoretical, some of which I will consider here. The film analyzes cultural constructions of gender, deconstructing patriarchal discourse related to aging and difference, especially as it is falsely grounded in women's bodies. It also questions women's conventional construction of self, specifically as constituted through relationships to male power and privilege. Concentrating on women who are doubly marginalized, the film explores the experiences of aging women and women of color, shifting between diverse perspectives that question one another. Rainer's film engages viewers in a feminist analysis that positions all women with double differences "on the other side of privilege." Through this analysis, age and racial and ethnic difference are recognized as interrelated concerns in a critique of privilege and, therefore, as crucial, fundamental factors in feminist theory.

Throughout her filmmaking career, Rainer has developed her experimental films through an antinarrative strategy that assembles and abruptly juxtaposes a variety of fragmentary materials. *Privilege* continues and elaborates upon this technique. The film is a collage of fragments that include documented interviews, enacted narrative sequences, film clips imported from other works, printed notations, and offstage commentary. These multiple materials and methods function both to reinforce and to mutually deconstruct one another. Development of the film takes place primarily through a series of interviews of postmenopausal women, who are diverse in race, ethnicity, and class. Action is minimal and discontinuous but is largely concerned with the interview of a middle-age, white woman named Jenny, who recounts—and reenacts—her experiences as a young woman. These sequences are interrupted and repeated and juxtaposed with a number of documentary film clips and other imported materials that add to and contradict previous scenes. Rainer's strategies effectively block the prevalent tendency of audiences to become engaged with the narrative or empathetic with a central character; by contrast, they enforce distance and enhance the viewer's critical capacity.

The opening scenes of *Privilege* establish the experimental context of Rainer's film and introduce the audience to a different way of viewing. In between the opening credits, the middle-age filmmaker stares into the camera as if it were a mirror, and to the romantic strains of "My Funny Valentine," slowly, methodically applies lipstick in ever-widening arcs on and around her mouth until the image becomes grotesque. The image effectively ruins expected cinematic representations of women and conventional modes of viewing and directly confronts a culture saturated with representations of women as unreal objects of sexual desire. This is no object amenable to the consumerism of the gaze. Countering the objectification of women as well as the cultural invisibility of older women, the image insists not on effacement but on expressivity. The defiantly grotesque and humorous image inducts the audience into the carnivalesque realm of the film, where the calculated chaos of Rainer's experimentalism subverts hierarchies, questions cultural codes, and provides a space for presenting alternative perspectives and voices.

As this introductory image indicates, Rainer is concerned with women's subjectivity and the conflict between the social construction of female identity and self-construction, particularly as it affects aging women. In the film, the interviews of the women are juxtaposed with fragments from documentary films about menopause, in which a number of white male physicians, along with the token woman physician, expound on the "problem." They describe the presumed physical and sexual difficulties caused by menopause, and the aging woman's consequent loss of self-esteem and diminished social status, particularly in relation to her husband, even though, as one woman interviewee points out, "it's the men who have problems sexually." Aging women are treated as deficient or diseased, the disease beginning, as another woman comments, "when we can no longer make babies"—a condition that the film notes was diagnosed by Dr. Helen Deutch as "woman's partial death."

Rainer's strategy is to intersperse throughout the film a number of documentary film clips presenting repetitively similar statements by many different male "authorities" on women and aging. This technique leads the viewer to an awareness that the construction of identity is influenced by incessantly reproduced images and discourse. The presumption of objectivity in documentary film technique and the staging of the visual-verbal presentation of the physicians as authority figures become apparent, disclosing the process through which patriarchal perspectives and discourse have actively constructed the cultural conception of aging women.

It also becomes evident that the female body is the site of this construction. In our culture, the body is regarded as the basis of personal identity, so that markers of difference, such as those of race and gender, tend to be viewed as constituted by the material body. But as Judith Butler has argued in *Bodies That Matter,* discourse performs on matter; and in this context, what is perceived to be essentially grounded in the body is actually discursively constituted. This is the process that Rainer dramatically discloses in the construction of the postmenopausal woman: as the physicians locate their opinions in the female body, the offscreen interviewer's voice warns against "confusing biology and patriarchy." Rainer's technique of fragmenting the repetitious documentaries opens spaces within the discourse that disturb the codes for the representation of older women and reveals the process of cultural construction from conditions presumed to be essentially grounded in bodies.

The juxtaposition of the physicians' presentations with the women's own voices in their interviews also opens spaces between the discourse and actual subjectivities. Feminist methodology has depended upon women's experience as a touchstone for critique, and the tension evident between the women's self-presentation and the physicians' opinions provides the viewer with the means for deconstructing cultural discourse and representations of womanhood and aging. It becomes apparent from the testimony of the women interviewed that, in most cases, they feel comfortable with their age. Indeed, they often seem to feel "younger" than they previously had—that is, their experience coincides more with those characteristics traditionally labeled "young" than with characteristics labeled "old." Although they express a range of responses to aging, a number of the women report experiencing themselves as more spontaneous, freer—"off the hook," as one woman says, "free from needing to please other people in all kinds of ways." And many report aging as a positive experience: feeling more focused and less controlled by psychological and emotional forces; being more open, less judgmental of different perspectives, and more willing to act outside prescribed gender, class, ethnic, and sexual norms.

The self-presentations of these older women throw into question not only the physicians' statements but also conventional conceptions of youth and age. In recent feminist and queer theory, thinking has pushed beyond binaries: masculinity/femininity, male/female. Yet the hierarchical opposition of youth/age continues unabated. As we view the women's presentations and listen to their voices, the rigid binary opposition of youth/age gives way to a continuum of aging, and the self is seen to comprise a range of ages—youth in age, age in youth. Moreover, it becomes evident that age is not simply a circumscribed period in one's life, that regardless of the subject's chronological age, aging is a fundamental and continuous factor in the individual's construction and re-construction of self-identity throughout life.

But if aging is not simply a social construction, neither is it wholly a self-construction. As Kathleen Woodward points out in her introduction to *Figuring Age,* aging is theoretically complex in that it cannot simply be deconstructed as a conception. There are real physical, social, and economic issues in aging. In opposing negative representations of age, it is important to avoid replacing them with practically and philosophically limited "positive" views. In their interviews, the women acknowledge problems as well as opportunities, expressing both positive and negative responses to menopause and growing older. In an imported film clip, a woman muses to a friend, "I finally have my head together and my ass falls apart." And the interviewees voice a variety of opinions, ranging from various declarations of liberation to Faith Ringgold's cheerfully delivered pronouncement that "getting older is a bitch." Aging may bring physical disabilities, and often, particularly for women, aging has economic and social consequences—as Rainer reminds us, reading a list of statistics: fifteen million older women live on $5,000 or less, and in the richest country in the world. It is important to recognize that these women's experiences have taken place within the context of particular political, social, and economic circumstances. As one woman acknowledges: "I realize that one of the things that has made [aging] . . . a positive experience is that my life is so very comfortable. And so I have genuine alternatives now that I can take advantage of and I think it would be very different if I didn't." And, indeed, it is evident in the interviews that the women who assume they have fewer alternatives view their experience much less positively.

The perception by older women that alternatives are being closed off is often connected to shifts in a woman's relationship to male centers of power, a process disclosed by tracing these relations during the course of a woman's life. To explore these changes, the film focuses in particular on the interview of Jenny as a middle-aged woman and the story of her life as a young woman. These scenes record one woman's attempts at self-construction during different periods in her life and, at the same time, reveal more generally the sociopolitical forces at work in women's relationship to patriarchal power structures.

Jenny's interviewer is a middle-aged African American woman known as Yvonne Washington. In the film, the interviews are conducted by Rainer, who is white, and by this interviewer, and both are called Yvonne, creating a significant doubling and difference. One of the credits even states that this is a film by Yvonne Washington, replicating exactly the format of the credit that announces Rainer as filmmaker. Yvonne Washington plays an active role in questioning, even confronting, Jenny. The camera is often positioned just behind this interviewer, in a technique that self-consciously situates the audience to observe Jenny, a member of the white, middle-class majority, from Yvonne's "different," more "marginal" perspective.

Jenny's story is a discontinuous narrative, developed through a fragmented series of flashbacks, featuring opposing camera perspectives and conflicting versions of the same events. In the enacted narrative flashbacks, the youthful Jenny is actually the same age as in the current interview, an anachronism noted by Yvonne. This presentation of Jenny, as both aging and young, again puts pressure on the binary, reinforcing a recognition of young in old, old in young, and undermining cultural conceptions of the body as ground of the self. Jenny's presentation also throws into question the stability of subjectivity as she constructs and re-constructs her identity over time. We come to see identity and personal history not as a unified entity or reified fact but as an open process, continually under construction, continually under pressure from new insights and interpretations, and therefore continually in movement in relation to age.

We also see the movement and instability of a woman's "self" in relation to patriarchal systems of power. But it is only as Jenny tells about a particular incident in her life as a young woman living in New York City that we are able to trace the trajectory of that relationship to power. In Jenny's story, a lesbian friend who lives in the same building is apparently (there are several different versions of the same scene) sexually accosted by a Puerto Rican male who lives in the less costly apartment building next door. Jenny presents herself as helping her friend by phoning the police and pounding on her door. When the door is opened, the man is not there; but we later learn that Jenny nevertheless testified that she saw the intruder in the room, perjuring herself at the trial. We also learn that Jenny began dating the young assistant DA who prosecuted the case and soon became involved in a love affair with him. Jenny mentions the thrill of having a relationship with a man above her class and educational level. But she also admits that she accepted without protest or comment the DA's biased opinions regarding people of color and homosexuals. Confronted by Yvonne as she discloses the details of her relationship, Jenny wonders about herself: "Who was that woman who put up with such vicious twaddle?"—adding that she has told the story hoping to find an answer to that question.

The relationship, though, as becomes evident in a scene of Jenny and the DA in bed, is a manifestation of what Aida Hurtado has termed "subordination by seduction" ("Relating to Privilege"). In analyzing differences between the subordination of white women and women of color, Hurtado draws on the insights of Audre Lorde, who in *Sister Outsider* noted the difficulties and differences in women's relationship to white male privilege.

> White women face the pitfall of being seduced into joining the oppressor under the pretense of sharing power. This possibility does not exist in the same way for women of color. The tokenism that is sometimes extended to us is not an invitation to join power: our racial "otherness" is a visible reality that makes it quite clear. For white women there is a wider range of pretended choices and rewards for identifying with patriarchal power and its tools. (118–19)

In a perceptive essay analyzing privilege, Hurtado points out that each oppressed group in the United States is positioned in a particular relationship to the power structure, dominated by white upper- and middle-class men. The power structure is a complex hierarchy with many culturally constructed markers of group identity—race, class, ethnicity, and sexuality are only the most obvious. In this structure the subordination of different groups is based on their relational position to the male centers of power as it affects them economically, socially, and politically (833–34). Working out of a conception of gender roles and status as a process accomplished through social interaction, Hurtado focuses on differences between white women and women of color in relation to the power structure. Warning that these groups cannot be thought of as undifferentiated categories, she analyzes the relational position of women and finds that in general white women are subordinated through "seduction" and women of color are subordinated through "rejection" (839–44). Explaining these relational positions, Hurtado points out that white men relate to white women as lovers, wives, and mothers, relating in a way in which they do not need to relate to women of color, particularly if there are pressures for white offspring. And white women in general are socialized to become the lovers, wives, and mothers of white men, whereas women of color are trained to relate to men of color, who themselves are in a subordinate position to white men. Class, too, obviously affects relational positions and daily social interactions, as does sexual identity, influencing the probability of obtaining the privileges of seduction or the obstacles of rejection. These complex social interactions create differences among diverse groups in their distance from and access to the sources of power and privilege dominated by white men (842–46).

Rainer's film discloses the differential power relations of white women and women of color and extends the analysis of privilege and power relations to include aging women. Through a strategy that juxtaposes opposing perspectives and camera angles, the filmmaker introduces the audience to diverse viewpoints capable of deconstructing one another. At times the director focuses the camera on the perspectives and opinions of white female or male characters and then, reversing the camera position, provides opposing perspectives and opinions of diverse "others," the various points of view putting one another under pressure. This strategy is employed in her casting and filming of Yvonne, the African American interviewer, who questions Jenny and provides confrontational observations. The perspective of the "other" and its deconstructive potential is particularly effective in a sequence involving Digna, the Puerto Rican wife of the man accused of sexual assault. Although a victim of domestic abuse, she has been stereotyped as the emotionally unstable Latina and committed to the psychiatric ward of Bellevue Hospital. Upon her return, she visibly assumes the semblance of the Hollywood stereotype, appearing in a ruffled rumba gown topped by an elaborate headdress made of fruit. In a visually dazzling and amusing scene, she surreptitiously accompanies

Jenny on a dinner date with the DA. In the revealing sequence that follows, Digna metaphorically and literally turns the table (and the camera) on Jenny, pointing out her obsequiousness in the presence of her powerful male companion. Suddenly the complicity of the young white woman in a patriarchal system of privilege is disclosed.

Digna notes that Jenny "is unable to recognize, much less analyze, her own blind spots," her ignorance of her own efforts to position herself close to male power and the ways in which this affects her sense of self. Digna's analysis is incisive. "Isn't it amazing," she states, "how we agree to inferior status in our daily lives. [Jenny] made no objection not even to herself. She didn't even ask herself the question: must a woman's feelings about herself depend on a man's assessment about her body? The doors of her thought storage tanks clanged shut. In total abjection she handed over the keys." As the older Jenny tells the story, though, she admits that the biggest shock in reaching middle age was the realization "that men's desire for me was the linchpin of my identity." If a young woman grounds her identity in her relationship to males and male power, as Jenny does, then as she becomes older, she may well experience a diminishing self-esteem and decreasing rather than increasing life choices. As Jenny says: "Aging has been such an emotional subject for me. No one ever told me how many hours of the day I'd spend mourning for—what?—myself." Not only did she willingly agree to subordination through seduction, she based her sense of self on her privileged relationship to white male power.

In aging, though, Jenny has moved, as Yvonne tells her, to "the other side of privilege," a social and political position that, like the position of women of color, is even further removed from centers of male power. Reinforcing the point, the film incorporates a printed script, scored by an operatic aria, that unrolls a cautionary tale about a man's rejection of a middle-aged woman for a younger woman at an academic conference. Contemplating the incident later as she looks out upon the Rio Grande, the older woman realizes that she "was on two different sides of two frontiers. Economically she was on the advantaged side overlooking a third world country. And sexually, having passed the frontier of attractiveness to men, she is now on the other side of privilege." Her access to white males—and consequently her relationship to patriarchal power—has changed.

In *Borderlands: La Frontera,* Gloria Anzaldúa develops the idea of a consciousness that, like the *mestiza* (a person of mixed parentage, generally Spanish and native American), inhabits both sides of a border. She points to the necessity for subordinated groups to apprehend both sides at once: "It is not enough to stand on the opposite river bank, shouting questions. . . . At some point, on our way to a new consciousness, we will have to leave the opposite bank, . . . so that we are on both shores at once" (78–79). If this awareness of the other side is necessary for ethnic and racial groups, it is even more necessary for white, middle-class, heterosexual feminists to comprehend perspectives from the other side and integrate them into an analysis of privilege and theories of gender subordination.

Rainer's exploration of privilege in this film expands feminist analyses of gender, racial, and ethnic subordination to include issues of aging. The film not only discloses the social construction of the aging woman through patriarchal cultural representations; it also deconstructs the youth/age binary opposition. Questioning the construction of female identity in relation to male power, the film gives voice to diverse women's experiences. Their heterogeneous perspectives put pressure on one another, providing insights into the differences within women's relations to patriarchal power structures and the instability of those relationships over a lifetime. Most important, the film incorporates into feminist theory the diverse perspectives of women with multiple differences, women on "the other side of privilege," so that we may clearly analyze privilege and its relationship to women's subordination.

As Rainer's film leads the audience through these perceptions, we come to construct a theory of women's relation to power that positions age, along with race, ethnicity, class, and sexuality, as fundamental critical factors of feminist analysis. Rainer's experimental techniques demand the viewers' participation, leading us to become actively engaged in perceiving and conceptualizing our diverse social and political positions as women and in recognizing our own relationship to privilege. In *The Coming of Age,* Simone de Beauvoir speaks of the need for women of various ages to apprehend the self in the other, an identification that she believes will have significant political consequences. And Gloria Anzaldúa speaks of the possibility of a new consciousness that can at once perceive different experiences and multiple realities. Rainer's film *Privilege* helps us to recognize the self in the other, to acknowledge diverse realities, to arrive at new insights, and to construct more comprehensive feminist theories.

REFERENCES
Anzaldúa, Gloria. *Borderlands: La Frontera.* San Francisco: Aunt Lute Books, 1999.
Beauvoir, Simone de. *The Coming of Age.* 1972. New York: Norton, 1996.
Butler, Judith. *Bodies That Matter: On the Discursive Limits of "Sex."* New York: Routledge, 1993.

———. *The Psychic Life of Power: Theories on Subjection.* Stanford: Stanford UP, 1997.
Hurtado, Aida. "Relating to Privilege: Seduction and Rejections in the Subordination of White Women and Women of Color." *Signs* 24.4 (1989): 833–55.
Lauretis, Teresa de. Foreword. *The Films of Yvonne Rainer.* By Yvonne Rainer. Bloomington: Indiana UP, 1989.
Lorde, Audre. *Sister/Outsider.* Trumansburg, NY: Crossing P, 1984.
Rainer, Yvonne, dir. *Privilege.* Zeitgeist Films, 1990.
Sontag, Susan. "The Double Standard of Aging." *Saturday Review* Sept. 1972: 29–38. Rpt. in *No Longer Young: The Older Woman in America, Occasional Papers in Gerontology II.* Ann Arbor: Inst. of Gerontology, U of Michigan; Detroit: Wayne State UP, 1975. 31–39.
Woodward, Kathleen, ed. 1999. Introduction. *Figuring Age: Women, Bodies, Generations.* Bloomington: Indiana UP.

Gwen Raaberg *is professor of English and director of women's studies at Western Michigan University. She is editor, with Mary Ann Caws and Rudolf Kuenzli, of* Surrealism and Women *(MIT Press) and has published extensively on feminist theory, women writers and gender issues in twentieth-century literature and is currently writing a book about experimental strategies in contemporary feminist literature, art, and film.*

Copyright © 2002 by Gwen Raaberg

"I'm a Wheelchair Girl Now"

Abjection, Intersectionality, and Subjectivity in Atom Egoyan's *The Sweet Hereafter*

Vivian M. May and Beth A. Ferri

> Since form cannot be separated from content—the form of the story being (integral to) the story itself—there is no other way to say it without reforming it (that is, un/intentionally modifying, augmenting, or narrowing it).
>
> —Trinh T. Minh-ha

Introduction

Our analysis of the 1997 film *The Sweet Hereafter* explores the formal techniques employed by director Atom Egoyan in his "retelling" of Russell Banks's 1991 novel of the same title. We focus on how Egoyan's use of interruption, haunting, and visual and aural simultaneity does more than push viewers to acknowledge their active role in meaning-making—these formal techniques also allow space within the narrative for oppositional consciousness and for reconfigured power relationships. Our interpretation combines insights from both women's studies and disability studies to enable us to attend to the political and theoretical implications of the film's form and content and thus explore one of the central paradoxes of subjection and power—that each contains the seeds of its own undoing. More specifically, we focus upon this possibility, even necessity, for agency within constraint in connection with the character Nichole, who self-consciously moves "from object to subject" (hooks 9) by the film's end.

Our reading of *The Sweet Hereafter*, which highlights the simultaneity of the politics of knowledge and the politics of disability and gender, engages a "both/and" epistemology because it challenges binary thought and "additive models of oppression" (Collins, 1st ed. 225). In addition, we draw upon psychoanalytic theories of "constitutive" parameters of subjectivity (Butler, "Imitation" 15) and, from disability studies, theories of "extraordinary bodies" that prompt "double responses" of fascination and repulsion (Thomson 115). Without a both/and framework that focuses on both gender and disability as loci of abjection, Nichole—a character who experiences both incest and disability—might simply be interpreted as a victim, an object of pity. We are not suggesting that Nichole is unaffected by or does not suffer from disempowering, oppressive relationships within her family and her community. However, we do want to emphasize that Nichole does not simply survive "experiences with intersecting oppressions[;] . . . she clearly rejects their ideological justification" (Collins, 2nd ed. 201). Our goal is to underscore the potential of intersectional political and analytical frameworks not only because they help us to understand the nuances of Nichole's subjectivity, but also because thinking "at the intersections" is a productive methodological practice. Without intersectionality as a critical tool, it would be impossible to fully grasp the radical agency that Nichole claims as she skillfully negotiates the double negation of the ableist stare (Thomson 25) and the sexist gaze. Before delving into a more detailed analysis of the character Nichole, whose story is, to us, the most memorable, we first introduce several related interpretive "facets" or narrative layers in Egoyan's film. We structure our essay in a matric approach not only because Nichole's character needs to be understood within a "matrix of domination" (Collins, 1st ed. 222–30), but also because this layering technique best parallels the film's nonlinear form.

Fragmented Narratives, Disrupted Stories

The Sweet Hereafter tells the story of a school bus accident that kills all but one of its fourteen passengers (all the town's children) and the subsequent arrival of a lawyer from outside the town who pushes the community toward a class-action lawsuit to compensate it for its loss. The sole survivor of the accident, aside from the bus driver, Dolores, is Nichole, a teenager who acquires her disability in the bus crash. Because she is the only surviving passenger, Nichole's testimony becomes central to the success of the lawsuit. Although this is the basic plot summary of the film, it is not the whole story. Because the film has multiple layers and narrators, it could be characterized as a film about the definition of community, a critique of father-daughter relationships, or even a film about incest. Rather than being a unified, linear tale, *The Sweet Hereafter* is a collective of narratives that intersect and interrupt one another. The film neither begins nor ends with the bus accident, which remains unresolved in terms of established guilt or innocence. When the lawyer, Mitchell Stephens, arrives from the "big city" after the accident, he repeatedly claims that "there are no accidents," and that he is there to help give voice and focus to the community's anger. However, the film's multiperspectival narrative structure resists the causal explanation and neat closure that the lawyer, the community, and even the viewing audience might desire.

The continual interruption of past and present and of one story with another highlights the impossibility of resolving the meaning of the bus accident or of reconstructing an event or moment in time: meaning, identity, and perception remain unstable and nonlinear. Further, the plural community narrative prevents any one story from gaining absolute authority. Egoyan's narrative techniques differ from those of Banks's novel. The novel's narrative method, although multiple, is more static than the film's visual and narrative multiplicity. Unlike Egoyan's, Banks's story is told in turn by the town's various residents, with, however, each person's standpoint contained by chapter breaks such that we have many viewpoints, but one at a time, in successive juxtaposition, in contrast to Egoyan's more deconstructive, fragmented juxtaposition. In addition, Egoyan makes the story his own in many other ways. For example, he adds significantly to the narrative's affect and effect by incorporating Robert Browning's "Pied Piper of Hamelin" as an intertextual frame.

The film's interconnected narratives and subjectivities destabilize the relationship between the "real" and the "fictional" as well as between private and public realms, individual and social experiences, and personal and collective knowledge. Rather than passively consume a readymade tale, viewers of *The Sweet Hereafter* must piece together contradicting, fragmented perspectives in order to create meaning out of the community's response to the accident. Egoyan's methods engage the politics of knowledge to challenge paradigmatic epistemological models of acontextual, disembodied, "neutral" knowledge. Egoyan encourages a self-conscious, located, and contextual model of knowing and perceiving that attends to questions of power, interest, and accountability. *The Sweet Hereafter* asks viewers to negotiate among several contradicting and juxtaposed stories, pushing us to become more aware of our role (Pevere 15) in selecting what to focus on, both visually and narratively. The film, therefore, offers a productive space to explore feminist theoretical insights about knowledge, embodiment, and agency.

Visually, *The Sweet Hereafter* disallows the possibility of a seamless, unified tale by encompassing multiple views within one camera angle. Moreover, stories that take place offscreen overlap with ones onscreen—thwarting any attempts to separate a central story from the multitude of subplots. For example, once the lawyer arrives, he visits the homes of all the parents who lost children as well as the home of the bus driver, Dolores. Our visual understanding of this visit is not "centered" on or contained in one character or even one part of Dolores's house. The camera moves back and forth between the lawyer and Dolores, but it also encompasses a wide and deep view of Dolores's living room that emphasizes both the scene's foreground and background. On one side of the room, tinkering with some food, is the lawyer, gently and then more forcefully prodding Dolores to tell the story he wants to hear so he can move forward with the lawsuit. Behind Dolores, who is sitting down, is a wall full of photographs of children. Upon close inspection, viewers realize that rather than being photos of her biological children, these are pictures of all of her school bus kids. The details of these pictures, which portray Dolores with children at the fair, at school, and on field trips, underscore the guilt and agony Dolores is living with not only as the only other survivor aside from Nichole, but also as the driver of the careening bus. In another background area, in the upper right-hand corner of the screen, sits, in a wheelchair, Dolores's husband, Abbott—a decorated war veteran whose seemingly unintelligible speech and gestures can only be understood by Dolores. In a big-screen theater, viewers have to move their heads in order to "see" the scene: kinesthetically, we have to make choices about where to focus our attention. Meanwhile, we become aware of all that we are *not* seeing—or are only seeing out of the corner of our eye: if we focus on Dolores's husband, we cannot pay attention to the photographs behind Dolores on the wall; if we focus on Dolores, we miss the husband's nonverbal participation in and reaction to the dialogue with the lawyer; if we focus on the lawyer, we miss the photographs of all the children as well as the subtle visual and physical exchanges between Dolores and her husband.

Without a narrowly framed or focused picture, viewers must attend to multiple visions and versions and actively and self-consciously participate in the construction of the story. Egoyan's approach contrasts traditional modes of representation, which tend to obscure the interest and influence of both the camera's look and the audience's look, thereby denying the skillful strategies employed by both filmmaker and viewer to prevent questioning the reality and perceptions they coconstruct (Trinh 54–55, 93–94). As de Certeau asserts, "Representation thus disguises the praxis that organizes it" (in Scott 399). In contrast, Egoyan's wide, slow-moving camera angle pushes us to actively recognize the role we play in interpreting and constructing meaning. Meaning, as a collaborative project, is not given, determined, or fixed:

the film's fragmented multiplicity allows multiple interpretations, but it also creates space for transgressive readings.

By using a heterogeneous structure, Egoyan highlights the doubleness and ambiguity of power to explore the radical possibilities for subjectivity and agency within the context of subjection. The film's asynchronicity leaves reality, subjectivity, and meaning momentarily defined rather than clearly delineated and static. Within provisionality and instability, possibilities emerge for knowing across the boundaries dividing self from other, agency from victimization, and innocence from guilt. Although Egoyan's polyphonic, asynchronous, and multiply layered approach to truth and reality could be interpreted as negatively emblematic of the "crisis of reason" (Grosz 192–194), within a both/and framework, such fragmentation can be understood to be symbolic of a "crucial and potentially hopeful incoherence" (Kaplan 42), a space for creating new narratives or for allowing suppressed stories to emerge. The film therefore reframes "threat and disruption . . . as a critical resource in the struggle to rearticulate the very terms of symbolic legitimacy and intelligibility" (Butler, *Bodies* 3).

Just as the narrative is multifaceted and unstable, all of the characters are contradictory and variously flawed. Stories of father-daughter relations, of individual and community failures, and of love and exploitation overlap with the narrative of the bus accident. Thus the genre of the film can best be described as one of continuous interruption or haunting. As each character's individual "phantoms" come to the surface, clear distinctions between self and other, abled and disabled, past and present, good and evil, insider and outsider, are shaken. The blurring of these regulatory dichotomies highlights the fragility of the normative center. This porosity can seem quite ominous to those who benefit from the (unearned) privilege and power of normative identities, but recognizing porosity can also be liberating for those who have been marginalized. Both viewers and characters come to see the transitory nature of their own identities, to understand the "exclusionary matrix by which subjects are formed . . . [that] requires the simultaneous production of a domain of abject beings, those who are not yet 'subjects,' but who form the constitutive outside to the domain of the subject" (Butler *Bodies* 3).

Thus the film's various hauntings signify fears and suppressions that are both personal and social, private and public. They erupt from an "abject domain that continually threatens to overrun its carefully established borders" (Weiss 42). Egoyan asks viewers to attend to the excess, to the negated, subordinated, "constitutive outside" at the edges of each character's story and at the edges of the town's sense of self or community (Grosz 190; Butler *Bodies* 3). Frequently, "the very project of demarcating the 'I' from what it is not relies upon a dualistic metaphysics" (Weiss 445), but Egoyan strategically refuses binaries through deconstructive juxtaposition. *The Sweet Hereafter* makes room for viewers to reflexively engage with suppressed stories and subjects: in creating indeterminate spaces within his film, he pushes us to acknowledge the politics of subject formation.

Thus Egoyan's techniques, including the slow, wide camera angle, asynchronous juxtaposition, and interconnected yet contradicting narrative interpretations, are politically significant. In particular, *The Sweet Hereafter* offers feminist scholars a productive site in which to further explore intersectionality and the politics of domination within the discursive fields and lived experiences of both gender and disability. Egoyan's *The Sweet Hereafter* can be understood to be a form of liberatory practice because it "engage[s] critically the stories informing people's lives" while also "[encouraging] vulnerability to the stories of others" (O'Connell 74), yet not in a simplistic or romanticized way. The liberatory aspects of these multiple stories can be found in the contradictory, ambiguous spaces among the narrative threads.[1]

Haunted Selves and Ghost Stories

In an early scene, the lawyer interviews hotel owners Resa and Wendell to begin to generate a list of "good citizens," whom he defines as "folks like you . . . sensitive, loving parents" who would make a good impression on the judge for the class-action lawsuit against the bus manufacturer. During the ensuing conversation, both reveal secrets about their neighbors (including incidents of spousal abuse, theft, alcoholism, drug use, promiscuity, and adultery) such that no one in the town emerges as a model citizen. Then, when the lawyer receives one of the many phone calls in the film from his desperate, drug-addicted daughter, Zoe, the camera angle shifts from Resa and Wendell's living room (one space) to encompass three visual spaces and two aural narratives. In the foreground, we watch Mitchell Stephens listen to Zoe's desperation, while in the background (at the end of a long hallway that serves as an interstitial third space in the center of the screen) we watch and hear Resa and Wendell begin to fight bitterly about who is and who isn't an "upright citizen," ironically highlighting the flaws in their own embattled marriage. Visually, we are asked to view three spaces within one space; while aurally, we take in two dialogues, one across the continent, the other yelled across the living room in the background. This rupture in the scene, where flaws in both families and in the town as a whole emerge, is an early example of the film's deconstructive fissures, which emphasize how interest and power shape justificatory standards of knowledge production, from town gossip to court testimony. These narrative and aural disruptions also provide room, however marginal or small, for questioning—for thinking about who or what is left out of the story as it unfolds.

Interestingly, although the lawyer is, at first, understood to be an outsider to the town's space as well as its values, the qualities distinguishing stranger from neighbor become fuzzy, demonstrating slippage among the seemingly distinct categories of insider and outsider. Billy, the town mechanic, a recent widower whose twins die on the bus while he helplessly watches from his truck, comes to be seen as an outsider for refusing to join the class-action lawsuit because he is sickened by the greed and hatred he sees in his neighbors' desires for financial gain and causal closure. At the same time that Billy defines himself as a community "insider" in opposition to the greedy lawyer from the "outside," the community brings the lawyer inside their homes, rejecting Billy's claims that they should act in a more neighborly manner toward one another. Billy feels accountable to the town and the community and not to his individual situation and needs, although he is not entirely "neighborly" in an altruistic sense, as he is having an affair with Reesa, who is married to Wendell. Billy is shunned by the community, whereas the lawyer, who appears to be a failed father and husband as well as a solicitor with less-than-angelic intentions, gains entry to people's homes to influence family philosophies, mores, and decision-making. Ironically, the town's overwhelming desire for closure and resolution of the tragedy, via a class-action lawsuit, results in more fissures and discontent.

These unstable, malleable categories underscore the limits of the constructs we rely upon to define and describe ourselves and our surrounding reality: there is always something that does not fit, that gets pushed to the "outside," acting as an excess or shadow to the stories we devise. *The Sweet Hereafter* highlights how the "real" is always haunted by the fictions that it simultaneously depends upon and denies, a dynamic that Toni Morrison outlines in American social thought and fiction in terms of the "Africanist character as surrogate and enabler" (51) who "is the vehicle by which the American self knows itself as not enslaved, but free; not repulsive, but desirable; not helpless, but licensed and powerful; not history-less, but historical; not damned, but innocent; not a blind [*sic*] accident of evolution, but a progressive fulfillment of destiny" (52). In the context of disability, Rosemarie Garland Thomson analyses how the normative body is defined in opposition to the disabled other in ways that uphold the "natural" superiority, freedom, autonomy, and agency of the abled (40).

Egoyan emphasizes the role of fiction as the "necessary outside" of the real by intermingling Browning's poem "The Pied Piper of Hamelin" into the "real time" of the film. Browning's verses reenter the film at several key points in the form of a voice-over by Nichole, who will become, as in the rhyme, "the one left behind"—the lone child survivor after the bus accident. The voice-over is another example of haunting in the film. Hearing Nichole's voice reading this prophetic tale to Billy's children the night before the accident brings back memories of all the children now missing from the town. But the voice-over also foregrounds Nichole's own lost childhood. Immediately after putting Billy's children to sleep with the story, she changes into a more adult, tight-fitting dress and stockings. Driving her home later that evening, her father Sam stops at a barn, viewers assume, to drop Nichole off for band rehearsal. But as she follows her father into the darkened barn we once again hear Nichole's voice reading fragments of Browning's "Pied Piper":

> A wondrous portal opened wide . . .
> "It's dull in our town since my playmates left;
> I can't forget that I'm bereft
> Of all the pleasant sights they see,
> Which the Piper also promised me . . .
> And everything was strange and new. (401–8)

Bridging the divide between safety and exploitation, the voice-over creates a disturbing contrast between the just-past image of Nichole reading the children a bedtime story and the unfolding image of father-daughter incest in the candlelit barn. Egoyan's use of Nichole's voice-over juxtaposes the idyllic safety and comfort of a nursery rhyme with stories of incest, loss, and vindication. By choosing to interject this bedtime story into the film, Egoyan eerily connects seemingly disparate stories to emphasize innocence lost. Childhood is not necessarily apolitical or unfettered: it, too, entails politics of domination.

The nursery rhyme of the one "lame" child who survives comes into play again when Nichole survives the crash but is paralyzed as a result. Once Nichole is home from the hospital, her father is awkward and uncomfortable: his past incestuous fantasies of Nichole as the beautiful "rock star" cannot mesh with his post-accident perceptions of Nichole as an asexual "wheelchair girl." However, both images of Nichole still exist. Thus each objectifying image or construct of

Nichole haunts its opposite, its other. In addition, Sam is repelled by Nichole's disability and, at the same time, attracted to it because he thinks he can gain financially from this "misfortune." Sam's double response of simultaneous attraction and repulsion (Mitchell and Snyder 15) is reminiscent of typical responses to "extraordinary bodies" who straddle conventional categories of embodiment (Thomson 55–63).

Like Nichole's father, the lawyer, too, is troubled by his own past and present contradictory images of his daughter Zoe, another "ghost" who, like Nichole's reading of the "Pied Piper," haunts the narrative. From its opening scene, the film emphasizes the contested nature of father-daughter relationships by immediately introducing Zoe's drug addiction and continual invasion of her father's reality through his own troubling memories and her disturbing phone calls. Their painful conversations also symbolize love gone astray and childhood lost. In a flashback, the lawyer recalls an idyllic image of his former happy marriage and of parental comfort and care: he, his wife, and Zoe are asleep on a bed in a vacation home. However, his rosy recollection is shattered by his remembering how, on that vacation, he had to prepare to save Zoe's life "at all costs," to go "all the way" after she was stung by a baby black widow spider. He races his young daughter to the hospital singing her nursery rhymes, knife in hand, readying himself, if necessary, to cut into her neck to open her windpipe for oxygen. His memories of a sylvan past torment his disconsolate present, for he can no longer save Zoe, his marriage has ended in divorce, and his ethics as a lawyer are compromised by the paradox that the law's power is built on the need for financial gain and revenge.

The interweaving of the past with the present combined with the film characters' recognition of and dismay at the blurred and fuzzy line between self and other, insider and outsider, good and evil, and love and domination remind viewers of the partiality and multiplicity of all apparently seamless narratives. Attending to these disruptive ghosts that destabilize normative oppositions within the film allows unexpected insights about subjectivity to emerge, creating possibility for our intersectional reading of Nichole's critical consciousness. In the fissures where the seamlessness of the real and of the self are broken apart, fault lines develop in which aspects of identity, such as gender and disability, and their constructed meanings can be renegotiated. In other words, because the film's fragmented and nonlinear format refuses artificial coherence or homogeneity, interruption and disruption yield spaces for alternative subject formation. This dynamic is particularly evident in the character of Nichole as she sorts through the implications of entering the cultural space of the "third term . . . ambiguously positioned both inside and outside the category of woman" because of her acquired disability (Thomson 29).

Tropes of Disability in Film

Disability scholars contend that characters with disabilities are most commonly enlisted as exotic spectacles of otherness: ciphers for ableist fears and anxieties about vulnerability, dependency, and loss of control (Crutchfield 286; Darke 186; Mitchell and Snyder 13; Norden 11; Thomson 6–9). In these analyses, the disabled body absorbs whatever is refused or rejected by the normative position (Thomson 41). In other words, through the attention given to disability, the norm emerges from its otherwise transparent location within the text. Among the three disabled characters in the film (Nichole; Shawn, Reesa's young son; and Abbott, war veteran and husband of Dolores, the bus driver), Nichole is the most complex and fully developed. Because Nichole acquires her disability, viewers are reminded of the way ability, like other aspects of normativity, is always haunted and threatened by its other.

Far from there being a problem of invisibility, disability studies scholars document the pervasive use of disability as metaphor and symbol in literature and film (Darke 185–86; Davis 151–153; Norden 377–84; Safran 468; Schuchman 44). Disability is at once everywhere (in terms of representation) and nowhere (in terms of critical analyses within film studies, cultural studies, and feminist studies). Disability is a well-worn trope of filmmakers, and has been even more so in recent history (Safran 472). One reason for this preoccupation with disability and film is that the combination often yields box-office success (Darke 189) and critical acclaim (Safran 472). In fact, since 1987, twenty Oscar nominations have been awarded to disability portrayals, almost exclusively played by nondisabled characters (Crutchfield 284). This success could be attributed to the fact that disability in film not only reinforces everyday ableist stereotypes, but also shores up the normative center for viewers and critics alike.

The relentless use of the disabled body as a repository of cultural meaning has resulted in predictable and identifiable genres, motifs, and social archetypes that function as "lightning rod[s] for . . . pity, fear, discomfort, [or] guilt" to affirm the illusion of the "normalcy of the reader or [the] more significant character" (Thomson 15). The idea that disability functions to "buttress" the normative position (8) has been influential—so much so that films employing disability have been described as following a highly predictable "normality genre" by Darke (184). The conventions of this genre focus on the plot of overcoming disability through individual struggle, cure, or rehabilitation—usually aided by an able-bodied rescuer. Characters who cannot or will not assimilate are eradicated, such that either way, normality is restored and valorized.

The options available to disabled and nondisabled female characters are similar—the nondisabled female character must, in the end, either marry, go mad, or die, whereas the disabled female character must either be cured, go mad, or die (Herndl 15). Obviously, the marriage plot is replaced by the cure plot for the disabled woman character, who is deemed to be asexual rather than a sexual object. Other conventions of the genre include social isolation of the disabled character, both from able-bodied characters and from other characters with disabilities. The rule is one disability per film, a "divide-and-quarantine" approach described by Norden (2) that constructs an artificial border or barrier around disability. This paradigm places disability and "normalcy" in an oppositional relationship, reinforcing the notion that disability is about personal tragedy rather than oppressive social and political relationships.

Despite the proliferation of disability in film, available roles for characters with disabilities remain limited. Norden first described what have come to be understood as archetypal disability roles, which have been in use since the silent film era and across every conceivable genre, from Disney cartoons to dramas. Some examples of disability archetypes include the "sweet innocent," invariably a young unmarried woman or a child, characterized as humble, gentle, pure, respectful, childlike, asexual, and most important pitiable (33–35); the "saintly sage," a pious older person who serves as the "voice of reason and conscience in a chaotic world" (131–32); the "noble warrior," a hypermasculinized figure, commonly a veteran, who is characterized by the ability to heroically overcome disability to achieve fully restored manhood (318); the "obsessive avenger," again a role most often given to male characters, who are villains or monsters seeking revenge, often eliciting in viewers a double response of repulsion and fascination (52); and finally, the "comic misadventurer," a character whose disability causes trouble or problems, used for comedic effect (20).

The rhetorical effects of such representations most commonly assume and reinforce the idea that physical "defects" are synecdochal stand-ins for flawed character traits (Sutherland 17). This is a problematic or limited understanding because it precludes the possibility of disability as a site of subjectivity and agency: disability becomes simply an explanatory device, rhetorical tool, or symbolic repository. Such approaches to disability limit its role to that of an instrument for or mirror of others' subjectivity, or as a metaphor for subjection, deviance, or lack. The instrumentalization or objectification of disability denies disability as a site of subjectivity.

Although it is easy to focus on the oppressive representations of disability in film because of their sheer numbers, Thomson (7–9) and others remind us that there is liberatory potential in representations of disability. Characters with disabilities *can* be read as radical subjects who straddle and transgress categories and resist normalization—they can be seen metaphorically and corporeally as "non-conformity incarnate" (44). Reducing and obliterating complexity ignores the political and dialectical relationship between identity and difference, as noted by Trinh T. Minh-ha (73–76). More complicated readings of disability in film therefore turn the ableist gaze back upon its source to examine how representations of difference reinforce and demarcate more privileged normative identities (Darke 183; Davis 24; Sutherland 18; Thomson 8).

Subverted Stereotypes, Subversive Subjects

At first glance, as the paralyzed survivor who is kind, soft-spoken, and caring, Nichole seems to be a perfect candidate for the conventional disability role for women, the role of the "sweet innocent" who is asexual, childlike, and pitiable (Norden 33, 316). For example, a reviewer from the *Dallas Morning News* describes Nichole in this patronizing way, referring to her as a redemptive "brave, crippled teen" (Sumner). We contend, however, that Nichole's character does not completely conform to the sweet innocent role or to other conventional film roles for disabled characters such as the "brilliant mind in the crippled body"— one who sees beyond the visible because of her disability (Morris 27). Rather, she simultaneously evokes and subverts ableist and gender stereotypes as a means of challenging their power to define and delimit.

Individuals with disabilities are frequently portrayed as full of resentment and anger at the world for their misfortune who only come to accept their "lot in life" with the help of a wiser and more reasonable nondisabled character (Darke 193; Morris 28; Klobas 192). In contrast, Nichole is self-contained, calm, and in no need of assurance from others—she is self-assured. Nichole's characterization also strays from another convention of disability in film in which disability completely transforms the character's identity and reshapes his or her entire life. Instead, Nichole has an atypical continuity of character, particularly in the way she continues to care for herself and others, rather than become the object of care. In its narrative multiplicity, *The Sweet Hereafter* departs from the filmic trope in which disability is the central problem that can only be "resolved" by cure, death, or eventual acceptance with the help of an abled-bodied character.

Recognizing and even playing up the ways in which social roles are fictions made real through social practices, Nichole uses roles of presumed powerlessness and subjection (girl, disabled, exploited) to renegotiate her subjectivity. In other words, as a survivor of incest who is also disabled and female, Nichole comes to recognize one of the key paradoxes at the heart of subjection. As Judith Butler explains, "Power is not simply what we oppose but also . . . what we depend on for our existence. . . . Subjection consists precisely in this fundamental dependency on a discourse we never chose but that, paradoxically, initiates and sustains our agency" (*Psychic* 2). In other words, because "subjection is the account by which a subject becomes the guarantor of its resistance and opposition, ... no subject comes into being without power" (*Psychic* 14). Nichole clearly recognizes how power contains within itself the seeds of its own undoing (*Psychic* 15) and uses this antilogy to her own ends.

The Sweet Hereafter therefore mitigates determinist interpretations first of disability as a signifier of tragedy and second of gender as a signifier of the "ground" against which autonomy and freedom are defined and delimited (Martin 41, 93). Rather, disability and gender are interdependent sites of *both* agency *and* marginality: because they are ambiguous locations, possibility for change lies in their indeterminacy. Nichole exceeds and subverts ableist conventions and the stereotypes and expectations associated with them in order to assert agency. For example, when she returns home from the hospital she finds a garishly painted ramp and an over-the-top hyperfeminine new bedroom on the first floor of her family's house. Nichole is somewhat underwhelmed by the overdone nature of the ramp and her new bedroom, both of which her father has been working on for weeks. Her first words to her father, in a matter-of-fact tone, are "The door needs a lock." When he quickly and somewhat nervously returns and begins to install the lock too high for her to reach from her wheelchair, she demands that he hang it lower. Asserting a newfound ability to "lock him out," and clarifying that she will be the one to determine access to her space and her self, Nichole also tells her younger sister, who will now be alone in their old bedroom, that she can always come and sleep in her room.

Later, Nichole's father tells her that she has become "hard to talk to" and "distant." She responds, "We didn't used to have to talk a lot, did we, Daddy?" and then adds, "I'm a wheelchair girl now and it's hard to imagine I'm a beautiful rock star." Nichole actively espouses the terms of her subjection—her paralysis, her father's sexual objectification of her, and her girlhood—as a means of claiming subjectivity. As Judith Butler writes, "I am led to embrace the terms that injure me because they constitute me socially.... As a further paradox, then, only by occupying—being occupied by—that injurious term can I resist and oppose it, recasting the power that constitutes me as the power I oppose" (*Psychic* 104). Nichole reminds her father of the way he used to think of and look at her, while simultaneously refusing that sexually objectifying role and gaze by inviting his asexual and ableist stare. Thomson explains: "If the male gaze makes the normative female a sexual spectacle, then the stare sculpts the disabled subject into a grotesque spectacle." She adds that the ableist stare is "the gaze intensified, framing [the disabled female] body as an icon of deviance" (26). Nichole subverts the ableist convention of the "stare" and its stereotype of asexuality and abjection and at the same time negates the sexually objectifying "gaze" that allowed her father to eroticize his domination of her. Although her experiences with incest and her accident do marginalize Nichole, she also recognizes that subjection is never total, nor is power simply unidirectional. She creates subjective space for herself by turning one oppressive gaze onto another in a way that cancels out each one's ability to define and fix her as an object reflecting and reinforcing someone else's subjectivity.

Having lived through the socially sanctioned, if not mandated, secrecy of incest, Nichole also understands the power of voice and makes sure her father knows that if asked to testify in the lawsuit, she plans to "tell the truth . . . no matter what I'm asked." She signals to her father that she has taken hold of the rules of telling and not telling, this time on her own terms, not his, even though incest remains one of the more taboo arenas of social experience and, thus, is usually erased, negated, or refused articulation. By making sure that her father is aware that she will break the normative rule of silence to bring shame upon him if need be, she keeps their secret, but shifts the meaning of the silence and whose interest it will serve. Rather than being a locus of shame and invisibility for her, her silenced experiences now become also a place of power and self-determinization.

Later, at the deposition, Nichole finesses the "law of the father"—the conventions of testimony, truth, and objectivity—to enact her own ethics and to breathe life into the agential possibilities she sees for herself as a "wheelchair girl." She manipulates common assumptions about testifying and truth-telling that presume the "evidence of experience" to be a site of transparent meaning (Scott 400). However, the lawyer and her father overlook the possibility that the law can be "cited" differently "in order to reiterate and coopt its power" (Butler, *Bodies* 15). Judith Butler describes how contentious practices of queerness can be used to rework abjection into political agency and thus act as a kind of "demanding resignification" (*Bodies* 21–23). Patricia Hill Collins describes this dynamic as rearticulation: "redefining social realities by combining familiar ideas in new ways" (2nd ed. 118). In the film, Nichole's deposition statement is a "demanding resignification" or "rearticulation" of disability and gender: she re-presents incest, paralysis, and girlhood from symbols of abjection to sites of defiance and legitimacy.

On the day of the deposition, Nichole overplays the "good girl" and sweet innocent roles. She passively sits in the backseat of the car, wearing an uncharacteristic schoolgirl dress complete with ankle socks. While we again hear her voice-over reading of the "Pied Piper," she actively makes her body completely limp, forcing her father to struggle to carry her "dead weight" from the car into the (ironically) inaccessible community center where the deposition will take place.[2] Once the deposition begins, however, she is anything but passive. She carefully reconstructs the story of the accident in such a way that while no one believes her, neither can anyone refute what she "remembers." Her testimony, in which she claims to remember Dolores, the bus driver, driving too fast, places the blame on the person with the shallowest pockets, thereby subverting the much larger and more profitable lawsuit the lawyer and her parents had had in mind. By recognizing the uncertainty of memory and by manipulating the stereotypical ways she is perceived and treated as a disabled girl, Nichole is able to derail the lawsuit and prevent her parents, the lawyer, or the town from making any financial gain from the accident. In other words, Nichole takes away others' ability to commodify her marginality for their own gain (see Collins, 2nd ed. 289), even though she still asks to keep the fancy computer the lawyer bought in an early attempt to mollify her.

After the deposition, the lawyer, knowing that she has lied, says to her, "You'd make a great poker player, kid," to which she replies, "Thanks." Then she looks at her father and says, "Let's go now, Dad." For the first time in the film, Nichole calls her father "Dad" instead of "Daddy," implying that she will no longer be either his rock star or his little innocent wheelchair girl. Moreover, this is the first time we see her pushing her own wheelchair. Both these acts signify a shift in agency and power. She uses her experiences of gender, disability, and sexual domination as points of resistance and agency not only to subvert her own positionality and narrative, but also to disrupt the divides between fact and fiction, past and present, and good and evil to reconfigure the narratives and identities of her family, her community, and the law.

Conclusion

Although disability is not a yet a central concern in feminist film studies or in much of feminist theory, our reading of *The Sweet Hereafter* points to the necessity of looking at dis/ability as an integral part of identity formation and of power relations. Without a consideration of how disability and gender interdepend, our analysis of the film could not have explained how Nichole uses gendered ableism to counteract and defuse ableist sexual exploitation. The negation of the ableist "stare" combined with the negation of the sexually objectifying "gaze" is, in the end, a double negative, creating for Nichole a positive site of agency and power.

By focusing on multiple aspects of knowledge, identity, and power all at once, intersectionality offers a more fruitful exploration of the paradoxes of subjection and agency while also allowing further appreciation of the productive and liberatory possibilities of multiplicity, porosity, and ambiguity. Such insights are encouraged in *The Sweet Hereafter* by Egoyan's asynchronous, fragmented, and many layered narrative methods and visual techniques. Egoyan emphasizes visual and narrative hauntings, including a focus on how the excess and the marginal both frame and support the center. He also attends to how our social, legal, and philosophical categories are more porous and unstable than we usually acknowledge, such that distinctions between good and evil, insider and outsider, and self and other become blurred and open for redeployment.

A cross-categorical methodology that recognizes the ways "political consciousness can emerge within everyday lived experience" (Collins, 2nd ed. 209) is important to an emerging feminist disability studies because it fosters an understanding of how each facet of identity or of experience has another, negative space to which it is connected and upon which it depends. Conventionally, disability forms an absent presence in feminist theory, and conversely, gender analysis and feminist theory tend to haunt disability studies. However, intersectionality "reminds us that oppression cannot be reduced to one fundamental type, and that oppressions work together in producing injustice" (Collins, 2nd ed. 18).

A feminist disability studies perspective grounded in intersectionality offers a synergistic scholarly model able to account for multiple and interconnected sites of "othering" and subject formation. Because intersectionality is not additive and because it is a theoretical approach developed out of lived experience and aimed at social justice (Crenshaw), it can be understood to function, like Nichole's strategic redeployment of oppressive identities, as a "strategy" that is "employed for particular purposes in particular contexts at particular times" (Spivak 4). Like Nichole's rearticulation of her own marginality, strategizing as a methodology or pedagogy is pragmatic and necessary, but not necessarily celebratory or easy. Spivak describes it as "the useful but semimournful position of the unavoidable usefulness of something that is dangerous" (5), recognizing the "mournful" facts of negotiating subjection and oppression.

This is not a cynical methodology, but rather an approach grounded in survival as a form of resistance sparked by the desire to imagine or sustain "an independent consciousness as a sphere of freedom" (Collins, 2nd ed. 205). Chela Sandoval articulates this approach as the "methodology of the oppressed" and describes a "differential mode of social movement and consciousness" at the center of this methodology. She explains that this "differential mode of social movement and consciousness depends on the practitioner's ability to read the current situation of power and self-consciously choosing and adopting the ideological stand best suited to push against its configurations" (60). We conclude by asserting not only that this "methodology of the oppressed" is illustrated and deployed by Nichole, but also that the complexity of Nichole's oppositional consciousness can best be understood within Sandoval's notion of "differential consciousness," which "permits functioning within, yet beyond, the demands of dominant ideology" (44). As interdisciplinary fields committed to social justice, disability studies and women's studies have much to gain from an intersectional "differential" methodology for further identifying and teaching practices of resistance.

ATOM EGOYAN FILMOGRAPHY
Director

The Blind Assassin. Icon Entertainment. 2002.
Ararat. Miramax. 2002.
Felicia's Journey. Artisan Entertainment. 1999.
Yo-Yo Ma Inspired by Bach, Sony Classics. 1998.
Bach Cello Suite #4: Sarabande. Rhombas Media. 1997.
The Sweet Hereafter. New Line Studios. 1997.
A Portrait of Arshile. BBC. 1995.
Exotica. Miramax. 1994.

Calendar. Kino Video. 1993.
The Adjuster. Alliance Communications Corp. 1991.
Montréal vu par . . . Atlantis Films 1991.
Speaking Parts. Fox Lorber. 1989.
Family Viewing. Fox Lorber. 1987.
Men: A Passion Playground. Ego Film Arts. 1985.
Next of Kin. Connoisseur, Meridian Films. 1984.
Open House. Ego Film Arts. 1982.
Peep Show. Ego Film Arts. 1981.
After Grad with Dad. Ego Film Arts. 1980.
Howard in Particular. Ego Film Arts. 1979.

Writer

Felicia's Journey. Artisan Entertainment. 1999.
The Sweet Hereafter. New Line Studios. 1997.
Exotica. Miramax. 1994.
Calendar. Kino Video. 1993.
The Adjuster. Alliance Entertainment. 1991.
Montréal vu par . . . Atlantis Films. 1991.
Speaking Parts. Fox Lorber. 1989.
Family Viewing. Fox Lorber. 1987.
Next of Kin. Connoisseur, Meridian Films. 1984.
Open House. Ego Film Arts. 1982.
Peep Show. Ego Film Arts. 1981.
After Grad with Dad. Ego Film Arts. 1980.
Howard in Particular. Ego Film Arts. 1979.

NOTES

1. Because the film's ambiguity allows multiple readings, reception of the film among disability and feminist scholars has been mixed. However, we feel that the discomfort of ambiguity is a productive tension and not a sign of the film's failure—particularly if expectations of "celebration" or "redemption" aren't the markers of a film's quality of success, commercially or intellectually. Similarly, reception of earlier versions of this essay has been varied. Several people have disagreed with our perception of Nichole as an agential subject—to many, she seems to exemplify the stereotypical or stock disabled female film character; to others, our focus on her agency denies the painful realities of surviving incest.
2. Of course, the inaccessible community center only emphasizes how abled our concepts of community membership really are.

REFERENCES

Banks, Russell. *The Sweet Hereafter.* New York: HarperCollins, 1991.
Browning, Robert. "The Pied Piper of Hamelin." *The Illustrated Treasury of*

Children's Literature. Ed. P. Edward Ernest. New York: Grosset and Dunlap. 1955. 401–408.

Butler, Judith. *Bodies that Matter: On the Discursive Limits of "Sex."* New York: Routledge, 1993.

———. "Imitation and Gender Insubordination." *Inside/Out: Lesbian Theories, Gay Theories.* Ed. Diana Fuss. New York: Routledge, 1991. 13–31.

———. *The Psychic Life of Power: Theories in Subjection.* Stanford: Stanford UP, 1997.

Collins, Patricia Hill. *Black Feminist Thought: Knowledge, Consciousness, and the Politics of Empowerment.* 1st ed. New York: Routledge, 1990.

———. *Black Feminist Thought: Knowledge, Consciousness, and the Politics of Empowerment.* 2d ed. New York: Routledge, 2000.

Crenshaw, Kimberlé. "Mapping the Margins: Intersectionality, Identity Politics, and Violence against Women of Color." *Stanford Law Review* 43 (July 1991): 1262–65.

Crutchfield, Susan. "Film Studies and Disability Studies." *Disability Studies Quarterly* 17.4 (1997): 284–287.

Darke, Paul. "Understanding Cinematic Representations of Disability." *The Disability Studies Reader: Social Science Perspectives.* Ed. Tom Shakespeare. London: Kissell, 1998. 181–197.

Davis, Lennard. *Enforcing Normalcy: Disability, Deafness, and the Body.* London: Verso, 1995.

Grosz, Elizabeth. "Bodies and Knowledges: Feminism and the Crisis of Reason." *Feminist Epistemologies.* Ed. Linda Alcoff and Elizabeth Potter. New York: Routledge, 1993. 187–216.

Herndl, Diane Price. *Invalid Women: Figuring Feminine Illness in American Fiction and Culture, 1840–1940.* Chapel Hill: U of North Carolina P, 1993.

hooks, bell. "Talking Back." *Talking Back: Thinking Feminist, Thinking Black.* Boston: South End P, 1989. 5–9.

Kaplan, Caren. *Questions of Travel: Postmodern Discourses of Displacement.* Durham: Duke UP, 1996.

Klobas, Laurie E. *Disability Drama in Television and Film.* Jefferson, N.C.: McFarland, 1988.

Martin, Biddy. *Femininity Played Straight: The Significance of Being Lesbian.* New York: Routledge, 1996.

Mitchell, David T., and Sharon L. Snyder, eds. *The Body and Physical Difference: Discourses of Disability.* Ann Arbor: U of Michigan P, 1997.

Morris, Jenny. "A Feminist Perspective." *Framed: Interrogating Disability in the Media.* Ed. Ann Pointon and Chris Davies. London: British Film Institute, 1997. 21–30.

Morrison, Toni. *Playing in the Dark: Whiteness and the Literary Imagination.* New York: Vintage, 1992.

Norden, Martin F. *The Cinema of Isolation: A History of Physical Disability in the Movies.* New Brunswick: Rutgers UP, 1994.

O'Connell, Sean P. "Claiming One's Identity: A Constructivist/Narrativist Approach." *Perspectives on Embodiment: The Intersections of Nature and Culture.* Ed. Gail Weiss and Honi F. Haber. New York: Routledge, 1999. 61–78.

Pevere, Geoff. "No Place Like Home: The Films of Atom Egoyan." *Exotica: The Screenplay by Atom Egoyan.* Ed. Atom Egoyan. Toronto: Coach House Press, 1995.

Safran, Stephen, P. "The First Century of Disability Portrayal in Film: An Analysis of the Literature." *Journal of Special Education* 31.4 (1998): 467–479.

Sandoval, Chela. *Methodology of the Oppressed.* Minneapolis: U of Minnesota P, 2000.

Schuchman, John S. "Deafness and the Film Entertainment Industry." *Framed: Interrogating Disability in the Media.* Ed. Ann Pointon and Chris Davies. London: British Film Institute, 1997. 43–48.

Scott, Joan W. "The Evidence of Experience." *The Lesbian and Gay Studies Reader.* Ed. Henry Abelove, Michele Aina Barale, and David M. Halperin. New York: Routledge, 1993. 397–415.

Spivak, Gayatri Chakrovorty. *Outside in the Teaching Machine.* New York: Routledge, 1993.

Sumner, Jane. "The Sweet Hereafter: Tragic Tale is Beautifully Told." *Dallas Morning News* 24 Dec. 1997: 1C.

Sutherland, Allan. "Black Hats and Twisted Bodies." *Framed: Interrogating Disability in the Media.* Ed. Ann Pointon and Chris Davies. London: British Film Institute, 1997. 16–20.

The Sweet Hereafter. Dir. Atom Egoyan. Ego Film Arts and the Canadian Film Development Corporation, 1997.

Thomson, Rosemarie Garland. *Extraordinary Bodies: Figuring Physical Disability in American Culture and Literature.* New York: Columbia UP, 1997.

Trinh, Minh-ha T. *When the Moon Waxes Red: Representation Gender and Cultural Politics.* New York: Routledge, 1991.

Weiss, Gail. *Body Images: Embodiment as Intercorporeality.* New York: Routledge, 1999.

Vivian M. May, *Ph.D., is assistant professor of women's studies at William Paterson University. She is coeditor, with Beth A. Ferri and Barbara McCaskill, of a forthcoming special issue of* Womanist Theory and Research *titled* Black Feminist Theorizing across the Disciplines; *she has contributed articles to* NWSA Journal *and* Callaloo; *and she is currently working on a book tentatively titled* Lessons for Liberation: Contemporary Literature and Social Change. **Beth A. Ferri,** *Ph.D., is assistant professor of education at Teachers College, Columbia University, in the Department of Curriculum and Teaching. Her publications include articles in* Women's Studies International Forum *and* Disability Studies Quarterly.

Copyright © 2002 by Vivian M. May and Beth A. Ferri

Films by Tracey Moffatt
Reclaiming First Australians' Rights, Celebrating Women's Rites

Cynthia Baron

Although Tracey Moffatt's name is not likely be found on the marquee of your local multiplex, the Australian Aboriginal photographer, video artist, and filmmaker is, in the contemporary art world, "one of the most popular artists of the moment" (Versloot 1). Seen today as "Australia's hottest artist internationally," Tracey Moffatt first received wide recognition in 1989. During that year, the Australian Centre for Photography exhibited her photographic series *Something More* in a one-person show that toured galleries across Australia. That same year, her experimental narrative film *Night Cries: A Rural Tragedy* was selected for official competition at the 1990 Cannes Film Festival. The film received a Golden Palm nomination for Best Short Film. Since 1989, art galleries throughout the world have been a primary exhibition venue for Moffatt's films and videos. Representative of recent exhibitions of her work, the *New Works by Tracey Moffatt* exhibition at San Francisco's Yerba Buena Center from 5 August to 22 October 2000 featured two of her films and two videos that she co-directed along with her 1998 series of hand-tinted photogravures titled *Laudanum*, the *Invocations* series of silkscreens she created in 2000, and a documentary that provides an overview of Moffatt's career.[1]

Moffatt's imaginative work as a director of photonarratives in a range of art forms has prompted film scholars and art historians to discuss the boundary-crossing power of Moffatt's authorial vision. Feminist film scholar Patricia Mellencamp has argued that filmmakers such as Tracey Moffatt "use the affective quality of photography—of composition and the close-up—to make intellectual arguments" ("Empirical Avant-Garde" 179). Writing about an exhibition of Moffatt's work last year at the Roslyn Oxley Gallery in Sydney, an *Artspace* critic explained that the strength of her work results from the fact that "with Moffatt, there's always a conversation between photography and cinematography" ("2000 Shows" 1). That interaction means, in part, that Moffatt is a directorial photographer who sets "up her

Tracey Moffatt portrays one of the characters haunted by a ghost train in "Choo Choo Choo Choo," the second of three stories in her 1993 feature film *Bedevil*.

Photo courtesy of *Women Make Movies*

shots like a filmmaker: storyboarding them, constructing sets, casting and directing characters" (1).

The interaction also means that in Moffatt's films, the mise-en-scène elements, sound-image combinations, and sequence-to-sequence relationships are so dense with meaning that they invite, require, and reward the kind of contemplation often reserved for one's leisurely or studied encounters with art gallery exhibitions. In the discussion that follows, I take time to look more closely at three films by Moffatt, *Nice Coloured Girls* (1987), *Night Cries: A Rural Tragedy* (1989), and *Bedevil* (1993). Taking into account the films' production and reception contexts, I will discuss selected elements of the films as instances in which Moffatt gives vivid expression to First Australians' vital place in contemporary Australian culture, and to aesthetic strategies often found in women's art.

Reclaiming First Australians' Rights

These three films by Moffatt provide the basis for a coherent and potentially illuminating study in part because they represent important developmental moments in her career. They also represent instances in which Tracey Moffatt and other artists have contributed to Aboriginal politics and Australian film culture in ways that have reshaped the country's cultural identity and national cinema.[2] Moreover, the three films provide glimpses of a movement within her country to create a more egalitarian society that has, for more than a century, depended on women's participation in the public sphere.[3]

Moffatt's film *Nice Coloured Girls* has overlapping significance because she produced this first film during the time she was involved in the production of a film commissioned by the Australian Bicentennial Authority to celebrate "the diversity of women's contributions to Australian life over the past two hundred years" (French 4). Given that convergence, local audiences saw *Nice Coloured Girls* as a new mode of artistic expression for Moffatt and as another contribution by Moffatt as an activist in Aboriginal politics (see French 4). The Golden Palm nomination given to Moffatt's second film, released the same year in which her photography was given national recognition, represents the moment that Australian Aboriginal artist Tracey Moffatt joined the elite rank of internationally recognized women filmmakers, for the nomination positioned Moffatt alongside Jane Campion, the New Zealand filmmaker whose first international recognition came with the Golden Palm nomination given to her experimental narrative *Peel* (1982). The multidimensional significance of Moffatt's third film, released just months after the Australian High Court recognized Aboriginal and Islander claims to land ownership, and nominated for a Golden Palm Award in the feature film category, comes from the fact that *Bedevil* is "the second feature film to be directed by an indigenous Australian[,] ... the first to be released commercially" (Haslem 322), and the first and only feature film to be directed by an Australian Aboriginal woman.

Australian film scholar Tom O'Regan explains that for his country's postnational multicultural project, "there is no more important figure than Aboriginal and Islander Tracey Moffatt[, whose work] incorporates difference in a national space [in which] Aboriginal and non-Aboriginal subjects negotiate the meaning and future of this space" (326). Her work invites audiences, especially those cognizant of the Fourth World struggles of indigenous peoples across the globe, to see the films as participating in the movement created by the poetry, novels, and dramatic productions of First Australians whose work (in English) since 1929 and increasingly from the 1960s to the present "belongs largely to the realm of symbolic politics" (Shoemaker 275). Artwork created by Aboriginal Australians such as Moffatt has contributed to establishing the more diverse national identity reflected by landmark decisions such as the government's declaration of a National Agenda for a Multicultural Australia in 1989 and the 1992 Mabo decision, in which "the Australian High Court overturned the doctrine of *terra nullius* to [ostensibly] recognize prior Aboriginal and Islander ownership" (O'Regan 20).[4]

It is possible to see at least three ways in which Moffatt's films articulate Aboriginal Australians' right to full and equal participation in contemporary postcolonial Australian. The films continually reassess the history of encounters between black and white Australians, giving special attention to the legacy of Australian policies of protection and assimilation.[5] They also consistently raise the issue of land rights in more and less overt ways. Moreover, Moffatt's films invariably and brilliantly challenge "previous styles of representation of Aborigines in film[, especially] the realist documentary mode usually reserved for the 'ethnographic subject'" (Rutherford 155, 148).

All of Moffatt's films explore connections between the past and the present to reassess the history of dispossession that began with the arrival of British convicts in 1788 and the British Empire's claim to the continent in 1829. The films look at public and personal histories to analyze the legacy of British expansion, which became increasingly genocidal as the white population doubled during the gold rush of the 1850s and 1860s, and increasingly exclusionary when the Eurocentric nation was formed by the declaration of the Australian Commonwealth in 1901. Moffatt reinterprets conventional views of Australia's past in *Nice Coloured Girls,* as, for example, she interweaves the story of three shrewd Aboriginal girls in present-day Sydney with a recurring, static image of a nineteenth-century European print of the Australian landscape and a voice-over of excerpts from the diary of a British explorer, which, over the course of the film, sounds more and more naive. In *Night Cries: A Rural Tragedy,* Moffatt connects past and present, public and personal, by using a repeated clip of Aboriginal singer Jimmy Little, who was a crossover success in the 1960s, and flashback sequences that reveal the complex relationship between a middle-aged Aboriginal woman and her now very elderly white foster mother.

Moffatt's feature film, *Bedevil,* presents a multifaceted picture of Australian history. In two of the three short stories that make up the film, Moffatt shows how social policies of past shape the personal experience of individuals in the present by intercutting faux documentary sequences from the present with flashbacks to traumatic moments in the characters' youth. In the third story, Moffatt makes that point by having events from the past become a vivid feature of the present through parents' memories. Moreover, this last short story shows how the racial polarities at the heart of Australian protection policies, implicitly designed to eliminate Aboriginal people by assimilating them into white culture, open onto other damaging polarities: the lovers have died because their union transgressed tribal boundaries; the teenager who is sympathetic to the lovers' plight is shunned by other boys because he is Greek; the last remaining inhabitant of the warehouse haunted by the lovers' ghosts is a Frida Kahlo cross-dresser who has been ostracized because he has transgressed conventional gender boundaries.

Moffatt's films also call attention to the issue of land rights, which has, from the 1966 Wave Hill Station stockmen's strike forward, become a fundamental political concern for Australian Aboriginal activists. The films take a particularly incisive look at the dimensions and consequences of white land development. For example, by making King's Cross, "the mythical center of prostitution in Sydney" (French 3), the setting for the present-day story in *Nice Coloured Girls,* Moffatt invites audiences to see that British settlement not only failed to improve the Aboriginals' land, it actually brought to Australia the squalor found in urban trading centers throughout the British Empire.

In *Night Cries: A Rural Tragedy,* Moffatt suggests a comparison between British colonial adventure and present-day tourism. The film contrasts the confinement that the middle-aged Aboriginal woman experiences in caring for her elderly white foster mother with the freedom suggested by the bright colors of the glossy travel brochures she flips through in disgust as she tends to the old woman amid the clutter in the shack that the two women inhabit. The contrast between the confinement of servitude and the freedom of tourism serves as a concrete visual metaphor for the profound distinction between colonists' and tourists' romanticized views of the Australian landscape, and First Australians' experience of subjugation and despair in seeing outsiders waste the land that had sustained Aboriginal people since 80,000 B.C..

In *Bedevil,* Moffatt repeatedly makes the point that land development has also led to the destruction of people and land. In the first story, the building of a movie theater over a haunted swamp sets up the traumatic experience that ruins the life of an Aboriginal boy. In the second story, the young Aboriginal couple are haunted by the ghost of a child who has been killed on train tracks that whites had built to cut across the bushland. In the third story, the ghosts of ill-fated lovers are threatened by modern-day entrepreneurs who want to build an ocean-side casino on the site that has been their home.

The film does not, however, present audiences with an image of First Australians as victims. With its highly stylized, theatrical images creating an allegorical and symbolic mode of address, the ghosts that inhabit the swamp, the railroad track, and the seaside warehouse in the fictional spaces of *Bedevil* seem to represent the ghosts that reside in the sacred sites throughout Australia that have been built over, cut across, and sold off by European settlers over the course of the past two hundred years. The haunting return of those ghosts begins with the opening credit sequence. Parodying the title sequence of the arch-imperialist narrative *Dr. No* (1962), Moffatt's film supplants the figures of exoticized women on display with vibrant, dancing figures who kick back and who will be given full form in the film's final story. Ghosts that resist land development can be found in the film's first story, for the Oasis Cinema, built by the clownish white workers over the haunted swamp, never opens, because it is vandalized by Rick and haunted by Mr. Chuck. In the second story, the railroad tracks integral to white expansion into the interior of Australia are never completed. In the third story, the ghosts of the young Aboriginal-Islander lovers whose deaths haunt the warehouse change the direction of future land development by scaring off the businessmen who want to build an ocean-side casino.

In addition to exploring ways in which the two-hundred-year history of dispossession has left all Australians possessed by ghosts from the nation's past, Moffatt creates films that "avoid the clichés and didacticism of earlier films" about Aboriginal Australians (Rutherford 147). Film scholar Karen Jennings explains the ways in which the portrayal of First Australians in white Australian films has been dominated by three recurring, obfuscating myths. First, by eclipsing the profound influence of social circumstance, mainstream Australian films have suggested that Australian Aboriginal characters are shaped exclusively by psychological factors. Second, films produced by and for white Australians have consistently conflated "Aboriginal culture with Nature" (Jennings 2). Third, white Australian cinema has consistently dramatized the opposition between full-blood Aborigines and half-castes that depends on the "essentialist notion of Aboriginality [and] a romantic nostalgia about a 'natural' uncontaminated past" (2).

Moffatt points out that even films by well-meaning white Australians often simply reinscribe the rigid categories of racial difference. She explains that a film such as *Fringe Dwellers* (1986), directed by Bruce Beresford and based on the 1961 novel by white author Nene Gare, who developed the story through "substantial first-hand knowledge and field work" (Shoemaker 95), is an example of what she seeks to supplant by her work. Beresford's social realist film follows the story of Trilby Comeaway, a young Aboriginal woman who resists the stifling social pressures caused by living on the fringe of white civilization. When the novel was first published, its recasting of relationships between Aboriginal and non-Aboriginal people in an urban setting signaled white Australians' belated awareness of "the changing demographic realities of the Aboriginal situation" (Shoemaker 95). Beresford's 1986 film led to Gare's novel becoming standard reading for many students in Australian secondary school. Yet precisely because of their earnest, ethnographic tone, the novel and the film reveal the limitations of non-Aboriginal people speaking for Aboriginal Australians. Articulating the response of many First Australians, Moffatt explains that for all its good intentions, *Fringe Dwellers* "is a very Hollywood version of Aboriginal life. There's an attempt to show Aboriginals as human beings with human emotions . . . but it just annoyed a lot of Aboriginal people" (Rutherford 148). By comparison, Moffatt's films give audiences anything but a Hollywood version of life. One of her films' most salient features is the disturbing vividness of lived experience that has emerged from her determination to create images that result from a conscious and direct "reaction to traditional images of Aborigines by white Australians" (Rutherford 148).[6]

Celebrating Women's Rites

Given their textual richness and complexity, the three films by Moffatt discussed here also invite audiences, especially those attuned to the strategies of women's narratives, to consider the films as contributing to a disparate but vibrant tradition of work by women artists. Several features of Moffatt's films exemplify strategies often found in artwork by individuals who, because of their gender, ethnicity, or both, have been silenced, objectified, dispossessed, and positioned as the other. Moffatt's films consistently use, for example, autobiographical details in fictional narratives that examine intersections between public and private narratives. In their explorations of the dissonance created by the disparities between official stories and lived experience, her films also often take the form of ghost stories. In addition, Moffatt frequently uses experimental elements to disrupt conventional viewing habits that have been shaped by one hundred years of cinema practice dominated by male-centered, imperialist, illusionist conventions.

It is possible to see Moffatt's films as building on local traditions established by First Australian novelists such as Mum Shirl (also known as Shirley Smith) and Ruby Langford, who are known for their autobiographical work, for Moffatt uses cinematic representation as a canvas on which to superimpose personal and Australian history. In all her films, details from her lived experience serve to qualify, complicate, or contradict official stories. For example, *Nice Coloured Girls* overturns stereotypical images of Aboriginal women as victims by contrasting the orthodox "myth of the white seducer" (French 2) with Moffatt's assertive rereading of relationships between black women and white men. The account provided by British explorer Lieutenant William Bradley that is presented in a voice-over reading of his dairies fades into the background once it is juxtaposed with a story drawn from Moffatt's teenage years about three girls who, in Moffatt's words, "pick up a 'Captain' which is an Aboriginal term for sugar daddy, have a good night and in the end roll him" (Rutherford 152). With the young black women turning the tables on the white man, who assumes that the girls are there for his pleasure, the film provides droll rather than pedantic commentary on a two-hundred-year history in which Aboriginal women "were physically and sexually exploited by the whites who were 'civilizing' them, or 'employing' them, or 'protecting' them" (Pattel-Gray 192).

As if to exorcise personal demons at the same time that she confounds simplistic conceptions of Australian history, in *Night Cries: A Rural Tragedy* Moffatt superimposes Australian social policy, her own autobiography, and the opening scenes of the 1955 film *Jedda*, by

Australian director Charles Chauvel. Chauvel's film used Australia's social policy of mandated assimilation for Aboriginal people only as a point of departure, for his film focused audience attention on the sexuality of the noble savage, who in this film rescues a half-caste girl from a white foster mother. By comparison, Moffatt makes assimilation policy the focus of her film. Moffatt's own foster care by an Irish Australian family was provided with her own family's consent. The assumptions and realities that led to that consent, however, were the same assumptions and realities that caused thousands of other Aboriginal children to be taken by force from their parents and placed in institutions and foster care as late as 1980. Using her memories of being a foster daughter as one of the layers superimposed on the film's narrative, Moffatt makes the interracial mother-daughter relationship central. With memories of her own experience serving as a palimpsest, she presents a view of Australian assimilation policies that is more dense, more poignant, and more multivalent than an official account could ever be.

Moffatt's third film discussed here, *Bedevil*, also features autobiographical elements. She notes that "in the second story, for example, I play my mother who actually lived out west in a ramshackle house like the one you see in the film" (Conomos and Caputo 28). Complicating that simple identification, the white nightgown that Moffatt's character wears establishes a link with Jedda, the eponymous character of Chauvel's film, who, like Moffatt, was sent to live with a white foster mother. Shuffling once more the autobiographical elements in *Bedevil*'s second of three stories (a location that makes it seem the most transitional or most transformative, the most embedded or most central of the stories), Moffatt designs the piece so that audiences see the happily-ever-after future of the young woman who was once bedeviled. As a grown woman, she is smart, outgoing, and completely comfortable with her past.

Moffatt's films establish connections between personal ghost stories and national nightmares. To do that, they feature a particular form of storytelling that has allowed individuals to articulate the complexity of the experiences they have endured in circumstances that have challenged and threatened them in every aspect of their lives. Cross-cultural studies have shown that women's fiction often takes the form of ghost stories. For example, Wendy Kolmar points out that supernatural stories by women "seem to be one more place where women writers and thinkers explore the doubled or multiple vision that their insider/outsider status forces upon them" (Carpenter and Kolmar 237). The supernatural is especially integral to *Nice Coloured Girls* and *Night Cries: A Rural Tragedy*.[7]

Night Cries: A Rural Tragedy begins by announcing itself as a ghost story. The distorted white outlines of the letters used in the film's title follow the conventions found in cheap horror films. The comic tone evoked by the title's graphic design quickly changes to one of horror as we hear the sound of bird cries dissolve into a child's cries, which in turn are transformed into the lonely sound of a train whistle. The cluttered shack and tin outhouse that stand isolated on the dark glossy floor of the set create an eerie, minimalist picture of a haunted house. The film has no dialogue. Instead, we hear wind blowing, a coyote howling, a whip cracking, a woman cackling, a train's whistle, a child sobbing. Sounds that should be soothing are frightening: in the flashback, waves crashing onto rocks at the shore sound like guns firing. The soothing sounds we expect to hear drop out: as the film progresses, the footage of singer Jimmy Little is accompanied by silence and radio static.

Discussing *Bedevil,* Australian film theorist Lesley Stern points out that the film "captures the allusive quality of parochial, local, familial ghost stories" (37). She explains that it circulates the kind of stories "that are passed down through generations, that are repeated and embroidered upon so that eventually they are woven into quotidian discourse and a passing reference can evoke a complex texture of ghostliness" (37). In the first short story within the film, faux interview sequences allow two characters to repeat and embroider upon a ghost story that has been in circulation since World War II. In the second story, we get details of the ghost story from townspeople, a Chinese Australian antique collector, an old alcoholic named Mickey, and the central character, older now and beyond bedevilment. In the third story, audiences learn about the ghosts of the ill-fated couple through the stories told by the mother of the young man who died mysteriously and the mother of Greek teenage boy who lives across the street from the haunted warehouse.

Moffatt uses other aesthetic principles found in work by women artists to express her vision. Moffatt explains that she belongs to the generation that has "benefited from the work of Kath Walker and so many others like her" (Rutherford 152). There are many ways that artists such as Walker contributed to the environment in which Moffatt and others like her now work. One of the most important is that the poetry of Walker (whose Aboriginal name is Oodgeroo Noonuccal), first published in 1964, provided concrete evidence that strategies central to imagistic Aboriginal oral traditions could speak to modern Australians. It is possible to see Walker's poetry serving as a model for Moffatt films, which are marked by a metaphoric richness that is embedded in their expressionistic settings; hyperbolic and memorable color designs; sometimes archly iconic character types; orchestrated levels of stylized performances; sound designs, which are haunting and gleefully parodic by turn; and narrative structures, whose logic depends concomitance rather than consequence.

In all of Moffatt's highly elliptical films, laconic surfaces invite audiences to make connections between individual, highly charged moments. Carefully orchestrated, her films contain dense structures that insure that nuances and images central to the poetic text are illustrated many times over, until the layers of expression render metaphors that are both apt and enduringly memorable. For audiences who follow the conceptual sight lines suggested by her films, Moffatt's work embodies a clever, sometimes gentle, sometimes disturbing style that features strategies that are experimental insofar as they are emblematic of Aboriginal and feminist art. Using principles integral to primitive-modern dance, music, poetry, and visual design, Moffatt has been able to speak to disparate constituencies in contemporary, multicultural Australian society.

Moffatt's use of experimental form is, in part, ideologically motivated. She explains that after going to art school, being involved in "the independent film making scene" in Australia, and working as a photographer with the Aboriginal Island Dance Theatre, she became convinced that serious issues could be treated in experimental ways (Rutherford 153). Citing the dense work of Aboriginal novelist Colin Johnson (Mudrooroo Narogin) as a precedent, Moffatt explains that straightforward documentary cannot express the complex perspective she wants to bring into the public sphere. Moreover, as she points out, "I don't believe in having to talk down to Aboriginal people. I don't want to make my films simplistic, assuming that people can't understand them unless they are simple" (Rutherford 153).

Using experimental form to reclaim First Australians' contributions to Australian society, and to celebrate women's contributions to artistic expression, Moffatt sets aside well-intentioned social realism to create films that are visually inventive and filled with incisive humor. In *Nice Coloured Girls,* she creates a mischievous response to British colonial narratives, which have informed Australian structures of power since the eighteenth century. The film's multilayered storytelling gives center stage to the three teenage Australian Aboriginal girls who cruise Sydney's red light district. Setting aside strictures to produce only positive images of Aboriginals, Moffatt has the girls rob the drunk they've picked up, and then, entirely self-satisfied, go on their way.

Night Cries: A Rural Tragedy is a black comedy about an elderly white woman (played by Agnes Hardwick) who has no one to care for her except her adopted, now adult Aboriginal daughter, played by Aboriginal scholar Marcia Langton, author of a 1993 study on films by and about Aboriginal people that was commissioned by the Australian Film Commission. Yet the film complicates the dark humor of the old woman's situation. It gives audiences glimpses of the affection that once existed between the white mother and the Aboriginal daughter. It also shows the outward thrust of the Aboriginal woman's anger at the white woman being turned back in on itself: the film ends with the image of the caretaker lying next to her dead mother and the sound of a child sobbing. The film's conclusion makes audiences feel the conflicted sense of loss that the daughter feels when her foster mother dies. Her loss is doubly painful because the woman who dies is not her real mother and so she has lost nothing, and yet that fake mother, that false mother, that nothing, is all she has ever had. The film's diffuse exploration of Moffatt's relationship with her own white foster mother allows even outsiders to see Aboriginals' perspective on the dark history of Australia's protection policies precisely because it invites audiences to use their own childhood experiences as the basis for understanding the pain of separation and loss that Australian Aboriginal children experienced as pawns in assimilation policies.

Writing about *Night Cries: A Rural Tragedy,* Australian film scholar Peter Kemp finds that "the orchestrating touch, the boldly extreme, creative vision of its talented, justifiably acclaimed auteur [are] central to the film's disquieting epiphanies" (3). Filmed entirely on an almost empty sound stage, *Night Cries: A Rural Tragedy* generates its symbolic power by presenting audiences with a painted backdrop that features "the saturated ambers and lavender purples of Albert Namatjira's kitshily redolent watercolours with [props and set pieces that] might or might not constitute a stylised rendition of the living room interior of the 1995 Chauvel classic *[Jedda]*" (Kemp 2). The film creates its poignant and oppressive atmosphere in part by repeating a clip that shows Australian Aboriginal singer Jimmy Little performing his 1960s hit song "Royal Telephone," sometimes accompanied by his melodic voice in sync sound, other times presented as counterpoint to silence or the grating sound of radio static. As if replicating the process of dreamwork, the film also repeats sequences that show the Aboriginal woman as a child with her youthful white foster mother, both of them at the ocean's edge as huge waves break against the rocks among which they stand. Over the course of the film, the mood conveyed by these briefly glimpsed sequences becomes progressively darker and more frightening. The first time we see the girl she is carefree and playing with two other Aboriginal children. The last time we return to this scene, the little girl is being strangled by rolls of black paper that look like ropes of kelp or seaweed (or film or videotape).

In *Bedevil,* Moffatt uses an experimental, multilayered aural and visual style to give expression to postcolonial and feminist perspectives on official stories that have sustained social, political, and economic structures in Australia for the past two hundred years. The film's nonnaturalistic images, stylized performances, and elliptical narrative design bedevil conventional modes of absorption and identification. Its lush visuals, intricate music scoring, and bursts of anarchic parody open lines of communication with audiences acclimated to cultural tourism and postmodern humor. The film features a segmented, self-referential structure that consists of three distinct stories that are introduced by the titles "Mr. Chuck," "Choo Choo Choo Choo," and "Lovin' the Spin I'm In." Like Moffatt's other photonarratives, each of the stories has an independent meaning at the same time that it contributes to a larger significance. The film invites audiences to think about cinema ontologically, for each of the stories exists as a series of moving pictures, with all frames carefully composed, with all shot-to-shot relationships thoughtfully selected, with all sound-image combinations chosen to create a resonant emotional and intellectual experience.

Bedevil imaginatively explores the following questions. What has bedeviled First Australians? What has bedeviled white Australian history? What will continue to bedevil multicultural Australia? How might Australian Aboriginal artists bedevil the colonial gaze? Spinning out the nuances of the core metaphor of bedevilment, the film's three stories introduce audiences to Aboriginal and non-Aboriginal characters, all of whom are bedeviled in some way. Some characters appear to be bedeviled in the sense that they seem harassed, driven frantic, and possibly possessed by devils. For example, the young lovers in the third piece are not only driven to suicide; their ghosts harass anyone who threatens to occupy the space in which they performed their dance of death. For other characters, social circumstances have caused their lives to be bedeviled, that is, spoiled and changed for the worse. Illustrating this form of bedevilment, the first story gives painful expression to the horrors caused by Australia's policy of assimilation as it moves between documentary-like sequences of the old man who scars or tattoos himself in the asylum, and expressionist sequences that forcefully convey the abuse and isolation that marked his childhood. As suggested by the sometimes zombielike young husband and wife in the second story, other characters are bedeviled in that they are confused and bewildered by the nightmarish circumstances in which they find themselves. Several of the non-Aboriginal characters are bedeviled in yet another way. The well-meaning woman who narrates part of the troubled boy's story in "Mr. Chuck" is bedeviled insofar as she is impervious to and bewildered by the consequences of her ostensibly kind behavior.

Bedevil perhaps presents Moffatt's clearest statement about the fact that Aboriginal people have been bedeviled by whites. Moffatt's story "Mr. Chuck" links Rick's destructive behavior as a boy and his mental instability as an old man (played by Kenneth Avery and Jack Charles respectively) to the meager handouts he received from the protective white woman (played by Diana Davidson) whose faux interview also serves to tell Rick's story. The film establishes a clear connection between Rick's bedevilment as an old man and the beatings he received as a boy from the angry uncle he was forced to live with as a foster child. The film conveys the horrible, haunting power of that uncle by never clearly picturing him. We see only his shadow; we hear only the garbled sounds of his terrifying voice. By making the protective white woman and the angry uncle key figures in Rick's story, Moffatt makes it clear that Rick's troubled life is representative of the effect of Australia's protection and assimilation policies. Framing her presentation in highly personal and aesthetically imaginative terms, Moffatt is able to dramatize a point made by dry academic studies, namely, that throughout the twentieth century in the name of protection and assimilation, Australian Aboriginal children were "deprived of the influence of their parents and of the opportunity to care for their siblings and peers. Physical and sexual abuse occurred in many of the institutions, and, thus, patterns of violence between and toward children were introduced into the parenting behavior of the next generation of aboriginal peoples" (Armitage 208).

The "Mr. Chuck" story also gives audiences a condensed look at the haunting effect that white commercial cinema has had on Australian Aboriginal children. The film illustrates selected encounters between Rick, the quiet, serious-minded Aboriginal boy, and the ironically named Oasis Cinema, a movie theater built over a swamp that is haunted by the ghost of an American service man known as Mr. Chuck. Rick steals candy from the theater as soon as its construction has been completed by a crew of white carpenters whose comically squeaky-clean 1950s costumes and highly stylized, carefully choreographed buffoonish performances make them appear to be not simply stereotypes but in fact nonhuman cartoon figures. Alone in the Oasis Cinema one night, Rick strikes out in frustration at his hopeless situation as a black boy in a white world by vandalizing the theater. He rips through the canvas of the deck-chair theater seats, beginning in an absentminded way, then more aggressively, until he has torn through every seat in the theater. In spite of his aggressive act, the toxic power of the cinema overpowers him. The story ends with a scene of Rick in the empty theater again late one night. He falls, and with his legs caught in a hole in the theater floor, he suffers the horrifying experience of having the ghost hold him tight by the legs as it licks his feet.

Moffatt's highly elliptical story suggests that for boys like Rick, the tantalizing world of white commercial cinema is one of the many ghosts that haunt the lives of Australian Aboriginal children. Rarely if ever even pictured in the onslaught of alluring images, Aboriginal children bear the brunt of social changes brought on by the increased domination of white commercial culture. In Moffatt's dense photonarrative, the threat of losing one's identity in the sweep of white cinematic images might be a metaphor for the threat that Australian social policies of assimilation represent for Aboriginal Australians. As linked or distinct threats, their effect is made plain by the interview scenes with Rick as an old man, confined to an institution built to house those people who cannot break free of the ghosts brought to their shores by white society.

Moffatt does not leave audiences with an image of First Australians as victims. Her next two stories suggest that, while Aboriginal people have been consistently harassed by whites, made frantic by whites, and bedeviled by whites, they have found ways to transcend and transform their encounters. In the second narrative, the story's central character, Ruby Morphet (played by Tracey Moffatt), is haunted by the ghost of a blind white girl. When she matures, however, that bedevilment becomes nothing more than material for a good ghost story, a transition that marks another step forward in the long journey to celebrating herself. In the faux documentary scenes that show Ruby as a grown woman (played by Auriel Andrews), it is clear that she enjoys life and has a great sense of humor.

In contrast to the muteness that marks Ruby as a young woman, the older Ruby knows how to communicate with an audience. She has composure and presence and is quite a talker. Throughout the present-day sequences, Auriel Andrews directly addresses the camera. To provide wry commentary on the filmmaking process and to show that the older Ruby is a woman who is always in charge, a passing moment in one scene includes an instance in which Andrews walks up to the camera, wipes dust off the glass filter in front of the lens, and shakes her head to show minor disgust that she has to take care of everything, all this without missing a beat in her monologue.

This direct address moment is part of a scene that is one of the most clever and succinct passages in feminist, postcolonial cinema. In the scene, Ruby and her women friends prepare a gourmet meal as part of their trip back to the place where Ruby had lived when she was bedeviled by the ghost of the blind white girl. The scene parodies highbrow cooking shows on television by juxtaposing incongruent elements. For example, the polished silver and heavy white porcelain plates rest on a table, draped in a white tablecloth, that stands, not in the middle of a modern television studio, but instead outdoors, amid debris left behind in the deserted settlement.

Moreover, the scene establishes connections between Julia Child and the scene's expert chef, a gray-haired woman who only speaks what seems to be Koori. Serving as the cook's interpreter, Ruby explains away the bottles of wine lined up on the table by saying that the woman is especially fond of using wine in her cooking. Moffatt gives that connection a wry twist, for when two women friends poking through the bush nearby gleefully announce that they have captured a snake, Ruby gives us the recipe for the snake dish that the cook will prepare in a tureen once they return home. To cap the joke on conventional distinctions between civilized and uncivilized people, the scene ends with the ostensibly more civilized Ruby huddled off to the side, tearing into a crayfish she holds in her hands, then pouting after the "Queen Victoria of bush cuisine" berates Ruby for pouring the hollandaise sauce over the crayfish improperly.

Building on the middle story about Aboriginal characters who transcend and come to terms with their haunting encounters with white society, the third segment moves even further away from the image of Australian Aboriginal people as helpless victims, for here we get a story about non-Aboriginal characters bedeviled by the ghosts of two Aboriginal lovers. The ghosts are very selective in using their powerful magic. They never threaten the family members who pay a last visit to the warehouse. The ghosts do not disturb the Greek family that lives across the street from the warehouse. But they do use their power to scare off the foreign (Greek and Asian) land developers who want to build a casino on the now valuable waterfront property. The warehouse that was once the place where the lovers' bedevilment was tragically acted out now becomes the place where their ghosts are able to change the direction of offshore-directed land developments. After a few moments in the swirling fog that fills the warehouse, the two businessmen run for their lives. They jump back into their car, but even here they are under the ghosts' spell. The film ends with a bird's-eye view of their car spinning around and around on a spot in the pavement painted with a huge right-turn arrow, which perhaps suggests that they turn back or make a right turn, or at least recognize that they are bedeviled by expansionist visions.[8]

Given their conceptual density and artistic complexity, all three of Moffatt's films discussed here participate in the contest for power that shapes Australian discourse. Cleverly postmodern and constructed of self-reflexive elements that frustrate "illusionistic viewing strategies and gendered pleasures embedded in the dominant cinema" (Jacobs xxii), Moffatt's films use cinema in ways that are a refreshing departure from the discursive practices in which gendered and racialized polarities of self and other have been used to sustain privilege. Her films represent occasions when those threadbare polarities are reframed so that audiences are given an Aboriginal woman's view of Australia's internecine history and fraught national identity. Using playful allusions and vivid imagery to secure the clarity of their metaphors, Tracey Moffatt's films seem to supersede "current theory, including feminist film theory, by fashioning new models of history, politics, and subjectivity for transnational women of color and white women" (Mellencamp, "Empirical Avant-Garde" 176). Her films most certainly signify occasions for celebrating women's aesthetics and postnational, multicultural identity.

TRACEY MOFFATT FILMOGRAPHY, PHOTOGRAPHIC EXHIBITIONS, AND PUBLICATIONS

Filmography

Guniwaya Ngigu. Documentary. 64 minutes. (Assistant editor/production manager). 1983.
The Rainbow Serpent. Television documentary. (Still photographer). 1985.
Nice Coloured Girls. Experimental film. 16 mins. 1987.
Spread the Word. Documentary video. 9 mins. 1987.
Watch Out. Experimental/documentary dance video. 5 mins. 1987.
A Change of Face. Television documentary. 1988.
Moodeitj Yorgas/Solid Women. Documentary video. 22 mins. 1988.
It's Up to You. Documentary video. 9 mins. 1989.
Night Cries: A Rural Tragedy. Experimental film. 17 mins. 1989.
Bedevil. Feature film. 90 mins. 1993.
The Messenger. Music video for INXS. 1993.
Let My Children Be. Music video for Ruby Hunter. 1994.
My Island Home. Music video for Christine Anu. 1995.
Heaven. Co-director Matt Jacobson. Experimental video. 28 mins. 1997.

Artist. Co-director Gary Hillberg. Experimental video. 10 mins. 1999.
Lip. Co-director Gary Hillberg. Experimental video. 10 mins. 1999.

Selected Photographic Exhibitions: Group Shows

Pictures of Cities. Artspace, Sydney, 1984.
Aboriginal and Islander Photographs. Aboriginal Artists Gallery, Sydney, 1986.
Art and Aboriginality. Aspex Gallery, Portsmouth, England, 1987.
Shades of Light. National Gallery of Australia, Canberra, 1988.
Satellite Cultures. New Museum of Contemporary Art, New York, 1990.
From the Empire's End. Circulo de Bellas Artes, Madrid, 1991.
The Boundary Rider. Ninth Biennial of Sydney, Sydney, 1993.
Prospect 96. Shirn Kunstalle, Frankfurt am Main, 1996.

Selected Photographic Exhibitions: One-Person Shows

Something More. Australian Centre for Photography, Sydney, 1989.
Pet Thang. Mori Gallery, Sydney, 1992.
Scarred for Life. Karyn Lovegrove Gallery, Melbourne, 1994.
Guapa (Good-Looking). Mori Gallery, Sydney, 1995.
Free-Falling. Dia Center for the Arts, New York, 1997.
Invocations. Roslyn Oxley Gallery, Sydney, 2000.
New Works by Tracey Moffatt. Yerba Buena Center, San Francisco, 2000.
Tracey Moffatt. Museum of Photography, University of California at Riverside, 2001.
Tracey Moffatt. University of North Texas Art Gallery, 2001.
Tracey Moffatt. Conner Contemporary Art Gallery, Washington, D.C., 2001.

Published Collections of Photography

Fever Pitch. Sydney: Piper Press, 1996.
Tracey Moffatt. Berlin: Hatje Cantz, 1998.
Laudanum: Photographs by Tracey Moffatt. Berlin: Hatje Cantz, 1999.

NOTES
1. Representative instances of critical commentary on Moffatt's place in the art world can be found in "2000 Shows: Tracey Moffatt" at the Web site of Artspace, the Auckland, New Zealand, contemporary art center; James; and Haslem. In the documentary *Up in the Sky: Tracey Moffatt in New York* (1999), media artist Jane Cole articulates Moffatt's important role in Australia's postcolonial avant-garde. Looking at a collection of Moffatt's work, Cole surveys Moffatt's dazzling reinterpretations of sources rang-

ing from Victorian photography to the Australian Mad Max films, starring Mel Gibson, to the controversial work of Italian novelist-filmmaker-theorist Pier Paolo Pasolini. The connections made by people writing about Moffatt depend of course on their critical perspective. In her analysis of Moffatt's films as examples of "empirical feminism," feminist film scholar Patricia Mellencamp proposes that in Moffatt's work it is possible to see "an emerging aesthetic that can stage national, political debates within the everyday lives of women; invoke emotional and spiritual values that illuminate cultural differences; and unite rather than divide through differences" (*A Fine Romance* 277). Fine-art critics sometimes compare Moffatt with American photographer Cindy Sherman because she occasionally casts herself as an actor in her own film, video, and photographic narratives. For example, as part of Moffatt's 1997 exhibition at the Dia Center for the Arts in New York, a billboard on West Twenty-second Street between Tenth and Eleventh Avenues featured the image of Moffatt as a combat photographer, dressed in fatigues, with scores of cameras hanging from her neck, surrounded by marshland reeds. Australian cultural studies scholars find that Moffatt's video productions have contributed to her stature as an artist working in several forms, noting, for example, that Moffatt made her first videos as an Aboriginal activist. In *Spread the Word* (1987), an AIDS-awareness piece commissioned by the Aboriginal Medical Service, Moffatt used Aboriginal humor "to get the message across, little 'in' jokes and Aboriginal English" rather than a standard health video format (Rutherford 154). In *Watch Out* (1987), a short that won the *Frames* Best New Australian Video Award, Moffatt used a "dance sequence intercut with family photographs of the girl who choreographed the piece" rather than documentary form to illustrate a story in the history of Australian women (Rutherford 153). In the past few years Tracey Moffatt has produced a collection of inventive pieces. In *Heaven,* a 1997 video co-directed with Matt Jacobson, Moffatt presents audiences with an irreverent look at the power of the female gaze in a playful and sometimes frightening narrative that centers on a collection of brawny Australian surfers who preen for, turn from, and flirt with the filmmaker as they change in and out of bathing and wetsuits. In *Artist,* co-directed with Gary Hillberg in 1999, Moffatt uses clips, graphic design, and musical commentary to present a send-up of Hollywood's depiction of "the artist." In another video co-directed with Gary Hillberg in 1999 titled *Lip,* Moffatt creates a collage that reexamines moments in Hollywood films when black women cast as maids have found ways to express the depth, humor, and intelligence of their characters.

2. Since the founding of the Australian Commonwealth 1901, the country's mainstream film practice has been markedly Eurocentric and male-centered. Australian cinema began in 1896 with a travelogue piece shot by a visiting cameraman who was employed by the French company owned by Louis and August Lumiere. Not surprisingly, the "earliest extant footage

shot in Australia is of a horse race, the 1896 Melbourne Cup—a national sporting and cultural event of such significance [for transplanted Europeans] that it has been recorded on film or videotape every year since" (Rattigan 4). Since that beginning, Australian cinema has featured a collection of manly films, among them the ultraviolent, apocalyptic adventure trilogy directed by Dr. George Miller, *Mad Max* (1979), *The Road Warrior* (1981), and *Mad Max Beyond Thunderdome* (1985); the western/adventure films *The Man From Snowy River* (George Miller, 1981) and *The Man From Snowy River II* (Geoff Burrowes, 1988), based on Banjo Paterson's immensely popular poem first published in 1895; and the international blockbuster hits *Crocodile Dundee* (Peter Faiman, 1986) and *Crocodile Dundee II* (John Cornell, 1988), which polished and enhanced the television personality that Paul Hogan had developed during his long tenure (1973–84) on the weekly comedy-variety program *The Paul Hogan Show*, Australia's counterpart to England's *The Benny Hill Show*.

For many domestic and international audiences, the exploits of Australian warriors, cowboys, and bushmen are an extension of the country's historical films, which establish an Australian national identity defined by its history as a member of the British Empire. In Australian historical films, national coming-of-age narratives identify the country's history with international military conflicts in which Australian men descended from British colonists prove their mettle. That Anglo-Celtic vision of Australian history and national identity is embodied in films such as *Breaker Morant* (Bruce Beresford, 1980), which explores the court-martial of three soldiers to portray Australian men's valiant but thankless participation in Britain's imperial army in the Boer/South African War (1899–1902); and *Gallipoli* (Peter Weir, 1981), which memorializes the Australian soldiers who joined the Allied forces in World War I and died in the catastrophic Allied defeat during the Gallipoli campaign of 1915–16.

A review of the country's cinema reveals that while tough-guy narratives have been Australia's biggest box-office successes, "some of Australia's highest profile directors are women [and] some of its most popular and famous films have been women-centered: *Picnic at Hanging Rock, Caddie, My Brilliant Career, The Piano, Muriel's Wedding*" (O'Regan 36). Citing the influence of the "unusually significant though still minor presence of women directors and producers in Australian film," film scholar Tom O'Regan notes that the continuing production of films such as *The Last Days of Chez Nous* (directed by Gillian Armstrong, screenplay by Helen Garner, 1992) and *The Piano* (written and directed by New Zealander Jane Campion, 1993) sometimes leads the "public and critics alike [to see women-centered film narratives] as representative of Australian cinema" (172). O'Regan also explains that the "special training, access and equity provisions and sometimes funding programmes [that became available beginning in the 1970s] to women, people of [a non-English speaking] background, Aborigines, the disadvantaged, and people in regional areas

... provide one of the reasons why Australia produces many more women directors and producers than do other comparable countries" (177). Thus, following their support for such directors as Gillian Armstrong and Jane Campion, the Australian Film Finance Corporation sponsored Moffatt's feature film, *Bedevil,* even though the film's commercial prospects were limited. As a feature to be directed by a woman whose short film had been nominated for a Golden Palm Award, as a film to be directed by a woman whose avant-garde photography had secured national recognition, *and* as the first feature to be directed by an Australian Aboriginal woman, *Bedevil* held the kind of "significant cultural capital" that would enhance the prestige of Australian national cinema (O'Regan 14).

Prior to Moffatt's films, Aboriginals and especially Aboriginal men had served only as authentic accessories in the adventures of Anglo-Celtic Australians, such as Mick Dundee, or as frightening apparitions in the spiritual journeys of white Australians, in films such as *The Last Wave* (Peter Weir, 1977) and *Dead Heart* (Nick Parsons, 1996). At the same time, there had been a tradition of Aboriginal-centered narratives even in English that reached back to David Unaipon's 1929 monograph *Native Legends* and the widely respected novel *Coonardoo* by white author Katharine Prichard that was also published in 1929. The state funding for Moffatt's work represents an interesting development in Australian national identity because for two hundred years, fiction produced by white Australians has disclosed the presence of "an Aboriginal subject that cut[s] right into the centre of their doubts, fears, hopes, traumas [with white-black relations in Australia existing as] a penetration so massively reflected upon that their fictions became narrative battlegrounds in which conscience fought itself into a kind of consciousness" (Healy xv).

3. A dissident tradition of Australian women artists can be traced back to the novels of Miles Franklin (*My Brilliant Career,* 1901), and the poetry and short stories of Barbara Baynton (*Bush Studies,* 1902). One of the closest aesthetic corollaries to the visceral quality of Moffatt's cinematic ghost stories is to be found in Baynton's short story "The Chosen Vessel." Jane Campion's short films, *Peel* (1982), *Passionless Moments* (1983), and *A Girl's Own Story* (1984) represent other cultural contributions that, because of their shared density and symbolic power, connect to Moffatt's films. Moffatt, who explains that the New Australian Cinema movement in the 1970s sparked her interest in making art, notes that it was "very inspirational [to see] people like Gillian Armstrong, a woman, directing" (Conomos and Caputo 32). Antecedents to Moffatt's women-centered narratives can be found in such films as Gillian Armstrong's *My Brilliant Career* (1979), *Starstruck* (1982), and *Hightide* (1988), and Jane Campion's *2 Friends* (1986), *Sweetie* (1989), and *An Angel at My Table* (1990).

Moffatt sees herself working in a global tradition of women artists, a tradition she has been exploring by reading one biography after another, "usually of a woman artist" (Moffatt 2). Writing in 1997 about the biographies she had studied, Moffatt explains that "in 1984 it would have been Zora Neale Hurston, in 1985 Diane Arbus, in 1986 Frida Kahlo, in 1987 Anais Nin, in 1988 Pauline Kael, in 1989 Carson McCullers, in 1992 Maya Deren, in 1993 Anne Sexton, in 1994 Georgia O'Keefe, in 1995 Leni Riefenstahl, and lately it has been turn-of-the-century Californian pictorialist photographer Anne Brigman" (2). Given Australia's two-hundred-year history of white oppression, some observers might not believe that an Aboriginal artist would draw on cross-cultural points of contact. As Anne Pattel-Gray points out, "Aboriginal women's experience of white women during [the first part of the twentieth century especially] was classified as part of the white oppressor system, and often the women were more ruthless than the men" (173). To imagine connections between the work of Aboriginal and non-Aboriginal women is to recognize but look beyond the profound division that has resulted from the fact that Anglo-Celtic women have often been the most direct agents of white privilege in the institutions and domestic labor settings in which Aboriginal women have been victimized. Second, imagining cross-cultural points of contact between the work of Australian women artists involves rejecting conceptions that have developed because whites have viewed Aboriginal culture through and in terms of white patriarchal society. The inaccuracies created by using white patriarchal norms to analyze gender relations in Aboriginal culture are outlined in Brock; Gale; and Smith.

4. Given the films' reassessment of Australian history; their consistent use of humor; and their intensively theatrical visual, audio, and narrative design, Moffatt's films can be compared to many of the Aboriginal theater works that have been produced since the 1970s. For a useful introduction to these productions, see Gilbert. Selected poetry, fiction, and drama by First Australians includes work by poet Oodgeroo Noonuccal (Kath Walker), *We Are Going* (1964); poet and dramatist Kevin Gilbert, *The Cherry Pickers* (1971); poet and dramatist Jack Davis, *The Dreamers* (1973/1982); novelist Faith Bandler, *Wacvie* (1977); autobiographer Margaret Tucker, *If Everyone Cared* (1977); novelist Monica Clare, *Karobran: The Story of an Aboriginal Girl* (1978); novelist Sally Morgan, *My Place* (1987); novelist Mudrooroo Narogin (Colin Johnson), *Long Live Sandawara* (1979); novelist Archie Weller, *The Day of the Dog* (1981); autobiographer Elsie Roughsey, *An Aboriginal Mother Tells of the Old and the New* (1984); autobiographer Ida West, *Pride Against Prejudice* (1984); and autobiographer Glenyse Ward, *Wandering Girl* (1988).

5. When the New South Wales colony was established in 1788, there were more than 300,000 Aboriginal people living on the continent; by the 1930s there were 30,000. At the present time, First Australians are about 2 percent of the Australian population. Control over that small percentage of the population has, throughout the country's history, prompted extreme measures. For example, the Australian Aborigines Protection Board in New South Wales, active from 1883 and 1940, was formed to establish and maintain "a deliberate systematic effort to train, educate,

and employ Aboriginal children" that by 1911 included the power to separate children from their parents (Armitage 42–43). Most children who were removed from their homes lived in single-sex dormitories, with family visits discouraged or prohibited; some children were placed with "European families to assist with farm labour or domestic service" (43). Social scientist Andrew Armitage explains that institutional life for Aboriginal children "segregated the children from their parents, from their peers of the opposite gender, and from their younger and older siblings. The use of English was enforced, and aboriginal languages were suppressed through the extensive use of corporal punishment and various forms of humiliation" (205). Armitage reports that, during what social scientists have termed the "protection period" (1860–1920), there was a high rate of children taken from their families, but actual numbers are unavailable. During the "assimilation period" (1920–40), all half-caste children were removed from their families and the placement of Aboriginal children in dorms was extensive. In New South Wales 400 out of every 1,000 children were placed in dorms; in Queensland 600 out of every 1,000 children were removed from their families. In the "integration period" (1960 to the present), the dorms were closed, but in 1970 100 out of every 1,000 children were removed from their homes in the Northern Territory and as late as 1980, 65 out of every 1,000 Aboriginal children were taken from their homes in Queensland (see Armitage 206–7). Between 1967 and 1972, all Australian states except Queensland repealed their protection policies and power of wardship over Aboriginal children. In 1958, two years before Moffatt was born in Brisbane, Queensland, 300 to 400 Aboriginals out of every 1,000 were taken from their parents and put into institutional settings (see Armitage 20, 52). Australian public official H. C. Coombs explains that "the assimilationist objectives of white Australian policies and the deeply ingrained attitudes and patterns of behavior of Aborigines" are so fundamentally opposed that the enforced regime of assimilation has induced in many Aboriginal people "a state of mental confusion and emotional stress amounting often to psychiatric disorder: a disorder that lies at the heart of many of the issues which underlie the more immediate causes of incarceration and deaths in custody" (21–22).

6. Moffatt is, of course, not alone seeking to overturn white images of Aboriginal Australians. In the 1970s a collection of films began to look at encounters between Aboriginal and non-Aboriginal people. The films helped to change public discourse, for the political demands of First Australians "gained publicity through the Australian cinema... through commercial releases such as *Walkabout, The Chant of Jimmy Blacksmith, Backroads* (starring black activist Gary Foley), *Manganinnie*" (Suter and Stearman 8), and adaptations of autobiographies such as Elsie Coffey's *My Survival as an Aborigine* (1979). Other works that were efforts to revision images of Aboriginal Australians include: *Lousy Little Sixpence* (Alex Morgan and Gerry Bostock, 1981); *Two Laws* (Cavadin and Strachan,

1981); *Women of the Sun* (1982, miniseries); *A Change of Face* (Franco di Chiera, 1988); *Island of Lies* (Gillian Coote, 1990); *Cry for Justice* (Anne Pattel-Gray, 1991); *Maria* (Barbara Chobocky, 1991); *Special Treatment: Locking Up Aboriginal Children* (Margaret Smith, 1991); *Bigger Than Texas: The Ghosts That Never Die* (David Noakes, 1992); and *Exile and the Kingdom* (Frank Rijavek, 1994).

Films that attempted to counter racist images of Aboriginal Australians also contributed to the revival of Australian cinema in the 1970s. The most important film in this regard is British director Nicolas Roeg's visually stunning depiction of cultural encounter in *Walkabout* (1971). With its emphasis on landscape as a central character in the film, *Walkabout* helped to establish "Australian cinema as an international territory in cinema and provided directly for an Australian place" (O'Regan 58). Tom O'Regan explains that "Roeg's emphasis on the uncanny and the otherworldly, the mundane and the spiritual, and the tragic clash of Aboriginal and non-Aboriginal peoples in the Australian continent opened directly onto Weir's *The Last Wave*, Schepisi's *The Chant of Jimmy Blacksmith*, Moffatt's *Night Cries—A Rural Tragedy* (1989), the children's films *Storm Boy* (Safran 1976) and *Manganinnie* (Honey 1980), and even Barron Film's remake of *Bush Christmas* (Safran 1983)" (57–58). Moreover, Roeg's use of metaphoric logic conveyed by striking visual design has been the film's primary legacy to Australian cinema and to Tracey Moffatt. Discussing the surreal qualities of her films, Moffatt has told interviewers, "When I think of directors who have influenced me the most, I would have to say Nicolas Roeg. I saw *Walkabout* (1971) when I was thirteen and the visuals have always stuck with me. I love that movie . . . because of its open texture, the juxtaposition of images . . . and its play with time" (Conomos and Caputo 30). Given that Roeg made *Walkabout* after working for years as a cinematographer, and given his modernist concern with reimagining the moribund form and message of the novel from which his film was adapted, it is not surprising that *Walkabout* anticipates in many ways films created by Tracey Moffatt, who moved from photographic composition to film directing and has also taken it upon herself to imaginatively re-vision the formal and ideological uses of cinema.

7. Ghost stories have been an integral part of Australian women's fiction. For example, the ghost stories of W. W. (Mary Fortune), "The Ghostly White Gate" (1885) and "The Illumined Grave" (1867), use the form to work against patriarchal modes of envisioning women's place in the Australian bush. In Fortune's stories, the landscape is, like conventional bush literature, infused with female figures and imagery. The felt presence of these images, however, is not naturalized but instead remains to haunt the characters in the present. To place Moffatt's and Fortune's ghost stories in larger contexts, see Carpenter and Kolmar; and Gelder.

8. To imagine that Moffatt's films represent the harmonious culmination of continuous progress toward a social ideal in Australia is to misinterpret Australia's historical realities. Literary scholar Adam Shoemaker explains

that the final decades of the twentieth century represent "an era of frustrated ambitions for Black Australians, who saw the advances seemingly promised by the referendum of 1967[, which empowered the Commonwealth to protect Aboriginal rights when threatened by special interests in the Northern Territory and six individual states,] remain largely unfulfilled, and who witnessed a white backlash to many of those positive developments which did take place" (104). He points out that in 1971 Australian courts ruled that "the doctrine of communal native title . . . does not form, and never has formed, part of the law of any part of Australia" (109); that in 1974 the Woodward Commission ruled that Northern Territory Aboriginals "could not block mining in their traditional areas if [mining] was deemed to be in the 'national interest'" (113); that in 1982 the Northern Territory chief minister led a campaign to set a time limit on Aboriginal claims to land rights (117); and that in 1985 the states of Queensland and Tasmania "dismissed the concept of land rights outright" (118). Echoing Shoemaker's observations, postcolonial scholars Bob Hodge and Vijay Mishra explain that as Aboriginal and non-Aboriginal Australians move into the twenty-first century, "there has been no essential change in the formal legal position between the two peoples, and until a treaty is agreed, that will continue to be the case" (70). Moffatt herself underscores the fact that in some parts of Australia "nothing's changed [and Aboriginals continue to find that] you're not allowed into the pub because you're black" (Rutherford 156).

Still, scholars such as Hodge and Mishra argue that from the 1970s to the present there has been "massive and fundamental change in the relations between Aboriginal and non-Aboriginal Australians" (70). While much of the change is the result of overt political activism by both white and black Australians, additional pressure has been applied by First Australians' cultural-aesthetic activities. Shoemaker explains that in published work that articulates a "respect for traditional culture, pride in Aboriginality, and an awareness of the existence of a symbolic Aboriginal nation . . . Aboriginal writers are making a most noteworthy contribution both to their own people and to Australian society as a whole" (121). Their work on Aboriginals' past and present place in Australia has been especially pertinent to visions of Australia's national identity, for, as literary scholar Kay Schaffer points out, precisely because "the concept of national identity [is not] a fact of history to be revealed but [instead is] a social and ideological construct" (16), Aboriginal claims in the realm of discourse affect the conceptual frameworks through which all contemporary Australians approach the country's social, political, and economic policies.

REFERENCES

"2000 Shows: Tracey Moffatt." Feb. 2000. Online. Available: <http://www.artspace.org.nz/shows/00_02.htm. 19 Oct. 2001.

Armitage, Andrew. *Comparing the Policy of Aboriginal Assimilation: Australia, Canada, and New Zealand.* Vancouver: U of British Columbia P, 1995.

Brock, Peggy, ed. *Women's Rites and Sites: Aboriginal Women's Cultural Knowledge.* Sydney: Allen and Unwin, 1989.

Carpenter, Lynette, and Wendy Kolmar, eds. *Haunting the House of Fiction: Feminist Perspectives on Ghost Stories by American Women.* Knoxville: U of Tennessee P, 1991.

———. *Ghost Stories by British and American Women: A Selected and Annotated Bibliography.* New York: Garland, 1998.

Conomos, John, and Raffaele Caputo. "*Bedevil:* Tracey Moffatt." *Cinema Papers* 93 (1994): 28–32.

Coombs, H. C. *Aboriginal Autonomy: Issue and Strategies.* Melbourne: Cambridge UP, 1994.

French, Lisa. "An Analysis of *Nice Coloured Girls* (Tracey Moffatt, 1987)." *Senses of Cinema* 5 (April 2000). Online. Available:<http://www.sensesofcinema.com/contents/00/5/nice.html. 19 Oct. 2001.

Gale, Fay, ed. *We Are Bosses Ourselves: The Status and Role of Aboriginal Women Today.* Canberra: Australian Institute of Aboriginal Studies, 1983.

Gelder, Ken, ed. *The Oxford Book of Australian Ghost Stories.* Melbourne: Oxford UP, 1994.

Gilbert, Helen. *Sightlines: Race, Gender, and Nation in Contemporary Australian Theatre.* Ann Arbor: U of Michigan P, 1998.

Haslem, Wendy. "Tracey Moffatt." *The Oxford Companion to Australian Film.* Ed. Brian McFarlane, Geoff Mayer, and Ina Bertrand. South Melbourne: Oxford UP, 1999. 322.

Healy, J. J. *Literature and the Aborigine in Australia.* St. Lucia, Queensland: U of Queensland P, 1989.

Hodge, Bob, and Vijay Mishra. *Dark Side of the Dream: Australian Literature and the Postcolonial Mind.* Sydney: Allen and Unwin, 1991.

Jacobs, Katrien. "The Status of Contemporary Women Filmmakers." *Women Filmmakers and Their Films.* Ed. Amy L. Unterburger. New York: St. James Press, 1998.

James, Bruce. "Interview: Australian Artist Tracey Moffatt." *Arts Today.* Australian Broadcasting Corporation Radio. 9 January 2001. Transcript. Online. Available: <http://www.abc.net.au/rn/arts/atoday/stories/s229128.htm. 19 Oct. 2001.

Jennings, Karen. "Aboriginality and Film." *The Oxford Companion to Australian Film.* Ed. Brian McFarlane, Geoff Mayer, and Ina Bertrand. South Melbourne: Oxford UP, 1999. 1–5.

Kemp, Peter. "*Night Cries: A Rural Tragedy.*" *Senses of Cinema* Oct. 2000. <http://www.sensesofcinema.com/contents/00/10/cteq/night/html. 19 Oct. 2001.

Mellencamp, Patricia. "An Empirical Avant-Garde: Laleen Jayamanne and Tracey Moffatt." Ed. Patrice Petro. *Fugitive Images: From Photography to Video.* Bloomington: Indiana UP, 1995. 173–95.

———. *A Fine Romance: Five Ages of Film Feminism.* Philadelphia: Temple UP, 1995.

Moffatt, Tracey. "Dear Lynne: A Letter from Tracey Moffatt to Lynne Cooke, curator of Dia Center for the Arts, New York." Fall, 1997. Online. Available:

<http://www.diacenter.org/exhibs/moffatt/project/traceymoffatt.html>. 19 Oct. 2001.

Murray, Scott, ed. *Australian Cinema*. St. Leonards, New South Wales: Allen and Unwin/Australian Film Commission, 1994.

O'Regan, Tom. *Australian National Cinema*. London: Routledge, 1996.

Pattel-Gray, Anne. *The Great White Flood: Racism in Australia*. Atlanta: Scholars P, 1998.

Rattigan, Neil. *Images of Australia: 100 Films of the New Australian Cinema*. Dallas: Southern Methodist UP, 1991.

Rutherford, Anne. "Changing Images: An Interview with Tracey Moffatt." *Kunapipi* 10.1–2 (1988): 146–57.

Schaffer, Kay. *Women and the Bush: Forces of Desire in the Australian Cultural Tradition*. Melbourne: Cambridge UP, 1988.

Shoemaker, Adam. *Black Words, White Page: Aboriginal Literature, 1929–1988*. St. Lucia, Queensland: U of Queensland P, 1989.

Smith, Claire. "Negotiating Gender in Aboriginal Australia." Presentation. Five College Women's Studies Research Center, Mount Holyoke College. 12 February 2001.

Stern, Lesley. "When the Unexplained Happens: Tracey Moffatt's *Bedevil*." *Photofile* 40 (1993): 36–38.

Suter, Keith D., and Kaye Stearman. *Aboriginal Australians*. London: Minority Rights Group, 1982.

Tracey Moffatt: Free-falling. October 9, 1997–June 14, 1998. Exhibition Guide. New York: Dia Center for the Arts. Online. Available: <http://www.diacenter.org/exhibits/moffatt/moffatt>. 30 November 1999

Versloot, Anne. "Roller Queens and Narrow-Minded Machos: The World of Tracey Moffatt." *Themes: Culture*. Radio Netherlands. 2 June 2000. Transcript. Online. Available: <http://www.rnw.nl.culture/html/moffatt000602.html>. 19 Oct. 2001.

Cynthia Baron is an assistant professor in the film studies program at Bowling Green State University in Ohio. Her recent publications include "Buying John Malkovich: Queering and Consuming Millennial Masculinity" in The Velvet Light Trap, *"The Cybernetic Logic of the Lumiere Actualities" in* Quarterly Review of Film and Video, *and chapters in* Headline Hollywood: Perspectives on Scandal and American Film and Screen Acting. *She has co-edited a forthcoming volume of original essays titled* More Than a Method: Trends and Traditions in Contemporary Film Performance *(Wayne State University Press, 2002).*

Copyright © 2002 by Cynthia Baron

Political Filmmaking
Talking with Renee Tajima-Peña

Interview by M. Rosalind Sagara

Renee Tajima-Peña has become a chronicler of the American scene with her films *Who Killed Vincent Chin?* the Academy Award–nominated investigation of the beating death of a Chinese American in Detroit, and *My America . . . or Honk If You Love Buddha,* which won an award at the Sundance Film Festival. Tajima-Peña has written and lectured widely on Asian American and independent film and was the founding director of the Asian American International Video Festival and former director of Asian CineVision. This interview with her dates from July 2000 and was revised in October 2001.

What inspired you to get into filmmaking?

When I first got into filmmaking as a twenty-one-year-old, it was because I wanted to make propaganda. I was an activist in school where I was growing up. I had so much anger inside, and I just wanted to say these things, and I thought film would be a good way of doing that. I figured I could make a film, and just put all my ideas out there, and I wouldn't have to hear it! But it's like anything, once you get in to it and start maturing, after a few years, of course, I was much more interested in the gray areas, rather than the black-and-white, "I'm right, and you're wrong," aspects of filmmaking. I started getting interested in questions you can't answer, and with facts that have a thousand different interpretations. That made me interested in what other people had to say, and what the audience had to say.

Almost from the very beginning, I started traveling with my work, and presenting it to audiences big and small, and talking to them afterwards, listening to what they hated, and what they loved about the film. That's been half of what I do as a filmmaker. Also, there were very few Asian American filmmakers when I started out, and I was such a rebel, that made me want to do it even more because it wasn't done. I got into it at a time when the independent film movement that we know today was just starting to blossom. It's almost like Web production is now. It was in its pretty early stages. This was before the Sundance

Festival. It was just a lot of very energetic young people who had really strong ideals. We just wanted to make movies.

Can you talk more about coming out of the Asian American movement, so to speak, and your thoughts on how the social climate has changed?

I grew up in the 1970s, during the height of the Asian American movement, and people were very politicized by the Vietnam War, the Civil Rights movement, the Black Power movement, the Chicano movement, the Young Lords on the East Coast, the national movements around the world, the feminist movement. I remember when I got to college in the late '70s, the one film course I ever took was one semester of film production at MIT, and it was being taught by Ricky Leacock, who's a famous cinema verité documentary filmmaker. He'd already been around a while and was known for his very political documentaries. But at that time he was just filming young women—what they did when they woke up in the mornings. Putting on makeup, or whatever. And he wanted to film me, and I said sure because he was a famous documentary filmmaker. I thought it would be interesting to see how he operated. He asked me what kind of work I wanted to do, and I talked about political filmmaking. And he said, "Darling, that's passé, nobody does that anymore!" I said, "Well for us, it's just starting!" And really, in the late '70s, Asian American filmmaking really was just starting. That's when all the advocacy media organizations like Asian CineVision and Visual Communications were just a few years old, and NAATA [the National Asian American Telecommunications Association] hadn't been born by that time. So, we were in a parallel universe, I think.

Today, the conventional wisdom is that the activism of that time, and of the '60s and '70s, no longer exists in the new economy. But, I've been making a film about these young Asian American women labor organizers. They're not simply an exception, but they're part of this new generation that's becoming active. Asian Americans have been historically excluded from the American labor movement. The American Federation of Labor, one hundred years ago, was actually one of the main forces to push forth the Chinese Exclusion Act. In 1905, Samuel Gompers said, "Caucasians are not going to let their standards of living be destroyed by Negroes, Chinamen, Japs, or any others."

During the past few decades, organized labor has been on the decline. But, it's being reenergized by, particularly, immigrant workers. The women organizers I've been filming are daughters of immigrant workers. The numbers of Asian Americans active in the labor movement have just skyrocketed in the past few years. So in a way, it's kind of similar, because the '60s were a prosperous time, and right now we're in a prosperous time in the country. There's more of a comfort level, I think, for people to become active. At the same time, there's a seduction for getting on the dot-com gravy train, and making money. But a lot of people are not giving in to the seduction. They don't get a lot of press, but I think a lot of people are still out there making change.

Given that you identify yourself as an Asian American independent filmmaker, do you find you are approached to do projects that center on race, more so than gender, or class, for that matter?

I make films because something pisses me off. And racism, more than anything, has really pissed me off my entire life. Also I am attracted to particular stories, and in general they have to do with race, especially Asian Americans. For the most part, my productions are independently produced. But when I am commissioned, yes, quite often the project deals with race, because those are the kinds of films I am known for. It doesn't bother me. I remember a time when you couldn't dream of getting a documentary about Asian Americans on the air, so I don't take the opportunity for granted. However, the key factor here is choice. What matters is if I have the choice to pick the subject matter I want to deal with in films, or if I'm straitjacketed into doing only work about Asian Americans.

Can you talk more about being a woman filmmaker of color, and how that has presented itself as a challenge over the years?

Being a woman of color certainly excluded me from power and access to the industry. I graduated from Harvard in 1980. At the time there was a whole slew of [white male] Ivy League graduates surfing into Hollywood and landing big jobs and big bucks as TV writers. I wanted to get into filmmaking, too, and wrote every movie studio and every television network on the face of the planet for a nonpaid-serve-your-coffee internship. Didn't even get a call back. Who wanted a Japanese American female in their mail room? No one. It was only twenty years ago, but the degree to which we were invisible, a nonentity in the culture industry, cannot be underestimated. To be an Asian American woman was to be a nobody.

So I got my first job as a secretary to "The Mr. Bill Show," a recurring *Saturday Night Live* character made out of clay. That's about as far as I ever got in Hollywood. But then I joined the independent film movement. So being an outsider paid off in the end. Asian Americans were excluded, so we created our own institutions and our own alternatives.

How has your approach to filmmaking changed over the years?
I've tried to vary my approach. *Who Killed Vincent Chin?* was non-narrated, as is my newest project, *Labor Women*. *My America* was very heavily narrated and personalized. *Who Killed Vincent Chin?* was very journalistic. *Labor Women* is much more of an organizing-advocacy documentary. When I did *The Best Hotel in Skid Row*, it was structured as a tone poem. It didn't necessarily have any overt political themes. Mostly, I've changed lately in terms of technology, testing DV [digital video], being more hands-on. And shooting [the labor film] myself, that was a big change.

Who Killed Vincent Chin? was my first film. I wanted to balance making a social-change documentary with trying to reach as large an audience as possible. If you've read theories of Third Cinema, financing and venue have so much to do with diluting the political themes. The more money you need, the bigger audience you have to have, the more diluted the political themes have to be, since you have to reach a lowest common denominator dictated by your financing sources. Also, Asian American subject matter is so marginal to American culture. People don't really know much about Asian Americans and are not necessarily that interested either. So you have to find ways of making it interesting to them. *Who Killed Vincent Chin?* was a murder story. You've got sex and violence because it happened in a strip club. So there's the prurient underside that people were attracted to. *My America* was structured as a road movie because that's something Americans just love—being on the road—that whole pop culture element. With *Labor Women*, I said screw the mass audience, I don't care. I like these characters and what they're doing. And maybe this film will only be seen by other activists, or college students, or people who are trying to organize in their communities; maybe it'll be a smaller audience, but I really felt compelled to talk about what these young activists were doing. The whole stereotype of young people is that they're slackers, or making a million dollars in the new dot-com economy. And also of Asian Americans, either they're in Silicon Valley being technonerds, or very passive and apathetic. It's just not true. I go to colleges all around the country and people are standing up all over. I want people to know that.

Are audiences more, less, or equally receptive to the political themes you speak to in your films?

When I make a film like *My America,* or *Who Killed Vincent Chin?* a feature-length documentary, where I've got to really spend some money on it, it's financed by television and has to reach something amounting to a mass market, even if it's only a million people on PBS. And, I want to reach not necessarily an Asian audience, but a general audience. I don't want to preach to the converted all the time. But at the same time, I do make smaller projects that are more targeted, for example, this documentary on Asian American labor activists. It's probably not going to be on PBS. It's not going to be picked up by the Discovery Channel, but it's going to have a much more focused viewership and be used more as an organizing tool, which is just as important.

What are your thoughts on film being used as a teaching tool?

I think film should be used to promote discussion, because a film can't answer all questions. In fact, a film should mostly ask questions and not answer too much. One, because a film is fixed, and things change. Two, because I think anybody who depends on a filmmaker to answer too many questions is not doing their job. Filmmakers are very limited, and the filmmaking process is very limited because it's part entertainment, and to the degree that it's entertainment, it is not very factual, or very valid in a scholarly kind of sense. It really negates a lot of the scholarly credibility when you have to edit people so nobody gets bored, when you have to edit their sound bites down, or you have to shape their stories in a dramatic arc, a narrative arc, in order to make the film more interesting. All this mitigates against a drier, but more salient, scholarly analysis. I think films can help take people to places they can't go to through books, or any other way. It humanizes a subject matter. And because it's very concise and compact, and can have that power of being in thirty, or sixty, minutes, film can provoke a lot of discussion and debates.

Can you talk about how you went from making* My America, *a personal piece that addressed Asian American identity, to* Labor Women, *a film you have described as an "organizing-advocacy documentary"?

Working on *My America* took a good part of the 1990s. And toward the end of the '90s, I was really sick of the whole question of identity. It seemed to me that the Left, being so subsumed by academia, and this whole idea of cultural studies and that kind of environment, and also the arts, was really starting to get very removed from its roots in social justice and social change, and people weren't even going out to talk with people. It was just looking at media, and looking at objects, and referring to media, and referring to objects, and referring to culture, rather than actually engaging people and experiencing things. You know, talking with people. I thought identity was fun to look at and make fun of, but on the road I was meeting people like Pang Ku Yang, who was a Hmong refugee in Duluth, Minnesota. She didn't have any question about who she was. She knew exactly where she came from. She knew what her culture was; she knew what her history was. But she had very deep survival issues: feeding her family, getting off public assistance, getting a job. Her husband only worked as a farmer and soldier in Laos, and here he was in Duluth, Minnesota, in the cold, with no skills and no training. And they just had to have a life. This really made me question this whole identity search as being such a luxury for middle-class Asian Americans like myself to kind of wallow in. Also, I was meeting people like Alyssa Kang, who's a young activist, and re-meeting Yuri Kochiyama, who's an older activist. Despite the whole fashion of looking at culture, and looking at identity, they were out there organizing against racism, organizing hotel workers and garment workers, and organizing against racist immigration legislation. They were doing something, and it really inspired me. And I just wanted to get back to my own roots of making social change media.

In **Labor Women,** *you follow three Asian American labor activists through the course of their respective campaigns as they fight for social justice and workers' rights in Los Angeles. Given your background as an activist, was it difficult for you to remain objective when working on this film?*

It's a highly editorialized film. I don't go into the merits or lack of merits of the campaigns themselves. It comes down on the side of worker justice and economic justice. It's not a journalistic film. It's really more a film about Asian Pacific participation in the labor movement, which is rarely talked about. People don't even think about Asian Americans when you think about labor justice. Also, I think you're really going to know about these women in twenty or thirty years. I think that it's just the tip of the iceberg of what's going to be in terms of not only the labor movement, but also activism in the United States. So I wanted to look at these women while they were still starting out.

The three women you focus on in **Labor Women** *are young college graduates working as labor activists. What has motivated this generation of women to join the labor movement?*

I think that similar to the older veteran women activists, Quynh Nguyen, a Vietnamese immigrant who organizes meatpackers; Jun Chong, a Korean American now working with a grassroots welfare rights group located right near the corner of Florence and Normandie, the flashpoint for the Los Angeles riots; and Karla Zombro, the daughter of a Sri Lankan immigrant and a Kentucky coal-mining family, wanted to pay tribute to their parents, but also change things because of what they witnessed growing up. Their parents had come to this country and busted their asses as janitors, garment workers, messengers, doing Chinese take-out delivery, every kind of job, and they really paid the price. So these young women took their college education and turned it into ammunition, rather than turning it into a bank account. In terms of why they did it, another thing which I don't really go into in the film, is that a lot of them were really mobilized in college in Asian American Studies, in Asian American student activism. And this was true of this first generation that went to college in the 1960s. All of them said, "I took an Asian American studies course, or I took a women's studies course and it just changed my life." It opened their eyes to how society works, how the economy works, and how it works against working people. They decided to change.

Did you relate more to the younger, or veteran, activists, and why?

Both. I started out as an activist and very much related to their anger and drive to make social change. Also, I related to their connection to their families. People love this mythology of the Asian (mostly Chinese) American young woman, and the conflict with her immigrant mother and father. You know, the Asia/Bad, America/Good paradigm. I personally come from a very close-knit family that respected the good and rejected the bad of both cultures. There was no difference between how the boys or girls in my family were raised. If anything, I had more freedom than my brothers, and I was encouraged to pursue traditionally male interests. I got involved in social change with the support of, and in tribute to, my family. That was true with many of the activists I interviewed. It ain't the Joy Luck Club.

Is **Labor Women** *a "woman's film"?*

Interestingly, it was commissioned by Asian Women United, which is mostly comprised of the generation of women who came out of the

Asian American Feminist movement in the '70s and '80s. They asked me in earlier cuts to focus on the organizers and what they had to deal with in terms of being women. But Quynh, Jun, and Karla didn't really have much to say about their experience in the conventional "feminist" framework; sexism was a factor, but did not seem to be a big deal to them. It's a new day, and there are a lot of women organizers in the labor movement. Everybody knows that the labor establishment is primarily white and male, but I think for a lot of the younger women, they see these people as part of history, that they're on their way out. They're not that worried about it. They're operating in a completely different venue. And I really relate to that because this is the first time that I've made a so-called woman's film. I've always focused my work on race. That was defining for me when I was growing up, not gender. Being a little younger than that first generation, being "postfeminist," I came of age in a time when men were different. All the men I ever knew really supported me having a career, supported strong women. I grew up in an era where there was much more sexual equality, particularly for middle-class women. Also my family was very unusual. For instance, my father always encouraged me to be a lawyer, or get a Ph.D. in economics and take traditionally male types of jobs. You know that Ms. Foundation "Take Your Daughter to Work" campaign? My dad did that thirty years ago.

The young organizers I filmed may have dealt with male patriarchy from their fathers, who were raised with old-country values in Asia. But their experience here is much more complicated. They deal with race, class, sexism, and in Karla's case, homophobia. These multiple identities really color their activism. At the same time I think they also feel much more empowered than women of color twenty or thirty years ago. Each one of them was politicized in Asian American studies in college, at a time when Asian American studies was beginning to flourish. They took leadership roles as students, they have had support within the labor movement from both older men and women. It's just always been different for Asian American women, this idea of feminism. All three—Quynh, Karla, and Jun, all name a male, Kent Wong, who founded the Asian Pacific American Labor Alliance, as one of their mentors.

What challenges presented themselves in the making of **Labor Women***?*

This film was not as difficult as other films I've made. Part of the reason why I made it was that what was happening was happening close to home. I also made it while I was pregnant. You can imagine, I'm out there eight months pregnant, shooting it by myself with a DV camera, shooting these rallies, it was wild! Physically, it was hard. It was also the first time I shot my own film. I've always hired cinematographers, but it was so low budget, and I wanted to see what I could do with the new DV technology.

What are your thoughts on the current state of documentary film production? What do you feel is lacking, or exciting, in documentary right now?

I think it's really healthy in that there's a lot of production going on. You've got very commercial reality types of programming like *Survivor,* or even the network magazine shows. There's cable, HBO, National Geographic, the History Channel. All the way down to kids who are making documentaries because of the new technology. These are non-filmmakers, nonprofessionals who have access to the medium. People in communities are able to make documentaries, so that's really good.

What I think is lacking, is documentary production, for whatever reason, has become an Asian American ghetto. Even in terms of PBS documentaries, there are actually quite a few Asian Americans making them. But in terms of other groups of color, African Americans, Native Americans, and Latinos, there are very few people making documentaries. I think it's very hard to sustain a life making documentaries. I don't know why some Asian Americans have been able to do that. I know there has been a lot of support from Asian American media organizations. Also, I think a lot of Asian Americans end up in documentaries because they haven't had any access to features, for example, or episodic television. I think for Latinos and African Americans, it might be because people do have a tiny little bit more access to working with say, UPN sitcoms, or a few more features being made.

What's next?

I have a new long-term project, which is a documentary *Grapes of Wrath*–type story for the new millennium. The film will follow parallel stories of meatpackers in the Midwest: a Vietnamese refugee family and a Mexican migrant family. It's about their stories of coming to the U.S. and working in what is the most dangerous industry in America, meatpacking, for very low pay, and having to live in little, desolate, out-of-the-way towns. It's about their inner lives, their hunger to reunite with their families, and the memories of what they've left at home, which is often very rich, but very devastating, like war and poverty. It'll be a feature-length documentary shot on film.

RENEE TAJIMA-PEÑA FILMOGRAPHY

Producer

Kansas, Doi Moi. In production for PBS series *The New Americans,* by Kartemquin Films.
Labor Women. Asian Women United. 2001.
The Last Beat Movie. Sundance Channel. 1997.
My America . . . or Honk if You Love Buddha. PBS. 1997.
Declarations: All Men Are Created Equal? PBS. 1993.
The Best Hotel on Skid Row. HBO. 1990.
What the Americans Really Think of the Japanese (Americajin no Tainichikanjo no Tatamae to Honne). Fujisankei. 1990.
Yellow Tale Blues. Filmakers Library. 1990.
Monkey King Looks West. Filmakers Library. 1989.
Who Killed Vincent Chin? PBS. 1988.
Haitian Corner. ZDP television network, Germany. 1987.

Director

Kansas, Doi Moi. In production for PBS series *The New Americans.* Kartemquin Films.
Labor Women. Asian Women United. 2001.
The Last Beat Movie. Sundance Channel. 1997.
My America . . . or Honk If You Love Buddha. PBS. 1997.
"The Ballad of Demetrio Rodriguez." Segment of *Declarations: All Men Are Created Equal?* PBS. 1993.
Jennifer's in Jail. Lifetime Television. 1992.
The Best Hotel on Skid Row. HBO. 1990.
What the Americans Really Think of the Japanese (Americajin no Tainichikanjo no Tatamae to Honne. Fujisankei. 1990.
Yellow Tale Blues. Filmakers Library. 1990.
Who Killed Vincent Chin? PBS. 1988.

Writer

The Last Beat Movie. Sundance Channel. 1997.
My America . . . or Honk If You Love Buddha. PBS. 1997.
Jennifer's in Jail. Lifetime Television 1992.
The Best Hotel on Skid Row. HBO. 1990.
What the Americans Really Think of the Japanese. (Americajin no Tainichikanjo no Tatamae to Honne). Fujisankei. 1990.
Monkey King Looks West. Filmakers Library. 1989.

Participating Artist

Those Fluttering Objects of Desire. Audio/video installation conceived by Shu Lea Cheang and exhibited at the 1993 Whitney Museum of American Art Biennial Exhibition.

M. Rosalind Sagara *has received degrees from the University of California, Riverside, and the University of Iowa. She has written and lectured on Asian American film and was a founder of WAVES: An Asian/American Film Festival at the University of Iowa. She is currently producing a short documentary exploring the experience of working-class Chinese in Mexico.*

Copyright © 2002 by M. Rosalind Sagara

Remembering *Barbie Nation*
An Interview with Susan Stern

Susan Stern with Wendy Kolmar

After a twenty-year career in journalism in Boston and the San Francisco Bay Area, Susan Stern was inspired to begin work on her first film when her daughter, Nora, invented the game "Jealous Barbie." In this interview, Stern tells the story of the genesis, production, and marketing of *Barbie Nation: An Unauthorized Tour* (1998), a film that documents the American (and world) obsession with the Barbie doll and its iconic version of femininity.[1]

How did you come to make **Barbie Nation**?

I didn't think much about Barbie until my daughter, Nora, was three years old. Nora was given her first Barbie for her birthday by her four-year-old cousin, Katie, and all I remember thinking was, Isn't it a bit young?—as if this was a rite with a specific time in life, like menstruation. But, of course, it was the 1990s. Nora was in the prime contemporary Barbie demographic, much younger than in 1959 when Barbie debuted, and I, at age six, first zipped the zipper of her gold brocade gown.

So were you also thinking about your own Barbie experiences when you started on the film?

Barbie was always tactile and sexual for me. There were only two types of people in the world, I would decide later: Barbie glorifiers and Barbie defilers. And I am both of them. But I didn't think about my own past when my daughter got her first Barbie. That didn't happen until she invented the game "Jealous Barbie."

By this time, Nora had several Barbies we played with. In Jealous Barbie, Nora insisted we play that her Barbie had everything better than mine—better hair, better boyfriend, better imaginary car—and my Barbie was jealous. My Barbie was jealous for hours on end. Amused and intrigued, I gave Nora what I have come to call "Feminist Lecture #205: Women Don't Have to Be Jealous of Other Women." Nora listened to me patiently. "Okay, Mom," she finally said. "How

Director Susan Stern burns a Barbie doll on a shoot for *Barbie Nation: An Unauthorized Tour.*

Photo by Sibylla Herbrich, copyright © 1998 by El Rio Productions LLC.

about we first play Jealous Barbie—and then we can play what you want to play?" When I told this story to other people I was surprised to find out that virtually everyone—men as well as women—had a story to tell involving Barbie. And each "Barbie story," as I came to call them, revealed a facet of life between 1959 and the present. I was, at the time, an ex–newspaper reporter who had gone back to City College to learn video production. I was also writing television news for a CBS affiliate and didn't like it. I knew I had the subject for my first film.

I began to film Barbie people and events, gathered artifacts from the hidden history of Barbie, and gained the cooperation (but not control) of Mattel Inc. And Barbie creator Ruth Handler. Eventually, I filmed some of the many X-rated Barbie stories we had heard. As the film progressed, I learned more and more. I learned how Mattel was suing or threatening people who satirized Barbie. I learned how Barbies are made by Third World girls sometimes in sweatshop conditions. I saw how Barbie could be an instrument of cultural conquest, and how Barbie could be an instrument to express creativity. And though I didn't succeed in exploring all the issues I had discovered—for instance, the issue of race and beauty is missing—I tried to get as much of it in as I could.

Who did you see as the audience for the film? Who were you making the film for?

I thought I had a film with wide appeal. I knew my core audience was girls, women, and gay men—the people who had either played Barbie, refused to play Barbie, or been refused Barbies. I thought these people, like me, would be entertained by the campy, glitsy parts of the Barbie world, and also appreciate the insights into gender roles, body image, and sexuality afforded by Barbie stories and play. My research also showed me that heterosexual men had Barbie stories—usually as brothers or fathers of Barbie players. When I screened early clips of *Barbie Nation*, heterosexual men, along with women and gay men, were interested in what *Barbie Nation* revealed about sexuality, gender roles, male violence against women, nostalgia for the 1950s, and American cultural and business history.

Was it difficult to get funding for the film? Where did you find funding to complete it?

The most difficult part of independent filmmaking is raising money. In 1994, when I began *Barbie Nation*, I was optimistic. Though I did get a few small grants (including one from the Women in Film Foundation),

I knew that I'd have to go elsewhere for the big money that filmmaking requires. I hoped to get a presale to cable television, which, in the early 1990s, was expanding. The History Channel, the Learning Channel, HBO, Showtime, Lifetime (for women!), A & E, and Bravo: there was the promise that more channels would allow for more viewpoints and in-depth programming.

So, in 1994–95, I shopped around a fourteen-minute sample reel of *Barbie Nation*. At that point it was relatively PG. The film did not yet include its lesbian Barbie players with their fabulous S&M creations, or the infamous X-ray of Barbie heads in a patient's descending colon. The project did have two gay male Barbie players, a recovering anorexic Barbie artist and college student, and Ruth Handler.

I was excited when the Learning Channel said they would like to buy *Barbie Nation*—giving me the money to finish the documentary. But when it came time to close the deal, it became clear I had been naive.

The producer for the Learning Channel said that *Barbie Nation* would be wonderful as "an art house film," but had to be changed to make it suitable for "Joe six-pack." Having two gay men wouldn't do. I could have one—but only if he didn't mention that he was gay. The anorexic had to go, the producer said, "because she's a downer." The story of the criminal conviction of Handler and the near-bankruptcy of Mattel would also have to be cut, the producer said. It was also "too depressing."

Of course, I put up a fight. But the producer wouldn't budge, though he did admit in a startling conference-call confession that he was gay and would himself enjoy the "art house" version of *Barbie Nation*. This did not, however, alter his conviction that *Barbie Nation* must be turned into, in his words, "mind candy" for the American public.

My partner, Trish Harrington, and I said we'd think about it. And think we did, sorely tempted by the prospect of finishing the film and getting it seen. I thought about making two versions: one "blanc" for the American market; and one "noir" for the more sophisticated European market.

That night my friend the author Susie Bright came to dinner. I told her my quandary, and she told me how she too had recently been offered money to do work she thought was compromised. She said that she couldn't do it—she had a reputation to preserve. But I had no fame. I could, she suggested, take the money and run this time—and fight the good fight the next time. Or I could believe that there was, hidden perhaps, but sizable, an alternative American audience.

After a difficult night, I made a decision. I can't say that I was sure there was any place that would ever show *Barbie Nation*. All I knew, as I turned down the Learning Channel, was that I was too old to be a hack.

So I borrowed the money to finish the movie. I thought it would cost $40,000 but it cost $130,000—still cheap for a one-hour documentary. And I decided that since I had no assurance that anyone would ever see *Barbie Nation*, I would make the movie without compromise. I would make *Barbie Nation* only for me—and for Nora, who is the brunette five-year-old in *Barbie Nation*, and for Susie, and for the "two gay men"—Franklin and Allen—and Kerry, the "downer" anorexic, and all the others in the Barbie world who had trusted us and let us film them.

I hoped that when the film was finally finished, someone would be interested in it. Then *Barbie Nation* was rejected by the Sundance Film Festival and I was sunk in gloom: what if there wasn't an audience there? But within two months, *Barbie Nation* was bought by PBS's *P.O.V.* series and accepted to the first of many film festivals around the world.

Did you think of the film as intended for women's studies classrooms when you made it? Did you think that it might be used in women's studies?

I wish I could say that I thought about women's studies when I was making *Barbie Nation*, but I had forgotten about women's studies when I dreamed up *Barbie Nation*, just as I had forgotten about Barbie for years before I conceived of the film.

When I arrived at the University of California at Berkeley in 1971, it was the beginning of women's studies. I co-edited *Libera,* the campus feminist literary journal. As a reporter for the student newspaper, I covered the first statewide meeting of the National Women's Political Caucus. I joined the Berkeley Poet's Coop and went to poetry readings by Susan Griffin, Judy Grahn, and Alicia Ostriker. In the atmosphere of early 1970s campus feminism, I began to learn women's history, began to practice feminist analysis, and found a community of like-minded friends.

And then I graduated. I spent twenty years as a journalist, and I didn't think too much about women's studies, until I had to pay the bills for *Barbie Nation*. After the film was sold to *P.O.V.*, I decided to distribute it to colleges and universities through New Day Films, the thirty-year-old filmmakers' co-op distributing feminist and progressive independent film to the educational market. That's what has paid the bills for the film—sales to women's studies programs and showings in courses on sociology of gender, psychology of women, women's history, and business courses in more than four hundred U.S. colleges and universities.

Because of women's studies, I've had the confidence and income this year to write my first screenplay, for a fiction film I hope to make about a woman who challenges sexual conventions. And I'm far from the only feminist filmmaker who owes thanks to women's studies. As a volunteer promotion director this year for the New Day Films cooperative, I can see that women's studies is one of the leading users of film and video in college and university education. Women's studies has, as the dot-comers like to say, "aggregated an audience" that makes feminist film possible. As the history of New Day Films shows, feminist film and women's studies have developed together.

Julia Reichert and Jim Klein, who made the classic films *Union Maids* and *Seeing Red*, founded New Day in 1971. "The whole idea of distribution was to help the women's movement grow," said Reichert. "We could watch the women's movement spread across the county just by who was ordering our films."

So you think of yourself as a feminist filmmaker? Is **Barbie Nation** *a feminist film?*

I have been a feminist and a writer since I was a child. Looking back on it now, these things seem related. I think that I first realized I was a feminist during family dinner-table debates in the mid-1960s when I was about thirteen. My father was—is—a big, smart, aggressive, egotistical man. Ultimately he taught me a strong sense of my own power—and undercut it. My father made an argument that was common at that time. That the proof of the fact that women were inferior to men in every important sphere was that men were more famous. "Where," he argued, "was the woman Shakespeare?"

Except for Emily Dickinson, Carolyn Keene (Mildred Wirt), Louisa May Alcott, and Madeleine L'Engle, I'm sure I couldn't name many women writers then. But I had my own poems, and, like any child, I knew about secrets. I knew, fiercely and surely, that women were, had been, or could be great in all fields of endeavor. Their stories, therefore, must be hidden. It all fit: being a writer, I knew the best stories were hidden ones; being a feminist, I knew women's stories were among the most hidden.

As for whether *Barbie Nation* is a feminist film, there are as many answers to that as there are types of feminism. I think *Barbie Nation* is a feminist film. I did get a review in *Cineaste* saying the film was insufficiently critical of Barbie's negative effect on girls. I disagree. I think *Barbie Nation* is critical, but not didactic. I think *Barbie Nation* is in the feminist tradition that is "sex positive" and recognizes people's power to subvert popular culture along with that culture's power to shape people.

How do you see the current situation and the future of feminist film and filmmakers?

As a filmmaker, it seems to me there are limited prospects for feminist and other progressive filmmakers in a world of increasing numbers of channels controlled by decreasing numbers of owners.

In August 2000, after seventeen years of distributing independent documentaries to television, Jane Balfour Films went into liquidation. Balfour blamed the proliferation of cable-television outfits driving down prices and making independent filmmaking and distribution economically impossible.

And Hollywood is no haven. In 1920, nearly half of all the films produced in the U.S. were written by women.[2] That figure has declined. And though the number of U.S. women directors appears to have increased in the past few years, they seem to suffer from a strange invisibility.

I've been struck in the past year by the difference in the media attention paid to two filmmakers at the same stages in their careers: Mary Harron, director of *I Shot Andy Warhol* and *American Psycho;* and Paul Thomas Anderson, director of *Boogie Nights* and *Magnolia.* Both have had critically acclaimed first features and bigger, even more controversial second features. But Harron has been virtually ignored, even as both her films have been critically acclaimed, while Anderson has been hailed as a "new talent bursting on the screen" even as his second feature has been panned.

NOTES
1. *Barbie Nation* runs 53 minutes and is available through New Day Films.
2. *Without Lying Down: Frances Marion and the Power of Women in Hollywood,* dir. Bridget Terry, based on the book of the same title by Cari Beauchamp, Turner Classic Movies, 2000.

Susan Stern *has a degree in journalism from the University of California, Berkeley. She is married to underground cartoonist Spain Rodriguez and lives in San Francisco where she heads her own production company, El Rio Productions. She is currently working on a documentary about her father and can be reached at vividpictures@attbi.com.* **Wendy Kolmar** *is professor of English and director of women's studies at Drew University. Her most recent book is* Feminist Theory: A Reader *(1999), coedited with Fran Bartkowski.*

Copyright © 2002 by Susan Stern

María Novaro on the Making of *Lola* and *Danzón*

Interview by Isabel Arredondo

Mexican filmmaker María Novaro (born 1951) trained as a sociologist before attending film school in Mexico City. A prolific director—her films include *Lola* (1989), *Danzón* (1991), *El Jardín del Edén* (1994), and *Sin dejar huella* (2000)—Novaro has also written most of the scripts for her films, in collaboration with her sister Beatriz. With *Danzón*, a widely distributed film that was selected to be shown at the Cannes Film Festival, Novaro gained international recognition. These excerpts from an interview with Novaro present her views on motherhood, cinematographic technique, and the importance of her characters' emotions. Originally published in Spanish, the interview has been translated into English by Mark Schafer, Jim Heinrich, and Isabel Arredondo.[1]

Let's begin now with your first feature film. There are people who said nothing happened in Lola. *What do you attribute these comments to?*

It would have been more revealing had they said that nothing interesting happened, for that would have showed that they didn't find motherhood to be an interesting topic. When I took the screenplay for *Lola* to different institutions to get funding, they said that it wasn't about anything and so *Lola* wasn't worth anything. These people didn't see anything about the life of this young mother who has to take care of her six-year-old all by herself as meaningful or worthy of being told. I think that behind that great nothing with which they received the screenplay for *Lola* was a very generalized social attitude of disinterest regarding the issues of motherhood. Motherhood is taken as being something natural that doesn't need to be explored or that poses no questions. Nevertheless, we authors who are women are reclaiming things from daily life, apparently mundane things, and giving them their fair due in terms of our lives. I tell my stories as a pretext to speak of something much vaster. In the case of *Lola*, for example, I'm interested not only in the particular story of Lola and her child: *Lola* is also the means by which I can reflect profoundly on women, motherhood, and Mexico City.

Which plays the greatest role in Lola's crisis: the economic aspect of her subsistence or Omar's emotional abandonment?

For me the trigger is not the economic situation. The crisis really occurs because Omar leaves and Lola experiences a brutal, emotional vacuum. She is not experiencing an economic crisis. She goes on selling clothes, just as before; she was screwed before and she is still screwed economically. Where there is a complete change—at first, in the development, and also at the end—is in her emotional makeup. Some feminists were bothered by the fact that Lola's crisis is related to the emptiness that she feels when she finds herself without a partner. I think that I'm very sincere; I'm not judging her, I'm speaking about what I have observed in the lives of a great many women. Being abandoned creates a very serious emotional problem for us, and I reflected on this in the movie, with much pain. Maybe it is possible one would want things to be otherwise. I simply told it as I've experienced it and seen it happen around me. I could have changed the story of Lola's depression, but I think that rather than mythologize that emotional emptiness, it's very important to reflect on it. I don't think it works for us women to wish to be what we aren't, but rather, to look at what is happening to us and to transform ourselves from there. The main idea that we had in mind when creating Lola's character was that she had to act according to how she felt and not according to reason. Lola's character, we thought, didn't analyze or reflect; rather, she did things very impulsively and followed her gut, her emotions. We came up with a woman who, when she thought about things, thought about them afterward, who was constantly acting out of rage, anger, jealousy, desperation, emptiness, loneliness, sexual desire. Even her relationship with her child is very visceral; after the culmination of her crisis, when she needs to relate again to her daughter and build a life with her, she isn't thinking, "My daughter needs me" or, "I ought to . . ." Lola is acting based on her immediate feelings.

Could Lola possibly have ignored her emotions and mastered her situation when it began to topple? Were you not interested in this type of option?

I came up with Lola's reaction intuitively. First I created Lola and only afterward, as I reflected on the character, did I understand the aspects I had wanted to deal with through that character. I now think that to have Lola in control of her emotions would have been to ask her to have an attitude toward her life that would be more male than female. According to my way of thinking, we women are much more in contact with our emotions than men are. We let them possess us and carry us off. They have a far greater effect on our lives. There are all kinds of women—there are women who are stronger, more intelligent, more self-controlled, but there are also women who act more from the gut. Even so, let me be so bold as to say that within the entire range of variations that might exist, there is a common trait among women: our emotions are much more a part of our lives. We let ourselves be carried off much more by depression, we allow ourselves to cry more, we allow at least a part of our lives to be swept away by our emotions. Lola is—I don't know if this is the right word—quite typical. She is like many women are—at least, at certain times in our lives, when we don't recover from our emotions. We let them sweep us away, although they might be destructive emotions; we let our lives be completely controlled by these emotions.

With men, we see much less importance placed on the emotions, and that's why I think it is one of the traits that distinguishes us. It's funny: often what we ask of men is that, as far as their feelings go, they be like us. I believe that women have learned that part of being masters of our own lives is to accept that emotion matters to us. It is a shame and a little dishonest to deny it, although in some countries there may be a generation of women who have lost touch with the power of their feelings and have played at being equals in a male world. Perhaps that wasn't the option. Those women might feel they have changed into something else at the cost of renouncing other things. A certain sector of feminist critique disagrees with the way *Lola* ends and thinks it should be different. It seems strange to me that this feminist criticism is in agreement with a segment of the male audience that is bothered when Lola starts to cry and can't control herself. For a man, it would have been much easier to watch a movie in which the woman is abandoned but lifts herself up, works, and deals with things. If the woman lifts herself up, he bears no responsibility nor does he have to consider certain issues. However, when you let that woman be destroyed by some guy's selfishness, then the men get awfully irritated. To make Lola reason and overcome her abandonment is to make it easy for everyone: for women, because it gives them a model character to follow, and for men, because then they don't have to deal with the conflict. In *Lola* I did, according to my own parameters, what had to be done: stick the knife right into ourselves and say why we suffer so much, why we let ourselves be dragged around so much, why our hearts, our feelings, get the better of us so often, why we are so fragile. I wanted to explore it in depth and, in this way, enlarge the hole so as to see in better. One must also keep in mind the response of the female audience that did like the movie—the many women coming out with their eyes all swollen and speaking freely about their lives after seeing the movie. Essentially, the movie is a trigger. Now, a person who doesn't like seeing this won't like it. I understand that. I know there are many people who don't like to think about things. But for others, it's an important source of reflection, precisely because I talk about things as they are, at one extreme of female vulnerability.

Tell me a little about the end of Lola. Why did you choose that ending?

To tell you the truth, when one writes stories the characters grab the reins of their lives. As a director, you can guide them, but you can't really interfere with their desires and their natural development. It would have been completely contrived if Lola, such as she develops in my story, were to come up with a different solution for her life. It wouldn't ring true. The character finds herself with very few possibilities for self-realization: the only thing she had to counter a dead-end life was the love she felt for her daughter. Things are as they are; Lola shows her life the way it is and works with whatever possibilities she has at hand and no more. I even had written a much harsher ending for the movie but it seemed too strong to me and I changed it to one that allowed you a glimpse of hope, an opening in the sky. I really dislike that cinema of tacked-on happy endings where we have to be fools to believe the denouement because the story is leading us in a different direction. Although there might not be a happy ending, and Lola doesn't become the woman who will solve every problem, she does show a certain strength; there is an evolution in what she does. Lola is one person at the beginning, another at the middle of the movie, and another the end.

Lola *and* **Danzón,** *your second feature film, are very different movies. Could you explain to me what the differences are between them?*

My emotional state was very different when I was doing *Danzón*. While I was still editing *Lola*, I commented to my sister—with whom I always write the scripts—that we had to write something very happy, which would fill us with joy and love of life. After all the emotions we had touched upon in Lola's story, my heart was torn apart and I felt like doing something completely the opposite. One of the first things we talked about was that it had to be a movie with a lot of color, with music, with dancing, with laughter. Almost immediately we had the idea of giving it the form of a comedy or of a melodrama played throughout as a comedy. The script for *Danzón* was the opposite of the script for *Lola*—it concerned a woman who could forge her own path, virtually without limits. Although she was a woman from as limited an environment as Lola was, she was able to do almost whatever she wanted, because of her fantasy, her generosity, her openness to life....

Why did you choose the world of the danzón as the main subject for your second feature film?

I chose it because it is a very rigid, very conventional world. It seems to be structured differently for men than for women: women have to dress in a specific way and men have to dress in another, men are in charge and women obey them. The men lead and the women follow. Many dancers of the *danzón* even think that real life is like this, and they live their lives according to those rules.

The *danzón* seemed to me a perfect structure to use as a framework and to play with. I wanted to show how, even within this framework, a woman could be in charge of her life. People who dance the *danzón* say, "In dancing, as in life, the man commands and the woman obeys," and I translated it as "In dancing, the man commands and the woman obeys, but not in life." For me that was essential: yes, we can live together, we can dance, but that doesn't mean that you order me around in my life.

Julia [played by María Rojo] dances the *danzón* and does so by following the man, because that's the way one really enjoys this dance. What's the problem there? Julia is a passionate *danzón* woman and is able to follow these rules—to dress like a real woman, to be the one who obeys in the dance, who follows the man. Nevertheless, she is also totally and absolutely the master of her own life—that is, according to how her life has shaped up and the possibilities she would logically have, given who she is. She lives her life according to what she is given, and she is so open, so generous, and so full of life ... She is so willing to take what comes to her in life and to react according to it that, ultimately, she's in charge of her life. She's more in charge of her life than she even realizes. Julia shows this ability to choose on her trip to Veracruz, when she chooses her young lover and when she leaves him, and also by dancing with Carmelo, this very elegant gentleman.

I even found myself affected by the rules of the *danzón*. The high heels one wears to dance it, which characterize Julia, turned into a game that became explicit: the *danzoneros* told me I should wear high heels to dance. I responded, "I'm sorry, but this is how it is: I'm learning to dance the *danzón*, I'll follow the rules, but I don't wear high heels."

In addition to playing with the rules of the **danzón**, *you also played with the rules of melodrama. Why is that?*

It is a genre that thrives among Latin Americans. My sister and I—we've talked a lot about this—have said that the emotional upbringing of Mexican women is totally bound up with melodrama. We were raised on melodrama, grew up on melodrama; it is a form that has dominated cinema for a very long time. Perhaps the Latin American militant cinema of the '70s broke that somewhat and turned, in my opinion, to pamphleteering, weeping, and dispensed with many of the values inherent in melodrama as a form of expression. On the other hand, if one never leaves melodrama, the genre can become somewhat limiting. What we do is to work with this genre, make fun of the forms melodrama takes. In *Danzón*, we certainly were playing constantly with a melodramatic form, but then we took another tack and the movie ended up going in a different direction. The scenes were constructed very much in the style of the Mexican cinema of the Golden Age, but we came up with totally different, and I hope surprising, endings.

When we made *Danzón*, on the one hand, we took elements from our emotional upbringing, but on the other, we distanced ourselves from those elements. So, through humor, we were able to accept our culture, yet, at the same time, we freed ourselves from what our emotional education taught us to feel when we were growing up....

By playing, we explore all the things we have inherited. With this method, it doesn't weigh on you: "This is how I was raised, this is my tradition and I recognize it as part of me, but I'll make fun of it and won't let it run my life." I am not like a woman from melodramas, and I don't understand motherhood in that way—I broke that mold. However, I recognize that melodrama has affected my way of being, my dreams, and some of my characteristics. We were always playing with that contradiction by applying humor, and it worked for us because we had a good time and was quite enjoyable.

We also wanted to use humor to handle the relationship between Julia, an older woman, and Rubén, a young sailor. We wanted to laugh at Julia's need to say a pile of lies and get caught in them, to invent a younger daughter in order to appear younger when she spoke with Rubén. What I didn't know was that later that same mechanism would work for the audience: that the audience itself, because of this humor, would take the melodrama they were used to and loosen up, have fun, feel really good. When you finally recognize your whole heritage, you feel good; you see all the profile types here, arranged in a friendly way, and they weigh on you a lot less. In *Danzón* I wanted to rejoice, to be moved by my cultural legacy, by what it means to be a woman in Mexico. I even wanted to praise a part I no longer identify with at all because I'm at another point. Despite my distance, I wanted to play with looking at Mexico that way, through those eyes.

What do you see as the most essential elements of cinematic narrative?

When I saw the cinema of Andrei Tarkovsky or the old Michelangelo Antonioni or Theodoros Angelopoulos, I realized that cinematic narrative is far more related to poetry than to dramaturgy. Tarkovsky explains that if one wants to put pieces of life on the screen, poetry is a much more accurate tool than dramaturgy. I think Tarkovsky was right. I believe that film is precisely another artistic form related to literature and painting and that it contains a lot of literature but has its own forms. However, there are people who believe that things must be told in film in dramaturgical terms.

An example of this tendency is North American scriptwriting, which evolved from dramaturgy. One is commonly asked to organize a narrative dramaturgically, almost as if it were a recipe; one must structure that hour and a half to tell something and get to the end . . . I don't believe one should judge whether a movie is well narrated based on that sort of dramaturgy. That "proper" way of narrating bores me. I studied "proper" narration in school, I could do it, but I didn't see any point to it. Since I made *Lola*—above all here in Mexico but also in the United States—I constantly run into certain critics who say that my narrative is weak, that I don't know how to tell a story. For them, a good narrative is one based on recognized conventions . . . It's true that there are marvelous North American movies, excellently narrated, but they don't know that there is a much vaster cinematic narrative. It's not that my narrative is weak in *Lola* and *Danzón*, but rather, that I'm not using a conventional narrative design.

What importance do you place, in the progression of the narrative, on things happening?

The truth is that I'm not concerned about things happening, but I feel somewhat forced to put in more action, because I know that if I don't, people will miss it and will feel disconnected or think that what I am doing is weird. I try to negotiate in order to survive, but my natural way of setting up the narrative has always been based on what I want to be looking at. As I've thought about it, I've come to the conclusion that often the most significant memories of a person in real life or in the life of the character I'm writing are not powerful actions or events. Sometimes things are more subtle, almost imperceptible. What is important is how we are affected by them and what our reception of them is. For me, the way in which events affect us is more important than the action itself, because the action distracts; when there is no action, your attention focuses on something else. In the manuals on how to write screenplays, by contrast, a different view is taken: spectacular events are set in place and then things are forcibly made to mesh. First you program what is going to take place and then, in the action, you fit in the characters, their experiences, and their feelings. I don't see life this way and I don't like to narrate like this.

I don't impose a given action on the characters. I let them guide me to whatever might happen in their life. To give you an example, I hadn't planned for Lola to break a bottle over the head of that guy on the beach. I had the idea that she was going to the beach to get better, to breathe, even to get depressed to her heart's content. But at one point, this guy was bothering her so much—without him being anything close to the worst guy in the world—that suddenly Lola has no choice but to smash him with the bottle. And that's what she does. I wrote the Lola incident this way, because it made sense that Lola would react in that way, not because the script required it. For me, what takes place in a script is a consequence of the factors that come together. Like life itself, they happen . . . Things take place and one always has explanations, but there are much blurrier motivations than the one employed in conventional screenwriting. Those blurrier motivations are the ones that really move people to act.

My desire to explore certain topics through my characters also influences the way I write my scripts. In a movie like *Danzón*, my constant guide as I was writing the script was my desire to explore Julia's naive view of life, optimistic in the extreme. As a director, I shared the view of my characters, regarding Mexico, dance, women, happiness, love, fate, coincidence, the generosity certain people have toward others. That was our attitude. In writing the script, that naïveté and endless optimism was much more important than any specific action. Julia's way of looking at the world was the reason I made *Danzón*. Really, Julia is traveling because she feels like it; she is allowing herself something that few of us allow ourselves, something that probably only children allow themselves to do. When I wrote the script, I thought, "There it is, this is the state of mind in which she travels." I'll give you another example. When I have Julia get off the train in Veracruz, I use a classic framing to indicate that she has arrived at her destination: I put the camera on the steps of the train and the character gets off. However, I also add an important detail: Julia's high heels. For me, this scene offers a different reading than would a conventional scene that simply would say, "The character arrives at her destination." With the high heels, I'm suggesting that, although the character arrives and gets off the train—the way all characters do—this character is different. Julia's very high heels, which are characteristic of her throughout the movie, symbolize the way she perceives the world. The high heels let me link her descent from the train with her feeling that the men are looking at her; so much so that it seems that when Julia arrives in Veracruz, the station is full of no one but men. When we shot this scene there were a number of extras—women and children—whom I didn't want to include in the shot. People recommended that I not exclude them, but I didn't follow their advice because the fact that there were only men in the scene was important to represent the spirit of the trip. It had to convey the sensation Julia was feeling, that there were no one but men looking at her. The essential thing was to respect the state of mind with which she got off the train. Whether or not it is true that there are only men looking at her in Veracruz isn't important. What is important is that those little feet in high heels that get off the train believe that is the case.

In general, what has been the most difficult for you in terms of directing?
When I'm directing, the most difficult thing for me is to create a space in which I can hear my own voice. It seems difficult for me to maintain a type of shell or internal niche from which to continue speaking with my creative being. I'm not referring to a dialogue with your cameraman, with your assistants, or in the best of cases, with your actors: that is not speaking with yourself. I once clipped out a quote by Ingmar Bergman that said that when a director no longer hears his internal voice, he's lost. I think Bergman was right regarding the need to protect the artist's voice so that it can express itself. Over time I've learned to realize that when the pressure was such that I couldn't listen to myself, I would lose touch with myself and do things mechanically. And over time, I've created a mechanism to avoid that. After those terrible days of filming, I go to my room and review the recording on "video assist," a recording made through a video tap, in black and white and with poor sound quality. I used to do it to see what I'd done and how

it had turned out, but I've slowly realized that it's also a form of discipline that requires that I get back in touch with myself.

This dialogue with myself is crucial because I have a particular creative process. My method is intuitive, absolutely emotional. What moves me is tenderness. If what I see when we are doing a scene moves me, I know how the camera should move. If the actor gives me goose bumps, if he makes me feel a knot in my throat, I immediately have the camera follow this character. This process is not exclusive to filming; tenderness also moves me in my life. The same thing that happens to me in the filming happens when I see something in the street, when I'm looking at children, with a dog that walks by, with trees. As a movie director, apart from making sure that things happen on time, the planning, solving problems, and making decisions, one must not lose that internal dialogue. I try to perceive that tenderness that means so much to me and organize my story around it. I think it has to do with the way one was as a child, with what is deepest, truest, and most hidden inside.

When you are sitting at your desk alone, thinking, listening to your music, it is easy to get in touch with yourself, but when you are filming, it is very, very difficult. People don't imagine the work required to make a movie. It is a titanic, almost military, and even hellish job, because it is extraordinarily expensive and involves a large amount of stress and demands made by the technology used in filming a movie. You have to adapt to an overwhelming and crushing reality: people ask you if the cable can go here or if you want them to put green eye shadow on the actress or if the actor should say his lines in such-and-such a way. A thousand things, even those that supposedly aren't your job but come to you simply because you're the head of it all: that certain equipment trucks got stuck and won't arrive on time, that this actor is suffering a nervous breakdown. In short, everything.

It's a process that's a bit schizophrenic: you must have a part of you functioning artistically, allowing your most natural perception of things, your intuition, to work. You have to nurture the part of you that is always alert to what you are seeing—like visual composition and a sense of time—so that it keeps working, and to do that, you have to create a niche for it. At the same time, another part of your being has to be absolutely practical and always be thinking in terms of money. Since making films is quite expensive, you have to know what you can't permit: that this take can't be repeated because it uses so much material, that you have to do it with just one camera because you can't afford two, that the sun is going down and you only have three minutes to do the take because there's no way you can even think about coming back tomorrow. It's like going crazy: you have to function skillfully and intelligently, be director of the ship and make everyone do his job, and on the other hand, be engaged in your interior dialogue. The most difficult thing is that the two parts must function efficiently and clearly as you are doing the scene and the day's filming is coming to an end. It's difficult, because one part fights brutally with the other, one wants to annihilate the other. When you want to make personal movies, when you truly believe in the language of film as a specific and unique artistic manifestation, you must safeguard the artistic part against the infernal machinery. It is essential to be able to say something that makes sense, but to do that, one must be able to listen to the reason why you thought up this scene.

With practice, I am creating my own way of telling things, my own internal security: I'll take this and leave that. It's a process that produces a lot of insecurity and problems for me. At times I think there's probably no point to what I'm doing or that it's not taking me anywhere. There are moments in which that commitment to developing the language of film as art is very difficult; particularly, because you feel a huge loneliness. Can you give me concrete details regarding this dialogue with yourself?

One of the things that grabbed me in *Lola*, and that I think I was right about, is the scene on the beach when Lola is looking at the old man who goes into the water and pulls down his shorts. I was told that this wasn't appropriate, that narratively—in the classical sense—it wasn't crucial to the story. It so happened, besides, that this scene was very complicated to film because we couldn't get anyone who would agree to let his shorts drop. There are so many women willing to take off their clothes for a sex scene, and yet we couldn't find an actor who would simply play in the water, let his shorts slip off, and let it all hang out. No one would do it, and less so for a small role. There was a moment when I was told, "Don't film it, it's very complicated, what's the point?" But at times like that I think you must listen to that internal voice of yours that says, "Yes, it serves a purpose, I'll sacrifice this other scene, because you must know how to tell what you shouldn't suppress, however crazy it might seem."

When I made *Danzón*, I had some conclusions I had drawn from my work on *Lola*, which I continued to modify. The dialogue with myself was much stricter and I tried to be more careful so I could distinguish when I would allow myself digressions, like the one of the old man in the waves, and when I wouldn't. For example, in *Danzón*, changing the names of the ships to film them was torture: we had to get the captain's permission, permission from the ship's country of origin, permission from the harbormaster—it was an awful mess of red tape! In addition, we could barely afford to paint the names, film them, and repaint them. The producers tried to convince me, they told me, "María, film the ships with the names they have. Look, it's a pretty name, it's called *Milano*, but I said, "No, it has to be called *Puras ilusiones* [Pure Illusions] or *Amor perdido* [Lost Love]. That's got to be the name." But inside, in this loneliness I was talking about before, I asked, "Do the ships really have to be named like that, or am I exaggerating?" In this case I told myself, "Well, it's a mess, everyone will have to work triple, the permits are a real hassle, this is going to cost more than what I was figuring, but the ships have to have those names. Yes, it's important to the story: they're not normal ships. We're in this woman's fantasy. . . ."

Given that working with the actors is so important, tell me how you have worked with them.

I have my own way of casting and I also do exercises with video. Before doing *Lola*, I didn't care if the actors were professionals or not; I thought that anybody could do it. But when I saw the results and realized—especially at the Sundance Institute—that Mexican actors were poorly trained, I began to reconsider. In Mexico there is little tradition of preparing actors. Many young actors get their training entirely from the theater and they have a very hard time dealing with film, especially the filming itself. To make *Lola* I needed a group of very young actors, but, with the exception of Roberto Sosa, who has been an actor since he was a child and works very well with the camera, they didn't have a clear idea of what film was all about. Even in casting I didn't have many choices of experienced actors. In the case of Ana, Lola's daughter [played by Alejandra Vargas], even fewer. I wanted a girl who was not an actress because I had seen how the children who have worked in commercials or movies are little monsters; they are children with little spontaneity who think that acting is reciting. For *Lola*, since there were no experienced actors, I began to prepare them myself using games with the video camera. For example, with Alejandra Vargas, I spent entire days recording her. At times I asked her very open-ended things—to do whatever she felt like. Other times, I asked her to do specific things. But the condition was always that she couldn't look at the camera; if she looked at the camera, she lost. I realized that Alejandra was fantastic because she could go for hours without looking at the camera. If the game was not to look at the camera, then she didn't look at it and that was that. No problem. Not looking at the camera was also like forgetting that I was there, and she was able to do that very well. I spent a lot of time videotaping her or getting her on video. I went to pick her up at her house, I kept her company while she ate, and I took her to get ice cream, to the subway, to the park. Later I did a lot of video tests in order to choose the rest of the actors, particularly Lola. Leticia Huajira, who was going to play the part of Lola, was a young woman who had only done theater, so I gave her a lot of tests to see if she was going to cause me problems. There are people who simply can't work in front of the camera; it causes them a lot of anxiety. Since the tests with Leticia went well, I began to put her together with Alejandra. I wanted to see if they looked like mother and child, because I hate this cinematic convention that the mother and daughter don't seem to know each other at all but you're supposed to believe that they're related. I took them both for ice cream in the park and saw that, in fact, they did make a good pair. . . .

Since getting to know the actors in *Lola* using the video camera worked very well for me, I adopted it as my method. Nevertheless, *Danzón* was a different situation. Since the actors had a lot of experience, I was afraid that they would feel they knew more than I did and would be hesitant to let me direct them. In contrast to *Lola*, in *Danzón* the games with the video camera beforehand and the casting helped, not so the actors could face the camera, but rather, so I could face them. With María Rojo, for example, it really helped me get to know her. I spent months going to the Salón Colonia, taping her dancing, watching her expressions, her smile, the angles of her face, her moods, knowing when she was uncomfortable, when she could be spontaneous, when something was bothering her. Knowing her was important because she's a very intelligent woman and very sincere in her work, and if she didn't like what she was doing, it showed. She would do exactly what I would say, but you could see it in her eyes that she didn't like it. I learned a lot from this work and it made me be sincere with myself. I learned to say, "No, that's no good. Let's fix it. . . ."

I just taught an acting class for film students. I had no time to prepare and was following my intuition, because I've never studied anything in the field. Nevertheless, I've reflected a lot on how an experienced actor finds his or her place in the medium of film. I've been able to think about the extent to which they are not prepared to work as actors in film, the amount of cobwebs and fear they carry around in their heads, and even the atmosphere of scorn for film in which they have been trained. They adore the movies and are dying to make them, but their teachers—and there are great teachers of theater in Mexico!—have told them, "In film, actors do tricks, they don't have to act." I have explained to them that that's not the case. Film requires a different language—there are many fewer deceptions, there are techniques, there is fragmentation, one must work with great sincerity, and one must have a fine control of one's gaze. This course forced me to reflect on my own experience with Mexican actors, because it's a different case with North American actors. North Americans are sometimes better trained for film and television than for theater; the camera is not a problem for them. By contrast, in Mexico it's an important topic because there's an acting tradition that creates a lot of short circuits in film. This acting tradition that is very Mexican and Latin American, and that originally we inherited from Spain, is very exaggerated, very melodramatic. For many people in our countries good acting is considered being very spirited, saying things well, and not so much sincerity or making the character believable. While Latin American and Spanish cinema is full of examples of very exaggerated, very heavy-handed acting, in American cinema—even in the totally superficial movies—you can generally believe what you are watching. This is marvelous for a film performance because the cinematic convention is that you believe what you are seeing.

Let's move now to another topic related to the image: what has your relationship been with cinematographers?

The cinematographer of *Lola* and *Danzón*, Rodrigo García, in addition to being a good cinematographer, is a very sensitive man and one in whom I have a lot of confidence. In *Lola* he was kind of shocked when I asked him to have the camera follow the girl and, as if the camera were the girl's eyes, have it look around at all her toys, which are on the floor. It wouldn't have occurred to him to move the camera this way, but I was interested in Ana's little hands, her face, and how she related to her toys. I placed a different value on these details than do certain movies made by men, where children are made to say certain things but what they feel is not included. I wanted to present the girl as I believe boys and girls really are, and Rodrigo liked that and accepted it.

There have been more difficult situations, like in the scene in *Danzón* where Julia is in her hotel room with Rubén [Victor Carpinteiro]. In that case, the different ways in which Rodrigo and I see things became an obstacle. I told Rodrigo to have the camera linger over the half-naked body of a man: "It's as if you were caressing his thigh, his calf; you move up his naked back and then move back to María Rojo." But Rodrigo couldn't get the camera movements I was asking him for. It was as if, in effect, I were asking him to touch the man. When I got up on the camera and showed him graphically—so he could see on the monitor the movement I wanted—he almost died laughing, because it was almost as if he couldn't get it. He wasn't willing to caress the body of a man with the camera! It was his own resistance. He only wanted to watch María Rojo but not to caress the body of the young man. We resolved this difference because in our work relationship we have constantly talked things over, discussed them. Afterward, we even joked about what happened. It is all about different ways of seeing but . . . of course, the look that I want is the one that comes most naturally to me. . . .

Would a female cinematographer have helped you find the viewpoint you seek?

It's possible, but I don't know, because in Mexico there simply aren't any female cinematographers working in 35 mm, the industry standard. I don't think we're trusted or allowed to do it. Or is it that women are unable to use cameras or think in terms of emulsions? Does it go against our way of being? Discrimination has been broken down considerably with respect to directing—where it existed before as well—but it persists in the technical fields in positions of responsibility: there are no female sound people or cinematographers. There are assistants, but they don't have any responsibility. It's true that there are concrete reasons why women are not familiar with particular fields. For example, a woman can be clumsier with a camera than a man because, as a child, she didn't play with tools or didn't receive encouragement. But she can look at where her lack of ability occurred within her own line of development. It's natural: it's like a man who doesn't know how to change a diaper. It's not something he can't learn to do. He's probably clumsy and grabs the baby without the faintest idea of how to do it, but it can be learned.

What can be done about the lack of female cinematographers?

I have asked myself that question throughout my career. In the first 35 mm movie I made, I asked the woman who had been my cinematographer for my shorts in 16 mm, María Cristina Camús, to do the filming. I insisted, but she refused because she had never filmed in 35 mm and felt unsure of herself. I would have taken any woman who could have filmed in 35 mm, because I think that we must create more opportunities and we ought to help each other. But she wouldn't do it and there was no one else. I have always asked the cinematographers with whom I work to take on female assistants so they get trained and participate in feature films.

When I did a little five-minute short called *Otoñal* (Autumnal), I did use a female cinematographer who had never filmed fiction before. The result wasn't very good. It was her first filming, and it was a very complicated film about ghosts, which required a certain technical ability. It turned out fine, but the producer of the shorts told me, "You should never have taken on that girl, you should have hired so-and-so" (a guy). He made me feel guilty for having used a female cinematographer. It's a vicious circle: women don't take on these things and when we do, the pressure and our inexperience are such that, effectively, we can't do a good job from the outset. Then comes the reproach and the lack of confidence: "It's a matter of fact: they don't know how to do it." We must continue, however, until we break the vicious circle.

I'm proud that, to the best of my abilities, I engage in a certain amount of activism and struggle because I'm aware that we haven't had the opportunity to learn how to use movie technology. It's the same as before, when men had no confidence that women could direct. In my first movie the electricians would look at me . . . as if I were mentally retarded. For them, a woman directing is just like a child directing. It's as if they were saying, "How could she possibly direct? She doesn't know how to order people around, she doesn't know how to demand things." It's true that, perhaps, it was like that because it was my first film, but with a man they might have had a little more confidence.

Directing is an authoritarian job and to do it, you must have a certain energy that, supposedly, women don't have. I worked as an assistant to a few directors here in Mexico, and my experience was that they are a bunch of shouters and swearers. I don't want to name names, but I would include in this group almost the majority of the people in the generation prior to mine. They are directors who ask for things by shouting, who run people off the set, mistreat the actors. Well, things work out in the end, the movies get made, but I always told myself, "I don't think that this is the only way to deal with this business of directing." And, I have shown that it isn't. I have never shouted at anyone, but I've managed the movies I've made very well, on time and on budget. I have always created a work plan, there has been even a good working environment. I encounter people, however, who think that I don't know how to direct because they haven't seen me shouting. But you have to show them that it's another style and that, in all likelihood, everyone will come out ahead with this other style. It's much more pleasant to be working shooting with someone who gets the job done without kicking or screaming than to be shooting with someone who does it bragging about their abilities.

NOTES

1. The complete, Spanish-language interview can be found in the collection *Palabra de Mujer: Historia oral de las directoras de cine mexicanas (1988–1994)*, Madrid: Iberoamericana and Universidad Autónoma de Aguas Calientes, 2001, edited by Isabel Arredondo.

Isabel Arredondo *is associate professor at Plattsburgh State University. During her sabbatical year, 2001–2, she is working at the McGill Center for Research and Teaching on Women.*

Copyright © 2002 by Isabel Arredondo

Documenting Race and Gender
Kym Ragusa Discusses *Passing* and *Fuori/Outside*

Interview by Livia Tenzer

In her two award-winning short documentaries *Passing* (1996) and *Fuori/Outside* (1997), New York–based filmmaker Kym Ragusa explores the limits of the documentary genre in order to portray the centrality of race and ethnicity in U.S. women's experience.[1] Employing the narrative techniques of storytelling and the imagery of personal memory, Ragusa's films relate a past that is broadly historical, yet anchored in the intimate relationships between a granddaughter and her grandmothers. Each film emerges from Ragusa's research into the life of one of her grandmothers and reveals the social pressures and prejudices the older woman confronted. As her grandmothers' lives connect to the present through the filmmaker, their stories provide crucial insight into how race and ethnicity continue to shape identity both inside and outside the family.

Passing records a story told to Ragusa by her African American grandmother about an incident that occurred in 1959 during a trip she took from New York City to Florida. Using still images, archival footage, and a soundtrack that mixes blues and gospel, Ragusa evokes the racial tensions of the time and creates a multilayered narrative around gender, class, and color. Traveling with an African American male friend (her then lover), the grandmother encounters the segregated and racially hostile South for the first time when her companion sends her into a diner in North Carolina to purchase food for a picnic. Inside, two white male customers repeatedly confront her with the question "What side of the tracks are you from?" When she realizes that they are asking her race, Ragusa's light-skinned grandmother also realizes that her companion has presumed that she will be able to "pass." Her courageous response to the people in the diner carries with it an aftermath of fear—will the two white men pursue them?—and unsettling questions about the supposed community among people categorized as racial outsiders by white social norms.

In *Fuori/Outside* Ragusa depicts the life of her Italian American grandmother, the person in her family who most resisted accepting the racially different Ragusa as belonging and of the same blood. Posing the film as "a letter to you," Ragusa addresses her grandmother directly with evidence of her own origins among New York's immigrant Italians, her own experiences of prejudice and deprivation. Piecing together the past from family pictures, historical footage, and broken memories, Ragusa moves back in time from the working-class New Jersey house where her grandmother now lives to her impoverished childhood in East Harlem as the daughter of Calabrian immigrants, her arranged marriage at sixteen, her long working life as a hotel maid, and the family's flight in the 1970s from the Bronx, where they had settled, to the "safety" of New Jersey. The borders of race and class align with the geography of New York City in this story, as neighborhoods come to define the whiteness of their inhabitants. Because the women in the film share New York's history of shifting borders and sometimes explosive racial friction, however, the boundaries between them seem to dissolve through their collaborative exploration of the past.

Your documentary films **Passing** *and* **Fuori/Outside** *examine issues of race and ethnicity as reflected in the lives of two women. Why did you choose to focus on women's experiences?*

I have always been interested in women's stories, particularly in the hidden histories of working-class women, whose daily acts of courage and resistance have often gone unacknowledged. In *Passing* and *Fuori/Outside,* I was talking about the ways in which issues of class, race, and ethnicity are inextricably linked to issues of gender—that you can't separate out each factor and say that was the defining element in this person's experience. My grandmothers' lives were emblematic of this interconnection; in *Passing,* the tensions in the diner are due not only to my African American grandmother's racial ambiguity, but also to her sexual desirability to these white men. My Italian American grandmother's revelation about her father's physical abuse of her mother illustrates the ways in which an impoverished immigrant man still had power over an immigrant woman through the force of his body, even though they were both marginalized on the basis of ethnicity, language, etc.

Watching the two films together, I was struck that your grandmothers both faced intense marginalization or exclusion on the basis of race or ethnicity, although they were of different races, and their communities responded to this pressure in different ways. Do the two films reply to each other, showing opposite sides of the experience of race in the U.S.?

Yes, I see them as mirror images of each other. Partially, this has to do with the ways in which both women were marginalized on the basis of race and ethnicity, and also in the ways that each story defies expectations: a light-skinned, mixed-race woman who doesn't choose to pass, even though her life may depend on it, and an Italian American woman whose life doesn't follow the familiar narrative of the American Dream.

Your grandmothers seem to have very different personalities. Was it very different working with each of them, and how did they each react to you as a filmmaker?

Miriam Christian, my African American grandmother, was a prolific storyteller, and I think she enjoyed the process of making *Passing*. Gilda Ragusa, my Italian American grandmother, was not lucid when I was making *Fuori/Outside*—she wasn't well. So it's not really a question of different personalities, but rather different life circumstances. I was just beginning as a filmmaker when I shot both projects, so I don't think either one had a real sense of me as a filmmaker. I think they were mostly amused, but sometimes annoyed!

Both films, but especially Fuori/Outside, have an autobiographical dimension. Did you see these projects as a form of self-exploration, and did you worry about diverging from classical norms for documentary, which suggest that the filmmaker should be an objective recorder of events?

In each piece, I was trying to look at the relationship between personal memory and "official" history: what are the stories that get left out of the history books, and how do "regular" people live within and respond to history? So I wasn't interested in making a traditional "objective" documentary, instead I was interested in subjectivity and intimacy. Each piece is also very much about the act of storytelling—how do women pass these stories on to one another, and how do we make meaning from them across the generations.

Although some of the footage in Passing *is new (as opposed to archival), you've chosen to make the film black and white throughout, and you've incorporated a lot of grainy footage that looks historical, even if it's new. What were you aiming for here, and why did you mix black-and-white with color footage in* Fuori/Outside*?*

I shot *Passing* with black-and-white film because I wanted to give it the feeling of being in the past, but also as a commentary on the artificial racial binary of black and white. Some of the footage is archival, but I degraded it so it looks grainy and unclear, which is about memory and the unconscious. In *Fuori/Outside,* I mixed black-and-white film with color video, which was about the relationship of the past to the present.

In Passing *your African American grandmother rejects the pressure to identify as white, defiantly proclaiming as she leaves the diner, "Well, you have just served a nigger!" While I initially read this as a gesture of courageous self-definition, I later wondered how much choice she had in defining herself. I'm thinking of the image of railroad tracks that you repeat throughout the film and the absolute binary division it suggests.*

That's a good point. In a sense, no matter how light her skin was, or how straight and red her hair was (you don't see that in the black-and-white), her "black blood" would always be used to identify her as black in this nation that is obsessed with the binary of black and white. Still, I wanted to focus on her choice, her political identity, her sense of solidarity with African Americans as an oppressed people struggling for freedom. Her choice put her in that struggle—she could have passed and sat it out.

Is the notion of "passing" something that also applies to your Italian American grandmother? Does her yearning for safety, for well-defined borders around her family, her house, her neighborhood, involve maintaining a certain facade of identity?

Absolutely. In the U.S., southern Italians were not viewed as white by the dominant culture until relatively recently. Many Italian Americans are unaware of or uncomfortable with this history. This was certainly the case with my family. The move from the Bronx to New Jersey was definitely a move toward whiteness.

You explain in **Fuori/Outside** *that your father originally introduced you to his family as a niece, not as his daughter. Did anyone believe this fiction? If not, what purpose did it serve? Do you think his lie made it harder or easier for your grandmother to accept you?*

I don't know if anyone believed it, and I don't know what purpose it served. My father doesn't have a good answer for that. It was basically a lack of courage on his part. What made it so hard for my grandmother was the lying—ultimately that was much more an issue than my racial difference. Understandably, she felt betrayed and was angry at my father—I was caught in the middle.

Does the difference of courage and fear between your two grandmothers have anything to do with class? Do you see class as shaping their personalities and abilities to react to racism?

No, of course not. In discussing my grandmother's fear in *Fuori/Outside,* I was absolutely not saying that she was not also courageous, or that she was fearful because she was working class. I was saying that fear and isolation led to her own racism, and in a larger sense to some Italian Americans' identification with whiteness and the dominant culture instead of a politicized otherness.

In both films you bring out how violence, and the fear of it, compel people to stay inside racially defined identities. In **Fuori/Outside,** *for instance, you refer to lynchings of southern Italian immigrants. Where and when did this happen, and was it connected to similar treatment of African Americans?*

There are many documented cases of lynchings of southern Italians in the U.S., the most notorious being a mob lynching in New Orleans at the turn of the century. I think eleven Italians were lynched on that occasion. Often lynchings occurred when Italians were attempting to organize with African Americans against oppressive working conditions. I think Italian Americans got the message early on that to identify with other marginalized groups was to court violence.

Both in **Passing** *and* **Fuori/Outside** *a kind of secret history of oppression by men emerges alongside the story of racial/ethnic oppression. How would you evaluate the actions of the male companion in* **Passing***, and what effect does his part in the film lend to the larger story of southern segregation and violence? In* **Fuori/Outside***, do you see the revelation that your grandmother's father physically abused her mother (a dramatic moment in the film) as connecting to the themes of race and class?*

In *Passing*, my grandmother's male companion was playing a strange kind of game. He knew it was a segregated diner, and he sent her in there anyway. There was a lot of secrecy between them in that sense. She also didn't tell him what happened inside. I wondered what effect the constant threat of racial violence had on the relationships between men and women, as each was affected differently by that violence (it was mostly, but not exclusively, men who were lynched). In this case, the threat of violence didn't bring them closer together, but instead drove a wedge between them that was characterized by silence and dangerous risk taking. With *Fuori/Outside,* as I said before, violence along lines of gender was definitely connected to issues of class and race—her father took his rage against being economically marginalized as an immigrant man out on her mother, who he believed could not fight back because she also was marginalized. Where could she go without economic resources and no English? But in the end she ended the violence by throwing him out of the house.

In **Fuori/Outside** *you employ some archival footage of a saint's day festival in New York. We see a crowd of women streaming out the doors of a large church and a statue of the Virgin Mary carried in procession through the street. As your grandmother watches this on a TV screen, she seems to recognize a forgotten piece of her past; as we viewers watch it, replayed on our screen to the accompaniment of traditional southern Italian chanted music, we too can feel connected to this past and its ancient cult of motherhood. Why did you stage this screening for your grandmother, and what significance does the footage have for the film as a whole?*

It was footage from the feast of the Madonna of Mount Carmel in East Harlem, where my grandmother grew up. The church, Our Lady of Mount Carmel, was a space of central importance to my family. My grandparents were married there, my father and his siblings were baptized there, and my great-grandmother, who went there to mass every day and was devoted to that particular Madonna, died on the steps of the church. For me, it's a place filled with history and also with a kind of magical spiritual power.

My grandmother had lost so much of her memory, and I was searching for a way to "give" her back some of her past. The footage was from 1937; she would have been living there then, and I hoped that she would recognize it on some level. Unfortunately, the screening of this footage failed; I was hoping it would unleash in her a flood of memory, for some kind of epiphany, that these images would unlock some door in her mind and her life would come rushing back to her. She vaguely remembered the church, but she didn't connect with the footage. So that moment in the film was very much about the impossibility of going back to an idealized past. But it was also about the power of the women's faith, the strength it gave them not only to survive but to make meaning and beauty from their lives.

Can you comment on your use of sound—both music and voice-over—in **Passing** *and* **Fuori/Outside** *and on your unusual technique of interspersing silent moments or gaps in sound across the narrative?*

In each piece, music tells a parallel story. In *Passing*, blues and gospel songs tell of black women who defied the laws of slavery and segregation. In *Fuori/Outside*, the songs are in the dialect my grandmother spoke in her own home, in her own community, and they relate back also to peasant life in southern Italy, from which she was only one step removed. I like to use silence as breathing space, to let the audience have time to reflect on what's been seen and said, and to bring their own stories into the one that I'm telling, so that the viewing is active and intimate.

What new projects do you have under way, and how do these works in progress connect to **Passing** *and* **Fuori/Outside** *?*

I'm working on a piece about immigrant women (Puerto Rican, Mexican, Italian, and Haitian) in East Harlem and their relationship to the Madonna of Mount Carmel, to which I refer in *Fuori/Outside*. I'm just in the beginning stages now, but it's going to look at how these women create community through faith, across lines of race, ethnicity, and language. It will have autobiographical elements as well. In addition, I'm finishing up a project that I began two years ago in Sicily, about recent immigrants from Africa and Asia in Palermo. It juxtaposes ideas of Sicily as an unchanging, timeless place with the realities of Sicilian life in the twenty-first century. It also reflects on my desire to return to this homeland that lies between Europe and Africa, and the impossibility of that return.

NOTES

1. *Passing* runs 9 minutes, and *Fuori/Outside* runs 12 minutes. Both films are available through Third World Newsreel. For more information, see www.twn.org.

Kym Ragusa *holds an M.A. in media studies from the New School for Social Research and has taught writing and film studies at Eugene Lang College and at the City University of New York. Her publications include "Geographies of Memory and Race: The Making of* Fuori/Outside *" in* The Politics of Race-Making in the United States *(forthcoming, Routledge) and "Baked Ziti" in* The Milk of Almonds: Italian American Women Writers on Food and Culture *(forthcoming, Feminist Press).* **Livia Tenzer** *is an editor at the Feminist Press.*

Copyright © 2002 by Kym Ragusa and Livia Tenzer

Women Make Movies Responds to Hate

Xochitl Dorsey

As is true for many nonprofit organizations located in Lower Manhattan, the tragic events of September 11 have had a profound impact on the staff and community of Women Make Movies. In the nearly thirty years in which we have distributed and supported films by and about women, we have never had to respond to a single event with such broad political, social, and cultural implications for our daily lives. For us as a New York–based arts institution, the destruction of the World Trade Center also signaled the entry into a new era of uncertainty for our organization and has prompted us to reflect on our mission as a feminist, multicultural distributor of films and videos.

Since 1972, Women Make Movies has encouraged progressive thought and creative freedom among women filmmakers from a wide variety of ethnic and cultural backgrounds. Many of today's most acclaimed women directors—including Jane Campion, Julie Dash, Kim Longinotto, and Trinh T. Minh-ha—began their film careers with us, only to later inspire other women to create films that explore themes related to art, identity, and politics. In the same vein, Women Make Movies was among the first to foster a feminist-friendly work environment for women entering the business of film distribution and promotion. This unique history, coupled with the organization's dedication to supporting the arts and education through alternative media, has not only made Women Make Movies a long-standing advocate for quality films by women, but also an organization dedicated to advancing social change.

Prior to 9/11, this precedent was the motivation for many of our current staff members to join the Women Make Movies team. However, in the wake of the World Trade Center disaster, returning to our offices presented numerous challenges to our ideals on work and activism. Many of our staff members questioned whether our aims were still relevant in the aftermath and felt conflicted about proceeding with our normal workday. Our purpose momentarily seemed inconsequential in the scheme of world events.

After we regrouped as an organization, we realized that like many other nonprofits in New York City, we held a collective feeling of dis-

Through encounters with three generations of women in filmmaker Fatima Jebla Ouazzani's family, *In My Father's House* (1997), one of the films included in Women Make Movie's "Response to Hate" campaign, explores shifts and changes in Moroccan and Islamic culture.

Photo courtesy of Women Make Movies

empowerment, coupled with an overwhelming need to respond to the tragedy in some form. Through numerous discussions we found that our immediate social and political concerns post–September 11 were quite similar: we saw a lack of representation of women in the mainstream media and felt deeply concerned about the effects of racial profiling on the Arab and Muslim communities. We were especially disturbed by representations of the Middle East on television, which presented this region as a territory inhabited only by men. Women were almost completely barred from view—except in footage featuring them veiled and running down war-torn streets—and seldom given an opportunity to speak authoritatively on political or foreign policy. As the distributor of a highly respected collection of award-winning films and videos about women in Islam and in the Arab world, we knew quite well that there existed an alternative perspective to the mainstream. It was our director of distribution and marketing, Vanessa Domico, who pointed out that our organization was capable of filling in the information gap about Arab and Muslim women missing on the nightly news.

When we first began to discuss our organization's reaction to September 11, many other educational distributors also began seizing the opportunity to announce the availability of films and videos related to the Arab and Muslim community. This posed a profound ethical dilemma for Women Make Movies. Was it appropriate to promote our films as a result of this event? Could we provide our educational resources without cost? It was generally agreed that informing people about educational resources—especially those that related to current events—would not compromise any organization's moral principals. However, as a nonprofit distributor, we felt compelled to find a way to provide our films and videos to the educational market free of charge. We were seeking a communal gesture that would allow our organization to give back after personally experiencing such a devastating event. The result was the creation of our special campaign, "Response to Hate."

The concept of "Response to Hate" was simple: provide free rentals on a selected group of Middle East titles to universities and nonprofit organizations for the purpose of educating the community at large about the Arab and Muslim experience. We would supply the tools for groups to organize teach-ins or screenings to foster communication; challenge cultural stereotypes; and, perhaps, prompt new forms of grassroots activism.

In a matter of days, all the staff members at Women Make Movies pulled their talents and professional skills together in solidarity to prepare our "Response to Hate" campaign and make this offer available to as many institutions and individuals as possible. This not withstanding, our most ardent supporters were our filmmakers, as well as the National Film Board of Canada (*Four Women of Egypt* and *My Heart Is My Witness*) and NOS Sales (*In My Father's House*), who generously donated their films and videos without a concern for monetary reward. The filmmakers who contributed their films to "Response to Hate" are listed here with the titles of the works included in the offer, the dates the films were made, and the countries represented in the films: Jeanne C. Finley, Mine Y. Ternar, Gokcen Hava Art, and Pelin Esmer, *Conversations Across the Bosphorous* (1995, Turkey); Tania Kamal-Eldin, *Covered* (1995, Egypt); Sabiha Sumar, *Don't Ask Why* (1999, Pakistan); Tahani Rached, *Four Women of Egypt* (1997, Egypt); Claire Hunt and Kim Longinotto, *Hidden Faces* (1990, Egypt); Fatima Jebli Ouazzani, *In My Father's House* (1997, Morocco); Maysoon Pachachi, *Iraqi Women: Voices from Exile* (1994, Iraq); Olga Nakkas, *Lebanon: Bits and Pieces* (1994, Lebanon); Louise Carré, *My Heart Is My Witness* (1996, Algeria, Mali, Morocco, Tunisia); Erica Marcus and Susana Blaustein Muñoz, *My Home, My Prison* (1992, Palestine); Kay Rasool, *My Journey, My Islam* (1999, India); Persheng Sadegh-Vaziri, *A Place Called Home* (1998, Iran); Haim Bresheeth and Jenny Morgan, *A State of Danger* (1989, Israel); Mehrnaz Saeed-Vafa, *A Tajik Woman* (1994, Afghanistan); and Norma Marcos, *The Veiled Hope* (1994, Palestine).[1]

In addition to these films on the Middle East, we also included two films on the Japanese internment camps of World War II: *History and Memory* (1991, U.S.A.) by Rea Tajiri, and *Who's Going to Pay for These Donuts, Anyway?* (1992, U.S.A.) by Janice Tanaka. We added these seemingly unrelated documentaries because they highlight an unfortunate period in American history when fear and prejudice prompted the removal of civil liberties on a targeted ethnic group. We believed it was important to provide these films in order to allow our viewers to discuss and reference the effects that racial profiling has had on public and cultural policy in the United States.

With the support of our filmmakers, staff, and board of directors, we posted the following statement announcing "Response to Hate":

Dear Friends,

The staff and Board of Directors at Women Make Movies would like to express our deepest sympathies to the families, friends and victims of the September 11th tragedy. Although our office is located just a few blocks away from the site, we were fortunate not to have lost any of our immediate family of co-workers and loved ones.

As the nation collectively responds to this horrific event, we have become increasingly concerned with the violence against Arab-Americans and Muslims, as well as the alarming trend toward racial profiling. We believe it is of utmost importance to sensitize people about the culture and traditions of the Arab and Muslim community, both abroad and in the United States, in order to avoid further prejudicial attacks and denouncements of any one ethnic group. To accomplish this feat, we believe it is vital to share educational resources that teach tolerance and an appreciation for cultural diversity.

At Women Make Movies we have chosen to contribute to this effort by providing *free* rentals on a selected group of titles on the Middle East and Arab culture through December 31, 2001. Also included in this offer are two documentaries on the U.S. Japanese internment camps of WWII, entitled *Who's Going to Pay for These Donuts, Anyway?* and *History and Memory*. We've added these titles in order to provide a historical reference to an episode in U.S. history when prejudice and fear dictated behavior and policy in this country.

It is our sincere hope that this gesture will assist to humanize the Arab-American and Muslim community and demonstrate the vast sources of alternative educational media available to the viewing public.

The reaction was overwhelming and immediate to "Response to Hate." Not only did nonprofit organizations and universities answer our call, they also forwarded our message to their constituents through e-mail campaigns and listserv postings. Rather than being limited to our community base, we were able to reach out to thousands more and screen our films at hundreds of universities, museums, festivals, and community organizations around the country. Many individuals, including our filmmakers who were not directly involved in the campaign, responded immediately simply to thank us for the gesture. Perhaps the most inspiring outcome of "Response to Hate" was hearing from a cross-section of the nation about how September 11 has affected their lives. There was an overriding sense of community and collective drive to foster tolerance, dialogue, and understanding. Schoolteachers, arts administrators, local activists all replied with simple messages such as "I am going to try and initiate a screening and discussion for our students, most of whom come from economically disadvantaged backgrounds and know very little about the Middle East/Arabs/Islam," or "I just got the message here in Istanbul . . . such a wonderful, thoughtful, generous response . . . just the idea lifts the spirits."

In the New York area, we had several opportunities to see firsthand how the viewing public received "Response to Hate." In one example, we presented films in collaboration with two local feminist groups, the Third Wave Foundation and WERISE (Women Empowered through Revolutionary Ideas Supporting Enterprise) in a program titled "Women for Peace and Empowerment: Movies Move Views." The attendance at this event was overwhelming, even standing room was occupied for the length of the two-hour program. After our films were shown, the screening room was alive with debate, as viewers one by one shared what they learned and how it fit into their understanding of the contemporary Arab and Muslim world. It proved without question the need for sharing information and creating open forums for discussion and debate about the events of September 11 and afterward. More important, it demonstrated to all of us at Women Make Movies that our mission and educational aims and the overall support of independent media are now more important than ever.

The experience with "Response to Hate" allowed us at Women Make Movies to reaffirm our long-standing support of films and videos that present the alternative perspectives and creative achievements of women from diverse cultural and ethnic backgrounds. As we approach our thirtieth anniversary, we will continue to promote the voices of women filmmakers who help us interpret the complexity, conflict, and beauty of the world we continue to inhabit.

NOTES

1. For complete production information relating to the films included in the "Response to Hate" offer, see the Women Make Movies catalog at www.wmm.com.

Xochitl Dorsey serves as marketing manager at Women Make Movies. She holds an M.A. in Latin American and Caribbean studies, as well as a professional certificate in museum studies, from New York University, where she founded the Center for Latin American and Caribbean Studies film series.

Copyright © 2002 by Xochitl Dorsey

Uncovering the Harem in the Classroom

Tania Kamal-Eldin's *Covered: The Hejab in Cairo, Egypt* and *Hollywood Harems* Within the Context of a Course on Arab Women Writers

Diya Abdo

In an effort to promote understanding in the wake of September 11, Women Make Movies undertook a special "Response to Hate" campaign. Under this initiative, the organization lent their videos relating to Arabs and Muslims free of charge to organizations and institutions wishing to educate on the experiences of Arabs and Muslims, especially women. The offer came to my attention as I was constructing a course on Arab women writers. From the Women Make Movies catalog, I selected two films by Tania Kamal-Eldin, an Egyptian-born scholar and filmmaker currently residing in the United States: *Covered: The Hejab in Cairo, Egypt* was included in the "Response to Hate" offer, and *Hollywood Harems* was a regular feature. In the following essay I examine these films and the ways in which I hope to utilize them in the classroom. In adopting them for my course, I accept the generous offer, and the challenge, presented by the "Response to Hate" campaign. The films, supplementing the literary selections that are the core of my course, will no doubt help to educate my students about Arab and Muslim women and counter the gross misunderstandings perpetuated by consistent misrepresentation of Arab and Muslim culture.

The Teacher, the Students, the Course

In the spring of 2002, I will teach a course, Arab Women Writers in English, at Drew University, a small liberal arts college in Madison, New Jersey. The course will focus on the ways in which Arab women writers negotiate their, as one writer so aptly put it, "feminist longings and post-colonial conditions" (Abu-Lughod). The course has emerged from my own location and experience and reflects the area that is increasingly my central academic focus. The course will be a first for myself as well as the university. Born, raised, and educated in Amman, Jordan, I am completing a Ph.D. in English literature at Drew. Since my arrival in the United States, my self-imposed exile and perpetual homesickness have honed my cultural and national identity. Regularly exposed to women's issues and discourses on feminism, I began to think of myself in terms of multiple identities: Arab/Palestinian and woman. As a result, my literary interests shifted toward twentieth-century Arab women's writing.

The syllabus I have devised includes seven novels by Lebanese, Jordanian, Palestinian, Syrian, Egyptian, Algerian, and Moroccan women writers, as well as an anthology of essays, short stories, and poems by women from these and other countries. The texts deal with historical, political, social, religious, and cultural aspects of Arab society. Our discussion will focus on, among other things, women and war, religion, patriarchy, colonialism and the colonial legacy, and sexuality. I hope that the students will come to formulate a vision of Arab feminism within the specific religious and political history of the region.

After September 11, however, it became clear that my course at Drew would need to encompass much more. Particularly in need of examination would be the politics of representation of Arab women, whether it be by the West or by Arab women themselves. Because the class meets a general education requirement, the nature of the audience becomes extremely relevant. My students may be male or female; Arab, Muslim, or neither; freshmen or seniors; women's studies or English majors; or anything else. Some of these students I know personally from previous courses or as residents in the Islamic Culture Theme House in which I serve as advisor. Others I will be meeting for the first time. Some students will have enrolled to learn more about their culture, about their religion, or about women in a culture. No doubt some students' interest will have been sparked by recent events and the now ubiquitous images of Muslims and Muslim women in the media. Many will enter with preconceived notions of Arab women and Arab culture, falsehoods that the media has largely reinforced since September 11. However, I maintain the hope that my students will be intelligent critical thinkers with open minds to learn about "other" women and other feminisms.

Recognizing the potential pitfalls of teaching Arab women's writing to such a diverse audience in a Western space, I decided that one or more short, powerful films could be an effective means of introducing complex issues in an engaging yet nonthreatening manner. After searching through available titles, I selected *Covered* and *Hollywood Harems* by Tania Kamal-Eldin because these films will serve to introduce the class to the Arab world in general, and Arab women in particular. Since the literature we will study is postcolonial, I must also address some concepts in postcolonial theory, the most relevant of which is Orientalism. *Hollywood Harems* offers an ideal introduction to this concept, confronting students with the very preconceptions that they will need to leave behind in order to appreciate the texts they will read in this course. *Covered* will serve to inform students on perhaps the most well-known, and most commonly misunderstood, Arab and Muslim women's issue: the hejab, or veil.

In developing this course, I will take into account not just the nature of my audience, but also my own role. Although I am an Arab woman raised in the Arab world, my viewing lens has been honed and shaped in the West, where I have been exposed to a largely Western model of feminism. Currently I am a privileged Arab woman studying other Arab women at an American college in a white upper-middle-class community. As such, I am simultaneously insider and outsider with regard to the subject of our study. As Amal Amireh observes, inappropriate Western feminist paradigms are often applied to the Arab world, even by Arab women scholars themselves (185). In my own attempt to examine Arab women through their lives and texts, I must not engage in the "elaboration of a victim discourse that fetishizes Islam [and] reifies Arab women" (186), such that they become "objects—of study, of pity, and of liberation" sans "agency and subjectivity" (185). Such an approach would replicate the condescending stance that First World women frequently tend to adopt toward Third World women (203). Just as oppression varies in type, degree, and circumstance, *feminism* is not a term that applies in the same way to all women across all cultures. Chandra Talpade Mohanty argues that "to define feminism purely on gendered terms assumes that our consciousness of being 'woman' has nothing to do with race, class, nation, or sexuality, just with gender,"(12) a frequent misapprehension among Western feminists. Many Third World women's apparent inability to speak out and rebel against their patriarchal communities finds its causes in a set of complex issues that go beyond gender. For example, the feminist struggle within the Arab world takes place against the backdrop of political struggles against imperialism.

To accommodate the particular nature of Third World feminism, avoiding simplification, I will maintain a holistic approach, neither privileging issues of gender over those of class and race (Amireh 185), nor privileging class and race over gender. The postcolonial, Arab, Muslim woman has much to negotiate in terms of her identity politics. The key is not to simplify any or all of these factors into cliches, such as the Arab woman's total oppression under Islam. A student not properly informed might easily perceive erroneously simple solutions to what are actually extremely complex sets of cultural, religious, and historical circumstances. The two films I have chosen to screen, one generously provided by the Women Make Movies "Response to Hate" campaign, will serve to help my students develop an appreciation for these complex realities, separate truth from media myth, and facilitate more complete understanding of the literature they will read. Below I discuss both films and place them within the context of the ideas and issues dealt with in my literature course.

Covered: The Hejab in Cairo, Egypt

The hejab, or veil, as it is commonly referred to in the West, is a problematic symbol. The West, and Western feminists in particular, fixate on this garment as a supreme symbol of oppression, seeing the covering of women solely as a gender issue. However, a more thorough understanding of the hejab is necessary to my course, since many of the novels we will read feature veiled or covered women as central characters.

Historically, the hejab has been a symbol for "Islamic" authenticity in the face of Western imperialism, since "European colonial and imperial powers that intervened in the Arab World in the nineteenth and early twentieth centuries often claimed that the advancement of women was a special concern of, and justification for, their intervention and rule" (Tucker x). Some Arab feminists see a disturbing similarity between colonial discourse and that of some Western feminists who "devalue local cultures by presuming that there is only one path for emancipating women—adopting Western Models" (Abu-Lughod 14). To this Western school, the hejab can have only negative, oppressive connotations.

The reality, however, is much more complex. The hejab can also be seen to put women in the position of representing the authenticity of the nation, if not Nation itself. During the Algerian struggle for independence, for example, the hejab became a tool for covert acts of rebellion (hiding guns, among others). Thus it stood for national independence in the face of imperialism, the fortification of a nation that must veil itself as protection from cultural rape by the imperial West. As one Algerian feminist states: "[F]aced with colonisation the people have to build a national identity based on their own values, traditions, religion, language and culture. Women bear the heavy burden of safeguarding this threatened identity" (Helie-Lucas 107).

However, as Helie-Lucas herself warns, "this burden exacts a price" (107). Thus, we must not idealize or romanticize the hejab as a noble symbol of anticolonial struggle and national independence. To ignore gender as a factor is also to disregard the sometimes oppressive nature of the hejab as it undermines women's agency and sexuality. Yet to view it simply as it relates to gender is to undercut its social, political, historical, cultural, and even economic significance. This is a complex phenomenon, the examination of which must be seen within the context of the region and its history. I would like my students of all backgrounds to engage in a discussion that examines and critiques the hejab in a more nuanced manner than one typically finds in Western circles. To this end, Tania Kamal-Eldin's film reveals some of the varied and complex reasons why women wear the hejab.

Covered opens to a panoramic bird's-eye view of Cairo. The narrator, Kamal-Eldin, is heard during this shot telling us that she was born in Egypt and returns there to visit occasionally. This time, she returns to Cairo to "find out the reasons behind the veil" (*Covered*). The filmmaker's biographical note establishes her as an "authentic subject" who can claim "the 'birth right' to represent [her] Arab sisters to a non-Arab audience" (Amireh 186). However, apart from this brief confession at the onset of the film, Kamal-Eldin's personality and identity are not revealed. On the contrary, she allows the women interviewed to speak for themselves. We do not hear her questions, and so cannot know how these conversations might have been initiated or manipulated. We are left to wonder about the filmmaker, whose quest it is to interrogate her subjects about their attire and appearance but who leaves us curious about her own. One is inclined to believe that Kamal-Eldin is not covered, but is that a safe assumption? Might her appearance on camera with or without a hejab damage the film's objectivity? Between sections of the film, we see artistic footage of a woman veiling and unveiling herself as the camera revolves around her; is this significant? I mention such things because I want my students not only to examine what is said in *Covered*—the reasons behind the wearing of the hejab—but also the way in which it is presented. What do they make of Kamal-Eldin's rhetoric, her choice of words and images, the absence of a visible interviewer or narrator? How does this Arab woman present and study her own society?

The women interviewed in *Covered* express varied reasons for donning the hejab. The hejab is an "order and injunction" from god, and therefore some comply in accordance with what they see as religious law. Others see it as a sign of respect for god and themselves or a symbol of spirituality. For others it is more clearly a duty. Some offer more practical reasons. It protects them from victimization by men, who because of poor economic conditions have turned to drugs. It protects them from harassment, temptation, pestering, vanity, changes in the weather, and unwanted male attention. (The narrator points out that, ironically, with regard to the last case, the hejab can have the opposite effect: men sometimes find covered women more mysterious and therefore more alluring.) Societally, the hejab legitimates women's appearance in the public space, says one interviewee, and thus allows them to participate in economic activity; hence the hejab "neutralize[s] that threat that comes from the male dominated society" (*Covered*). For some women, it is not a choice, but something imposed on them through pressure from family and peers.

Very interestingly, some women view the hejab as a powerful statement about their identity. They are proud to be Muslim and they want the world to know it. To one woman in *Covered*, the hejab is her rebellion and resistance against the "commercialization" of women's bodies that is so prevalent in the West. This particular interviewee, a journalist fluent in English, posits her feminism against the Western conception of women's liberation, which in her view has resulted in objectification, commercialization, and oversexualization of women. One point that I hope will emerge in class discussion is that this woman, despite her independent spirit, still defines herself in relation to the West. Her feminist identity is contingent on opposition to Western influence and a colonial legacy connected implicitly to veiling and unveiling. Certainly there are contradictions in the achievements of Western feminism, but ironically, in opposing this feminism, she has (like those who have opposed Western imperialism) reacted by embracing a traditional symbol of her culture. Can she really adapt that symbol to her own ends by discarding some of its conventional meanings? Either way, the students will see a strong, educated, clearly intelligent and independent woman who chooses to wear the hejab for well-defined, and feminist, reasons.

Another interesting interviewee is an American woman who converted to Islam upon marrying an Egyptian. She states that wearing the hejab is good for the survival of the family unit: if the husband sees only veiled women and therefore cannot compare his wife to anyone else, he will continue to find his wife desirable. I am hoping that the perspective of an American convert will give my students pause to think about how closely these ideas might relate to them. This woman grounds her belief in the notion that women are in fact more tempting and beautiful than men (an idea heard frequently in *Covered*), and that males are more easily tempted and perhaps not even fully responsible for their own actions. In this argument, one can clearly hear echoes of the "she asked for it" rape defense heard in Western courts. One woman in *Covered* speaks of "accidents," by which she clearly means sexual relations or perhaps rape. Her logical conclusion is that to prevent such accidents, women should cover or veil themselves. These covered women do not identify the other solution, offered by Shala Haeri, professor of anthropology at Boston University, that men should be educated on how to interact with noncovered women, to respect them regardless of their dress (*Covered*). I hope that my students will be able to identify these dilemmas, which are hardly unique to Muslim countries, and engage in a discussion of the shared similar experiences of women worldwide.

Another interviewee, who is completely veiled from head to toe, states that women must be protected from the "wounding" gaze of men; the hejab ensures her respectability and the sanctity of her private space. Such reasoning is quite attractive. However, it also assumes that the male gaze, the male desire, is more important than its female counterpart—if in fact, that female gaze and desire are perceived as existing at all. The male gaze, in contrast, is an assault that can take something away from its object. Not only does it exist, but it has a powerful, almost physical, presence. I hope to engage students in a class discussion of the "Gaze." Whose desire is important? Who is in control? Whose gaze is more significant and why? In attempting to deobjectify themselves, do these women in fact deny their sexuality and thus their agency and subjectivity, dismissing as well the female gaze, female desire, and female sexuality? How important is sexuality in the shaping of one's identity? How does it relate to other elements of identity such as class, race, and ethnicity? How can the students relate these issues concerning sexuality to their own lives and experiences?

These and other questions raised by *Covered* speak directly to issues that are central to a study of Arab women's literature. However, in addition to discussing the hejab itself, I want my class to critique and analyze the way in which Kamal-Eldin made this film. Is her goal simply to present points of view, or does the filmmaking and camera technique make judgments that are not made verbally? For example, at one point we see a slow-motion panorama of an Egyptian street in which a group of men stare lasciviously, even menacingly, into the camera. Their gaze seems truly "wounding," as one man slowly passes his palm over his mouth as if salivating. How are we to understand this scene? Does the camera, and by extension the audience, represent the uncovered woman being subjected to the hungry gaze of these "lions"? Is Kamal-Eldin's portrayal of Arab men objective? Stereotypical? Realistic?

In short, our class discussions of literature will involve the nature of the hejab; the way it is conceived in the West; the way it is conceived in the Arab world and the reasons behind it, implicit and explicit; and its historical, political, social, and sexual significance. *Covered* offers an ideal point of entry into such issues.

Hollywood Harems

The other film I will screen in class, *Hollywood Harems,* also by Tania Kamal-Eldin, will facilitate a graceful entry into discussion of Orientalism, a key concept in the examination of postcolonial literatures in a Western space. I hope that when students are confronted with one source of their own preconceptions—movies—they can begin to question those images of the East that through the years have been misused, distorted, or even invented by the Western lens. The film also highlights a myriad of issues of concern to Arab/Muslim women and women in general, for example, sexuality, agency, and subjectivity. Kamal-Eldin's film becomes even more directly relevant to the course, considering that several of our literary texts focus on harems, segregation, and confinement.

This short, intriguing film "takes critical aim at Hollywood's abiding fascination with and fantasies about all things east. Juxtaposing film clips from the '20s through the '60s, '70s, and '80s, Kamal-Eldin explores the organization of gender, race, sexuality in Hollywood's portrayal of the exotic East, an indiscriminate fusion of things Arab, Persian, Chinese and Indian" (Hartouni). To Hollywood, the "East" is a world of segregated women and vamps who perform "bizarre rituals." They are twirling dancers whose "eroticized performances were a hodgepodge of Arab, Persian, Chinese, and Indian dances." Hollywood presented "a collective portrayal of the exotic East undifferentiated by cultural plurality" (*Harems*). The women of this world are sexual, sensual, erotic, and sometimes violent. Their home, the East, is a world of orgies and lax morality. This world, and its women, are "hot," "exotic," "lavish," a "feast," and "wild" and are filled with "intrigue," "treachery," "beauty," and "glamour" as the 1942 trailer for *Arabian Nights* tells us. Such imagery catered directly to "Western male fantasies" (*Harems*). In a sense, these clips illustrate the power of the gaze—Western, male, and voyeuristic. The East is woman, the West is man, and the camera's lens the site of their heated liaison, the fulfillment of these male fantasies.

As Kamal-Eldin points out, Hollywood's film excursions into the Orient, especially ancient and biblical epics, were referred to as "T&S"

(Tits and Sand) movies. The very conjunction of these two words evokes the correlation between Woman and Land, and by extension Woman and Nation. In the colonial and colonized mentality, control of a woman and control of a land, the rape of a woman and of a nation, go hand in hand. Nowhere is this more clearly illustrated than in a song featured prominently in *Hollywood Harems*. The male singer declares in Vegas-lounge style, "Go east, young man!" in a clear reference to the pioneer cry of "Go west, young man." Kamal-Eldin sets these lyrics over a scene from *Son of Ali Baba* depicting exotic harem girls catering to the whims and fancies of a group of young males. Is the Eastern woman then uncharted territory in need of discovery, cultivation, and appropriation—just as indeed was their homeland to its European colonizers?

It would seem so, as Arab males are typically portrayed by Hollywood as primitive barbarians ruled by their sexual urges. As one clip taken from the silent movie *The Sheik* informs us: "When an Arab sees a woman he wants, he takes her!" Kamal-Eldin follows this with a number of scenes of Arab men ravaging and kidnapping tender exotic women—who are invariably later rescued by "white Western males" such as in *The Seventh Voyage of Sinbad*, *The Desert Song*, and *The Mummy* (*Harems*). Viewed in a larger context, it would seem that the white Western hero, in rescuing the Eastern woman from the Eastern man, undertakes the "white man's burden" of rescuing a colonized people from its own devices.

Another point in *Hollywood Harems* is Hollywood's paradoxical portrayal of the harem as a private female space that is nonetheless easily penetrated by men. Just as a woman's veil, "a symbol of inviolability" (*Harems*), is frequently seen being torn off, women are seen being denuded of their privacy in the harem quarters, historically off limits to men. Both transgressions elicit notions of rape, in which the woman's private sphere is subject to casual violation. In typical Hollywood fashion, the female often coquettishly repudiates the male while making it perfectly clear that she is quite happy to be "violated" or "taken." In fact, some clips portray women, often slaves or concubines, who are more than happy to oblige their masters and waive any rights they may have.

However, as the clips show us and as Kamal-Eldin tells us, "Eastern" women sometimes play more dominant roles; on rare occasions they are powerful femmes fatales whose aim is to bring about the "ruin of man and civilization" using their feminine and sexual wiles (*Harems*). Such assertive characters as Cleopatra, Sheba, Delilah, and Salome raise interesting issues about women's sexuality, its nature and power, and how it is perceived and presented. Does the representation of the sexually powerful Eastern vixen speak to any perceived relationship between East and West? Can the students identify a similar relationship between sexuality and politics in Western life and literature?

Before the close of this film, Kamal-Eldin reminds us that these images of the East from Hollywood's Golden Age have modern-day successors, with barbaric nomads and femmes fatales replaced by hijackers and terrorists, as in *Executive Decision* and *The Hostage*. These more recent films, given only brief mention in *Hollywood Harems*, will likely prove more relevant to my students, who are several generations removed from the *Sinbad* and *Ali Baba* epics. After September 11, the "Arab as terrorist" image has more power and more resonance than ever in Western media. Although it perhaps falls outside the scope of my course, we may continue discussion where Kamal-Eldin leaves off, applying her mode of critical analysis to more modern cinematic fare.

Finally, it is of stylistic interest that Kamal-Eldin's final narration in *Hollywood Harems* is accompanied by a black screen. We see neither the narrator nor a clip. How will students understand the significance of the filmmaker's refusal to allow us to gaze at her as she delivers her final monologue, rather presenting us with no image at all? Is she denying our gaze, our interest in her physicality as an Arab woman?

I hope that *Hollywood Harems* will first and foremost open my students' eyes to questions about their own preconceptions, and likely misconceptions, of the Arab world. How have they incorporated such images into their understanding of the Arab woman and the Arab world? How, as a result, do they relate to the Arab woman and the Arab world? Beyond these questions of personal subjectivity, the film raises several issues that will find echoes in the literary works we will examine. Of special interest is the way in which woman's sexuality is perceived and the role of that sexuality in the interaction between men and women. Does the power of the male gaze, in this case that of Hollywood, undermine or even eradicate the female gaze, and thus deny female agency? Is this indicative of a larger pattern? The film also touches upon the correlation between Woman and Nation, a significant theme with regard to novels on my syllabus that feature women relating to or taking part in nationalist movements. Finally, I hope the students will critique the gaze of the filmmaker herself: who is she; is she an insider or an outsider; what is she trying to do; how and to what end?

Visual Text, Printed Text

Although the examination of literary texts is the core of the course, the approach to these texts must take place within a cultural context.

Kamal-Eldin's films will help a class begin to establish that context. First, they invite us to critique ourselves and our misconceptions. Second, while not exhaustive studies, they do succeed in raising historical and theoretical ideas, which will be central to my course. *Covered* exposes us to some Muslim women's lives, their needs and ideas, providing a more complex approach to a commonly oversimplified phenomenon. *Hollywood Harems* invites us to explore representations of Arab women, the East, and Islam, and opens the door to Orientalist ideology. I hope that these perspectives will promote a better understanding of and appreciation for the complexity of the Arab world, Arab women, and Islam—an essential ingredient in approaching the literature. For example, the films will particularly inform our discussion of Assia Djebar's *Women of Algiers in Their Apartment* (Algeria) and Fatime Mernissi's *Dreams of Trespass: Tales of a Harem Girlhood* (Morocco). These two novels deal with issues of the harem (a real and not a mythical, idealized representation), the hejab, women's sexuality, the quest for independence in a patriarchal space, and women's role in national struggles. We can find similar themes in the other novels of the course: Ulfat Idilbi's *Sabriyya: Damascus Bitter Sweet* (Syria) also deals with the hejab, or veil, and national struggles; Hanan Al-Shaykh's *Story of Zahra* (Lebanon) deals with, among many other things, women's agency and sexuality in a state of war; Nawal El-Saadawi's *Woman at Point Zero* (Egypt) also focuses on sexuality and agency. Fadia Faqir's *Pillars of Salt* (Jordan) centers on women's confinement in a colonized, patriarchal community.

I have learned a great deal from watching these films and applying them in the formulation of this course. I have gained a more nuanced understanding of issues that even I, as an Arab Muslim woman raised in an Arab community, did not fully appreciate. I anticipate that the films will prove to be a nonthreatening, deceptively simple, vehicle through which a class can explore and discuss complex issues facing Arab women yesterday and today.

READINGS FOR ARAB WOMEN WRITERS COURSE SYLLABUS
Al-Shaykh, Hanan. *The Story of Zahra.* Trans. Peter Ford. New York: Doubleday, 1986.
Badran, Margot, and Miriam Cooke, eds. *Opening the Gates: A Century of Arab Feminist Writing.* Bloomington: Indiana UP, 1990.
Djebar, Assia. *Women of Algiers in Their Apartment.* Trans. Marjolijn de Jager. Charlottesville: Virginia UP, 1992.
El-Saadawi, Nawal. *Woman at Point Zero.* Trans. Sharif Hetata. London: Zed Books, 1997.

Faqir, Fadia. *Pillars of Salt.* New York: Interlink Books, 1997.

Idilbi, Ulfat. *Sabriyya: Damascus Bitter Sweet.* Trans. Peter Clark. New York: Interlink Books, 1997.

Khalifeh, Sahar. *Wild Thorns.* Trans. Trevor LeGassick and Elizabeth Fernea. New York: Olive Branch Press, 1991.

Mernissi, Fatima. *Dreams of Trespass: Tales of a Harem Girlhood.* Cambridge: Perseus Press, 1995.

REFERENCES

Abu-Lughod, Lila. *Remaking Women: Feminism and Modernity in the Middle East.* Princeton: Princeton UP, 1998.

Amireh, Amal. "Writing the Difference: Feminists' Invention of the 'Arab Woman.'" *Interventions: Feminist Dialogues on Third World Women's Literature and Film.* Ed. Bishnupriya Ghosh and Brinda Bose. New York: Garland, 1997. 185–212.

Covered: The Hejab in Cairo, Egypt. Dir. Tania Kamal-Eldin. 1995. Videocassette. Women Make Movies.

Hartouni, Valerie. Rev. of *Hollywood Harems,* dir. Tania Kamal-Eldin. Online. Available: <http://www.wmm.com/catalog/pages/c482.htm. 1 Nov. 2001.

Helie-Lucas, Marie-Aimee. "Women, Nationalism and Religion in the Algerian Struggle." *Opening the Gates: A Century of Arab Feminist Writing.* Ed. Margot Badran and Miriam Cooke. Bloomington: Indiana UP, 1990. 104–114.

Hollywood Harems. Dir. Tania Kamal-Eldin. 1999. Videocassette. Women Make Movies.

Mohanty, Chandra Talpade, Ann Russo, and Lourdes Torres, eds. *Third World Women and the Politics of Feminism.* Bloomington: Indiana UP, 1991.

Tucker, Judith, ed. *Arab Women: Old Boundaries, New Frontiers.* Bloomington: Indiana UP, 1993.

Diya Abdo *was born in Jordan, where she completed her undergraduate education in English literature and language at Yarmouk University. She is currently a Ph.D. candidate at Drew University and teaches composition and literature. Her doctoral dissertation will focus on Chicana and Arab women's literature.*

Copyright © 2002 by Diya Abdo

Motherhood, Desire, and Intimacy
Teaching Mexican Women's Films

Isabel Arredondo

I dedicate this article to the students in the honors seminar of spring 2000.

In the spring of 2000, I had the opportunity to teach an honors seminar, titled Motherhood, Desire, and Intimacy, at Plattsburgh State University in upstate New York. In the course I used North American and Mexican films to reflect on the ways in which images of women affect audiences. I wanted to provide students with alternatives to mainstream images of women and to discuss the importance of political and economic climate in the production of alternative images of women. In the curriculum, I sought to encourage students to write in creative and meaningful, but rigorous, ways, using both film and feminist terminologies.

The focus of the course was Mexican films created by female filmmakers during the presidential term 1988–94, a period during which several women made feature-length films. Their films represented mothers who could separate from their children, men who were the objects of desire of women, women who desired actively, and couples whose intimate life had become tedious. Given that I wanted the course to have a cross-cultural component and that I wanted to emphasize the new options offered by the Mexican films, I introduced several of the mainstream U.S. films of the classical period which are analyzed in Mary Ann Doane's *The Desire to Desire: The Woman's Film of the 1940s*. The Hollywood films of the 1930s and 1940s allowed for a teachable contrast; they also were more accessible to students than the films of the Mexican classical period and had been extensively analyzed by North American feminist film critics. The course, however, can be taught by offering a different contrast or by looking exclusively at films made by women.[1]

The course I taught focused on motherhood, desire, and intimacy, and was divided into three corresponding sections. In the first section, I used a U.S. film to get the students acquainted with a feminist analysis of motherhood: *Stella Dallas* (1937). Students were encouraged to respond to Doane's analysis of the film's representation of motherhood and afterward to use her analysis to read motherhood in the Mexican films. Comparing and contrasting *Stella Dallas* to *Una isla rodeada de agua* (*An Island Surrounded by Water,* 1985) and *El secreto de Romelia* (*Romelia's Secret,* 1988) went fairly smoothly. In the second section, on desire, I summarized Doane's interpretation of the visual mechanics of portraying female desire in the U.S. film *Humoresque* (1946). This time I asked for a written response from students: an essay about how the Mexican film *Danzón* (1991) represented female desire. In the third section, on intimacy, I reversed the order of film showings, presenting, first, the Mexican film *Sucesos distantes* (*Distant Happenings,* 1995) and, second, *Secret Beyond the Door* (1948). For their take-home final, I asked students to come up with their own theory of the way in which intimacy was represented.[2]

The assignments for the three-hour weekly class meetings were varied. They included readings from my book of interviews with Mexican filmmakers, *In Our Own Image: An Oral History of Mexican Women Filmmakers, 1988–1994;*[3] writing journal entries about the films we watched in class or the readings; and preparing three questions concerning the readings, the films we watched in class, or both. Students had to write three compositions, a five-page creative critical analysis, and a take-home final. They also had to make two presentations: one about a section of the readings and another about their creative critical analysis of the course's themes in films.

At the beginning of the course I gave out a list of the most important film terms from Timothy Corrigan's *A Short Guide to Writing about Film,* since there were several kinds of writing assignments that required the use of film terminology.[4] I described the use of the terms in class and asked students to create a reference card that they could easily consult when needed.[5] We talked about ways that film terminology could be used to detect the ideas that are behind films. For example, for their first composition I asked students to pick one scene of *An Island Surrounded by Water* and describe the filmic strategy that was most prominent. In their piece, they had to reflect on the psychological effect that that strategy could have on the audience.

In what follows I outline the connection of this course to my research, several of the central questions that I addressed in the course, the methodology I used, and some conclusions I reached from having taught the course. Finally, I include the course syllabus and a bibliography of additional readings.

Connection of This Course to My Research

The core idea for the course at Plattsburgh—to look at representations of motherhood, desire, and intimacy—came from my research. In 1994, delighted by the large number of active female filmmakers in Mexico, I decided to conduct an interview with the accomplished director María Novaro.[6] This interview, initially intended to be material for an article, burgeoned into a series of interviews and then into *Palabra de Mujer: Historia oral de las directoras de cine mexicanas (1988–1994)* (*In Our Own Image*), a book concerning five female filmmakers that includes biographies and filmographies. This book is divided into the three units that later defined my course. During the late 1980s, the topic of motherhood was predominant in Mexican women's films; in the early 1990s, desire was a common theme; and, by the mid-1990s, works on intimacy began to predominate.

My experience in conducting the interviews modified the way in which I viewed films. Whereas initially I had assigned a secondary importance to the economic and political climate, talking to the filmmakers made me realize that these were determining factors. High-quality artistic and technical films are considered part of the national patrimony in Mexico. Mexican filmmakers rely heavily on state support, to the point that the history of filmmaking can be divided according to presidential terms. The approach that each president takes toward the arts in general, and filmmaking in particular, determines the funds that are allotted to specific projects. The approach of each president and his/her team may even determine whether a given film can be made. Since female filmmakers had the opportunity to make films during the Salinas presidential term (1988–94), I attempted to understand the factors that allowed these women to make their films. After talking to the filmmakers, in designing the course I decided to give preeminence to the study of the economic and political conditions that allowed them to make films. I also decided to focus on the conditions of the film industry.

Introduction to the Course

I introduced the political and economic climate of Mexico by summarizing the introduction to *In Our Own Image*, where I had outlined these issues. The presentation, during which I also talked about how to summarize and present an outline, served as a model for the students' future presentations. I explained that during the 1940s, women in Mexico had serious difficulties in directing films. By state regulation, any film that was exhibited commercially needed to be made with the cooperation and approval of film unions. Since unions discriminated against women, women had to battle to direct. In my presentation, I argued that film schools, by giving female filmmakers confidence in themselves through democratic teaching, had a crucial role in encouraging these filmmakers to enter the film industry. Confidence alone, however, did not change state regulations. We read the interview with Alfredo Joskowicz (13–25), the director of one of Mexico City's film schools, in which he gives an overview of the situation faced by film school graduates. During the 1960s, film unions in Mexico were closed to film school graduates, and they allowed only union members to make movies commercially. Graduates and film buffs created a noncommercial circuit in and through film clubs that showed "quality" films. The gradual opening of the unions in the late 1970s, first to men from the film schools and eventually to women, and the disempowerment of the unions during the late 1980s, together with the state's privatization of the production, distribution, and exhibition of films, allowed graduates to enter the film industry.

Busi Cortés and other women, however, had built a system that allowed female students to direct, while complying with state regulations. Cortés, a student and teacher at one of the film schools, explains in her interview that, to make her first film, she used the film school Centro de Capacitación Cinematográfica (CCC) as a co-producer. Cortés had found a legal loophole: the participation of the school allowed her to disregard the regulation of using exclusively union members, while it permitted her to sell the film commercially. Cortés directed the film herself, hired small crews of union members, used students as technical workers, and obtained materials at low prices or even as donations. The school instituted her experiment as a contest: the *opera prima*. Winning graduate students thus had an opportunity to make their first feature-length films at the margins of the industry. The school had discovered a means by which they could help students produce high-quality films that were nevertheless low budget and legal. In her interview, Cortés explains that the *opera prima* was based on a lesson from home economics: a mother has to ask for food when her children are hungry; in the same way, a film graduate has to ask for film and workers in order to make a feature film.

Unit 1: Motherhood

While we were reading about the film industry in Mexico and the way in which it affected film school graduates, we watched films on motherhood. Given that I had decided to set up the discussion using North

American films, we started by talking about how motherhood was treated in *Stella Dallas*. I introduced the class to Doane's idea that the film presents the mother, Stella, as almost incapable of separating from her daughter. Doane contends that Stella finally learns how to separate only at the end of the film. Besides giving up her "unhealthy" attachment to her daughter, Stella is asked to give up her sexual desire. We concentrated on Doane's analysis of the last scene in the film, which portrays an otherwise flamboyant Stella wearing simple clothes, looking through a window at her daughter's wedding. We discussed the meaning of the smile on Stella's face and her stance at a distance from her daughter.

Stella Dallas set the contrast for *An Island Surrounded by Water,* a film by María Novaro in which adolescent Edith goes to Atoyac looking for her mother. In class we discussed the scene in which Edith's mother, who appears for a very short time, joins the guerillas and leaves the infant Edith with a neighbor. Our main question was, Are mothers inevitably attached to their children and unable to separate from them? What strategies and logic did both films use to ask and answer this question? I asked the students to reflect on strategies used by the film—such as positioning of the camera and use of frames, sounds, and editing—to represent attachment between mothers and children, and on whether the films "worked" on us as an audience.

After considering the images of infants and adolescents in *An Island Surrounded by Water,* we looked at the way in which adult women who are themselves mothers relate to their own mothers. We used *Romelia's Secret,* by Busi Cortés, a film that compares three generations' approaches to love. In 1938, Romelia marries Don Carlos, who sends her back to her parents' house, accusing her of not being a virgin. After this dishonor, Romelia leaves her provincial village and does not return until after the death of Don Carlos, when she returns to the house where she was born, accompanied by her daughter, Dolores, and her three grandchildren, Aurelia, Romelia, and María. There, Doña Romelia explains to Dolores that she had kept the sheets from her wedding night all these years as proof of her virginity. Dolores doesn't understand her mother's actions because she doesn't feel her mother owes her any explanation. The three grandchildren, who steal and read Don Carlos's diary, express their opinions about their grandparents' relationship.

While watching *Romelia's Secret,* we read the interview with its director. Cortés explains that in the short films she made at school, she was "'misogynist' towards men" and that she questioned masculine centrality by reducing males to the role of transcribers. According to her short *Hotel Villa Goerne* (1979), only women create stories. In *Romelia's Secret*, Cortés developed female characters who questioned the beliefs inherited from and by the women of a woman's family. In the interview, she explains her preference for melodrama as a way to approach a diverse audience, and she clarifies that she writes her scripts after first choosing an actress. After viewing and discussing the film, the students wrote a journal entry on their emotional response to the film, the interview, or both.

To wrap up the theme of the relation of adult women to their mothers, students had to answer the question, Does Dolores in *Romelia's Secret* reconnect with her mother? In their second composition, the students had to use film analysis to decide on how the film portrayed the separation between mother and daughter and the effects that that portrayal had on the audience. It surprised me, during small-group and general discussions of the compositions, that students believed that mother and daughter did not connect at all and that the students chose scenes in which separation was most obvious. I had analyzed the film as a portrayal of difficult but meaningful reconnection. Looking back, I think that I missed the opportunity to discuss the students' hope for, at least, one scene of complete reconnection between mother and daughter.

Unit 2: Desire

The unit on desire required sophisticated skills in film analysis. Somewhat naively, I had planned to present to the class a simplified version of Doane's analysis on the dynamics of desire on *Humoresque,* and then discuss the questions, Are women dependent on being a spectacle? and, What are the effects of having females as objects of desire for the audience? We watched a scene that takes place at a party in which a wealthy married woman, Helen, played by Joan Crawford, falls in love with violinist Paul (which Doane analyses in *The Desire to Desire*). I showed it several times to illustrate the point that the image that we see on the screen, a close-up of Helen in which her shiny lips and beautiful eyes are emphasized, does not correspond with what the film narrative seems to be saying. While the film narrative directs the audience to read that scene to mean that Helen is falling in love with Paul, what we see on the screen is not Helen's object of desire, the violinist, but the audience's object of desire: desirable Helen.

Almost all the journal entries for that class indicated the students' confusion during my presentation. They complained that they did not know who the object of desire was in the film, much less what I meant by *object of desire*. I then decided to give another explanation. I brought my video camera to school, connected it to a TV, and asked for two volunteers. I then shot a scene of looks of desire between a male and a female in first a 1940s and then a 1990s fashion. The students could watch the camera movement on the TV and simultaneously hear my explanation. In the 1940s version, which I shot first, I showed the woman as the audience's spectacle; I took an exaggeratedly long close-up of the female student. The female student, I explained, was the audience's object of desire—the camera concentrated its time and energy on her.

I then went on to shoot in the 1990s fashion (which represented the alternative image that we were going to see in the Mexican film *Danzón*). To make a contrast with the 1940s version, I took a very short shot of the female student and quickly moved and lingered on the male student, taking a exaggeratedly long close-up of him. The class started to laugh and feel uncomfortable when the male student became the camera's object of desire. I then asked the students which of the two versions they would choose to represent Helen's falling in love. Most of the class agreed that the second version worked better than the first. We went back to watch once more the scene in *Humoresque* in which Helen sees the violinist for the first time. This time, I turned the volume off and asked for a volunteer to explain to the class what she was seeing. After the student's explanation, most students agreed that although the film is supposedly narrating Helen's desire, what we are seeing on the screen are Joan Crawford's beautiful lips and shiny eyes, images that do not represent her desire but fulfill the audience's desire for her.

The Mexican film *Danzón* followed *Humoresque*. In *Danzón*, Julia, a telephone receptionist in Mexico City, goes off to Veracruz, apparently in search of her disappeared dancing companion, Carmelo. As the film progresses, however, the viewer realizes that Julia has other reasons for going. Instead of crying over the loss of her dancing companion, Julia takes advantage of being in Veracruz to discover the world of sensuality, to make new friends, and to have an affair with a handsome sailor.

I used the scene in which Julia is in her hotel room with the sailor, Rubén, to talk about an alternative way of showing feminine desire: one in which the male is the audience's and the female character's object of desire. I supported my explanation by referring students to an anecdote told by the director of *Danzón*, María Novaro, in her interview. Novaro explains that to shoot that particular scene she had to "retrain" the cinematographer and show him how to represent desire from a female point of view. The cinematographer was afraid to linger on the male body, almost as if he himself was touching this body![7] The students commented that the interview with Novaro, assigned to be covered in two days because of its length, helped them. Novaro explains that her work centers on women's emotions, on female characters who "own their own life." She also develops an emotional cinematic language through camera movements. Whereas traditionally, the camera movement tries to catch the actors at their best moments, Novaro subordinates the actors to the camera; she trains them to adjust to the camera movement so that she can focus on the characters' emotions. Novaro's work includes evaluating her emotional response as a spectator of her own work.

When the students had chosen one scene of *Danzón* on which to write their third composition on the dynamics of desire, they told me that they thought their assignment was easy. The compositions were excellent and some very insightful: one student, for instance, argued that the director places Julia in the shadows, where the camera can't enjoy her, so that the audience has to look at the body of the man who is lying with her in bed.

Unit 3: Intimacy

In the third section of the course, we talked about how to write a rigorous critical analysis that originated in an emotional response. I connected the assignment to Novaro's insistence on making work that is emotionally significant for her. I asked students to write a five-page critical analysis on issues that were emotionally significant to them. I wanted to discuss the advantages and the method of writing a rigorous, creative, and meaningful paper. As opposed to the topics of class compositions, for which I had asked very specific questions, the topic of the creative critical analysis was open. I asked the class to find a theme they were interested in. I suggested that in order to find out about their interests, they could read their journal entries looking for some moment of a film, response in an interview, or other things that they had either loved or hated. Once they found the theme that had overjoyed or infuriated them, they had to analyze their reaction. Finally, they had to transform that emotion into a logically organized explanation and a coherent argument.

For most students, this was the hardest part of the course. During the informal meetings that I held with them, they told me that they did not have any positive or negative emotional reactions either to the readings or the films and that they couldn't find any emotions in their journals either. A few students panicked. I offered to read as many drafts as necessary, and I extended the due date for their convenience. (Honors students are for the most part highly motivated; I wouldn't make this offer to every student.) While the research project was tough for some, when the time came to give presentations to their colleagues, they felt proud of themselves. Several students wrote about the importance of film schools and about the reasons that the female directors claimed that they were not feminist. If I were to assign a similar project, I would spend more time on the effects of and reasons for assessing an issue that we care about, and talk about the frustrations and extra time that it takes to do such a project.

By the time the creative critical analysis was due, we had been looking at the theme of intimacy for four weeks. For this third section, I asked the students to come up with their own theories to explain what the images of intimacy suggested to them. In order to facilitate their work, however, I presented several Mexican films (which were hard to "read") and left them to analyze the North American one. Consequently, I had to reverse the order in which I presented the material, beginning this time with the Mexican films.

We also looked at the way in which several interviews included in *In Our Own Image* answered questions such as, How do we view the intimate life of the couple? How much does the individual share with the partner? What is enough and not enough? Does sharing depend on gender? What happens to couples along long periods of time? How do everyday acts, such as waking up, change in a twenty-year-old marriage? We watched the films mentioned in the interviews.

First, we looked at Guita Schyfter's film *Distant Happenings*, in which the entomologist Arturo Fabre becomes obsessed with uncovering the past of his wife, the Russian actress Irene Gorenko. Fabre discovers a letter in Russian that contains a photograph of Irene with another man and begins to get jealous. His jealousy grows when Fabre receives a visit from Viktor Fet, who, supposedly, is Irene's second husband. Fet tells Fabre that he has come to warn Irene that her first husband is looking for her. Because of these intrigues, Arturo begins to distrust Irene, but is unable to discuss the topic openly.

By reading an interview with Schyfter, we learned that she was born in Costa Rica, brought up as a Jew, trained in a film school in England, and now lives in Mexico. Schyfter likes to look at cultures as an outsider. In *Distant Happenings*, for instance, Schyfter explores intimacy within a culturally diverse couple.

Our next reading was the interview with Schyfter's co-scriptwriter for *Distant Happenings*, Hugo Hiriart. Hiriart describes intimacy by using the metaphor of a "two-way, narrow road"; he means that each partner in a couple walks in opposing directions, but since the road is narrow, they constantly rub shoulders. This rubbing against each other is his figure for intimacy. Although Schyfter looks at the couple from a cultural perspective, and Hiriart emphasizes the differences between male and female, neither recommends sharing every secret with the other person in the couple.

Hiriart's work connected us to that of Dana Rotberg, who made one of Hiriart's plays, *Intimacy,* into a film. Rotberg's film *Intimidad* (*Intimacy*) presents an affair between Julio, a man in a long-standing marriage, and Tere, a woman in a newer couple. Julio, a high school teacher with literary aspirations, watches Tere, a housewife who has great sexual exuberance, through a peephole in the wall. His life is transformed; the peephole brings new light into the room, and Julio feels his creative capacity renewed. Nevertheless, once their affair is established, the passion disappears and the relationship becomes a nightmare. Tere demands that she be supported in the fashion she deserves, and the situation leads to ridiculous results. In addition to bearing the emotional consequences of having two families, Julio must take out both families' garbage. Through its use of humor, *Intimacy* insinuates that love is an illusion that must constantly be renewed.

Watching the film helped us to understand the dispute between Hiriart and Rotberg that had been mentioned in the interviews. Responding to Hiriart's claim that his meaning of intimacy in the play was lost in Rotberg's film, the female director explains that gender and generational differences between herself and Hiriart might have played a role in conceptualizing intimacy.

We continued discussing intimacy by looking at Eva López-Sánchez's work. According to López-Sánchez, the heterosexual couple needs to have private and common "territories." López emphasizes the need to respect restricted areas not shared with a partner because, in her opinion, having secrets does not impede loving each other. She also remarks on the importance of making intimacy a voluntary act. We watched López-Sánchez's *Objetos perdidos* (*Lost and Found*), in which two travelers, who do not know each other, mistakenly take each other's suitcase when they arrive at a station. They each try to contact the other to return the luggage, but as they have difficulty meeting each other, each begins to use the other's personal effects. By means of this device, López-Sánchez explores how identity is negotiated within the intimacy of the couple. While we were talking about intimacy, we continued to discuss film schools and their importance for female directors. Since López-Sánchez's worked as a student in

Cortes's first *opera prima*, she talks about the importance of having had Cortés as a teacher and also of following her path. When *opera prima* had became a contest, López-Sanchez won it and made her first long-feature film.

Many students, who were in their early twenties, were disappointed with the idea of completely domesticated love represented in these movies and wondered why couples were still living together. In the opinion of half the class, the films portrayed love very negatively. Only some took the opportunity, which both readings and films gave, to reflect on ways to cope with and change an intimacy that had become stale. The discussion on *Distant Happenings, Intimacy,* and *Lost and Found,* although very divided, prepared the class for writing their take-home final on the U.S. film *Secret Beyond the Door.* I chose to discuss *Secret Beyond the Door* because it presents a clear contrast with the Mexican films and also because of its use of a spatial metaphor to represent intimacy. While many 1940s film support the idea that the couple can't be happy until every aspect of the individual's private life is shared, *Secret Beyond the Door* establishes a parallel between the intimacy of the members of the couple and the structure of the house in which they live. Mark, for example, has a room that he doesn't allow Celia to enter, a part of himself that he doesn't want to share. I believed that the blatant spatial representation of intimacy issues would help the students to see a contrast between the representation of intimacy in the 1940s and 1990s films.

Watching *Secret Beyond the Door,* most of the students laughed at the rosy ending in which the male mind is finally "opened" by the committed female character, who is also an expert in psychoanalysis. Students were also critical about the fact that the last scenes of *Secret Beyond the Door* give the impression that the couple is going to share all aspects of their personal life undisturbed and forever.

It was an enlightening experience to share my research with this group of students. I thank them for their patience, feedback, and care.

SYLLABUS FOR MOTHERHOOD, DESIRE, AND INTIMACY
Course Description

This seminar will make students aware of the effect of images in our lives. The central questions will be, What is the relationship between ourselves and the images that surround us? and, If, as many film critics suggest, we create our identity through the images we see, how could a change in images affect us?

We will be looking at two groups of films. The first consists of North

American films from the 1940s. The second is a group of films made by a young generation of Mexican women filmmakers between 1988 and 1994. We will use these films to track a change in the representation of females. We will compare their mothering styles, the expression of their sexuality, and the representation of their intimacy. During the course we will watch several films, discuss them, and read a book of interviews in which the Mexican filmmakers discuss their struggle to create new images. We will talk about how these new images affect us also, and how potentially they can affect a larger audience.

Assignments

Reading. For each class, students will be assigned a minimum of fifteen, and a maximum of twenty-five, pages of the book of interviews *In Our Own Image.* Students will come to each meeting with three questions from the reading or from the films. We will use these questions for class discussion.

Writing. Every week, students will write in their journals what they thought of the films we saw, the reading assignment, or both (at least two pages). Students will choose a topic of interest from the readings and write a five-page critical analysis comparing and contrasting how the same topic appears in the work of several filmmakers.

Presentations. Students will give two oral presentations, one about an assigned reading and another on the topic of their research.

Portfolio. Students will keep a portfolio of their work to assess their progress. We will talk about the portfolio on the day of the final exam.

Schedule
Unit 1: Motherhood
Week 1

Course introduction
Film: *Stella Dallas.*
Discussion: Stella Dallas as a mother.

Week 2

The Movie Industry in Mexico (Presentation 1—Arredondo)
Film: *Stella Dallas*.
Assignments: Journal due.
Readings: Film terminology from Corrigan, *A Short Guide to Writing About Film*

Week 3

Readings: "The Film School Graduates," *In Our Own Image*. (Presentation 2)
Film: *An Island Surrounded by Water*.
Discussion: Early attachments.
Composition 1: Choose one scene in *An Island Surrounded by Water*, analyze its elements, and explain the meaning that the elements have for the spectator.

Week 4

Readings: First part of chapter on Busi Cortés and "Free Lunch" (interview), *In Our Own Image*. (Presentation 3)
Film: *Romelia's Secret*.
Discussion: Reading of one another's compositions.

Week 5

Readings: Second part of chapter on Busi Cortés, *In Our Own Image*. (Presentations 4 and 5)
Film: *Romelia's Secret*.
Discussion: Adulthood and reconnection.
Assignments: Journal due. Reading of one another's journals.
Composition 2. Does Dolores reconnect with her mother?

Unit 2: Desire

Week 6

Film: *Humoresque*.
Discussion: The sexual look.
Assignments: Turn in composition 2; read one another's compositions and give feedback.

Week 7

Roundtable: Chosen topics for critical analysis. Bring a page describing your interest. Film: *Humoresque.*
Discussion: Consequences of the sexual look.

Week 8

Readings: First part of chapter on María Novaro, *In Our Own Image.* (Presentation 7)
Film: *Danzón.*
Discussion: The sexual look.
Assignments: Journal due. Reading of one another's journals.

Week 9

Readings: Second part of chapter on María Novaro, *In Our Own Image.* (Presentation 8 and 9)
Film: *Danzón.*
Discussion: Consequences of the sexual look.
Composition 3: What is the sexual look associated with in *Danzón?*

Unit 3: Intimacy

Week 10

Reading: Chapter on Guita Schyfter, *In Our Own Image.* (Presentation 10)
Film: *Distant Happenings.*
Assignments: Turn in composition 3. Discussion of compositions.

Week 11

Readings: Chapter on Hugo Hiriart, *In Our Own Image.* (Presentation 11)
Film: *Distant Happenings.*
Discussion: The intimacy of *Intimacy.*

Week 12

Readings: Chapter on Dana Rotberg, *In Our Own Image.* (Presentations 12 and 13)
Film: *Intimacy,* part 1.
Discussion: Stereotypes overturned in *Intimacy.*

Week 13

Critical analysis due.
Roundtable presentations of students' work (five minutes each).
Film: *Secret Beyond the Door.*

Week 14

Readings: Chapter on Eva López-Sánchez, *In Our Own Image.*
(Presentation 14 and 15)
Film: *Secret Beyond the Door.*
Discussion: Intimacy in *Secret Beyond the Door.*
Assignments: Journal due.
Take-home Final: Answer the following question: Is the intimacy presented in the Mexican films similar to or different from the one presented on *Secret Beyond the Door?* Bring your final compositions to the class and we will discuss them. Individual meetings for portfolios.

REFERENCES

Arredondo, Isabel. *In Our Own Image: An Oral History of Mexican Women Filmmakers, 1988–1994.* (Unpublished English translation of *Palabra de Mujer*).
———. *Palabra de Mujer. Historia oral de las directoras de cine mexicanas (1988–1994)* Madrid: Iberoamericana and Universidad Autónoma de Aguas Calientes, 2001.
Ayala Blanco, Jorge "La mirada femenina." *La disolvencia del cine mexicano entre lo popular y lo exquisito.* México D.F.: Grijalvo, 1991. 461–51.
Chong, A. Noriega, and Steven Ricci, eds. *The Mexican Cinema Project.* Los Angeles: UCLA Film and Television Archive, 1994.
Corrigan, Timothy, *A Short Guide to Writing About Film.* New York: Longman, 1998.
Doanne, Mary Ann, *The Desire to Desire: The Woman's Film of the 1940s.* Bloomington: Indiana University Press, 1987.
Hersfield, Joanne. *Mexican Cinema/Mexican Women, 1940–1950.* Tucson: University of Arizona Press, 1996.
Hersfield, Joanne, ed. *Mexico's Cinema: A Century of Filmmakers.* Delaware: Scholarly Resources, 1999.
King, John. *Magical Reels: A History of Cinema in Latin America.* Critical Studies in Latin American Culture. London: Verso, 1990.
Kolker, Robert, *Film Form and Culture.* New York: McGraw-Hill, 1999.
Martin, Michael T., ed. *New Latin American Cinema.* Vol. 2. Detroit: Wayne State UP, 1997.
Millán, Márgara. *Derivas de un cine femenino.* Mexico D. F.: Programa Universitario de Estudios de Género, 1999.
Mora, Carl J. *Mexican Cinema: Reflections of a Society, 1896–1988.* Berkeley and Los Angeles: University of California Press, 1989.

Paranaguá, Paulo Antonio, ed. *Mexican Cinema*. London: British Film Institute, 1995.

Pick, Zuzana. *The New Latin American Cinema: A Continental Project*. Austin: U of Texas P, 1993.

Plazaola, Luis Trelles. *Cine y mujer en América Latina: directoras de largometrajes de ficción*. Río Piedras: Editorial de la Universidad de Puerto Rico, 1991.

Ramírez Berg, Charles. *Cinema of Solitude: A Critical Study of Mexican Film, 1967–1983*. Austin: U of Texas P, 1992.

Rashkin, Elissa. *Women Filmmakers in Mexico: The Country of Which We Dream*, U of Texas P, 2001.

Torrents, Nissa. "Mexican Cinema Comes Alive." *Mediating Two Worlds: Cinematic Encounters in the Americas*. Ed. Ana M. López, John King, and Manuel Alvarado. London: British Film Institute, 1993. 222–29.

NOTES

1. For setting a contrast with Mexican mainstream film, Hersfield and Ramírez Berg provide good resources. For an exclusive focus on films made by Mexican women, see Rashkin (if the audience is English speaking) and Millán (for a Spanish-speaking audience). These can be supplemented with Ayala Blanco's controversial but well-documented "La mirada femenina." To introduce other Latin American female filmmakers, see Pick or Plazaola.

2. The films for this course are available from FACETS (*Stella Dallas, Humoresque, Secret Beyond the Door, Danzón*), Woman Make Movies (*An Island Surrounded by Water*), and the Latin American Video Archives (*Romelia's Secret, Distant Happenings, Lost and Found*). For *Intimacy*, contact Metropolis Films at 212-888-3113.

3. *In Our Own Image*, an English translation of my book *Palabras de Mujer*, has not yet been published. Please contact me at arredondoi@westelcom.com for copies of the interviews in English. See note 6 regarding my interview with María Novaro.

4. Having taught several other courses on film, I would now use Kolker, because its explanations are clear, political, and accessible, and the CD-ROM that accompanies the book is a handy and powerful tool for students.

5. I would now recommend Kolker's CD-ROM as an aid in writing the paper.

6. See pages 196–212 of this volume for excerpts of this interview.

7. See pages 209–210 of this volume.

Isabel Arredondo is an associate professor at Plattsburgh State University. During her sabbatical year, 2001–02, she is working at the McGill Center for Research and Teaching on Women.

Copyright © 2002 by Isabel Arredondo

Whose Naming Whom

Using Independent Video to Teach about the Politics of Representation

Megan Boler and Katherine R. Allen

In this essay, we address how independent video can be used to help students recognize and contest the dominant culture's presumed right to represent the world. We examine how such videos provide alternative views, allow students to see how others contest dominant meanings, and help students to envision themselves and society with a sense of agency. From among the dozens of quality independently produced documentaries available for teaching about the intersections of race, class, gender, and sexuality, we select four documentaries on the basis of their usefulness and applicability in a range of classroom contexts and subject areas. The videos we analyze are *Tongues Untied* (1989); *Girls Like Us* (1996); *The Color of Fear* (1994); and *It's Elementary: Talking about Gay Issues in Schools* (1997).

We selected these videos based on our pedagogical experiences of using them in a variety of graduate and undergraduate courses in our respective departments, the Department of Teaching and Learning and the Department of Human Development and in our mutual affiliation with the Department of Women's Studies. Undergraduate courses in which we have used these films include Race, Class, and Gender; Schooling and American Society; Gender and Family Diversity; and Introduction to Women's Studies. Graduate courses include Feminist Social Theory; Schooling and Diversity; Perspectives on Human Sexuality; and Advanced Issues in Women's Studies. We have solicited feedback from students regarding their reactions to each of the videos for a variety of pedagogical purposes, including the assessment of how well students are learning to make connections among personal identities and political structures and assisting students in developing an informed reflexive consciousness (Allen; Boler).

Each of the videos we analyze enables educators to engage students in the following questions reflective of the politics of representation: Who has the power to name and construct social identities? How do the people depicted in the film challenge dominant representations of gender, sexuality, race, and class and thereby transform social identities? How does the film, as an independent representation not authored by Hollywood or other mass media, portray an alternative vision of social identities and political relations? Having watched this film, how do students engage in the contestation of dominant meanings and represent themselves with agency?

The four videos we analyze highlight these questions regarding the politics of representation in two central ways. First, simply by making independently produced documentaries available to students, the educator exposes students to images that have been marginalized from the mainstream of media and popular culture. Through exposure to independent video, students can begin to recognize the political importance of producing as well as witnessing alternative representations of identities and communities. Second, the documentary content of videos we examine highlights "who has the power to name," a question central to the politics of representation. Students are able to see the people represented in the documentaries struggle with the ways in which the dominant culture has named them or others. The experience of witnessing characters in the videos struggle with the politics of representation brings these issues to life and opens the possibility of engaging one's own students in similar direct struggles with the politics of representation.

Our theoretical understanding of the politics of representation is informed by the work of such theorists as Stuart Hall, Michel Foucault, and bell hooks. As Foucault states, "There is not, on the one side, a discourse of power, and opposite it, another discourse that runs counter to it. Discourses are tactical elements or blocks operating in the field of force relations; there can exist different and even contradictory discourses within the same strategy; they can on the contrary, circulate without changing their form from one strategy to another, opposing strategy" (101–02). While we may hope that by showing our students alternative representations of the world they will learn to recognize and resist painful and oppressive discourses, sometimes the opposite happens: they see the people represented in the videos only through the familiar "white supremacist patriarchal capitalist" gaze and quickly blame the victim (hooks 16). We find that our goals of social justice are often powerfully supported by using independently produced videos to expand our collective understanding of the power of naming, and how naming can be a source of oppression as well as a source of resistance to repression.

The discussions of the videos which follow are intended to illustrate how each documentary reflects the ways in which individuals and communities are named by the dominant culture, and, in turn, how individuals and communities resist the namings and stereotypes imposed by the dominant culture. Second, we hope to provide sufficient synopses of the films so that educators can decide if these documentaries are suitable to their own teaching context. Third, we integrate comments from our students to show the kinds of student engagement and critical reflection elicited by these documentaries.[1]

Tongues Untied

Beginning with its apt title, this remarkable documentary highlights the politics of naming. The video addresses how dominant voices are internalized, resulting in Black gay men's silence. "Silence is a way to grin and bear it," says a voice-over, while a Black man's grimace at homophobic and racist comments is shown. Naming is visually illustrated in the video when different voices are juxtaposed with very quick cuts, each voice shouting out a different name used to marginalize and silence Black gay men. *Tongues Untied* foregrounds the ways in which Black masculinities are constructed through contradictory cultural intersections. It reveals Black gay men as caught between the warring tensions of allegiance to the "Black community" (depicted in Riggs's autobiographical coming-of-age story that threads through the video, a story in which he learns that his forays with other young boys of his age warranted his being called "punk/faggot/homo"), religious values (depicted by the voice of the Black preacher quoting from the Bible and mouthing "Sinner!"), and racism (detailed in the story of Riggs's experience as the victim of a gay bashing and how a white man comes to his rescue, an event to which he attributes his "immersion in vanilla," his taste for "snow"—for white male lovers). The impact of this racism is foregrounded again when Riggs critiques gay porn for its hypereroticization and objectification of Black men. Then, in a very poignant scene, Riggs shows himself walking down Castro Street in San Francisco and passing another Black gay man, the two of them unable to look one another in the eye: "What are we afraid to see? One another's hurt and pain?"

One student offers a nice summary of the aesthetic structure of *Tongues Untied:* "Marlon Riggs's film is part testimonial, part spoken word/poetry, and part interview. The film is unconventional and nonlinear, but it is held together by the beauty of the poetry and spoken-word pieces that lace together the different parts to form a holistic view of gay Black life." Her summary foregrounds an aspect of Riggs's powerful social documentary that profoundly affects many viewers: the extensive intermingling of voice-over, rhythmic chants, poetry, and music with diverse images of Black gay men. The use of poetry—ranging from the work of Essex Hemphill to mantras in Riggs's own voice—creatively conveys the inner conflicts, humor, and vulnerability of Black gay men. Poetry eloquently voices the theme of the power of silence:

> Silence is my shield/it crushes
> Silences is my cloak/it smothers
> Silence is my sword/it cuts both ways

Other examples of the use of poetry include the film's opening and closing with a chorus of men's voices chanting "brother to brother/ brother to brother." Arguably, one of the most powerful culminating moments in the film is delivered through the chanted poetic lines: "anger unvented becomes/pain unspoken becomes/rage released becomes /violence cha cha cha . . ." Students invariably comment on their strong emotional reaction to this segment.

Tongues Untied is distinguishable from the other documentaries we examine in this essay by its unique aesthetic representations. In the distributor's review, Vito Russo, author of *The Celluloid Closet,* an excellent critical analysis of the representation of gay and lesbian characters in the history of Hollywood cinema, is quoted as saying, "Usually, politically and socially admirable films fall short of the mark in the aesthetics department. They are praised more for their good intentions. . . . Marlon Riggs has created that rarest of birds—a brilliant, innovative work of art that delivers a knock-out political punch." In part because of its unique beauty as a poetic film, *Tongues Untied* clearly offers an alternative to representations in mainstream film and documentary.

The subject matter of the video represents a taboo topic for many students (and indeed, its airing on the PBS program *P.O.V.* caused great controversy, as did Patrick Buchanan's use of this documentary to lambaste the National Endowment for the Arts). Educators—especially in the context of encouraging in-service or pre-service teachers to adopt lesbian-gay inclusive curricula—must work hard to counter the myth that to teach about lesbian and gay experience is to talk about sex. Riggs's film—produced, significantly, in 1989, and thus reflecting the AIDS crisis and its impact on gay men's experience of sexuality—invites such comments as the following, voiced by one of our students: "Why is this film so much about sex? Why doesn't it normalize black gay men by showing them with families and children?" Such a question allows discussion of how *Tongues Untied* represents a radical intervention in mainstream representation of Black male sexuality and of gay male sexuality. The documentary allows Black gay men the power of *self-representation* regarding their sexuality. It is about countering "silence = death."

The style of straightforward documentary combined with artistic license allows for unique exploration of the intersections of race and sexuality within different Black gay male cultures. Humor is used in the depiction of how some Black gay men use "finger snapping" to punctuate their speech. In another scene, Riggs talks about how dancing was historically a ticket for his assimilation into white culture, and is "now my passage back home." Another scene illustrates the "performance" of gender with men "voguing," doing dance/performance that "imitates" and incorporates "feminine" movements into engaging, slick, and polished artistic movement.

Students described the significance of the final refrain of the video: "Black men loving Black men is *the* revolutionary act." One student emphasized that Riggs is pointing out the "taboo" of this love of one Black man for another. "We are worth wanting each other," Riggs reiterates. The fact that the video ends with this revolutionary claim means that there is a positive conclusion to what has been depicted as a painful journey. This film encourages discussion of how an individual, or a marginalized community, can begin to reclaim a positive self-identity in the face of myriad attacks both from the dominant culture as well as, in this case, from within the African American community, as one student observed:

> One intersection of racism and homophobia is when the young men are asked to choose between their blackness and their homosexuality. This is not possible. As the poet says in the video, "choose between your left or right nut." This . . . is a mindless question. One cannot choose between two parts of themselves.

Girls Like Us

Girls Like Us illustrates the intricate ways in which discourses of religion, education, families, and peers construct and define norms of femininity and sexuality. This documentary—which won both an Emmy Award as well as Best Documentary at the Sundance Film Festival—shows the tremendous power of intersecting social structures as they shape four young women's lives. The four girls are interviewed in a variety of settings across a span of four years during their high school experience. In teaching the documentary, we asked students to identify "what people and institutions define what it means to be female for these girls." An undergraduate student captures this observation, saying: "In the movie, there was a strong notion that being female meant sexuality. In each girl's story, the topic of sex and pregnancy seemed to be the biggest issue. To me, it seemed that being female had to do with 'How are you going to deal with getting pregnant?'"

The experience of the adolescent girls in this video illustrates what Michele Fine calls the missing discourse of desire. In most cultures, and certainly within the culture of sex education in public schools, women are not given the language or the space to talk about their own desire. Rather, Fine identifies the three dominant discourses as victimization, violence, and individual morality. In the case of Raelene, a poor white woman, her notion of femininity privileges young motherhood over any other life choices. She became pregnant for the first time at age fourteen, had a child at fifteen, became pregnant again a year later, and did not consider abortion an option for her. A graduate student observes:

> The story about Raelene was very touching and made me want to reach out to her. She seems to want the right thing but she is not getting it and no one seems to tell her anything about life or show her where to learn. She seems like she is experimenting and failing.

Raelene's descriptions of sexual activity with male partners reveal a lack of knowledge about sexual agency, pleasure, and functioning. In one scene, she and her girlfriends confess to each other that they have never had an orgasm, despite having been sexually active for several years. Yet they all prefer sex with a man without a condom, as it allegedly feels less like a "dildo." In another scene, with her boyfriend, she describes requiring K-Y jelly in order to have intercourse with her previous boyfriend, because she had no passion for him, and sex with him gave her "sores."

Religious, societal, and family messages constrain the girls' ability to exercise a genuine sense of agency regarding their own sexuality and reproductive rights. Of the four girls, only De'Yona had been given accurate information about family planning, contraceptive choices, female sexuality, and the impact of teenage pregnancy on future life chances. Anna, a Vietnamese girl and the one presumed most-destined for college and medical school, admitted to having unprotected sex. Her friend chastised her, saying, "You know so much better than that."

The documentary contains many examples of contradictions within dominant discourses that the girls try to unravel. In terms of religion, there is a scene in which Lisa, an Italian working-class girl, and her friends are hanging out in a bedroom and talking about the contradictions they see between their Catholic education about the Virgin Mary and the reality of sexual intercourse and conception. There is a particular incident of resistance to the dominant culture's silence about female sexuality that stands out for nearly all of our students. This "counternarrative" arises with the one African American girl, De'Yona, and her grandmother, who is raising her. At the beginning, De'Yona is attending a high school for the performing arts, with plans to attend college and become a musical director. Her grandmother strongly supports De'Yona's creative aspirations. She explicitly instructs De'Yona to use birth control, provides condoms, and urges her to get monthly birth control shots. Our students consistently express a kind of surprised delight at the grandmother's frankness.

Yet De'Yona's narrative evokes significant pain and even despair for viewers, who, like her grandmother, invest great hope in De'Yona's musical talent. Early in her journey, De'Yona comments that she does not want to become a mother because there are so many little children already around her. After her favorite cousin, Man Man, is shot and killed, she becomes despondent, fails her senior year in high school, and gets pregnant. Her grandmother is hurt by De'Yona's pregnancy but does not take long to embrace the reality that a new baby is coming. She never wavers in her support for De'Yona, despite dashed hopes and dreams for the future.

We ask our students in what ways these girls have and use the power to shape their own lives. Almost without exception, the students parroted liberal individualism: they see the girls as having opportunities and choices. The students tend to blame the victim, accusing the girls in the video of failing to exercise free choice. They also blame them for the depressing circumstances in which they find themselves, but at the same time, some students could recognize the power of social structures in shaping girls' lives, as in the following student reflection:

> Watching the film, I felt like the girls did not have much power. Even though they had free will, they seemed to be caught in their surroundings. De'Yona was surrounded by her mother's children and her grandmother telling her to use birth control. De'Yona herself said she did not want children, yet she did not pass high school and ended up pregnant. They all have free will and exercise it. Several of them do this by having sex. However, none of the girls seriously branch out from what is expected of them.

Of all the videos we are examining, this one reflects the least hopeful portrait of possibilities of resistance to the dominant culture. Our students repeatedly commented on the sadness and hopelessness they found in the girls' lives. Clearly, early pregnancy and motherhood, school failure, postponement of college plans, and having to deal with death and other losses were realities that many of the more privileged white students watching this video found hard to swallow. They would prefer a more hopeful ending with De'Yona attending college and not having to face unplanned pregnancy, or Raelene stopping at only one child, or Anna being able to have a boyfriend and go to college. Despite a few hints of resistance that the students could relate to, including De'Yona's grandmother's direct support of responsible sexual behavior and Anna's homoerotic flirtation with her best girlfriend, only Lisa seemed acceptable to our students in that her life was turning out as expected. That is, compared to those of the others, her life most closely matched the normative heteropatriarchal ideal bought into by many of the students in our classes (hooks).

Despite the fact that many students tend to blame the girls for their so-called choices, they also acknowledge the power of social structures to shape life experiences. The ability to recognize how society and biography intersect and specifically how society constrains women's real choices is our shared pedagogical goal, and this video delivers that goal, as student comments reveal: "Society is a powerful machine that drives who we are and what we become. It's virtually inescapable and is almost always unpredictable"; "Especially in De'Yona's case, sometimes people and most definitely children don't have opportunities to change their own lives. The social structures shape it for them and they are left to survive under those conditions."

As teachers our goal includes helping students identify how the girls acted as agents, despite the social structures working against them. Many were able to pinpoint agency in the videos, even among the most poignant of stories, as one student observed: "These girls challenged the idea that girls should do as they're told and just sit and look pretty. These girls are all tough and regardless of how hard their situations got, they kept going (sometimes in the wrong direction, but nonetheless, they never gave up)." Another student noted that Anna was able to make her own choices, in spite of pressures from family and society:

> Anna definitely revolted against her parents and realized the inequalities in her life that she was experiencing by being female. Her father told her not to date but she did it anyway. She also down the road made the decision herself not to be sexually active which challenged the societal expectations for females to "put out."

In summary, *Girls Like Us* reveals the contradictory messages young women encounter as they struggle to find a sense of agency in the face of powerful social forces, as one of our students concludes:

> I believe the message that I can take from this film is how powerful *expectations* are. Expectations from society, from friends, from family members, and from ourselves all act to determine the choices we make (or are made for us). Resisting the expectations of others can be very powerful as well and can free us to do whatever we choose to do.

The Color of Fear

The Color of Fear documents a group of nine men of Anglo, Asian, Black, and Hispanic descent who, during a facilitated weekend retreat, confront issues of racism through an ongoing dialogue. The film portrays an unusually intimate and politically charged scenario, in which the viewer has the opportunity to witness emotionally harrowing and poignant conversations. As one student summarizes: "This was a compelling video about the devastating effects of racism on not only people of color, but whites as well. It was powerful, explosive, riveting." Another student observes: "This video was very beneficial for me to see. I had always heard of white privilege but never really was able to comprehend it. The video pointed that out as well as prejudices that other minorities have towards each other." While one might think that watching ninety minutes of men discussing racism would not be engaging, to the contrary, students find the film quite gripping. This is the one film most likely to be remembered by students when the semester is over. In fact, many of Megan's students show this documentary to their friends or teach it in their K–12 classrooms.

The video has some very heated moments, in particular, one in which the most articulate man in the film, Victor, who is African American, confronts David, the quintessential White Liberal. The heated exchange reveals David's privileged denial of racism. In effect, David's position can be characterized as follows: "I am not racist. I employ Mexicans. I am very friendly to them. I do not know why you colored people are so angry. You should not be angry. The white man does not want to stand in your way. If you are having trouble making progress in the world, you are standing in your own way." David's privileged liberal ignorance functions as a central focus of all of the men in the group. The group takes on the challenge of working to help David see his own racism, as one student remarks:

The white guy didn't have a clue to what he was talking about. It was so powerful, I thought Victor was going to get up and punch him out. The white man kept referring to the others as "you coloreds" apparently without thinking that that term itself is "racist." In the end he broke down and realized the feelings of hate and prejudice about persons of color that had been imposed upon him by a domineering and abusive father, and how today he is carrying that legacy.

The issue of whose naming practice carries authority, central to the conflict depicted in this documentary, is captured well by one student:

One of the major themes that caught my attention during the first half of the video was the idea of "being American." The young man of Japanese heritage commented that he strongly resisted applying for an American passport. According to Victor, being American means being white and privileged. The Mexican American man stated that he did not consider himself an American and that his ancestors were robbed of that title. The man of Chinese heritage commented that it is an insult to him to be called "American" because it denies him his Chinese heritage. The Black man with the short hair expressed his feelings about being an American by saying that he would "have to give up his ethnicity to become American." This theme especially interested me because of the rising feeling of nationalism expressed in the media since the terrorist attacks on September 11th. Currently there is a commercial on TV that includes many young men and women saying that they are "American." I wonder how many people see that commercial and are inspired by its message. I wonder how many watch it and are disgusted.

Another student's reflection on the invisibility of whiteness highlights the ways in which the film asks the viewer to contemplate how the dominant culture defines identity, and how the process of dominant cultural naming affects different people:

Victor, after having to explain to David that "being human" in the white person's mind requires people of color to "throw away" their identity and "to kill" themselves, asks David to define or name the White experience. David cannot, and instead replies, "we don't consider ourselves a part of an ethnic group." Victor goes on to tell David that "being white means you don't have to admit that being white is different from being a person of color. You step into a world that's already yours." Victor also goes on to say, "being white means you can blame minorities for their own victimization."

The video certainly offers a refreshing alternative to the stereotyped depictions of race and racism to which we are daily exposed by popular culture and the mainstream media. One student explicitly expressed her gratitude at seeing an alternative representation of racism:

> Among the refreshing things about the video for me as an Asian American woman was seeing a diversity of Asian American men, all willing to dispel the model-minority myths. This is not the case when I watch most visual media, which is why I gave up watching most of it long ago.

This film is best used later in the semester after racism and the construction of difference are discussed at some length because it evokes strong emotions. Students acknowledge the power of this video to address race and racism in ways that allow both white people and people of color to identify, to feel represented, and to think critically about the construction of racism, as seen in the following quotes:

> It was transforming for me to be a part of their experience. The camera work was spectacular. It came into things without being too intrusive. It showed the complexity of each man and the sameness of each man.
>
> As I cried, cheered, and ranted and raved at the different men in the video, I couldn't help but be reminded of Du Bois and the double consciousness of the African American and Ralph Ellison and the invisibility of the Black man. The discussion in the film reflected many themes . . . such as the oppressed having to liberate themselves and their oppressors without becoming the oppressors themselves, and the dominant group not having to worry about their place in the world because it is seen through their lens. The emotional impact of racism is also apparent in the film.

Although less explicitly, the film allows the viewers to witness embodied masculinity. Megan recalls a powerful experience one semester, when two male students were profoundly affected by witnessing men hug one another in what is a very emotional good-bye at the end of the film. Her young male students—who had, up until this point, not engaged in any critical discussion about issues of gender—now shared publicly that they were very moved by this simple embrace between men, and that they had never seen or experienced such intimacy between heterosexual men. Another student observed:

Each man was given the power and space to feel in this environment. David's progression from rational to feeling was a rare thing to see. The film provides a model for men, especially white men, to move out of their rational minds to feel how their power affects others and themselves.

Further highlighting the constraining norms of masculinity, *The Color of Fear* portrays men's emotional experience of racism, which contradicts the hegemonic depiction of men as nonemotional. It is instructive to ask students to consider this question: if *The Color of Fear* were depicting women's emotional confrontation of one another's racism, would the film have an equivalent impact? One could argue that it is precisely the vulnerability and emotional expressivity of the men in this video that conveys the powerful messages about how racism is internalized.

This video documents the unusual situation in which men of color have an opportunity to name and claim their own identity, and to express to members of the dominant white culture how it feels to be named. By the end of their weekend, David appears to go through a significant transformation. In a sense, he finally gets it. He recognizes to a limited extent how racism works; he manages to overcome his desire to deny these men the pain of their experience, and instead, begins to see what kind of work is involved in unlearning racism and identifying whiteness as a powerful yet frequently unnamed force.

It's Elementary: Talking about Gay Issues in Schools

It's Elementary, a film directed by Academy Award–winner Debra Chasnoff and produced by Helen Cohen, deals explicitly with how educational institutions and family and community groups can teach accurate and relevant information about sexual-orientation diversity. Beginning with the assumption that children hear distortions and prejudicial information about gays and lesbians, the premise of the video is to portray realistic examples of parents, students, and teachers engaged in open conversations about the lives, struggles, and contributions of gay people themselves. A variety of educational settings are depicted, with elementary through high schools and private and public school settings included. Students invariably notice that younger children are more open-minded than older children, as the following undergraduate explains:

> I was absolutely shocked at the sharp contrast of opinions between very young children and adolescents. Children at seven and eight are still open-minded when taught about gay and lesbian issues. But by

the time they are fourteen, and still haven't been exposed to serious discussions on gay and lesbian issues, they have very strong preconceived notions. I wish I had gone through an educational program that was inclusive. Some of my friends from high school are so homophobic that I won't even bring up the topic around them. It's like fighting a brick wall.

The question of naming and who gets to name is central in this documentary. Many of the educators engage their students in self- and group reflection to identify what kinds of names and stereotypes have been learned about lesbian and gay people. In a public third-grade classroom, a male teacher plays popular music and asks students to name the gay, lesbian, or bisexual singer/songwriter. Our students enjoy watching the children's excitement grow as they discover that famous pop stars such as Elton John and Melissa Etheridge are gay and lesbian. The same teacher uses the basic technique of constructing a "word web" to enlist students in his class to brainstorm gay-themed words, opening the door to discuss stereotypes associated with gay people, gay pride, prejudice, and homophobia.

Our students are also alert to the politics of representation in terms of whether or not gay and lesbian people are speaking for themselves, or whether heterosexual allies are speaking for them. The following student reflection is indicative of such insight:

> I really liked the diversity that they found in looking for teachers to be involved in this film. Some were gay but most were not, which I think was very important. The idea behind teaching the kids about gays and lesbians is to expose them to this different lifestyle but also to teach them to be accepting of others, even though they might be different. When a gay teacher taught about gays and lesbians I felt that it made the issue seem smaller and that the teacher was only interested because it dealt directly with them. When a teacher taught about the issue that was not gay or lesbian it brought it out as more of a community issue.

Students are quick to notice that the locations are characteristically "liberal" cities: Manhattan; San Francisco; Cambridge, Massachusetts; and Madison, Wisconsin. It is as if our students want to find a reason why curricular inclusiveness might be found in these environments, and not in their own southern or suburban backgrounds. There is a particular sensitivity on the part of religiously conservative students to the way such groups are portrayed in the video:

My reaction is that this video made Christians look horrible. I feel Christians can share their views in a loving way. For example, love the sinner, hate the sin. God has absolute love for us, yet we all sin. Who are we as sinners able to judge other sinners? Okay, I'll step off of my soapbox now and talk about the children.

It's Elementary offers an ideal avenue for students to grapple with the contradictions of their religious teachings and social justice goals. Students do not want to see themselves as homophobic, nor to identify with "hating homosexuals," yet they also do not want to "condone" homosexuality, as it goes against their religious teaching. Some students just lay out the contradiction without necessarily resolving it, as the following student reveals, but at least the video opens the door to further thought and discussion:

> The video mentioned a book called *My Two Mommies* [correctly *Heather Has Two Mommies*], which is supposed to make homosexual living a normal and accepted thing in the eyes of people of all ages. However, I was raised in a Christian home and went to a private Christian school from age three through twelfth grade and we were taught straight out of the Bible which states very clearly that homosexuality is not the lifestyle God intended for intimate relationships. We obviously were not read *My Two Mommies* at my school, and I am not a homophobic person and I do not hate homosexual people, I simply do not agree with their lifestyle. I was not exposed to homosexuality in my school system the way people want it to be now, and that did not make me completely oblivious to it. I learned about it through television, news, and of course, out in the world day after day.

Another student, however, was able to think more carefully about the nuances of what the filmmakers were trying to accomplish:

> I was surprised at how aware the children were about gay and lesbian issues. I found myself frowning on those children who held negative stereotypes about gay and lesbian couples and applauding children who seemed open-minded and accepting. It became clear to me that children are able to handle more than adults give them credit for, and that while they are still questioning life and figuring out what life is all about, is the time when teachers should be giving children the most information and the most options. This film separated sexuality from sexual orientation, which was great. It presented a way that sexual orientation is a part of development, hence, can be taught in a developmentally appropriate fashion. Why is it necessary for sexual orientation to be specifically addressed in schools, I wondered.

Is it truly in the academic arena where tolerance should be taught? I felt that the pretense for teaching sexual orientation behind the film was to educate children so that they might become more tolerant and accepting of diversity. I think that it really isn't tolerance that is being taught, or the issue about gay and lesbian lifestyles, it is about gaining knowledge about the world that children will be living in.

In the film, the politics of representation arise when a principal decides to put on exhibit a photography show called *Love Makes a Family*. At a parent-teacher meeting, some parents express their outrage at these images being publicly displayed in their school. A veteran teacher cautiously brings his class to view the exhibit and gains a more accepting attitude after he observes his young students attending to the photographs and family narratives with great interest.

In another discussion among teachers in a private Quaker school in Cambridge, Massachusetts, a woman of color raises the issue of whether or not all the teachers must explicitly address lesbian and gay issues, and if they do, does that mean the teacher must "condone" this lifestyle. Educators and administrators from all walks of life discuss their differences, and multiple opinions are aired and respected. When Gay Pride Day is held, during an all-school assembly, an openly gay soccer coach uses an analogy that first graders as well as university students can comprehend. He poignantly demonstrates how "I *could* play soccer if I had to hide one leg." He hops on one foot trying to kick the ball. "But," he says, putting his other foot down, "I can play soccer much better when I am able to use both legs." Students then understand that by sharing all of who he is, he can be a more effective teacher and friend.

Conclusion

Our educational agenda is to make intersections visible by helping students uncover the complexities of who has the power to name and construct social identities. The explicit content in the documentaries we have presented enables educators to engage students in discussion of the processes of naming, and how dominant cultural representations and stereotypes are constructed. By utilizing alternative representations in teaching, educators can urge students to think critically about the cultural images that dominate our visual, social, and perceptual horizons. Our analysis has emphasized how educators can use these documentaries to engage dialogue, challenge student assumptions about intersecting categories, and encourage agency in students themselves.

NOTES

1. The comments quoted in this essay are drawn from students' in-class written responses to questions posed by the instructor. The students' writing is published here with their permission.

REFERENCES

Allen, Katherine. "A Conscious and Inclusive Family Studies." *Journal of Marriage and the Family* 62 (2000): 4–17.
Boler, Megan. *Feeling Power: Emotions and Education.* New York: Routledge, 1999.
It's Elementary: Talking about Gay Issues in School. Dir. Debra Chasnoff. Prod. Helen Cohen. Women's Educational Media, 1997.
Fine, Michelle. "Sexuality, Schooling, and Adolescent Females: The Missing Discourse of Desire." *Beyond Silenced Voices.* Ed. Lois Weis and Michelle Fine. Albany: SUNY Albany P, 1993.
Foucault, Michel. *The History of Sexuality.* New York: Vintage, 1980.
Hall, Stuart, ed. *Representation: Cultural Representations and Signifying Practices.* London: Open University, 1997.
hooks, bell. *Killing Rage: Ending Racism.* New York: Owl, 1995.
Mun Wah, Lee, dir. *The Color of Fear.* Stir Fry Productions, 1994.
Riggs, Marlon, dir. *Tongues Untied.* Strand Releasing, 1989.
Russo, Vito. "Review of *Tongues Untied.*" Online. Available: <http://www.frameline.org/hv_ce_files/hv_tongues_untied.html
Wagner, Jane, and Tina diFeliciantonio, dirs. *Girls Like Us.* Women Make Movies, 1997.

Megan Boler *is associate professor of teaching and learning and adjunct professor of women's studies at Virginia Tech. Her work has focused on the politics of emotion in pedagogy, cultural and media studies, and philosophy of technology. Her book* Feeling Power: Emotions and Education *(Routledge, 1999) focuses on the politics of emotion in pedagogy; her essays appear in such journals as* Hypatia, Cultural Studies, *and* Educational Theory.
Katherine R. Allen *is professor of human development and adjunct professor of women's studies at Virginia Tech. Her books include* Single Women/Family Ties: Life Histories of Older Women *(Sage Publications, 1989);* Women and Families: Feminist Reconstructions *(with Kristine Baber, Guilford Press, 1992); and* Handbook of Family Diversity *(with David Demo and Mark Fine, Oxford University Press, 2000).*

Copyright © 2002 by Megan Boler and Katherine R. Allen

Women's Stories, Women's Films
Integrating Women's Studies and Film Production

Anne Orwin

We know we are without a text, and must discover one.

—Carolyn G. Heilbrun

Women working in creative fields today have the unique opportunity of creating the works that other artists will study in the future. But for students in artistic fields, exposure to the works of female artists of the past depends on the commitment of the instructor to seek out and show these works. This is particularly true for women studying film production. Because gender is, rightfully, not the first consideration in the selection of films to illustrate a point in class, teachers usually use the films they know best and that are most readily available. This has led inevitably to a situation in which the films shown are most often written, directed, and produced by men.

To increase awareness of women's films within the university setting and to address the gender imbalance of films shown in class, I developed and taught a course titled Women's Stories, Women's Films. The class was designed to introduce students of both genders to women filmmakers and to look at the stories they told and the narrative structures used in supporting their storytelling.

The course was offered at the School of Film and Animation (SOFA) at the Rochester Institute of Technology (RIT), a university that has a decidedly masculine student body. While most colleges and universities today have a fairly equal gender balance, with women predominating in many cases (*Barron's Profiles of American Colleges*), at RIT, perhaps because of the highly technical nature of the courses offered, the name of the institute, and the preponderance of males in the fields of science and technology, a high proportion, 65 percent, of the student body is male. Within the film school, although the faculty is evenly divided along gender lines, only 20 percent of the current students are female. The result is that women students in the film school are not only exposed to primarily male-created films but are also surrounded by male storytellers in every class. In this essay, I'd like to talk about my motivations for establishing this class, what I hoped to accomplish, my approach to the material and the class environment, and the successes and difficulties I encountered.

Premise

The impetus for the course came from the desire to offer women students the opportunity to view the work of other women. In showing these films and discussing the related material, I hoped to provide a basis on which students could evaluate their own creative impulses and to offer encouragement and inspiration to potential women filmmakers, who often find that their stories are not understood by their fellow students or their male teachers. Showing women's films that portray personal stories gives the women students permission, as it were, to explore their own stories in their own ways. Showing women's films also helps students and teachers understand the differences in narrative structure that appear in many women's films.

The class had four specific goals:

1. Familiarize students with the breadth of women's films
2. Explore the narrative structure of those films
3. Begin an acquaintance with feminist film criticism and such concepts as the *gaze*
4. Encourage students to access their own personal creative potential

Gender Differences

The course derived from a series of questions. Are there uniquely women's stories? If so, what are they? Are they really different from stories that men tell and enjoy? And if they are, what are those differences and how can we find a common ground for experiencing them?

As a teacher of scriptwriting I have noticed over the years a distinct difference in the scripts written by the women students in class and those written by the male students. More telling, perhaps, was that women were less successful in writing scripts that involved character and plot than their male counterparts. Their characters often became bogged down in a morass of emotions and relationships and were unable to act on their own behalf. In dealing with this, I came to wonder if there wasn't, perhaps, some other structure of storytelling that would work better for the kinds of stories women wanted to tell than

the traditional structure that has been in place since Aristotle.
At the undergraduate level, stories tend to come from two sources: personal experience and culturally imposed experience. In the case of personal experience, women's stories are inherently different from those of their male colleagues. Not surprisingly, the women students tend to tell stories that are relationship driven and family oriented. Often their stories concern a group of friends on an adventure. Scripts by male students are more impersonal, even when these students are dealing with stories about characters very like themselves. Male students, when writing about relationships, often write in terms of possession and betrayal—the girl who got away needing to be punished in some way, often graphically. The women who write about betrayal deal with how to go on living either alone or with the betrayer.

In the area of what might be called "culturally imposed" stories, plots tend to be less personal and more dramatic. *Culturally imposed*, in this case, refers to media-derived stories about experiences students have not actually had. For example, a good portion of male students write at some time a story about robbing or being the victim of a robbery at a convenience store or fast-food franchise. Through the media they have come to feel that this is a real experience for them, although for the most part they have never seen a gun up close. They often write genre stories—science fiction, mystery, and espionage. Many male students particularly like the idea of surprising and manipulating the audience, even if the ending is not justified by the story. Fewer of these stories come from female students, although because of the gender breakdown of the department in which I teach, there are fewer examples to draw from. Women's culturally imposed stories often become romances in which love triumphs at the end.

When stories are proposed in class and later read aloud, there is usually a noticeable difference in reaction to the proposals according to gender. Whereas the women can relate to the stories told by men, very often the males in the class seem befuddled by the stories told by women. It is almost as if women's films have become foreign films, a concept that is perhaps not terribly far-fetched. For many men, women's films are indeed foreign territory. They explore emotional realities that are unfamiliar. They tell the other side of the story. And that perhaps is the most important aspect of women's films. They are the traditional stories told from the other point of view. Instead of learning about the hero's journey, in women's films we witness the journey of the one who stayed behind. We see the nobility of the one who holds the home together. We see her hidden struggles and hidden dreams.

There are also differences in how stories are told. In stories by women students, characters often avoid conflict and therefore resolution. Since the accepted theory of drama from Aristotle to the present defines drama as conflict, women's films are often seen as incomplete and inadequate. The heroine's journey inward is not as active as the hero's journey outward, and therefore seems slow and tedious to an audience used to special effects rather than personal exploration.

Course Environment

Twenty women and five men were enrolled in the one-quarter (ten-week) class. This was an unusual gender balance for RIT, where most classes contain only one or two women students. The presence of the five male students provided an important gender balance for this class, even though the reason for their enrollment was that they needed the credits to graduate. Half of the women came from outside the film department. Most of the students were registered in film, photography, or theater. Four of the students were deaf.

The class was designed to be taught as a seminar rather than a lecture, with the assumption that the students already possessed a certain critical judgment, even if it was not yet mature. Before each class, readings related to the films were assigned. All readings were available at the reserve desk in the library and on electronic reserve. In-class work consisted of watching films related to the week's theme, discussion of the film from both an analytical and a personal point of view, and experiential class exercises, such as quilt making and a slow-motion race.

Because students of both genders often view anything feminist as also anti-male, a significant effort was made to focus the class on the positives of women's films while avoiding the negatives of male images of women, although the students often brought up the issues in discussion.

The class required three projects:

1. A journal in which students recorded their reactions to the material covered in class, films watched, and materials read
2. An analysis of a film made by a woman using one of the structures discussed in the class
3. A personal creative project or formal paper on a topic chosen by the student with instructor approval

Course Content

But for manly men, the very thought of screening after screening of so-called chick flicks is enough to make them burst into tears. And women, while they might not own up to it, can only stomach so much touch-feely-chatty before their ovaries implode.

—Jon Popick

The first challenge was the selection of films for the class. The title of the course refers to "women's films," so it was important to establish exactly what a woman's film was. Avoiding the idea that women's films are "touchy-feely-chatty" was easy. The real question was whether the film had to be the sole creation of a woman or a collaboration. For example, if the writer was a woman but the director a man, did that make a difference in how the film turned out? Because a significant focus of the class was women's creativity, the films selected were those in which a woman was the primary creative force. It also turned out that the subject of these films was women as well, but that was not the essential criteria used in selection.

To facilitate the selection process, the class needed an organizing principle, in this case one that was thematic rather than structural. The themes chosen were history, quilting, matrilineal history, myth and *midrash*, the heroine's journey and personal quest, the gaze, embodiment, and personal storytelling.

Readings assigned to accompany each film were intended to introduce students to concepts about women's psychology, mythology, and storytelling. Although the relationship of the readings to the films was often not obvious, the pairings were designed to provoke thought about women's creativity in general.

To be able to discuss women's films, the class first needed a common language. Because most of the students were not familiar with any of the films and readings, the early classes were structured around screening the films and discussing their themes and structures.

In the first class the historical perspective of women's films was presented through the showing of two films about early filmmakers: *Le jardin oublie* (*The Lost Garden*), a film about Alice Guy Blache, the first narrative filmmaker; and a documentary on Lois Weber produced by Barbra Streisand. These were followed by examples of Guy Blache's and Weber's work. The class discussed the importance of memory and how, in the case of these filmmakers, that memory has not been preserved. For the most part, their films have been lost or destroyed. Out of Guy Blache's 700 films, only a few remain. Lois Weber was less prolific, and much of her work, too, has disappeared. This information had a powerful effect on the class, especially the filmmakers and photographers, who couldn't bear the thought of someone's life work being lost forever.

The first theme to be covered was discussed in the section titled Quilting as Narrative Structure. Quilts are held together by common themes, patterns that repeat, and a border that ties the separate elements together. Films made like quilts tell disparate stories that are nevertheless linked by a common thread. To exemplify this concept the class watched *How to Make an American Quilt*, which told the stories of women in a quilting circle and how they dealt with their often difficult relationships. Their stories are told to the daughter of one of the women, who has come home to decide whether or not to commit herself to her own current relationship. For those with no experience of quilting, we read bell hooks's essay on her grandmother's quilts, which describes her relationship to the quilts created in her own family. Although her grandmother did not make story quilts, hooks says, she "believed that each quilt had its own narrative" (120). That connection of scraps to the whole can be seen as the same process in which the moments of a life can be turned into a story or film. It is the unity of meaning that can tie these elements together, creating a film that seems to wander yet remains true to its core.

The course section that followed was Matrilineal Heritage. The students were asked to take a moment and think back to the women in their own family and consider these questions: Do you know their stories? How far back can you go? What are their accomplishments? How were they valued against the men in your family? How did they succeed when deprived of the same educational and economic opportunities as the men? For some students the answers came easily. They knew their family histories, and the women played a part. Others had to go home and ask for stories that had long been kept secret in their homes. In *Writing a Woman's Life,* Carolyn Heilbrun discusses the ways in which women's stories, whether biography or autobiography or fiction, have been told and how those stories have been changed by feminism and feminist theory. The film shown was *Antonia's Line,* Marleen Gorris's Academy Award–winning drama that follows the generations of a woman's life as they are recounted on the day she is going to die. Later in the quarter, the class also watched Jan Oxenberg's *Thank You and Goodnight,* a film in which Oxenberg comes to terms with her grandmother's death. In the book *Leaving My Father's House* (Woodman et al.), three women offer their own personal narratives of individuation and growth. The message of these readings and films is that there is no one way to tell these stories. The material shapes the structure rather than being forced into the conventional narrative.

The section of the course titled Myth and *Midrash* dealt with how myths can shape lives and the power to create new myths. Myths are the stories of how what is came to be. There are personal myths, family myths, cultural myths. Again, the students were asked, think of your own lives. What are the myths of your heritage? The stories that your family has told you of how they came to be where they are? Did an ancestor come over on a boat, have trouble coming through immigration, have his or her house destroyed in a flood? These are your myths, the true source of your storytelling. In *Daughters of the Dust,* Julie Dash depicts a mythic moment in a family's history on the day they are about to leave the remote Georgia island of their ancestors and move to a new home in the North.

Other ways of dealing with myths are to create new ones or to fill in the gaps in the old ones. There is a tradition in Judaism called *midrash.* It is said that the Torah is written in black fire on white fire. *Midrash* is the white fire, the spaces between the words. The women within Judaism have embraced this method for giving voice to the silent women in the Bible and in history. Women filmmakers often fill in the blanks to tell the missing stories of long-silent foremothers. Charlene Spretnak's revisioning of myth provided an introduction to the concept of reworking old stories that no longer work.

The heroine's journey, dealt with in the section Heroine's Journey and Personal Quest, has become a kind of standard for a feminine quest. This model is derived from Joseph Campbell's Hero's Journey as applied to film structure by Christopher Vogler and the myths of the descent of the Goddess. The steps of the feminine journey, however, are inward to self, rather than outward toward a physical goal. When applied to film, this can produce a heroine who thinks rather than acts, and the result is often a less dynamic, and consequently less successful, film. In commercial films, the heroine's journey, therefore, is most successfully applied in a male narrative in which the woman finds her strength while the man is having his adventure, and by the end, no matter whether they come together or not, the audience has the sense that she will be just fine without him. To use a film more representative of a feminine approach to the journey as an illustration of the heroine's journey, the class watched Sally Potter's *The Tango Lesson,* in which Potter travels to learn the tango.

Although this was not a film studies class, it seemed important to introduce the concept of the gaze, which most students had not yet encountered, and which constituted the title of the following section.

To exemplify this concept, the class watched *The Governess.* The story of the film, which concerns a young Jewish woman who takes a job as a governess on a bleak island, is of far less importance than the way in which it explicitly employs the gaze in its use of photography. To understand the gaze in concrete terms, the class participated in several theater exercises using mirrors and looking (Aston 58–59), which were designed to supplement a reading of Laura Mulvey's "Visual Pleasure and Narrative Cinema."

In the section called Embodiment, this concept, which refers to using one's own body as the subject and object of the film, was covered. This relates as well to the concept of the gaze. What does it mean when one puts oneself on the screen to be looked at? To illustrate this, the class watched Maya Deren's experimental film *Meshes of the Afternoon* and Mara Alper's *Moving On.* It is notable that other films included in the course, such as *The Tango Lesson* and *Thank You and Goodnight,* also starred their makers.

The final classes, in the Personal Storytelling and Presentation sections, were a chance for students to show their own work. At a film production school, films are most often screened in an environment of criticism. In this class, however, the students were given the opportunity to screen their works and present their final projects without a critical response.

Experience

Overall, the course was successful, but it presented some challenges along the way and raised some unanticipated gender and diversity issues.

Much of what has been written about gender differences in learning (Belenky et al.; Goldberger et al.) was borne out by the class experience. Male and female students experienced the class differently and applied the material differently. One of the ways in which this was manifested concerned three of the male students who took the class. They were seniors and were preoccupied with the desire to complete the editing of their senior projects and show them at festivals. By week seven, they had missed more than half the classes. To make up for their absenses, they were given an extra assignment that included writing about their experience of the class—what it was like to attend a class dominated by women and taught without the usual lectures.

Their responses perpetuated the differences. They saw the extra assignment as an instance of gender bias, and they complained that not having regular assignments was a problem. Because of their resistance to the course, it remained difficult to integrate them into it. In addition, their absenteeism was noticeable to, and may have affected, other students. Among other things, it may have made students more conscious of gender differences in the classroom (though the topic was never discussed).

Gender differences certainly emerged in the students' final projects. Most of the women created something personal—drawings, poetry, stories. Three of the men, seeking to find something personal and assuming that it should be something to do with women, brought in work that their mothers had done—an autobiography, a painting—and showed that. One wrote about a family heirloom. Another, in an attempt to avoid gender stereotyping in language, came close to recreating Jung's theory of personality types.

The aspect of the course that seemed most problematic, however, was the freedom the class provided. In attempting to incorporate the ideas of Paulo Friere on liberating education and Agusto Boal's concept of turning spectators into participants (Boal 122), I created a class that was less rigidly structured than many other classes at the school. One result of this was that several students, both male and female, wanted more direction in creating their own projects. Some students, however, did exciting work, and one even said that she was changing to a women's studies minor.

Because Women's Stories, Women's Films was one of the few classes at RIT where women predominate, it was probably a unique experience for the students, even if they could not articulate this point.

The most common reaction to the class was the feeling that it was a shame that women's films had to be singled out, and that they should be somehow mainstreamed and included in the ongoing course curriculum. However, while many students are uncomfortable with having women's films taught as a separate subject, it is necessary to take a proactive approach in order to ensure not only that women's films are well represented in the curriculum, but also that ethnic diversity is honored.

A feminine aesthetic is not necessarily a provable phenomenon, but awareness is certainly the first step toward an acceptance of what is different. Most students had not seen the films shown in class. Now that they have and have been made aware that there is value in what is different, perhaps they will carry that lesson into other areas and ultimately will come to appreciate what they had heretofore ignored.

REFERENCES

Aston, Elaine. *Feminist Theatre Practice: A Handbook.* New York: Routledge, 1999.

Barron's Profiles of American Colleges. Hauppage, NY: Barron's Educational Services, 1999.

Belenky, Mary Field, Blythe McVicker Clinchy, Nancy Rule Goldberger, and Jill Mattuck Tarule. *Women's Ways of Knowing: The Development of Self, Voice, and Mind.* 10th anniversary ed. New York: Basic Books, 1997.

Boal, August. *Theatre of the Oppressed.* Trans. Charles McBride and Maria-Odilia Leal-McBride. New York: Theatre Communications Group, 1985.

Freire, Paolo. *Pedagogy of the Oppressed.* Trans. Myra Bergman Ramos. 20th anniversary ed. New York: Continuum, 1999.

Goldberger, Nancy, Jill Tarule, Blythe Clinchy, and Mary Belenky, eds. *Knowledge, Difference, and Power: Essays Inspired by Women's Ways of Knowing.* New York: Basic Books, 1996.

Heilbrun, Carolyn G. *Writing a Woman's Life.* New York: Ballantine, 1988.

hooks, bell. "Aesthetic Inheritances: History Worked by Hand." In *Teaching to Transgress: Education as the Practice of Freedom.* New York: Routledge, 1994.

Mulvey, Laura. "Visual Pleasure and Narrative Cinema." *Feminism and Film Theory.* Ed. Constance Penley. New York: Routledge, 1988.

Popick, Jon. "Tearing Down Stereotypes." *City: Greater Rochester's Alternative Newsweekly* Oct. 17–23, 2001: 12.

Vogler, Christopher. *The Writer's Journey : Mythic Structure for Writers.* 2nd ed. New York: Wieser, 1998.

Woodman, Marion, with Kate Danson, Mary Hamilton, and Rita Greer Allen. *Leaving My Father's House: A Journey to Conscious Femininity.* Boston: Shambhala, 1992.

SYLLABUS FOR WOMEN'S STORIES, WOMEN'S FILMS

Course Description

This course explores the ways in which women tell their stories and how that translates to the medium of film. Throughout the course, we will discuss the themes and issues of women's narratives. The hero's journey and traditional narrative structure will be contrasted with the heroine's journey and the more personal story telling style of the feminine. We will also examine whether a strong heroine exemplifies masculine or feminine values. In some cases, we will compare films made by women with films made by men about women. In addition to watching films written and directed by women, we will read works by feminist film critics, Jungian analyst Marion Woodman, and mythologist Joseph Campbell.

Course Requirements

1. Class Participation. Participation means regular attendance as well as participation in class discussion. This implies that you have read the assigned material and given it some thought before the class. Because this class is highly experiential, active participation in class exercises is essential for understanding the material.

2. Journal. During the course, the student shall keep a personal journal. This journal should include your personal reactions to the films shown in class and to the assigned readings. These journals will be collected and read during the quarter, so they should not contain any personal material that you do not wish to share with your instructor.

3. Analysis of a Film. At the end of the quarter, you will write an analysis of a film by a woman filmmaker discussing the heroine's journey as narrative structure and incorporating any other relevant narrative structures. This paper should reflect your understanding of the material presented in class and the assigned readings.

4. Final Project. At the end of the quarter you will create and present a project that reflects your own personal creativity. The project should tell a personal story in whatever medium you choose. If you do not wish to develop a creative project, you may write a paper instead on a topic relevant to the class. All projects and papers are subject to approval by the instructor. Projects and papers will be presented during the final three classes. The intent is for these projects to be presented in a nonjudgmental environment to allow for the open flow of creativity.

Texts

Dash, Julie, with bell hooks and Toni Cade Bambara. *Daughters of the Dust: The Making of an African American Woman's Film.* New P, 1991.
Francke, Lizzie. *Script Girls: Women Screenwriters in Hollywood.* London: British Film Institute, 1994.
Heilbrun, Carolyn G. *Writing a Woman's Life.* New York: Ballantine, 1988.
hooks, bell. *Yearning: Race, Gender, and Cultural Politics.* Boston, South End P, 1990.
Humm, Maggie. *Feminism and Film.* Edinburgh: Edinburgh UP, 1997.
Murdoch, Maureen. *The Heroine's Journey: Women's Quest for Wholeness.* Boston: Shambhala, 1990.

Penley, Constance, ed. *Feminism and Film Theory.* New York: Routledge, 1988.
Perera, Sylvia Brunton. *Descent to the Goddess: A Way of Initiation for Women.* Toronto: Inner City, 1981.
Ringgold, Faith. "Faith Ringgold: Images." *Art in Context.* New York: Art in Context Center for Communications, 1995-2002. Online. Available: <http: www.artincontext.org/artist/faith_ringgold/image.html/. 5 Feb. 2002.
Spretnak, Charlene. *Lost Goddesses of Early Greece: A Collection of Pre-Hellenic Myths.* Boston: Beacon P, 1992.
Vogler, Christopher. *The Writer's Journey: Mythic Structure for Writers.* 2nd ed. New York: Wieser, 1998.
Woodman, Marion, with Kate Danson, Mary Hamilton, and Rita Greer Allen. *Leaving My Father's House: A Journey to Conscious Femininity.* Boston: Shambhala, 1992.

Films

America's First Women Filmmakers: Alice Guy Blache and Lois Weber. VHS. Library of Congress/Smithsonian Video, 1995.
Antonia's Line. Dir. and screenplay by Marleen Gorris. First Look Pictures, 1995.
Daughters of the Dust. Dir. and screenplay by Julie Dash. DVD. Geechee Girls, 1991.
The Governess. Dir. and screenplay by Sandra Goldbacher. DVD. Sony Pictures Classics, 1997.
A House Divided. 1913. Dir. Alice Guy Blache. *America's First Women Filmmakers: Alice Guy Blache and Lois Weber.* VHS. Library of Congress/ Smithsonian Video, 1995.
How to Make an American Quilt. Dir. Jocelyn Moorhouse. DVD. Screenplay by Jane Anderson, based on the novel by Whitney Otto. Universal City Studios and Amblin Entertainment, 1995.
Le jardin oublie: La vie et l'oeuvre d'Alice Guy-Blache (The Lost Garden: The Life and Work of Alice Guy-Blache). Dir. Marquise Lepage. National Film Board of Canada, 1995.
Meshes of the Afternoon. Dir. Maya Deren. *Maya Deren: Vol. 1, Experimental Films, 1943–1959.* Mystic Fire Video, 1986.
Moving On. Dir. and screenplay by Mara Alper. 1997.
Reel Models: The First Women of Film. Dir. Susan Koch and Christopher Koch. Exec. prod. Barbra Streisand, Cis Corman, Marc Juris and Jessica Falcon. American Movie Classics, 2000.
The Tango Lesson. Dir. and screenplay by Sally Potter. VHS. Sony Pictures Classics, 1997.

Thank You and Goodnight. Dir. and screenplay by Jan Oxenberg. Red Wagon Films, 1991.

Too Wise Women. 1913. Dir. Lois Weber. *America's First Women Filmmakers: Alice Guy Blache and Lois Weber.* VHS. Library of Congress/Smithsonian Video, 1995.

Course Schedule

Introduction: The First Women Filmmakers

Le jardin oublie

Reel Models: The First Women of Film.

Too Wise Women; A House Divided; Francke, *Script Girls,* appendix.

Quilting as Narrative Structure

How to Make an American Quilt; hooks, "Aesthetic Inheritances"; Ringgold, *Story Quilts.*

Matrilineal History

Antonia's Line; Heilbrun, *Writing a Woman's Life,* introduction; Woodman et al., *Leaving My Father's House,* introduction, chap. 1, conclusion, "Allerleirauh."

Myth and Midrash

Daughters of the Dust; Dash, hooks, and Bambara, *Daughters of the Dust;* Humm, *Feminism and Film,* "Black Film Theory, Black Feminisms: Daughters of the Dust"; Spretnak, *Lost Goddesses of Early Greece,* introduction and "Demeter and Persephone."

Heroine's Journey and Personal Quest

The Tango Lesson; Murdoch, *The Heroine's Journey,* introduction; Vogler, *The Writer's Journey;* Perera, *Descent to the Goddess,* introduction and "Descent and Return."

The Gaze

The Governess; Mulvey, "Visual Pleasure and Narrative Cinema."

Embodiment

Meshes of the Afternoon; Moving On.

Personal Storytelling

Thank You and Goodnight; showing of films by women students in the class.

Presentations

Presentation of final projects and papers.

Anne Orwin *teaches scriptwriting in the School of Film and Animation at Rochester Institute of Technology, where she established the Women's Film Project. She has participated in the women's committee of the Writers Guild of America on both coasts and was a founding member of the New York Coalition for Professional Women in the Arts and Media. She regularly covers women's events for a local newspaper and has published essays on women's activism, educating women in film production, and women's psychospiritual development.*

Copyright © 2002 by Anne Orwin

Teaching What We're Not
Using Videos to Diversify the Women's Studies Curriculum

Ann Schonberger, Nancy Lewis, Mazie Hough, and Leslie King

Over the more than thirty-year life of women's studies as an interdiscipline, there has been a growing commitment in the United States to diversifying the curriculum—an effort certainly still in progress. Both the integration of the experiences of the diversity of women in the United States and the globalization of the curriculum have progressed with more or less success in programs with offerings ranging from an undergraduate minor or concentration to a Ph.D. Often the impetus for curricular diversity comes from the demands of the students or the interests and expertise of the faculty. In metropolitan areas with diverse populations, colleges and universities draw both international students and students of color from within the United States. They often (but not always) have a faculty reflecting such diversity. However, institutions in more rural areas, especially in northern-tier states with less racial diversity and with fewer international faculty and students, face challenges. More well developed women's studies programs with their own tenure lines can choose to hire faculty with a wide range of diversity, but women's studies programs without tenure lines have had to find other ways to offer a racially and ethnically diverse international curriculum.

The University of Maine, the largest and most comprehensive university in the state, certainly epitomizes that problem. The 2000 census identified Maine as the whitest state in the United States, and while the university is somewhat more diverse, the percentage of international students and students of color is still very low. Our students often come from towns smaller than the university in population, are often in the first generation of their families to go to college, and have not usually traveled much outside the state, let alone outside the country.

Our women's studies program offers an undergraduate major and minor as well as a graduate concentration but has no tenure lines. The director's position, although full-time, is defined as that of a faculty member with tenure in a department. The program offers its own Women's Studies (WST)-designated courses, cross-lists other interdisciplinary courses, and maintains a list of approved departmental electives. Cross-listed courses include American Indian Women and Franco-American Women's Experiences, taught by women from those areas. Jewish Women in History and Culture and Introduction to Lesbian, Gay, Bisexual, and Transgender (LGBT) Studies are offered in women's studies, pending the development of programs in Jewish studies or LGBT studies. A travel-study course taught by a German faculty member in family studies takes about a dozen students to Germany and the Netherlands every year during the two-week March break with whatever financial help we are able to provide them.

While occasionally U.S. women of color or international scholars can be recruited to teach the rest of the WST-designated courses, the bulk of the teaching has been done by white faculty. Since our women's studies program grew out of a curriculum transformation project aimed at decentering the male experience in the whole university curriculum, the language and conceptual frameworks to diversify and globalize the women's studies curriculum were part of at least some faculty members' consciousness; this time diversity was considered *as* the courses were being developed. Mindful of what Linda Alcoff (1991) has identified as "the problem of speaking for others," the faculty have chosen texts that integrate a variety of women's experiences into the discussion of each topic, have assigned extra readings to reflect diversity, and have invited guest speakers to their classes. And they have chosen videos from our program's collection to show in their classes. (We use the term "video" throughout this article although some of the titles we will mention are available as films as well. *All* are available as videos, which our faculty find much easier to use.)

Videos are particularly effective for several reasons. Our traditionally aged undergraduates are particularly image driven, and the videos really hold their attention. Although we are mindful of the mediating factors of the filmmaker's gaze and editing decisions and sometimes (in the case of international women's experience) the role of translation, videos come closer to portraying the perspectives and experiences of women in their own surroundings—women who have not written books or articles. When there are international students or U.S. women of color in the classroom, they do not feel as much pressure to represent their group, while they can, if they choose, compare their experience to that portrayed in the video. Finally the videos can also provide case studies to which can be applied concepts and theories developed in class.

What follows is an account of how some faculty use videos in WST-designated classes ranging from Introduction to Women's Studies to the senior seminar, which is the capstone course for the undergraduate majors and is required of the minors as well. Information on the sources for the videos is to be found at the end of the essay.

WST 101: Introduction to Women's Studies
Nancy Lewis

A Woman's Place (60 mins.) is a video about women working with the law to make important changes in women's status and their safety in their families. It is divided into three segments: the first in South Africa; the second in Duluth, Minnesota, in the United States; and the third in Bombay, India. The South Africa segment follows a woman who is a new magistrate in a rural district of the country. She is trying to publicize and enforce the new constitution, which declares that men and women are equal under the law. Tribal custom treats women as property with no rights of their own, and many tribal leaders are unwilling to accept this change. This segment shows the magistrate working to inform the women of the region of this change, trying to work with tribal leaders and informing the parliament of her concerns.

In Duluth, the video follows a public prosecutor who is trying to increase the conviction rate of perpetrators of domestic abuse. It follows her work over time, at first having little success and then finding ways to allow police officers' statements to be used as evidence in cases where the victim will not or cannot testify against the alleged perpetrator. It also shows her work with the local law enforcement and social services community to increase their awareness of the issue. The video underscores the high levels of domestic abuse, both in this community and in the United States as a whole.

The third, and final, segment introduces us to three women in Bombay. Two of the women are in the process of trying to obtain divorces from abusive husbands. The third woman is their lawyer and has been through a divorce procedure of her own many years ago. While law in India allows women to divorce, there are no provisions for any economic compensation. Thus many women are forced to choose between leaving their marriages and becoming destitute or staying and enduring the abuse. Despite the severe social strictures against divorce in the Hindu society portrayed in the video, it also shows how the women, with their lawyer's help, are transformed and empowered.

I use this video near the end of the semester to illustrate examples of activism. The video also allows the students to apply their understanding of violence against women, women's status in law, and the need for the economic empowerment of women. By seeing three culturally different situations, the students are able to view both the differences and the many similarities of the needs of women. These portrayals of women of different races and cultures, addressing problems specific to their locales, help students understand the varied emphases of feminist work around the globe. I find that the video helps many students synthesize the work we have been doing and also changes their perception of the status of American women as compared with that of women in other countries.

WST 101: Introduction to Women's Studies

Mazie Hough

In my Introduction to Women's Studies class, I always teach a unit on women and Islam. We may read *Dreams of Trespass* or *Will They Hear You When You Cry*, two very different depictions of women in Islamic countries. (*Dreams of Trespass,* by Fatima Mernissi, details the richly varied lives of women she observed while growing up in a harem in Morocco. *Will They Hear You When You Cry*, by Fauziya Kassindja, relates her struggle to gain asylum in the United States in order to avoid circumcision and forced marriage in Togo.) We may also read articles that portray Muslim women and their various strategies for resisting oppression and creating change. In all cases, I also like to show the students videos that portray the complex ways in which women are treated in and respond to their cultures' interpretation of Islam.

My favorite film so far is *Hidden Faces* (52 mins.), a collaborative documentary by Claire Hunt and Kim Longinotto, with Safaa Fathay. Originally intended as a video about the internationally renowned Egyptian feminist writer Nawal El Saadawi, *Hidden Faces* follows Safaa Fathay, a young woman then living in Paris, as she returns to her own country to interview her mother, aunts, and cousins, the young woman who works as a servant in her family's house, and Saadawi. The video combines footage of those interviews with scenes of a woman reading excerpts from Saadawi's novels, of a counseling session with Saadawi and one of her patients, and of a gathering of women exploring feminism.

With a quiltlike approach, the video presents a fascinating portrayal of Egyptian women's lives, one that suggests the complexities and contradictions of a society in which class, tradition, and modernity all affect women in different ways. Fathay's mother, for example, talks about her arranged marriage and her decision to return to the veil after twenty years, while her cousins and aunts talk about the reasons why they have accepted clitoridectomy. Segments about Saadawi's rural development project and the servant in Fathay's home reveal the distance that social class creates between Egyptian women. What the video makes absolutely clear is that Egyptian women do not all speak with the same voice. In their dissimilarities—in the conflicts that arise between young and old, rural and urban, middle class and poor and in the varied ways they respond to these conflicts—my students invariably find ways to find pieces of themselves. The Other—so far removed from our almost exclusively white, working-class campus—we find, is as varied as ourselves. The video provides an excellent starting point for discussing the contradictions inherent in any culture and provides grounds for discussing the way religion, culture, economics, and politics combine in defining women's experiences.

WST 340: Women and Globalization

Leslie King

The main goals of Women and Globalization are, first, to encourage students to think about how their own position in the global economic system is inextricably linked to that of others, in all parts of the world; and second, to call attention specifically to how women are faring under the major, global economic changes that have occurred in recent decades. I do not talk much about multiculturalism per se in the class but, in my own mind, I hope that students will increasingly come to value and be respectful of diversity of all kinds. Two of the videos I like to show in the course are *Hell to Pay* (52 mins.) and *Behind the Smile* (46 mins.). These videos enable students of women of various cultures to address the interaction between gender and globalization specific to each culture's context.

Hell to Pay was released in 1988, but its message is still utterly relevant. It focuses on how Bolivian peasants have suffered under foreign debt and structural adjustment. These issues are still regularly in the news. (For example, the new president of Argentina declared in December 2001 that the country would default on a $132 billion debt.) The background information provided in the film is helpful for understanding the current plight of many of the world's poor: the film explains how, why, and to whom private and public agencies and institutions lend money; how that money might typically be used; and how repayment systems have tended to disproportionately burden the poor. In Bolivia, indigenous peoples (and especially indigenous women), while rarely benefiting from international loans, have borne the brunt of structural adjustment policies designed to facilitate repayment of the loans.

Hell to Pay is organized around an activist's discussion of Bolivia's economic struggles. By focusing on a women's sewing cooperative and featuring the women's stories, the video shows real-life human beings who are both well informed about how they have been bilked by the country's ruling class as well as intensely angry about it, and they are actively seeking ways to resist the economic policies being imposed from above. The awareness that dollars held in U.S. banks (their parent's savings! their own future retirement funds!) may be lent to corrupt governments in developing countries makes the great divide between wealthy and poor countries begin to seem smaller. Acknowledging connections makes it increasingly difficult for the students to view people in "other" cultures, in "other" countries, as completely separate from themselves, and they are reminded that we are all linked together.

Behind the Smile describes the intersection of Buddhism and capitalist economic development in Thailand. Capitalist expansion there has been aided by a religious system that emphasizes duty to one's parents and a general acceptance of social hierarchy. Specifically, the video tells the story of young women who leave the countryside for Bangkok in order to earn money to send back to their families. One of the young women featured in the video works and saves, literally for years, to financially contribute to a monument honoring the village dead, one of them her mother. The video shows how hard she has worked and sacrificed, while the only requirement of her brother was that he become a Buddhist monk for a week. It also depicts the decline of farming villages, now populated almost solely by the elderly and by the children of those who have gone off to work in the city. It shows the stark contrasts between those who are better and worse off as a result of Thailand's booming economic growth. The economic exploitation of young women in this economy and the inhumane conditions in which these women live and work are also portrayed. Like *Hell to Pay, Behind the Smile* offers a glimpse of how women are resisting and shows how women are trying to unionize to battle poor wages and working conditions. It also reveals linkages between wealthy and less wealthy locales; we see that many items purchased by U.S. consumers, such as sneakers, clothes, and accessories, are made by workers in countries like Thailand. We talk in class about how wearing an article of clothing made by women in Thailand or elsewhere connects us to those people and them to us, in a bizarrely anonymous and extremely unequal relationship.

I use the videos to supplement articles on how women are affected by international debt and structural adjustment (policies instituted by the World Bank and International Monetary Fund to facilitate loan repayment) and how businesses in newly developing countries use young women as a docile and easily expendable labor source. For many students, these are new issues. Reading provides in-depth explanations; but videos provide sound and visuals that make the situations seem "real" in a way that articles and books often cannot. Students write essays and reaction papers in which they are asked to tie together information from assigned readings, videos, and when possible, their own experiences. I do not design assignments or discussions to directly or explicitly "teach about multiculturalism." However, one way to become more accepting and respectful of other ways of life is to be exposed to them.

Senior Seminar in Women's Studies: Women and Education

Ann Schonberger

The subject matter of this course includes the roles and experiences of women both as teachers and as students, now and in the past. As a capstone, its purpose is to have the students look back with their feminist consciousness over their own educations (K–12 and college) and to look forward to the roles in education they might play as teachers, parents, and taxpayers. It is also the course in which we look at various methodologies of developing new knowledge in women's studies.

We begin the course by reading three articles by Adrienne Rich— "On Claiming an Education," "Taking Women Students Seriously," and "Toward a Woman-Centered University," published in *On Lies, Secrets, and Silence* (1979). I show them a short clip from *Adrienne Rich*, one of the videos available from the Lannan Foundation. (See sources following.) While some may have read her work before, few have seen her or have heard her urban, Jewish voice.

In the history section we read and talk about the boarding schools that American Indians were coerced into attending in the nineteenth and early twentieth centuries in an effort to "Americanize" them. While there are photos (carefully posed) of those situations, the only video I know of is a fictionalized account. As we make the transition to a unit on the current educational situations for women and girls in Asia, Latin America, and Africa, we view the first segment of a five-part video (92 mins.) called *Voices of Change*. It portrays a woman who is part of a current movement of Aborigines to gain reparations for the experience of the destruction of their culture in similar, but more recent, Australian boarding schools. It is also a good example of the methodology of the personal narrative.

Later in the course we look at K–12 education using a combination of quantitative social science methods and personal narrative. While most of the students are familiar with the face of rural poverty in Maine and its ramifications for education, they are less so with the nature of urban poverty and schools. We view *Beauty in the "Bricks,"* a twenty-nine-minute portrayal of the lives of a group of black girls in a housing project in West Dallas whose participation in a girls' club influences their aspirations. One of the girls, with a talent for performing arts, is admitted to a magnet school for the arts at the end of the video. This leads to an interesting discussion of the similarities and differences of their "leaving home" for educational opportunities, which as first-generation college students they know something about. A follow-up video, *Beauty Leaves the "Bricks"* (46 mins.), interviews the women fifteen years later. If we have time to view that one also, it leads to discussions about educational outcomes and defining success.

Conclusion

Of course, there are complexities and opportunities for making mistakes when trying to diversify the women's studies curriculum in any predominantly white institution. Strategies, successes, and failures in diversity efforts are frequently discussed in our women's studies teaching group. One book we have read that has been helpful is *Teaching What You're Not: Identity Politics in Higher Education* (1996), a series of essays edited by Katherine Mayberry. Another useful article is Ann duCille's (1994) critique of the attitude among white scholars of the black experience that "anyone can play." Just as we resent other faculty who think anyone can teach women's studies, we recognize our responsibility to prepare ourselves to teach material about ethnic groups and cultures not a part of our graduate training, as well as the need for us to be both open and humble in our presentations to students.

Leslie has identified another set of issues of which to be wary. In the introduction to the recently published exchange *Is Multiculturalism Bad for Women,* Cohen, Howard, and Nussbaum (3) state that "'multiculturalism' according to one especially compelling formulation, is the radical idea that people in other cultures, foreign and domestic, are human beings too—moral equals, entitled to equal respect and concern, not to be discounted or treated as a subordinate caste. Thus understood, multiculturalism condemns intolerance of other ways of life, finds the human in what might seem the Other, and encourages cultural diversity." In the same book Susan Okin asks, however, whether multiculturalism implies tolerating the oppression of women, and as such is bad for women. Okin (12) argues that first, "the sphere of personal, sexual, and reproductive life functions as a central focus of most cultures, a dominant theme in cultural practices and rules" and second, "that most cultures have as one of their principal aims the control of women by men." She suggests that when cultures are intolerant of the idea of women's equality, those cultural practices that oppress women should be called into question. Leslie strongly feels that in advanced women's studies classes Okin's question *must* be addressed. Thus, in her course she tries both to foster multiculturalism and to problematize it.

Finally there is the issue of cost. It is expensive to buy videocassettes, but we have been successful in writing grant proposals to the university's instructional development fund for videos specifically about U.S. women of color and global women's issues. Vendors will often give discounts to programs ordering a group of videos at one time. The Lannan Literary Foundation offers a set of videos of American authors being interviewed and reading from their work for about twenty dollars each and will entertain proposals for giving them to you for free. We also videotape (with permission) speakers who come to campus, enabling those who could not attend to hear them, sometimes years later. Our web site (www.umaine.edu/wic/) offers a complete list of our video collection by title, with descriptions and a subject index.

Despite the costs—in both time and money—to do the diversity work we attempt, we think we cannot responsibly do otherwise. Preparing our students to leave Maine (which many of them do) requires that they have a sense for the world beyond the bridge over the river where the interstate highway leaves Maine going south. To those of them who stay and to us as well, such study brings us richness well worth the effort.

REFERENCES

Alcoff, Linda. "The Problem of Speaking for Others." *Cultural Critique* (Winter 1991–92): 5–32.

Cohen, Joshua, Matthew Howard, and Martha C. Nussbaum. "Introduction: Feminism, Multiculturalism, and Human Equality." *Is Multiculturalism Bad for Women?* Ed. Susan Moller Okin. Princeton, NJ: Princeton UP, 1999. 3–5.

du Cille, Ann. "The Occult of True Black Womanhood: Critical Demeanor and Black Feminist Studies." *Signs: Journal of Women in Culture and Society* (Spring 1994): 593–629.

Kassindja, Fauziya, and Layli Miller Bashir. *Do They Hear You When You Cry.* New York: Delacorte, 1998.

Mayberry, Katherine J. *Teaching What You're Not: Identity Politics in Higher Education.* New York: New York UP, 1996.

Mernissi, Fatima. *Dreams of Trespass: Tales of a Harem Girlhood.* Reading, Mass.: Perseus, 1994.

Okin, Susan Moller. "Part 1: Is Multiculturalism Bad for Women?" *Is Multiculturalism Bad for Women?* Ed. Susan Moller Okin. Princeton, NJ: Princeton UP, 1999. 9–24.

Rich, Adrienne. *On Lies, Secrets, and Silence: Selected Prose, 1966–1978.* New York: W. W. Norton, 1979.

Sources for Videos Cited

Adrienne Rich
Lannan Foundation
313 Read St.
Santa Fe, NM 87501-2628
(505) 954-5147
For the video donation program contact Small Press Distribution at (510) 524-0852, www.spdbooks.org.

Beauty in the "Bricks" and Beauty Leaves the "Bricks"
Cynthia Salzman Mondell and Allen Mondell
Media Projects, Inc.
5215 Homer Street
Dallas, TX 75206
(214) 826-3863

Behind the Smile
Filmakers Library
124 East 40th St.
New York, NY 10016
www.filmakers.com

Hidden Faces, Hell to Pay, and Voices of Change
Women Make Movies
462 Broadway, Suite 500 D
New York, NY 10013
www.wmm.com

A Woman's Place
Maria Nicolo
201 W. 85th St., #8C
New York, NY 10024
(212) 877-3253

Other companies we have found useful are these:

New Day Films
22-D Hollywood Ave.
Hohokus, NJ 07423
www.newday.com

Films for the Humanities and Sciences
PO Box 2053
Princeton, NJ 08543-2053
www.films.com

Ann Schonberger *is the director of the Women in the Curriculum and Women's Studies Program at the University of Maine and professor of mathematics. Besides offering a major, minor, and graduate concentration in women's studies, the program includes a faculty development curriculum transformation project. Ann is also working with the Maine Feminist Oral History Project on a book about the thirty-year-old domestic violence project in Bangor, Maine.* **Nancy Lewis** *is an adjunct faculty member in women's studies and the women's studies librarian at Fogler Library at the University of Maine. In addition to teaching, she gives library orientation sessions for many different university courses, especially those in women's studies.* **Mazie Hough** *is the associate director of the Women in the Curriculum and Women's Studies Program at the University of Maine. She teaches courses in women's history and research methodologies in women's studies, and is currently writing a history of community response to unwed mothers in Maine and Tennessee.* **Leslie King** *is assistant professor of sociology at the University of Maine. She teaches the course on globalization in women's studies as well as sociology courses. Her research and teaching specialty is the study of population.*

Copyright © 2002 by Ann Schonberger, Nancy Lewis, Mazie Hough, and Leslie King

The Films We Teach

Using *Rosie the Riveter, Global Assembly Line, Dreamworlds II,* and *Fast Food Women* in the Women's Studies Classroom

Wendy Kolmar, with teaching guides by Caitlin Killian, Debra Liebowitz, Lynne Derbyshire, and Carol J. Pierman

The most common and ubiquitous experience of film for women's studies students is the viewing of documentaries in core women's studies courses, particularly introductions to women's studies. Films and videos regularly supplement readings and discussion in introductory courses. Most women's studies faculty could make a long list of films used regularly in such courses, probably headed by *Still Killing Us Softly* and perhaps *Rosie the Riveter.* While we as faculty are not unaware of the politics of representation and the complexities of taking such documentaries as transparent and nondistorting lenses into particular women's lives or experiences, we also understand the power of such films and videos to bring the faces, voices, and environments of their subjects into the classroom, especially for a generation of students raised, for the most part, in a highly visual and media-oriented culture. We do use these films with the sense that, as Tania Modleski suggests, they can bring "real" women into our classrooms and give our students some sense of experiences and lives that are different from their own, whether the distance is marked chronologically or by location, race, or sexuality. This use of film is an important component of women's studies teaching. And women's studies programs and faculty remain an important, large, and reliable audience and market for the work of documentary filmmakers interested in issues of gender and other, intersecting forms of difference. I'd like to think that the growth of women's studies programs had both encouraged the production of such films and helped to train and inform the thinking of the filmmakers creating them.

In putting this *WSQ* issue together, it seemed to me important that this most common connection between film and women's studies be acknowledged and represented. In the short essays that follow, women's studies faculty in different fields responded to the following questions in relation to a film they teach and that is taught frequently in other programs as well: In what contexts do you teach this film? What readings do you use in conjunction with the film? What are the strengths of the film as a teaching tool? What are its drawbacks, or are there ways in which you feel you need to supplement the film in order to use it effectively? For those who have never taught these particular films, these short pieces will I hope offer a sense of the film and at least one way it has been taught. For those of us who use these films frequently, the essays may simply allow us to go back to the films next semester with a different perspective or to locate them differently in our syllabi and revitalize them for ourselves as teaching tools. Meeting these films again in the context of the other material in the issue may perhaps also remind us to ask our students to think about the ways in which the films we show function *as films* and to raise questions about how such films edit, control, or direct our attention as they re-present 'real' women's lives in the context of women's studies classrooms.

The Life and Times of Rosie the Riveter

Caitlin Killian

The Life and Times of Rosie the Riveter explores the participation of women in the American labor force during World War II and the consequences of their exclusion from manufacturing work when the men came home.[1] Interspersing interviews with five women employed in wartime industry jobs with shots of posters, songs, and film footage from the 1940s, the documentary is not simply entertaining but conveys a powerful message about the construction of gender roles. It provides an excellent example of how societal-level changes affect individuals and is an effective tool for provoking discussion of women's history, women and work, and gender role socialization.

Students are frequently under the impression that before World War II all women were full-time homemakers. *The Life and Times of Rosie the Riveter* counters this widespread perception and provides an opportunity to explore the employment patterns of poor and minority women. The film is particularly strong in its attention to racial differences in the hiring and treatment of white and black women and can easily be used in conjunction with Patricia Hill Collins' chapter, "Work, Family, and Black Women's Oppression," in *Black Feminist Thought*. Three of the five women interviewees are black, and the film offers a plethora of examples of racial discrimination.

The documentary shows how the government's need for labor during the war allowed women to escape unsatisfactory and underpaid jobs for skilled industrial work that provided camaraderie and the ability to improve working conditions through unionization. The women interviewed speak not only of the economic benefits they derived from their employment, but also of the pride and sense of accomplishment they took in their work and its importance for the construction of their identities. Listening to these women's feelings about working is a stepping stone for a discussion of identity theory and the benefits people derive from holding multiple roles (Thoits, "Multiple Identities"; "Identity Structures").

The other obvious use of the film is as an illustration of gender socialization and the transformation of gender roles orchestrated to fit the changing needs of the country. In a short period of time, "men's work," technical jobs that paid well, had to be redefined as "women's work." To do this, the government created propaganda that equated factory work with tasks in the home. A needle became a drill on the silver screen, and an authoritative voice told women that operating an industrial press is no more difficult than using a juice extractor. *The Life and Times of Rosie the Riveter* thus beautifully demonstrates how gender is a socially constructed category.

Given that women realized they were capable of doing men's work, the question becomes how they were rerouted back into domesticity at the end of the war. During the war, government propaganda promised the creation of child-care centers, and magazines counseled women on how to cut corners at home in order to devote more time to the war effort. Interviewees noted that messages in popular culture changed after the war to encourage women to spend their time cooking and caring for children. Articles began emphasizing the needs of children who suffered when mothers worked outside the home. In an especially ironic piece of propaganda, a female doctor provides a litany of reasons why paid work damages families and destroys femininity. One interviewee insightfully sums up the manipulation of women: "I think they prepare women psychologically for whatever role the society feels at that particular point they want her to play. After losing so many men, America wanted babies. And we wanted babies. That's okay. But we gave up everything for that. We gave up everything." Quotes like these make explicit the connection between the macro level and the micro level.

For the week in which the film is shown in class, I recommend having students read Sharon Hay's *The Cultural Contradictions of Motherhood*. This book traces the evolution of what Hays calls "intensive mothering," the type of caretaking of children that experts began to recommend after World War II. She makes an interesting argument about the seemingly paradoxical juxtaposition of the rational, commercial world of work with the time-consuming, yet unproductive (in monetary terms) world of raising children. Beginning with historical examples from popular culture that reinforce those of *The Life and Times of Rosie the Riveter* and concluding with explanations given by both mothers who choose to work and those who choose to stay home, Hays deconstructs our assumptions about the appropriate way to mother. This book and the film can thus be used in concert to push students further in their critical examination of the social construction of women's roles.

There are two potential problems with using *The Life and Times of Rosie the Riveter* in the classroom. The first is purely practical. The film runs sixty-five minutes (including the credits.) It is consequently perfect for a seventy-five-minute class, but must be cut for a fifty-minute class with discussion conducted during the next class period. The second problem is that students may find the example of the Second World War effort too dated and believe that because women now occupy diverse positions in the workforce, the points made in the film have no relevance today. To respond to this argument, I suggest using the film in connection with Susan Faludi's book *Backlash: The Undeclared War Against American Women,* in order to establish a broader pattern of women's gains repeatedly being undermined. This can lead to a discussion of what constitutes a backlash, how it is manifested, and what needs to be done to protect the advances that women achieve. While the film effectively highlights the disparities between the government wartime propaganda on issues such as equal pay, safety, child care, and women's reasons for employment with the actual experiences of female workers, the instructor needs to reinforce that these are the same challenges that working women face today. Questions of why salaries, for example, continue to be determined by the gender of those who hold the job rather than by the level of difficulty, engage students with the social construction of reality and with issues of power.

NOTES
 1. *The Life and Times of Rosie the Riveter,* dir. and prod. Connie Field, New Line Cinema, 1980, 65 mins.

REFERENCES
Collins, Patricia Hill. *Black Feminist Thought: Knowledge, Consciousness, and the Politics of Empowerment.* 2nd ed. New York: Routledge, 2000.
Faludi, Susan. *Backlash: The Undeclared War Against American Women.* New York: Doubleday, 1992.

Hays, Sharon. *The Cultural Contradictions of Motherhood*. New Haven: Yale UP, 1996.

Thoits, Peggy A. "Multiple Identities and Psychological Well-Being: A Reformulation and Test of the Social Isolation Hypothesis." *American Sociological Review* 48.2 (1983): 174–187.

———. "Identity Structures and Psychological Well-Being: Gender and Marital Status Comparisons. *Social Psychology Quarterly* 55.3 (1992): 236–256.

Caitlin Killian is an assistant professor of Sociology at Drew University, where she teaches courses on sociology of gender and the family. She is interested in women immigrants and ethnic and gender socialization.

The Global Assembly Line

Debra Liebowitz

Well before "globalization" became a trendy concept, feminist filmmaker Lorraine Gray worked to elucidate the gendered consequences of the international division of labor. Indeed, since the late 1980s, *The Global Assembly Line*, Gray's film about women's labor in export-oriented industries in the developing world, has been used in women's studies classrooms to expose students to the international dimensions of the sexual division of labor. This film takes viewers from Tennessee to Mexico's northern border, from Silicon Valley to the Philippines, to show that the internationalization of production relies on women's labor. The footage used is at least fifteen years old; however, the film has stood the test of time, raising important issues about the role of women's labor in facilitating processes of globalization, as well as highlighting gendered notions about the value and quality of women's work that undergird manufacturing for export. Using a series of questions that viewers of the film—both instructors and students—might ask, this essay spotlights some of the ways in which the context and the situation of women workers in export-oriented production has changed in the years since the film's production.

How has production for export in the developing world changed since the film was made?

While manufacturing for export still occurs in "zones"—particular geographic areas where foreign companies are given tax incentives, tax holidays, and other economic benefits—export-oriented industrialization is increasingly *the* development strategy of choice. The proliferation of free-trade regimes (such as that brought about by the North

American Free Trade Agreement [NAFTA], governing Mexico, Canada, and the United States, and that produced by the World Trade Organization [WTO]) has meant that production for export is increasingly geographically dispersed—both within and across national boundaries. Since *The Global Assembly Line* was produced, pressure to "develop" via export-oriented industrialization has only increased. Consequently, if a similar film were to be made today, it would explore the situation of women workers in more than just Mexico and the Philippines. The sources of the pressure to produce for export are extremely varied, ranging from various aspects of the "public" sector—international organizations such as the World Bank and the International Monetary Fund as well as bilateral intergovernmental relations—to "private" business interests in all areas of the world. While Mexico and the Philippines, as depicted in the film, remain key locations for such investment, the strategic sites of globalization (Sassen) have expanded to include less prosperous countries, among them Guatemala, El Salvador, Bangladesh, and Vietnam. In part, this move is the result of a seemingly never ending search on the part of transnational corporations for access to ever cheaper labor and lower production costs.

This increasing pressure to produce for export has dramatically increased the number of *maquiladoras* (assembly plants) located along the U.S.-Mexico border since *The Global Assembly Line* footage was shot. In addition, the number of maquiladoras located in other parts of the country has also skyrocketed in this time period. The number of employees in the maquiladora sector has increased from 60,000 in 1975 to 420,000 in 1990. By the year 2000, 3,600 factories employed 1.3 million people (Salas). In addition, those located outside the border region, for example, outside Guadalajara in central Mexico, have experienced similarly dramatic increases. Since the film's production, the Philippines has experienced a similarly impressive increase in the number of people employed in export processing zones, moving from nearly 230,000 employees in 1994 to more than 696,000 just six years later (Philippine Economic Zone Authority). The rapid increase in export-oriented production in Mexico and the Philippines is emblematic of globalization's direction in the past twenty years. At the same time, however, increasing employment in export-oriented factories in the developing world is not inevitable. Indeed, as the U.S. economy has slumped into recession, these factories have in many cases, experienced significant layoffs.

Do women now constitute the same proportion of employees in export-processing industries as when The Global Assembly Line *was made?*

While the overall number of women employed in export-oriented production in the developing world has grown, women no longer constitute upwards of 85 percent of this workforce. In Mexico's maquiladoras, current estimates suggest that the proportion of women workers has declined to between 50 percent and 60 percent (CorpWatch; Light). While many more men are now employed in the maquiladoras, one must be cautious of generalizations, as women remain the "paradigmatic workers" in many factories (Salzinger). Whether women workers represent 50 or 80 percent of employees in a factory can, in part, be explained by occupational sex segregation. For instance, in both Mexico and the Philippines, women predominate in the most labor-intensive industries (for example, making up 80 percent of the garment industry); however, they constitute a smaller percentage of the labor force where levels of technology or mechanization are highest (for example, in manufacture of wood products [34 percent] or in automotive assembly [Chant and McIlwaine]). In a study of women's labor in the Mactan Export Processing Zone in the Philippines, Chant and McIlwaine note that an electronics firm manager reported that he "preferred to employ men on the grounds that they were more adept at operating machinery" (153; see also Joekes and Weston). In other words, the percentages of women workers may be declining in some export-oriented factories, but gender discrimination and stereotyping persist.

Are present working conditions in export-oriented factories in the developing world the same as depicted in the film?

Conditions of work in this sector remain, more than fifteen years after *The Global Assembly Line*'s release, substandard. Frequent complaints are heard about union-busting activities; health and safety risks (Light); forced pregnancy testing (Human Rights Watch); and the inability of workers to survive on wages paid (Salas).[1] Yet analysts must resist the tendency to flatten women's agency—their capacity to be political and economic actors—in a rush to condemn the exploitative practices of transnational capital. Doing so leaves men firmly entrenched as the "true" agents of economic change (Fernández-Kelly). In recent work on the topic, researchers have begun to look at the ways in which narratives of gender are being reshaped by women's work in export-oriented industries. Salzinger, for instance, argues that by examining the production of gender in particular factories, it becomes clear that the "docile" woman worker can use the factory space to challenge narratives about the malleability of women workers. In other words, alterations in gendered subjectivities occur as the material conditions surrounding women's and men's lives change. When, for instance, young women become important family income earners, moving from rural areas to work in factories, microgender relations may begin to shift, giving young women more power in the family system.[2]

How can showing the film disrupt traditional hierarchies between the "developing" and "developed" worlds?

Showing a film such as *The Global Assembly Line* can be especially valuable, as it helps students recognize one of the consequences of globalization.[3] That is, the conditions of women's lives in Mexico, or the Philippines, are intimately linked to U.S. corporate strategies for maximizing profit. Acknowledging this link reduces the distance between "us" and "them" as it makes clear that as owners, investors, consumers, bargain shoppers, and corporate benefactors "we" are imbricated in systems of economic and political exploitation. However, one of the challenges of showing a film like this is to avoid reinforcing that which many students in the United States "know": that women in the developing world are exploited, undervalued, and generally worse off than women in the United States. Drawing sharp contrasts between "Western culture" and the culture of "others"—whether done explicitly or left to the imagination of students—simply re-creates the very hierarchies of class, gender, race, and nation that feminists are working to undo (see Narayan on this point).

One of the most effective methods for minimizing the tendency toward "othering" is to pair this film with readings about the labor conditions of women workers in the United States. Peter Kwong's work on women in the garment industry in New York's Chinatown is particularly appropriate, as the world of female immigrant labor that he describes mirrors that which the film depicts. This pairing can yield results similar to those described by Teresa Carrillo in an article about U.S.-Mexican cross-border organizing. Carrillo describes a tour of the Los Angeles and San Francisco garment districts by garment workers from Mexico City. The response of one of the Mexican garment workers to seeing firsthand the working conditions of garment workers in the United States was that "[c]onditions in Los Angeles were worse than . . . in Mexico. Garment workers there [in the U.S.] have to deal with being undocumented on top of everything else" (Carrillo 393).

And, calling into question our students' assumed hierarchies of gender, race, and nation is a key goal of *The Global Assembly Line*.

NOTES

1. For examples of union activities in Mexico's maquiladoras, see Kamel and Hoffman; in the Philippines' Export Processing Zones, see Maquila Network Update; in Guatemala, see Laslett.
2. For a discussion of related issues, see Melissa Wright's article on the subject.
3. The terms "developed" and "developing" in the heading above are in quotation marks to signify the inadequacy of both categories. There are at least as many underdeveloped areas in the "developed" world as there are wealthy areas in the "developing" world.

REFERENCES

Carrillo, Teresa. "Cross-Border Talk: Transnational Perspectives on Labor, Race, and Sexuality." *Talking Visions: Multicultural Feminism in a Transnational Age.* Ed. Ella Shohat. Cambridge: MIT P, 1998. 391–411.

Chant, Sylvia, and Cathy McIlwaine. "Gender and Export Manufacturing in the Philippines: Continuity or Change in Female Employment." *Gender, Place, and Culture: A Journal of Feminist Geography* 2.2 (1995): 147–76.

CorpWatch. "Maquiladoras at a Glance." 1999. Online. Available: <http://www.corpwatch.org/trac/issues/border/background/1999/factsheet.htm. 29 Sept. 2001. Fernández-Kelly, Patricia. "Reading the Signs: The Economics of Gender Twenty-five Years Later." *Signs: Journal of Women in Culture and Society* 25.4 (2000): 1107–12.

Human Rights Watch. *Mexico—a Job or Your Rights: Continued Sex Discrimination in Mexico's Maquiladora Sector.* New York: Human Rights Watch, 1998.

Joekes, Susan, and Ann Weston. *Women and the New Trade Agenda.* New York: United Nations Development Fund for Women, 1994.

Kamel, Rachael, and Anya Hoffman. *The Maquiladora Reader: Cross-Border Organizing since NAFTA.* Philadelphia: American Friends Service Committee, 1999.

Kwong, Peter. "American Sweatshops 1980s Style: Chinese Women Garment Workers." *Women Transforming Politics: An Alternative Reader.* Ed. Cathy J. Cohen, Kathleen B. Jones, and Joan C. Tronto. New York: New York UP, 84–93.

Laslett, Michael. "A Bitter Taste: Struggling for Just the Minimum." *NACLA Report on the Americas* 34.6 (2001): 8–11.

Light, Julie. "Engendering Change: The Long, Slow Road to Organizing Women Maquiladora Workers." 26 June 1999. Online. Available: <http://www.igc.org/trac/feature/border/women/engendering.html. 29 Nov. 2001.

Maquila Network Update. "Philippine Workers Demand End to Union Busting." Sept. 2000. Online. Available: <http://www.maquilasolidarity.org/resources/maquilas/philippines.htm. 29 Nov. 2001.

Narayan, Uma. *Dislocating Cultures: Identities, Traditions, and Third World Feminism.* New York: Routledge, 1997.

Philippine Economic Zone Authority. 2001. "Economic Zone Employment." Online. Available: <http://www.peza.gov.ph/news/pezanewsmain.htm. 29 Nov. 2001.
Salas, Carlos. "The Impact of NAFTA on Wages and Incomes in Mexico." *NAFTA at Seven: Its Impact on Workers in All Three Nations.* Briefing paper. Washington, D.C.: Economic Policy Institute, 2001.
Salzinger, Leslie. "From High Heels to Swathed Bodies: Gendered Meanings under Production in Mexico's Export-Processing Industry." *Feminist Studies* 23.3 (1997): 549–74.
Sassen, Saskia. *Globalization and Its Discontents.* New York: New P, 1998.
Wright, Melissa. "Maquiladora Mestizas and a Feminist Border Politics: Revisiting Anzaldúa." *Decentering the Center: Philosophy for a Multicultural, Postcolonial, and Feminist World.* Ed. Uma Narayan and Sandra Harding. Bloomington: Indiana UP, 2000. 208–25.

Debra Liebowitz *is an assistant professor of women's studies and political science at Drew University, where she teaches courses on global feminisms, gender and politics, Latin American politics, and international social movements. Among her most recent publications is "Constructing Cooperation: Feminist Activism and the North American Free Trade Agreement" in* Feminist Locations: Global and Local, Theory and Practice *(Rutgers UP 2001).*

Dreamworlds II: Desire/Sex/Power in Music Video

Lynne Derbyshire

Sut Jhally's examination of music videos in *Dreamworlds II* provides a welcome route for examining media representations of women and their sexuality.[1] In order to be effective in a college classroom, though, it is important to account for the overexposure to music videos that is characteristic of many students.

Many college students graduating this spring were born the year MTV debuted (1981) and were introduced to MTV with the exact videos highlighted in Sut Jhally's *Dreamworlds II* (1995). They recognize the video clips Jhally includes in the same way that another generation recognizes "Play it again, Sam," or "I love the smell of napalm in the morning." Whether they were allowed or forbidden to watch MTV, whether they viewed it surreptitiously, it is for most a significant part of their popular culture, a part of their world. *Dreamworlds II* offers an important challenge to what many students have seen as innocuous entertainment. Some quickly accept Jhally's analysis but others react as if it were an attack on *E.T.* or Disney's *Cinderella*.

Like the first *Dreamworlds* (1991), the sequel surveys what Jhally calls the male dream world of music videos that presents a story of female sexuality written by men. He contends that the messages of the dream world deny individuality and subjectivity to women, presenting them as interchangeable body parts. Women's story of sexuality is silenced. The evidence presented includes clips of music videos, without the music, accompanied by a voice-over, demonstrating and explaining the techniques of storytelling, the roles women play, camera angles and editing techniques, and an examination of real and implied images of sexual violence. The video concludes with a look at what Jhally believes to be the consequences of this dream world. Scenes from a gang rape in the movie *The Accused* are intercut with images from music videos that are presented as mirroring the gang rape scene; and then statistical data from surveys of attitudes regarding sexual assault are presented (for example, 60 percent of men believe that women provoke rape by their appearance or behavior, and 30 percent of women agree). Jhally argues that the ubiquitous message of music videos influences social attitudes.

Dreamworlds II may give the less experienced viewer of music videos the idea that the subject positions presented in the videos come from a clearer narrative than is generally true of music videos. The distillation of images of women's "nymphomania," objectification, and subservience, inevitably involving removing those images from the original context, also implies an almost exclusive focus on these images. Students more familiar with music videos may feel that this creates a misrepresentation. Even when inclined to agree with Jhally's basic message, they may discredit his analysis because of that perceived misrepresentation. Careful contextualization prior to viewing *Dreamworlds II* seems very effective in avoiding that pitfall. Also, a focus on the most objective section of the video, the analysis of camera angles and editing techniques, helps to lessen the negative effect that may otherwise occur.

The essentially non-narrative or very loosely narrative style of music videos enhances the opportunity for polysemic readings. Is Madonna transgressive? Is she co-opted by a culture that commodifies female sexuality? Is submission truly her fantasy, meaning that she therefore remains in charge? Are the roles she plays rooted in cultural norms that reinforce a lack of female subjectivity? Are hip-hop videos that display the essence of the "bling-bling" culture a satire of the fantasy of those who hope to "make it?" Do they celebrate the justly deserved rewards of success? Approaching Jhally's interpretation with some skepticism creates an opportunity to explore potential readings with less resistance from resistant students, and encourages students who are more accepting to work harder on their analysis.

The dry humor of the narrator ameliorates the tone some students find tiresomely moralistic, but also creates some discomfort. Are the images presented amusing or are they problematic? Many students already find music videos funny and suggest that the amusement they derive from them may contribute to masking the sexism. The narrative voice can reinforce that effect, though in some cases students report that it helps to delegitimize music videos. One student noted, "They have award shows so it must be an art form," but after seeing *Dreamworlds II* credited Jhally's sarcastic remarks for her recognition that music videos "make sex a spectacle rather than an intimacy," an effect she resented.

The study guide provided by the Media Education Foundation can be of assistance in overcoming some of the potential pitfalls of using *Dreamworlds II* with an audience that grew up with these videos. It emphasizes some of the issues that students raise, and it reiterates points that may be overlooked in viewing the video. It encourages viewers to consider the portrayal of male sexuality that is not analyzed in *Dreamworlds II,* argues for the need to increase democratic access to media so as to present a broader range of images of sexuality, and places music videos in a context of other influences. Use of the study guide undermines resistance and promotes more critical thinking.

With careful contextualization and use of the study guide, *Dreamworlds II* provides for effective classroom discussions of mediated images of women and sexuality. Discussions of mediated images of men and sexuality would require more preparation.

NOTES

1. *Dreamworlds II,* written, ed., and prod. Sut Jhally, Media Education Foundation, 1995, 55 mins.

Lynne Derbyshire is an assistant professor of communication studies and women's studies at the University of Rhode Island. She teaches courses in gender and communication, gender and media, and woman's rights discourse.

Fast Food Women

Carol J. Pierman

Whoever "pays mental wages" will control the people.

This dictum, glimpsed in passing during Anne Lewis Johnson's *Fast Food Women,* could serve as epigraph for this smart and sadly moving documentary film.[1] Shot in the interactive mode, the film makes the most of its footage. Featuring behind-the-scenes shots of franchise stores, interactions with the film's subjects, and expert analysis from author Barbara Garson, the reality of fast food jobs is laid bare. The phrase—*whoever "pays mental wages"*—graces a poster hanging in a fast food chain's corporate headquarters. On camera, a senior executive intones, "Suzy, sixteen years old, doesn't need benefits. She's got her father, working in the coalfields . . . he has every benefit under the sun."

And although the viewer has just learned from "Suzy's" supervisor that the coalfields are idle and workers laid off, the men in the corporate headquarters focus on how important it is to dress every hamburger in the exact same way: because "it affects the taste" of a sandwich.

From the film, we learn that the fast food industry is not looking for the worker who wants to be creative; it's looking for sameness, for someone "more content with following procedures"—procedures consisting of scripted, learned acts, including mandatory suggestion-sales, "Would you like cheese sticks with that? A large Coke and fries?" In this fashion, every worker becomes replaceable, a component part like the fry-vac or soft-serve machine, components that don't need health insurance, vacation pay, or retirement plans.

Symbolic then of so much of the doublespeak that passes for corporate philosophy, the company jargon hardly obscures the fact that from shop floor to fast food joint, jobs (and indeed workers) are broken down increasingly into disembodied tasks. The resulting routinization deprives workers of dignity, creativity, and—ultimately—a living wage.

These bitter truths are so clearly depicted by the camera work and interviews with the women employees in *Fast Food Women* that it never fails to provoke a lively, informed classroom discussion. The film touches on the serious issues that surround the topics of work, class, and gender. In fact, *Fast Food Women* is a documentary I have screened in a wide range of women's studies courses: Feminisms on Film; Women and Work; and Gender, Race, and Class. In a film course, *Fast Food Women* works exceptionally well with John Izod and Richard Kilborn's "The Documentary," which explicates the editorial effects a documentarist deploys "to fashion 'fragments of reality' into an artifact that has a specific social impact" (42–43). Students learn to "read" the technical interventions through which filmmakers manipulate point of view.

The video works equally well in Women and Work as well as Gender, Race, and Class for its clear understandings of social and economic class. Typically, I might screen the film at a point when students are reading material on the persistence of sex segregation in the workplace. They are quick to note that the film's salaried managers, who work with benefits and have more security, are male; and that the hourly and part-time workers, who earn no benefits, are female. This may be an obvious fact—one they can perceive without attending a class—but at the same time they are reading about the persistent and sometimes more subtle ways in which modern professions reinvent segregation within job categories, with women remaining clustered in similar jobs for lower pay.

With reduced lifelong earnings and low prestige, women fall into the more precarious economic class. Academic readings such as Christine Williams's studies of gender differences at work, Nancy Folbre's critiques of "caring labor," or Arlie Hochschild's explorations of the modern corporation reinforce this point. And once students begin their own research, they find much in a pervasive corporate structure from which even their higher educations won't protect them. Accordingly, the *Economist* notes that while McDonald's Hamburger University in Oak Brook, Illinois, might have been one of the first so-called corporate campuses, today there are 1,600 corporate universities in the United States, training their "workers [to] march to a single McDrum" ("Burger King" 78). (The academy itself is not immune to pervasive corporatization: part-time temporary employees and "continuous quality" schemes typify a diminished quality of life for academics on most college campuses.)

This film touches a raw nerve, especially for students at my Deep South university, many of whom come from mining or manufacturing communities. They can be heard murmuring, "There but for the grace of God go I." And yet they worry about the jobs they hope for in the professional sector, jobs that are filled increasingly by contract employees, by companies concerned mainly with squeezing profits from a division or subsidiary.

Filmed in various franchise stores—McDonald's, Kentucky Fried Chicken, Pizza Hut, Druther's (a Dairy Queen subsidiary)—*Fast Food Women* is set in eastern Kentucky coal country. The women, wives of laid-off miners, are now the sole providers for their families. With no benefits or wages they can count on, all earn just above the minimum wage. Nevertheless, they cannot rely on steady hours or pay; if it is a slow day, they might be sent home, and most work fewer than forty hours a week. Hence, even an inadequate minimum wage is beyond the grasp of the average fast food worker.

We learn that in Whitesburg, Kentucky, a town of about 1,600 residents, the manager of the local Druther's has 1,500 applications for his handful of minimum-wage jobs. "Most of the applications I'm getting," he notes, are from women whose husbands are laid off, and there's "no other income coming in." We learn that 99 percent of his applications are from women, because a man—even a laid-off man—won't work for such wages.

The irony of that corporate executive's comment becomes plain as the film introduces some of the far-from-sixteen-year-old Suzies who staff Whitesburg's fast food restaurants: Among them is Sereda Collier, a middle-aged cook, whose face is etched with exhaustion. "You can't stop for no reason," she says. "I'm real tired, my feet hurt, and I feel like I have about five pounds of grease on me." Jennie Gibson, also middle-age, shows her arms covered with burns "from dropping hush puppies" into the deep-fat fryer. Zelphia Adams, who states, "You have to keep moving. After I leave my job and come home, I've got another job waiting. So I'm exhausted." And Pam Banks, "It's a no-win situation. When you see a paycheck for $70 a week, it's pretty bad."

Finally there is Nellie Kiner, who once cooked in a real restaurant, where "they let you work eight hours." In her sixties now, she notes that in a "fast food restaurant, they won't let you work eight hours." Having no benefits, no retirement, no vacation pay "really bears on my mind, I grieve over it," she laments.

In *All the Livelong Day*, which students sometimes read in tandem with viewing the film, Barbara Garson notes that "people passionately want to work" (ix). They want to do a good job. "It is hard and uncomfortable to do a bad job" (xi). Despite the degrading rules—the insistence that every hamburger be dressed uniformly; that every batch of fried chicken be shaken six times, rolled ten times, and pressed seven times into the flour; or that the dough for every Pizza Hut Personal Pan Pizza weigh exactly 5 ounces—the women do take pride in their abilities and ask only that their work provide a living wage. "I can do about anything. I'm pretty sure of that," says Angie Hogg, who has worked at Pizza Hut for three and a half years. Asked about her prospects for finding a better job in Whitesburg, she just rolls her eyes.

Fast Food Women is a production of Appalshop Film and Video. Created as result of a 1969 War on Poverty program, Appalshop has as its mission training young people in central Appalachia in media production skills. Today Appalshop, Incorporated, comprises Appal Recordings, Roadside Theater, Appalshop Gallery and WMMT-FM.

Through its film and video series, Appalshop allows the people of central Appalachia to create and present work central to local concerns and culture. Appalshop films range from *Through Their Eyes:*

Stories of Gays and Lesbians in the Mountains, to *Evelyn Williams,* the story of black and white families working together to save their mountain village from destruction by mining interests. Their stories illustrate with clarity the maxim that politics is local, and that activism and creative work based in the local just might provide the best hope for our larger political culture. Folks—average people—do make a difference. Janet Zandy notes, "[W]orking-class people do not have the quiet hands or neutral faces of the privileged classes" (5). Indeed, grief and exhaustion line the faces of the poor women featured in *Fast Food Women.* The memory of those faces and their words lingers long after the film's screening. On hearing their stories, students come away caring far less about the women's poor grammar or the niceties of middle-class academic life, and caring far more about the implications of such a world in which personal worth is so disregarded.

NOTES
1. *Fast Food Women,* dir. Anne Lewis Johnson, Appalshop, 1991, 28 minutes.

REFERENCES
"Burger King." *Economist* 23 Oct. 1999: 78.
Garson, Barbara. *All the Livelong Day: The Meaning and Demeaning of Routine Work.* Rev. ed. New York: Penguin, 1994.
Izod, John, and Richard Kilborn. "The Documentary." *World Cinema: Critical Approaches.* Ed. John Hill and P.C. Gibson. London: Oxford UP, 2000. 42–49.
Zandy, Janet. Introduction. *Liberating Memory: Our Work and Our Working-Class Consciousness.* New Brunswick: Rutgers UP, 1995. 1–15.

Carol J. Pierman *is chair of women's studies at the University of Alabama. Her current project is a critical study of the All-American Girls Professional Baseball League. She is the author of two books of poetry,* The Age of Krypton *(Carnegie Mellon University Press) and* The Naturalized Citizen *(New Rivers).*

Wendy Kolmar *is professor of English and director of women's studies at Drew University. Her most recent book is* Feminist Theory: A Reader *(1999), coedited with Fran Bartkowski.*

Copyright © 2002, for their respective contributions, by Wendy Kolmar, Caitlin Killian, Debra Liebowitz, Lynne Derbyshire, and Carol Pierman

Women, Film, and Feminism
A Course Syllabus

Walter Metz

Course Description

This course introduces the issues that feminist theories pose for the analysis of films and culture. These issues are usually framed in reference to women's access to and roles in the production of media and women's representation within these media. Correspondingly, the course offers two major sections of investigation. First, we will explore the historical development of women's roles in the cinema as creative artists. Second, we will explore the various ways in which women's roles in the film industry intersect with the wider identity political issues of race, class, sexuality, and national identity. The course will conclude with a case study applying the feminist theories encountered to a recent popular film adaptation, Amy Heckerling's *Clueless* (1995). This "hands-on" conclusion will provide the impetus for students to finish their own term papers applying feminist theory to popular culture. The course will be rigorous, offering students the opportunity to engage with a vast array of important feminist theory, including the work of Kaja Silverman, Julia Kristeva, and Luce Irigaray.

Required Readings

Austen, Jane. *Emma*. New York: Bantam, 1981.
Waller, Robert James. *The Bridges of Madison County*. New York: Warner, 1997.
Weedon, Chris. *Feminism, Theory, and the Politics of Difference*. London: Blackwell, 1999.

In addition, students will read the following chapters and articles from recent scholarly books and journals:

Andrew, Dudley. "Adaptation." *Concepts in Film Theory*. New York: Oxford UP, 1985.
Awkward, Michael. "A Black Man's Place(s) in Black Feminist Criticism." *Who Can Speak? Authority and Critical Identity*. Ed. Judith Roof and Robyn Wiegman. Urbana: U of Illinois P, 1995. 71–91.

Butler, Judith. "Freud and the Melancholia of Gender." *Gender Trouble: Feminism and the Subversion of Identity*. New York: Routledge, 1990. 57–65.
Cixous, Helene. "The Laugh of the Medusa." *New French Feminisms*. Ed. Elaine Marks and Isabelle de Courtivron. New York: Schocken, 1981. 245–64.
Cook, Pam. "Approaching the Work of Dorothy Arzner." Rpt. *Feminism and Film Theory*. Ed. Constance Penley. New York: Routledge, 1988. 46–56.
Eckert, Charles. "Anatomy of a Proletarian Film." *Movies and Methods*. Vol. 2. Ed. Bill Nichols. Berkeley and Los Angeles: U of California P, 1985.
Flitterman-Lewis, Sandy. "From Fantasy to Structure of the Fantasm." *To Desire Differently: Feminism and the French Cinema*. Urbana: U of Illinois P, 1990. 98–112.
Freud, Sigmund. "Mourning and Melancholia." (1917). *The Standard Edition of the Complete Psychological Works of Sigmund Freud*. Vol. 14. Ed. and trans. James Strachey. London: Hogarth P, 1957. 239–58.
Gibson-Hudson, Gloria. "Aspects of Black Feminist Cultural Ideology in Films by Black Women Independent Artists." Rpt. in *Multiple Voices in Feminist Film Criticism*. Ed. Diane Carson, Linda Dittmar, and Janice R. Welsch. Minneapolis: U of Minnesota P, 1994. 365–79.
Heath, Stephen. "Male Feminism." *Men in Feminism*. Ed. Alice Jardine and Paul Smith. New York: Methuen, 1987.
Houston, Beverle. "Missing in Action: Notes on Dorothy Arzner." (1984). Rpt. *Multiple Voices in Feminist Film Criticism*. Ed. Diane Carson, Linda Dittmar, and Janice R. Welsch. Minneapolis: U of Minnesota P, 1994. 271–79.
Irigaray, Luce. "A Very Black Sexuality?" (1974). *Speculum of the Other Woman*. Trans. Gillian C. Gill. Ithaca: Cornell UP, 1985. 66–73.
———. "This Sex Which Is Not One." *New French Feminisms*. Eds. Elaine Marks and Isabelle de Courtivron. New York: Schocken, 1981. 99–106.
Johnston, Claire. "Dorothy Arzner: Critical Strategies." (1975). Rpt. in *Feminism and Film Theory*. Ed. Constance Penley. New York: Routledge, 1988. 36–45.
Kaplan, E. Ann. "The Avant-garde Theory Film." *Women and Film: Both Sides of the Camera*. New York: Methuen, 1983. 154–61.
Kristeva, Julia. "Psychoanalysis—A Counterdepressant." *Black Sun: Depression and Melancholia*. Trans. Leon S. Roudiez. New York: Columbia UP, 1987. 3–30.
———. "Women's Time." *Signs*. 7.1 (1981): 5–25.

Kuhn, Annette. "Intestinal Fortitude." Introduction. *Queen of the B's: Ida Lupino Behind the Camera*. Westport: Greenwood P, 1995. 1–12.

———. "Textual Politics." *Women's Pictures: Feminism and Cinema*. 2nd ed. New York: Verso, 1994. 151–71.

Mayne, Judith. "Lesbian Looks: Dorothy Arzner and Female Authorship." *How Do I Look? Queer Film and Video*. Ed. Bad Object Choices. Seattle: Bay P, 1991. 103–43.

Metz, Walter. "Another Being We Have Created Called Us': Point-of-View, Melancholia, and the Joking Unconscious in *The Bridges of Madison County*." *The Velvet Light Trap* 39 (Spring 1997): 66–83.

———. "A Totally Clueless Emma? How American Popular Culture Saved Jane Austen from Masterpiece Theatre." Unpublished MS. Bozeman, MT, 2000.

Mulvey, Laura. "Visual Pleasure and Narrative Cinema." (1975). Rpt. in *Feminism and Film Theory*. Ed. Constance Penley. New York: Routledge, 1988. 57–68.

Norden, Martin. "Women in the Early Film Industry." *Wide Angle* 6.3 (1984): 58–66.

Rabonovitz, Lauren. "Maya Deren and an American Avant-garde Cinema." *Points of Resistance: Women, Power, and Politics in the New York Avant-garde Cinema, 1943–71*. Urbana: U of Illinois P, 1991. 49–91.

Silverman, Kaja. "The Female Authorial Voice." *The Acoustic Mirror: The Female Voice in Psychoanalysis and Cinema*. Bloomington: Indiana UP, 1988. 187–234.

Williams, Linda. "A Jury of Their Peers: Marleen Gorris's *A Question of Silence*." *Multiple Voices in Feminist Film Criticism*. Ed. Diane Carson, Linda Dittmar, and Janice R. Welsch. Minneapolis: U of Minnesota P, 1994. 432–40.

Films/Videos

At Land, Maya Deren, United States, 1944.
Black Girl, Ousmane Sembene, Senegal, 1966.
The Bridges of Madison County, Clint Eastwood, United States, 1995.
Clueless, Amy Heckerling, United States, 1995.
Dance, Girl, Dance, Dorothy Arzner, United States, 1940.
How Men Propose, Lois Weber, United States, 1913.
Illusions, Julie Dash, United States, 1980.
Marked Woman, Lloyd Bacon, United States, 1937.
Matrimony's Speed Limit, Alice Guy-Blache, United States, 1913.
A Question of Silence, Marleen Gorris, The Netherlands, 1983.
The Smiling Madame Beudet, Germaine Dulac, France, 1924.

Superstar: The Karen Carpenter Story, Todd Haynes, United States, 1987.
Thriller, Sally Potter, Great Britain, 1979.

Graded Course Activities

Quizzes	15%
Midterm Exam	20%
Process Writing	25%
Oral Presentation	15%
Final Exam	25%

Description of Process Writing and Oral Presentation

Students will produce a ten-to-fifteen-page paper and a ten-minute oral presentation that (1) employs the methodologies presented in the class and/or (2) investigates the content of some portion of the class material. Students will be afforded the opportunity for feedback on their work as the semester proceeds according to the following schedule: By week 3, students will hand in a typed, paragraph-length sample thesis paragraph for the final paper. By week 6, students will hand in a typed, five-page analysis of one film that will serve as a significant case study within the final paper. By week 10, students will hand in a two-page précis for the paper. A précis is a document that tells the reader what the thesis of the argument is, what sources will be used, what methodology will be used, and what the case study analyses will be. By week 13, students will meet with the instructor, prepared with an outline of the oral presentation, including a film clip to illustrate support for the argument. A draft of the final paper is due by week 14. Students will receive written feedback and a grade on this draft. Students may accept the grade given or rewrite the draft for a new grade, with the due date for final revisions being the last day of finals week.

Schedule of Events

Section 1: Getting Our Theoretical Bearings

Week 1: Feminist Criticim

Discussion 1: Introduction to Feminist Criticism
Readings: Weedon, Chapter 1 ("The Question of Difference"); Weedon, Chapter 2 ("Challenging Patriarchy, Decentring Heterosexuality").

Discussion 2: Methodologies of Feminist Criticism
Readings: Weedon, Chapter 4 ("Psychoanalysis and Difference");
Mulvey, "Visual Pleasure and Narrative Cinema."

Week 2: Masculinity and Feminism

Discussion 1: Cards on the Table (or, What Business Does Walter Have Teaching Feminism?)
Readings: Heath, "Male Feminism"; Awkward, "A Black Man's Place(s) in Black Feminist Criticism."
Screening: *The Bridges of Madison County.*

Discussion 2: The Patriarchal Imagination in Waller's *Bridges*
Readings: Waller, *The Bridges of Madison County;* Metz, "Another Being We Have Created Called Us."

Week 3: A Case Study of The Bridges of Madison County

Discussion 1: Theories of Melancholia
Readings: Freud, "Mourning and Melancholia," Butler, "Freud and the Melancholia of Gender."

Discussion 2: Subverting the Patriarchal Imagination in Eastwood's *Bridges*
Readings: Irigaray, "A Very Black Sexuality?"; Kristeva, "Psychoanalysis —A Counterdepressant."

Section 2: Historicizing the Female Authorial Voice in Cinema

Week 4: The Female Authorial Voice

Discussion 1: Theorizing the Female Authorial Voice
Readings: Silverman, "The Female Authorial Voice."

Discussion 2: Women Directors in the Early Avant-garde Movements
Readings: Flitterman-Lewis, "From Fantasy to Structure of the Fantasm"; Rabinovitz, "Maya Deren and an American Avant-garde Cinema."
Screening: *The Smiling Madame Beudet; At Land.*

Week 5: Women Directors in Classical Hollywood Cinema

Discussion 1: Women Directors in the Early American Cinema
Readings: Norden, "Women in the Early Film Industry."
Screening: *How Men Propose; Matrimony's Speed Limit.*

Discussion 2: Dorothy Arzner and Ida Lupino
Readings: Johnston, "Dorothy Arzner: Critical Strategies"; Cook, "Approaching the Work of Dorothy Arzner"; Houston, "Missing in Action: Notes on Dorothy Arzner"; Kuhn, "Intestinal Fortitude," Mayne, "Lesbian Looks."
Screening: *Dance, Girl, Dance.*

Week Six: Contemporary Feminist Cinema

Discussion 1: The Feminist Avant-garde of the 1970s
Readings: Kuhn, "Textual Politics," Kaplan, "The Avant-garde Theory Film"
Screening: *Thriller.*

Discussion 2: Toward an African American Feminist Cinema
Readings: Gibson-Hudson, "Aspects of Black Feminist Cultural Ideology," Weedon, Chapter 7 ("Race, Racism, and the Problem of Whiteness").
Screening: *Illusions.*

Week 7: European Feminist Cinema

Discussion 1: The New French Feminisms
Readings: Irigaray, "This Sex Which Is Not One"; Cixous, "The Laugh of the Medusa"; Kristeva, "Women's Time."

Discussion 2: European Art Cinema
Readings: Williams, "A Jury of Their Peers."
Screening : *A Question of Silence.*

Section 3: Beyond Authorship (Identity Politics in Cinema)

Week 8: Feminism and Social Class

Discussion 1: The Intersection of Class and Gender in Feminist Theory
Readings: Weedon, Chapter 6 ("Class").
Screening: *Marked Woman.*

Discussion 2: Feminist Analysis of *Marked Woman*
Readings: Eckert, "The Anatomy of a Proletarian Film."

Week 9: Sexuality and Postcolonialism

Discussion 1: Queer Theory's Place in Feminism
Readings: Weedon, Chapter 3 ("Lesbian Difference, Feminism, and Queer Theory")
Screening: *Superstar: The Karen Carpenter Story.*

Discussion 2: Postcolonialism and Feminism's "Third Wave"
Readings: Weedon, Chapter 8 ("Beyond Eurocentrism").
Screening: *Black Girl.*

Section 4: A Case Study of the Female Authorial Voice in the New Hollywood

Week 10: Jane Austen in Hollywood

Discussion 1: The Cinematic Resurrection of Jane Austen
Readings: Austen, *Emma.*
Screening: *Clueless.*

Week 11: Feminism and Adaptation

Discussion 1: Theories of Cinematic Adaptation
Reading: Andrew, "Adaptation."

Discussion 2: Feminist Analysis of *Clueless*
Readings: Metz, "A Totally Clueless Emma? How American Popular Culture Saved Jane Austen from Masterpiece Theatre."

Week 12: Student Oral Presentations

Walter Metz is assistant professor of media and theater arts at Montana State University in Bozeman. He has had articles published in Literature/Film Quarterly, Film Criticism, The Velvet Light Trap, and The Journal of Film and Video *and is currently at work on a textbook about the relationships between canonical drama and popular film and television.*

Copyright © 2002 by Walter Metz

Feminisms on Film

Carol J. Pierman

Instructors of women's studies, like many others in the academy, rely frequently on film and video to generate—and sometimes direct—discussions of difficult or controversial subject matter. Because students are visually literate, one can sometimes forge a path into the written text by going through film.

As chair of a women's studies department, one in which graduate teaching assistants do virtually all the teaching at the introductory level, I became interested in the use our apprentice instructors make of the department's video library. The graduate students are required to enroll in a semester-long course in feminist pedagogy and to observe and perform some "practice teaching" in an introductory section before they take charge of their own undergraduate classroom in their second year. However, their training does not necessarily include any film theory or critique. It seemed that the strategic use of video as a supplement (or stimulant) to class discussions could be enhanced by a seminar on the medium itself. Even without a pedagogical aim, a course on the intersections of film and feminist studies might be a useful addition to the curriculum.

Although it had been several years since I last taught film and literature, I decided to adapt materials from that course and develop a seminar in film theory and pedagogy for women's studies graduate students at the University of Alabama. I proposed the class as a special topic, a pilot course for which I obtained funding from the College of Arts and Sciences for a video equipment upgrade and additional film purchases.

A list of films, readings, and comments on course design follow. Since this was a graduate course, each student was responsible for generating a significant number of critical and theoretical readings, which supplemented my own required reading list. Students designed and presented their own assignments and taught a film (or cluster of films) at the end of semester.

The films I selected were divided evenly between documentary and feature. Many, especially the documentaries, are used in our women's studies classes; and the feature films have engendered a substantial body of film criticism, including feminist criticism. Each of the films on the syllabus, except for George Butler's, were directed by women. The films reflected a broad range of film styles and techniques as well as subject matter. Consequently, to think about them, students had to engage with an equally broad variety of theory and criticism.

The class met once a week, and students were informed in advance that the length of our meetings could vary, depending on the length of the film and allowing ample time for critique and discussion. The course was open to all graduate students, regardless of discipline, and I ended up with a seminar enrollment of twelve; in addition to women's studies graduate students, two students were from telecommunications and film, one was from American studies, and one was a senior women's studies minor.

In our class discussion during the semester, I emphasized two kinds of critique, one focusing on the basics of film literacy, with a special interest in the ways in which cinematic technique is manipulated to fashion point of view; the other being on the problematic of the spectator-film relationship. For instance, the initial pairing of Annette Kuhn's "The Body and Cinema" and Izod and Kilborn's "The Documentary," along with *Pumping Iron II: The Women*, got us to the heart of film effects and the problem of spectatorship. One student spoke pointedly to the film's opening and its suggestive, almost pornographic tone. Others questioned the legitimacy of documentary's claims to the "truth." The director goes out of his way to provoke debate over definitions of such things as femininity, beauty, and female athleticism—the very "naturalness" of the body itself—and those debates continued over the semester.

By the term's conclusion, students had produced a number of outstanding teaching projects and topics, including gender and ethnicity in the earliest American silent films; film and literature, with a focus on Virginia Woolf's *Orlando;* films on gender and manual labor, with a focus on women in coal mining; women and documentary film art; gender and the road movie. The level of film critique had improved substantially; and those students who came from outside women's studies had increased their knowledge of feminist theory and criticism. It is too soon to know what impact the seminar had on graduate student instruction (it was taught only this past semester); however, it has kindled an informed interest on the part of students, one of whom is doing her thesis research on feminist directors.

SYLLABUS FOR FEMINISMS ON FILM

Objective: To introduce women's studies graduate students to film technique, style, and criticism; and to introduce students in other disciplines to feminist theory and critique, in order to create more informed viewers, critics, and instructors.

Films (Shown in this order)

Pumping Iron II: The Women, dir. George Butler, documentary, 107 mins., 1985.
A League of Their Own, dir. Mary Wallace, documentary, 27 mins., 1988.
A League of Their Own, dir. Penny Marshall, feature, 128 mins., 1992.
Regret to Inform, dir. Barbara Sonnenberg, documentary, 78 mins., 1998.
Daughters of the Dust, dir. Julie Dash, feature, 113 mins., 1991.
Mi Vida Loca, dir. Allison Anders, feature, 92 mins., 1994.
Ballot Measure 9, dir. Heather MacDonald, documentary, 72 mins., 1995.
Dying to Be Thin, documentary, 56 mins., PBS Video, 1999.
Clockwatchers, dir. Jill Sprecher, feature, 96 mins., 1997.

The class will also view selected half-hour documentaries, including *Freedom Quilting Bee* (Alabama Public Television), *Evelyn Williams,* and *Fast Food Women* (both from Appalshop Video).

Readings

Bordwell, David, and Kristin Thompson. *Film Art: An Introduction.* New York: McGraw Hill, 1990.
Miller, Toby, and Robert Stam, eds. *A Companion to Film Theory.* Oxford: Blackwell, 1999.
Kuhn, Annette. "The Body and Cinema: Some Problems for Feminism." *Grafts: Feminist Cultural Criticism.* Ed. Susan Sheridan. London: Verso, 1988.
Chatman, Seymour. "What Novels Can Do That Film Can't (and Vice Versa)." *Critical Inquiry* 7.1 (1970): 121–40.
Izod, John, and Richard Kilborn. "The Documentary." *World Cinema: Critical Approaches.* Ed. John Hill and P. C. Gibson. Oxford: Oxford UP, 2000.
Crofts, Stephen. "Concepts of National Cinema." *World Cinema: Critical Approaches.* Ed. John Hill and P. C. Gibson. Oxford: Oxford UP, 2000.
Mellencamp, Patricia. "Five Ages of Film Feminism." *Kiss Me Deadly.* Ed. Laleen Jayamanne. Sydney: Power, 1995.

Lane, Christina, *Feminist Hollywood*. Detroit: Wayne State UP, 2000.
Martin, Michael T. *Cinemas of the Black Diaspora*. Detroit: Wayne State UP, 1995. N.B.: Contains director's discussion and critical assessments of Julie Dash's *Daughters of the Dust*.
Taylor, Clyde. "Daughters of the Terreiros." *The Mask of Art: Breaking the Aesthetic Contract—Film and Literature*. Bloomington: Indiana UP, 1998.

Assignments

1. Annotated Bibliography

It will be a semester-long goal for each student to create a working annotated critical bibliography as a resource for teaching and discussing feminisms on film. At the final class of each month, your bibliography-in-progress will be due (minimum of two entries per week).

The bibliography must include the titles listed above and others of your own choosing from film criticism and theory and from feminist criticism and theory.

It should also include evaluative entries from a full variety of sources, including film journals, databases, critical and theoretical texts; film scripts, storyboards, and other primary documents.

The final bibliography should include a minimum of twenty-four entries.

2. Curriculum/Teaching Project

At the end of term you will be expected to assign materials related to a film you screen and teach in class. Submit along with this project a descriptive plan on how you will approach the film, assignments you would make, and outcomes you desire. Make sure each member of the class receives citations and resources in advance. Propose the topic in advance and arrange one meeting with me to discuss feasibility and strategy.

The plan must include the following:

1. a rationale and context for using the film in class
2. the lead-up and follow-up assignments you would make
3. accompanying readings and discussion materials
4. the key scenes and critical points that must be covered
5. desired outcome(s) and how they will be measured (exam, written assignment, special project or presentation; include examples).

Additional considerations might include

- What kind of class, and at what level?
- How many class sessions altogether?
- The rationale for using the film?
- The context (what else is being taught before and after) and how do you envision this film fitting with surrounding topics?
- And for you, what critical background readings or research interests inform your teaching of this project?
- What are the key scenes; what exchanges of dialogue, characterizations, and critical points will you cover?

Carol J. Pierman *is chair of women's studies at the University of Alabama. Her current project is a critical study of the All-American Girls Professional Baseball League. She is the author of two books of poetry,* The Age of Krypton *(Carnegie Mellon University Press) and* The Naturalized Citizen *(New Rivers).*

Copyright © 2002 by Carol J. Pierman

Redirecting The Gaze: Gender, Theory, and Cinema in the Third World, edited by Diana Robin and Ira Jaffe (Albany: SUNY Press, 1999)

Rama Lohani Chase

Diana Robin and Ira Jaffe's *Redirecting the Gaze* comes at a time when cinema studies is spreading its interdisciplinary wings and establishing itself as a crossroads for doing critical theory. *Redirecting the Gaze* is an invaluable addition to an area within cinema studies that has gotten very little press. This area is oppositional cinema in the "Third World" and its aesthetic, usually termed "third cinema aesthetic," that redefines the gaze as not only gendered, but also nativized, ethnicized, or anthropologized. *Redirecting the Gaze* makes visible unrepresented and underrepresented films and filmmakers and the world of existing differences, the nascent subjectivities, and the histories in the making they explore. The ten chapters in the book cover independent women filmmakers in Mexico, Cuba, the United States, Africa, Bolivia, Venezuela, China, India, and Argentina. In addition to analyzing the various films, almost all the essays provide a filmmaking history and tradition of the particular places of origin of the women creators and their films.

As the editors make clear in the introduction, the essays in the anthology explore the work of women filmmakers who "have moved beyond the totalizing, gender neutral, and dehistoricized discourses of Third Cinema. Their works foreground the *interconnectedness of race, gender, and class* in the context of discourses on nation, postcoloniality, and globalization" (2). The essays in the book provide students and teachers of cinema studies and women's and gender studies with critical tools and ways of thinking. At the same time, the information that the essays contain on the cultural, political, national, and gender history of the places of filmmaking will be invaluable in understanding the theory and praxis that gave birth to the filmmakers and their work.

The comprehensive introduction by the editors gives a brief history of Third World filmmaking practices and the trend of oppositional cinema, which seems to have started in Latin American films. As Robin and Jaffe suggest in their introduction, the manifesto *Towards a Third Cinema: Notes and Experiences for the Development of a Cinema of Liberation in the Third World,* produced in Argentina in 1968, and the 1989 text

Questions of Third Cinema, by Jim Pines and Paul Willemen, are useful places from which to begin to understand the conceptual and theoretical frameworks of the "Third Cinema." These sources also make it clear that the "third wave" of filmmaking seems to be perpetually open towards possibilities of change and movement.

Starting with the conceptual framework of the phrase *Third World,* Jaffe and Robin point out that the essays in the collection explore the windows to the world of these women filmmakers. The first two chapters, by Diane Sippl and Catherine Benamou, provide the unique history of Mexican and Cuban filmmaking traditions. Critical of "men's films about women" (74) even in those films with a postrevolutionary aesthetic, Benamou lets the subaltern speak by analyzing the works of Sara Gómez. Gómez is a documentarian whose "only feature film, *De cierta manera* (*One Way or Another,* 1974–1977), penetrated beneath the surface of the uniformly national and into the realm of the subcultural" (76). Admiring Gómez's open treatment of race and gender, Benamou says, "Unlike many of her male counterparts . . . Gómez did not thematize gender at the expense of race and cultural identity, but instead sought to demonstrate how historically they have been intertwined" (77). While Benamou's essay on women's filmmaking looks at Cuba's political, social, and cultural history to convey to us the spatiotemporal effects and moves in Cuban women's filmmaking practices, Diane Sippl in her essay, "Al Cine de las Mexicans: *Lola* in the Limelight," underscores women's participation "in the production of Mexican cinema from its pre-Revolutionary inception" (34). She puts Mexican cinema history into its cultural, political, and national context and also provides us with glimpses of the obstacles that come with being a Third World country. When borders are permeable, as are those of Mexico, cultural authenticity is only the constructed ideal of the outsider, and national boundaries are only imaginary homelands. Thus, when Diane Sippl discusses María Novaro's *Lola,* instead of borders and boundaries, she helps viewers to see *hybridity* as an identity, *bricolage* as a form, and *transnational* as a practice in filmmaking.

The desire to rewrite history is discussed in the essay by Patricia Mellencamp, the third chapter of the book. Mellencamp explores two films, *Illusions* and *Daughters of the Dust,* by African American filmmaker Julie Dash. Here again oppositional cinema, so different in style from that of Hollywood, works singularly in "making history" for an Afrocentric subjectivity as Julie Dash uses her camera to bring the past into the present. Robin and Jaffe explain that "Mellencamp sees *Daughters* as a film about the recovery of memory and the process of remembering for a new future. . . . Moreover, the focus in *Daughters* is on process, on becoming, and on living speech rather than the printed word—on what happens in the spaces between experience and thought, sound and image, and between women" (8–9).

The undertakings of decolonizing the screen and locating subjectivity are further elucidated in the essays by N. Frank Ukadike and Elena Feder. Speaking for the need to redefine black female subjectivity that is "constantly abused in films" made by the mainstream, Ukadike in "Reclaiming Images of Women in Films from Africa and the Black Diaspora" declares that "black women must take the lead in a revisionist dialogue, an alternative discourse that requires culture-based interpretation around questions of ethnic identity and representation" (129). While Ukadike sees the need to "move the questions of 'other' to the center" (128), Feder in her essay, "In the Shadow of the Race: Forging Gender in Bolivian Film and Video," analyzes a complexity encountered in Bolivian film practices in developing an identity that is inclusive of the local reality, one that is multiracial, multilingual, and multiethnic. While the "authentic" national and cultural identity within the contemporary construction of nation and culture might only be achieved with the homogeneity of people and cultures in filmic representations, the issues of gender are easily elided unless "looked at within the related contexts of racism, colonialism, and imperialism" (13). Feder's essay highlights the dyad of Bolivian history in which the majority, Indian people, have been ruled over by a minority, people with Western roots. Even though the oppositional cinema aesthetic is pretty new in the Bolivian cinema world, "the interlocking themes of race and class oppression and colonialism have been central to Bolivian cinema since its inception in the 1920s" (14).

If some essays focus mostly on the historical places of making and being, Karen Schwartzman's "The Seen of the Crime," Hu Ying's "Beyond the Glow of the Red Lantern," and Sumita Chakravorty's "Can the Subaltern Weep?" use or are informed by a poststructuralist critical lens. Schwartzman's analysis of the Venezuelan film *Macu, the Policeman's Wife* applies the psychoanalytic theory of Julia Kristeva in a powerful way. The interesting play between the camera and the spectator, or the spectator and the spectacle, is theorized in both Schwartzman's and Hu Ying's analyses. Following the critical trend of oppositional cinema, which is marked by anti-imperialist views and convictions against mainstream constructions of society, Schwartzman, in her psychoanalytic analysis of *Macu*, delineates the deconstruction and interrogation of the social. Hu Ying critiques the Sinocentrism in films that freeze a culture by denying change and transformation, as in the Chinese-made film *Raise the Red Lantern*. Ying's analysis redirects the gaze to interrogate spectatorial desires and uses it as a trajectory to critique the otherizing "gaze." Ying points to *The Bloody Morning* as "a different vision coming through at the intersection of culture and gender, a historicized culture and problematized gender system" (278). This disparate mode of representation in films and the equally new way of decoding such metaphors are also discussed in Sumita S. Chakravarty's essay on the Indian film *Rudaali* (The crier). In "Can the Subaltern Weep?" Chakravarty raises issues about the marginalized metaphors and symbols associated with the female body and voice to elucidate the unmourned state of the subaltern in postcolonial India. India has a huge film industry and produces more films than any other country in the world. The small number of women filmmakers is growing, and directors such as Mira Nair, Pratibha Parmar, and Deepa Mehta have gotten some limited press internationally. However, many independent women filmmakers and actresses from India are still known only locally.

The distribution of Third World–made films and films made by independent filmmakers is very limited, but learning about them can be an informative process of discovering the histories behind these women and their work. Following up on such landmarks as Gwendolyn Foster's *Woman Filmmakers of the African and Asian Diaspora* from 1997 and Brinda Bose and Bishnupriya Gosh's *Interventions: Feminist Dialogues on Third World Women's Literature and Film* from the same year, *Redirecting the Gaze* powerfully represents voices that ought to be heard. The book is essential reading for any serious student or teacher of women's studies or cinema studies. It is also an excellent place to examine film scholarship that looks at work that explores the intersections of race, class, and gender in a period of postcolonial anxiety and economic globalization.

Rama Lohani Chase, a native of Nepal, holds an M.A. in women's studies from Drew University, where she wrote a thesis on issues of representation in the films of Mira Nair, and where she is currently an ESOL instructor. Her interests include gender and development, issues of identity and subjectivity in film and literature, and postcolonial theories.

Copyright © 2002 by Rama Lohani Chase

Feminism and Film (Oxford Readings in Feminism), edited by E. Ann Kaplan (Oxford: Oxford University Press, 2000); Feminist Film Theory: A Reader, edited by Sue Thornham (New York: New York University Press, 1999)

Anahid Kassabian

Choosing a textbook for a Women in Film or a Film and Gender course is never easy. Students are rarely prepared for the high theoretical pitch of much of the literature, and they often don't expect to work hard in a film course to begin with. My approach has always been to warn students that the course is hard work and then to maintain my high expectations. But I have to find a textbook to support this approach, which until recently was a real challenge.

Two new anthologies—Thornham's 1999 *Feminist Film Theory: A Reader* and Kaplan's 2000 *Feminism and Film*—offer excellent choices. Prior to 1999, there were only a few viable classroom choices in print: *Feminism and Film Theory*, edited by Constance Penley (New York: Routledge; and London: BFI, 1988); *Issues in Feminist Film Criticism*, edited by Patricia Erens (Bloomington: Indiana University Press, 1990), and *Multiple Voices in Feminist Film Criticism*, edited by Diane Carson, Linda Dittmar, and Janice R. Welsch (Minneapolis: University of Minnesota Press, 1994). Erens and Penley offered collections of what has become the feminist film theoretical canon. *Multiple Voices* collected a wonderful range of voices, but can be too challenging if students have not read a collection like Erens's or Penley's first. I taught Penley's volume, once, and found that for my purposes, it did not engage psychoanalysis's critics enough, even though my own work is strongly influenced by psychoanalysis. Erens's *Issues* did noticeably better in that regard, but still didn't nearly suit my needs. I kept looking for some kind of combination, a book that would offer both canonical texts and challenges to them.

The notion of a feminist film theory canon may seem anathema to some, as it does to me in some ways. But as a teacher, I feel an obligation to walk my students through the intellectual history of the topic at hand, and they therefore must read the major debate-generating contributions. To find them collected in one volume makes everyone's life easier. Except that—as we've all learned—there's no *one* version of a canon, theoretical or otherwise. What that means, in practice, is that any anthology will have strengths and weaknesses, and as an instructor one has to make peace with them.

Enter the two volumes under consideration here. Amazingly, there are now two (!) volumes that I'm happy to teach from. What follows then, is a kind of kid-in-a-candy-shop discussion—all choices are good ones.

Of the two, E. Ann Kaplan's is, not surprisingly, the more "classical." Given the surfeit of essays eligible for inclusion, Kaplan chose as an organizing principle Laura Mulvey's 1975 "Visual Pleasure and Narrative Cinema." In the preface, she says:

> Many of the major essays in the field responded in one way or another—including outright rejection—to Mulvey's theoretical positions, so I could produce a book of coherent essays by printing work that debated, argued against, or built out from "Visual Pleasure and Narrative Cinema." (v)

By this logic, she compiled a collection that includes four large sections: "Pioneers and Classics: The Modernist Mode"; "Critiques of Phase I Theories: New Methods"; "Race, Sexuality, and Postmodernism in Feminist Film Theory"; and "Spectatorship, Ethnicity, and Melodrama." Each section begins with introductory notes, of about ten pages, which are enormously useful for scholars and students alike. Not only does she survey the essays she has included but also discusses some that she has not. This is a welcome way of combining the strengths of both textbooks and anthologies. There is also an ample "Further Reading" appendix, divided by section.

The body of theory generated in response to Mulvey's widely read essay revolves around questions of textuality and reception. Is a masculine position built into film, as her article suggests? If so, is it built into all film? Can women only occupy masculine positions in our engagements with films? What about genres addressed to women? What about films made by women? What about explicitly feminist films? These are the questions that generated the body of thought under consideration here, and they have as many answers as there are scholars grappling with them.

The coherence of the collection is both a strength and a drawback. Students can track a set of debates, around which it is feasible to organize a course, and this can give a welcome lucidity to teaching. However, it subsumes many attendant debates about theorizing culture and society—British cultural studies, for example—as a response to semiotic psychoanalysis, which is perhaps (at least in part) misleading.

Thornham's anthology is similarly organized in sections with introductions and recommendations for further reading. But the sections themselves differ noticeably. What Kaplan called "Pioneers and Classics," Thornham has separated into two sections, "Taking Up the Struggle" and "The Language of Theory." The former includes works by Molly Haskell, B. Ruby Rich, and others; the latter, Laura Mulvey, Mary Ann Doane, Teresa de Lauretis, and Kaja Silverman. This makes eminent sense to me, since these really were distinct moments in the intellectual history of feminist film studies—the opening of a terrain for debate on the one hand, and the development of a psychoanalytic, semiotic, Marxist theoretical approach on the other. There is obvious overlap—Claire Johnston, for example—but the separation will allow students to sense the historical differences in the field between the early and late 1970s.

In her third section, "The Female Spectator," Thornham includes the roundtable from *New German Critique* on feminist aesthetics, which is a welcome addition in both form and content. (Why is there so little multivocal feminist scholarship?) Also in this section is Mary Ann Doane's famous piece "Film and the Masquerade." Masquerade as a theoretical paradigm had a brief, hot flare, but it has always seemed to me to have been a path not taken and worth pursuing. Perhaps it has come back in another, more polished guise as "performativity," but I certainly welcome the presence of this important article in the collection.

The fourth section, "Textual Negotiations," reveals what is probably Thornham's most significant difference from Kaplan. The engagement of both British and American cultural studies with feminist film theory is treated here not as a response, but as an important, discrete intellectual entity. The articles by Christine Gledhill, Valerie Walkerdine, Jackie Stacey, and Janet Staiger create a coherent unit that offers a different theoretical direction, and the introduction to the section makes their contribution accessible and meaningful for students.

Whereas Kaplan chose melodrama for her genre case study, highlighting her own area of research, Thornham's section is titled "Fantasy, Horror, and the Body" and includes essays by Carol Clover, Barbara Creed, and Linda Williams. Horror as a genre has been an unusually productive area of feminist film scholarship, even more so than melodrama, and the essays here are all classics, if too few.

Thornham's final section, "Re-thinking Differences," covers both race and sexuality, and this is, I think, a shared weakness in both collections. While both editors take great pains to discuss differences other than the originary sexual difference posited by psychoanalytic orthodoxy, both package "other" differences together in catchall sections. This is quite simply no longer intellectually tenable. There are large bodies of scholarships at the intersections of feminist film theory and queer studies, critical race theory, and postcolonial theory, and they deserve to be treated distinctly. Thornham's collection includes only questions of black spectatorship; Kaplan at least includes postcolonial theoretical interventions by both Trinh T. Minh-ha and Pratibha Parmar. The absence in both books of work on the Middle East seems particularly poignant to me at this moment, especially since there is both outstanding scholarship (such as Ella Shohat's) and films (such as Mona Hatoum's).

Both also share a far more troubling absence, and that is the absence of sound. While there is not an enormous body of feminist scholarship on sound and music, there is certainly some important work, and it is a growing field. Film has never been a "visual" medium, despite feminist film theories' oculocentric approach. But Kaplan, in particular, treats it as such, stating at the end of her general introduction:

> [A]s new digital and computer-linked technologies grow apace, feminist research into these terrains *of the visual* are needed. . . . I believe knowledge of what feminist film scholars have produced—of the questions and areas our research has opened up—is crucial for continuing film research as well as for venturing into studying gendered and racial aspects of new *visual* practices and institutions. (14, emphasis mine)

It is clear that Kaplan considers film a resolutely visual medium, the millions of dollars of annual soundtrack sales notwithstanding. Thornham, while not quite as explicit about it, shares this same bias. While both collections contain essays by Kaja Silverman, neither includes her important work on women's voices from *The Acoustic Mirror*, and neither has excerpted Amy Lawrence's *Echo and Narcissus: Women's Voices in Classical Hollywood Cinema* (Berkeley and Los Angeles: University of California Press, 1991). Neither chose to include Mary Ann Doane's "Ideology and the Practice of Sound Editing and Mixing" (*The Cinematic Apparatus*, ed. Stephen Heath and Teresa de Lauretis.

London: Macmillan, 1980) or "The Voice in the Cinema: the Articulation of Body and Space" (*Film Sound: Theory and Practice,* ed. Elisabeth Weis and John Belton. New York: Columbia University Press, 1985). Nor have they included any work on music, such as Kathryn Kalinak's excellent 1982 article "The Fallen Woman and the Virtuous Wife: Musical Stereotypes in *The Informer, Gone With the Wind,* and *Laura*" (*Film Reader* 5) or an excerpt from Caryl Flinn's sadly out-of-print *Strains of Utopia : Gender, Nostalgia, and Hollywood Film Music* (Princeton: Princeton University Press, 1992).

Both volumes will make excellent teaching resources, and I would gladly order either one as a course text. I'll still be putting readings on reserve, but a lot fewer, thanks to Thornham and Kaplan.

Anahid Kassabian *teaches in the Department of Communication and Media Studies and in the Programs in Women's Studies and Literary Studies at Fordham University. She is the author of* Hearing Film *(Routledge, 2001) and numerous essays.*

Copyright © 2002 by Anahid Kassabian

WOMEN WITH VISION

KELLY HANKIN
The Girls in the Back Room
Looking at the Lesbian Bar

The first in-depth study of how lesbian bars are depicted in popular culture.
$18.95 paper • $52.95 cloth • 248 pages • 2002

ALEXANDRA JUHASZ, EDITOR
Women of Vision
Histories in Feminist Film and Video

Legends and rising stars of feminist film and video tell their stories.

Interviewees: Pearl Bowser, Margaret Caples, Michelle Citron, Megan Cunningham, Cheryl Dunye, Vanalyne Green, Barbara Hammer, Kate Horsfield, Carol Leigh, Susan Mogul, Juanita Mohammed, Frances Negrón-Muntaner, Eve Oishi, Constance Penley, Wendy Quinn, Julia Reichert, Carolee Schneemann, Valerie Soe, Victoria Vesna, and Yvonne Welbon.

$19.95 paper • $52.95 cloth• 280 pages • 2001
Visible Evidence Series, volume 9

DIANE WALDMAN AND JANET WALKER, EDITORS
Feminism and Documentary

"A valuable work that enhances discussion on both feminist documentaries and the history of women in documentary." —*Screening the Past*

Contributors: Michelle Citron, Gloria J. Gibson, Chris Holmlund, Alexandra Juhasz, Ann Kaneko, Anahid Kassabian, David Kazanjian, Susan Knobloch, Silvia Kratzer-Juilfs, Deborah Lefkowitz, Julia Lesage, Laura U. Marks, Paula Rabinowitz, Michael Renov, and Patricia R. Zimmermann.

$19.95 paper • $54.95 cloth • 372 pages • 1999
Visible Evidence Series, volume 5

MICHELLE CITRON
Home Movies and Other Necessary Fictions

A powerful and personal exploration of the line between truth and fiction, by one of the most influential independent woman filmmakers of our time.

"Citron's writing style is graceful, introspective, and accessible." —*Feminist Studies*

$19.95 paper • $54.95 cloth • 216 pages • 1998
Visible Evidence Series, volume 4

DIANE CARSON, LINDA DITTMAR AND JANICE R. WELSCH, EDITORS
Multiple Voices in Feminist Film Criticism

"An excellent balance between feminist film theory and the history of the women's movement."
—*Transformations*

Includes essays by B. Ruby Rich, Teresa de Lauretis, Janet Staiger, Beverle Houston, Chris Straayer, bell hooks, Linda Williams, and Julia Lesage, among others.

$22.95 paper • 560 pages • 1994

Now in paperback!
SARAH BERRY
Screen Style
Fashion and Femininity in 1930s Hollywood

"Sarah Berry's lavishly illustrated study is valuable for its encyclopedic grasp of the films of the studio system era and for its refusal to speak reductively of Hollywood's extravagant emphasis on the style of its female stars. Readable, comprehensive, and clearly argued." —*Film Quarterly*

$18.95 paper • 264 pages • 2002
Commerce and Mass Culture Series, volume 2

LOUISE BROOKS
Lulu in Hollywood
Expanded Edition
Introduction by Kenneth Tynan

"Brooks is brilliantly perceptive and articulate on everything from the art of film directing to the comedy of W. C. Fields." —*New York Times*
"A minor classic." —*Film Quarterly*

$19.95 paper • 184 pages • 2000

BARRY PARIS
Louise Brooks
A Biography

From her beginnings as a dancer to her years in Hollywood, Berlin, and beyond, Louise Brooks was hailed and reviled as a new type of woman: independent, intellectually daring, and sexually free.

"*Louise Brooks* is not simply a summary of her movie plots and love affairs but a serious work of film and social history." —*New York Magazine*

$19.95 paper • 624 pages • 2000

University of Minnesota Press
www.upress.umn.edu
773-568-1550

UNIVERSITY PRESS OF

Daughters of Abraham
Feminist Thought in Judaism, Christianity, and Islam

Edited by Yvonne Yazbeck Haddad and John L. Esposito

"Indispensable for those seeking to understand feminist theology. Jewish, Christian, and Muslim women share the historical reality of having been silent partners in their own traditions. By bringing their stories together, *Daughters of Abraham* suggests that they can forge a future characterized by mutual support based on a common bond."—Tamara Sonn, College of William and Mary
Cloth, $55.00

Tracing Arachne's Web
Myths and Feminist Fiction

Kristin M. Mapel Bloomberg

"I am particularly impressed with Bloomberg's insights about the ways in which women writers' urge to harness the power of women's myths has to some extent been aroused by historical forces. . . . She explains that women's desire to reinvent their identities requires that women writers take over the narrative tools (such as mythic allusions) provided them by male writers and use those tools to build their own textual 'house.'"—Mary Lowe-Evans, University of West Florida
Cloth, $55.00

The Major Novels of Susan Glaspell

Martha C. Carpentier

In a detailed critical analysis, Carpentier shows how six novels by the modernist American writer Susan Glaspell (1876-1948) speak to readers today, both in their focus on female sexuality and development and in their often subversive narrative form.
Cloth, $55.00

Women Poets on the Left
Lola Ridge, Genevieve Taggard, Margaret Walker

Nancy Berke

A theoretical framework, historical overview, and careful reading of the poetry of Ridge, Taggard, and Walker. . . . Berke describes the rich social, historical, and political context of their work, making the book an in-depth study of the gender issues, radical politics, and poetry of the modern period.
Cloth, $55.00

Order through full-service book sellers, our website at www.upf.com, or with VISA or M/C toll free: 1-800-226-3822

Gainesville, Tallahassee, Tampa, Boca Raton, Pensacola, Orlando, Miami, Jacksonville, Fort Myers

WE PUT WOMEN BEHIND THE CAMERA.

School of Film and Animation
Rochester Institute of Technology
www.rit.edu/~sofa

"*... democratize the sublime...*"
—Irving Howe, *The American Newness*
The COMMON REVIEW
The Magazine of the Great Books Foundation

"**N**ew Magazine Delivers Big Ideas
The Great Books Foundation, which for more than 50 years has been reminding the public that a book replete with sophisticated ideas and a 'good read' are not mutually exclusive, has brought that same philosophy to a new magazine." — POETS & WRITERS, JANUARY/FEBRUARY 2002

Look for these articles in future issues of **The COMMON REVIEW:**

- Morris Dickstein explores the roots of the Hollywood novel and the effect novels had on Great Depression era movies.

- Regina Barreca writes about fashion in academe and how clothes in the classroom reflect on larger issues of intellectual freedom and politics.

- Michael Kimmel reviews a spate of recent popular books in the field of "men's studies."

- Maria Russo discusses public intellectuals and their controversial role in the media.

*One year (4 issues) is only $9.
To subscribe, call 1-800-222-5870
or e-mail tcr@greatbooks.org.*

 The Great Books Foundation
35 East Wacker Drive, Suite 2300
Chicago, Illinois 60601-2298
www.greatbooks.org

camera obscura

Since its inception, *Camera Obscura* has devoted itself to providing innovative feminist perspectives on film, television, and visual media. It consistently combines excellence in scholarship with imaginative presentation and a willingness to lead media studies in new directions. The journal has developed a reputation for introducing emerging writers into the field. Its debates, essays, interviews, and summary pieces encompass a spectrum of media practices, including avant-garde, alternative, fringe, international, and mainstream.

Camera Obscura continues to redefine its original statement of purpose. While remaining faithful to its feminist focus, the journal also explores feminist work in relation to race studies, postcolonial studies, and queer studies. In addition, its understanding of visual media has expanded to include discussions of newly developing imaging technologies, such as those being used in medicine.

Special issues of *Camera Obscura* include "Black Women Spectators and Visual Culture," "New Imaging Technologies," and "Early Women Stars."

U.S. $27 for individual subscriptions.
Outside the U.S. add $12 for postage and handling.
Available directly from Duke University Press
Toll free 1-888-387-5765
subscriptions@dukeupress.edu
www.dukeupress.edu

Photographs: Paramount and Twentieth Century-Fox